THE NEW ARTIST'S GUIDE TO DRAWING

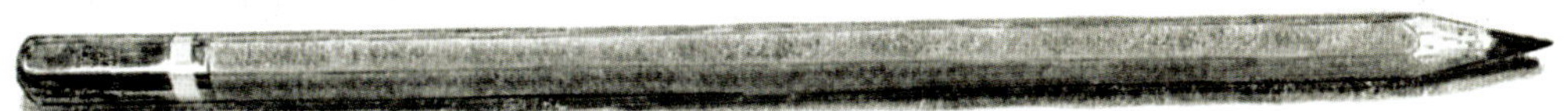

Learn How to Draw People, Animals, Landscapes and More **THE EASY WAY**

Mark Liam Smith

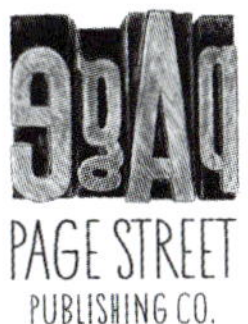

PAGE STREET
PUBLISHING CO.

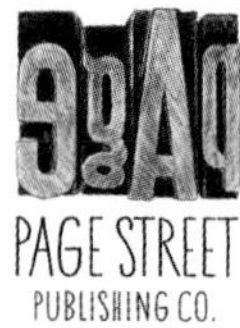

Copyright © 2024 Mark Liam Smith

First published in 2024 by
Page Street Publishing Co.
27 Congress Street, Suite 1511
Salem, MA 01970
www.pagestreetpublishing.com

Distributed by Macmillan, sales in Canada by The Canadian Manda Group.

29 28 27 26   5 6 7 8

ISBN-13: 979-8-89003-976-7

Library of Congress Control Number: 2023945409

Edited by Madeline Greenhalgh
Cover and book design by Caitlyn Boyd for Page Street Publishing Co.
Illustrations by Mark Liam Smith

Printed in China

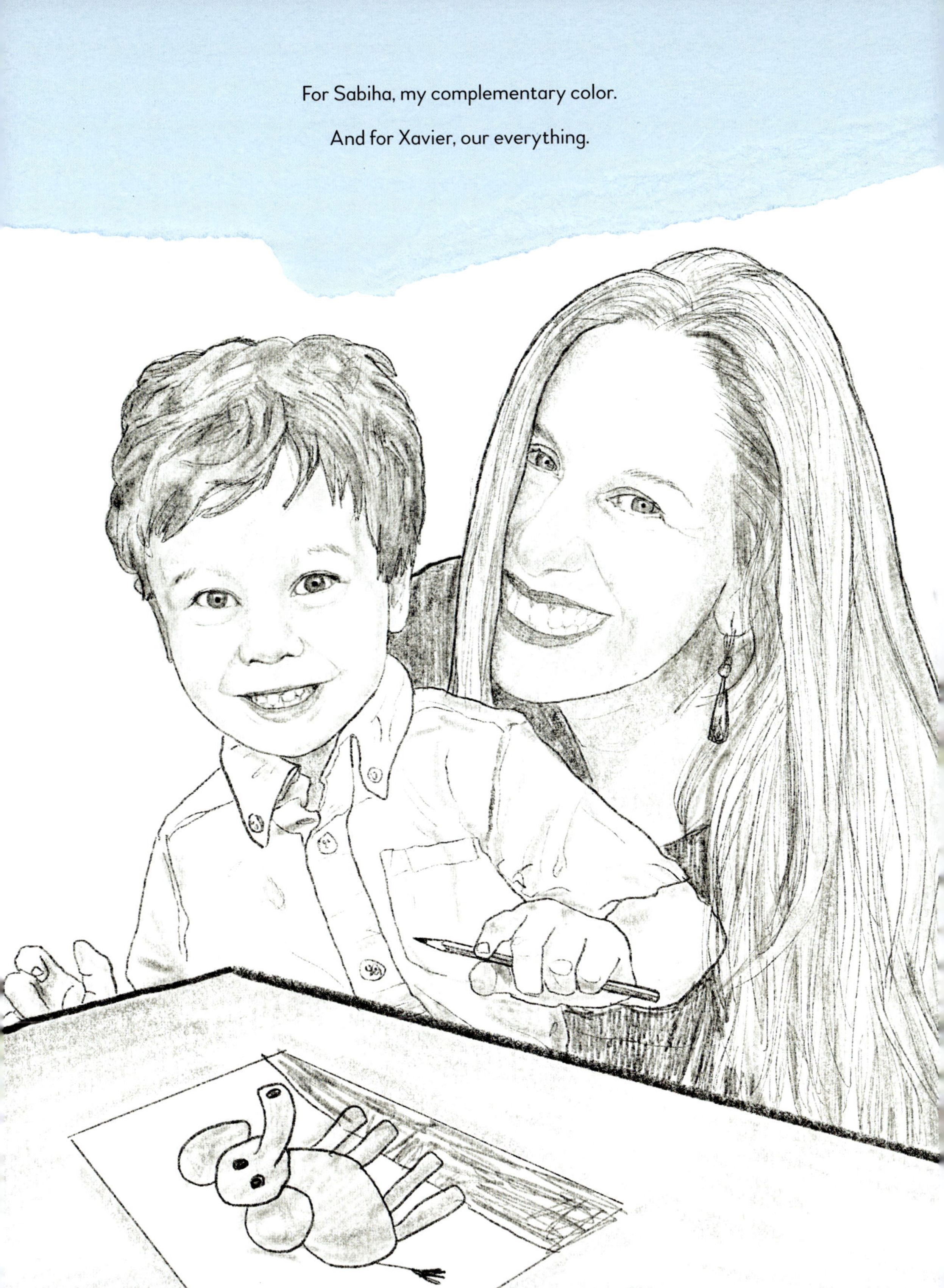

For Sabiha, my complementary color.

And for Xavier, our everything.

CONTENTS

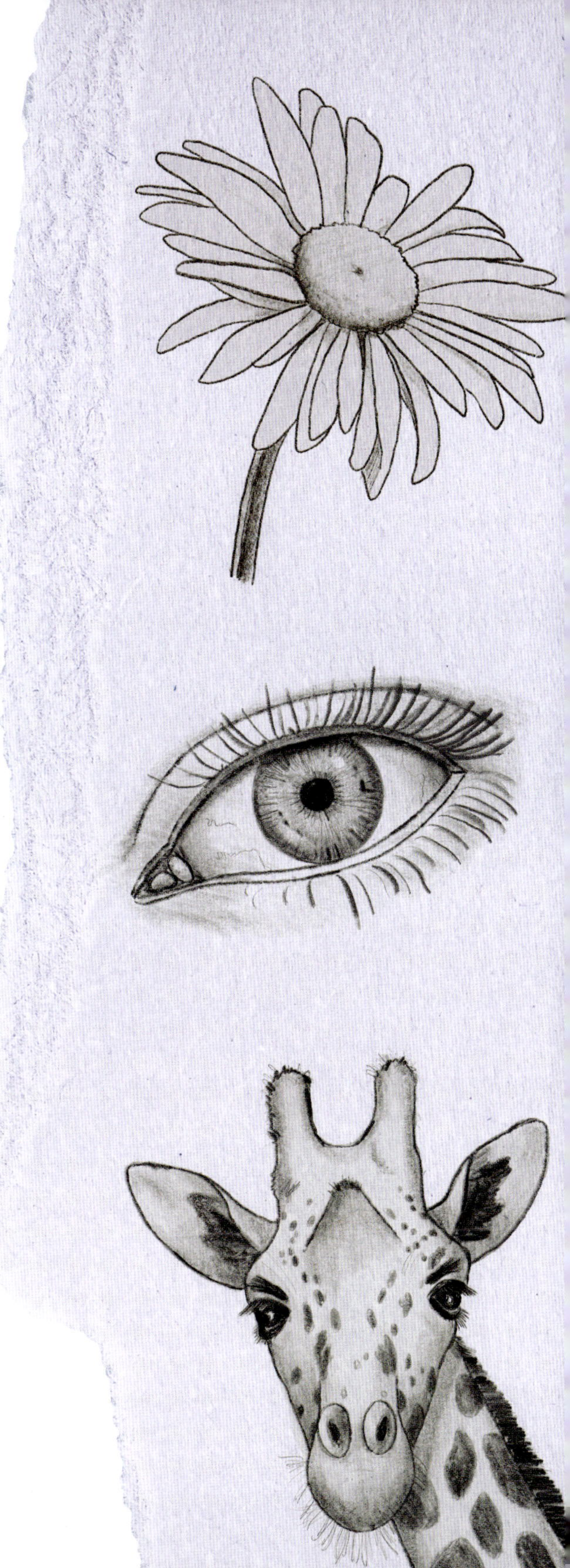

INTRODUCTION

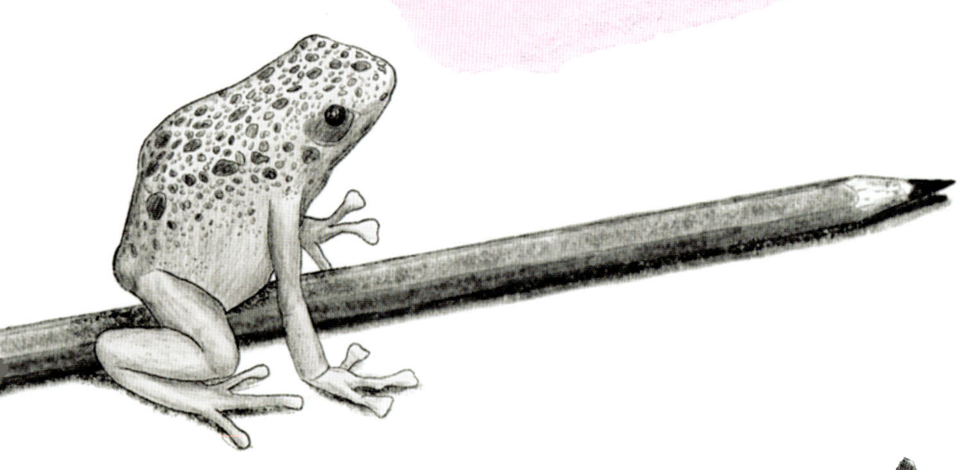

WHAT YOU'LL LEARN

Perhaps you want to learn to draw your pet, or a beautiful landscape, or the face of someone you love. The good news is that, by the end of this book, you'll have learned how to do those things.

The even better news is that you'll have learned so much more, too.

That's because drawing is about more than making pictures on paper. It's about learning to look at the world differently. Slowing down to appreciate the details all around us. Developing your creativity, patience and confidence. Turning your ideas into physical pieces of art. And, if you'd like, sharing that artwork with the world.

Drawing—especially realism—takes practice. You won't get it right the first time, or the second time, or maybe even the eleventh time. That's okay. Keep the parts that worked and discard the parts that didn't. As with most things in life, little adjustments each day add up to huge improvements over time. Before you know it, you could be hanging your drawings in galleries.

As you're learning to get your drawings just right, you'll also notice yourself learning to enjoy the process: finding the perfect reference material, picking up your pencil, looking at the blank page and imagining what it could be.

There's so much to learn when you pick up a pencil. Whether you're eight or 118 years old, *today* is always the best day to start your drawing journey.

Let's begin!

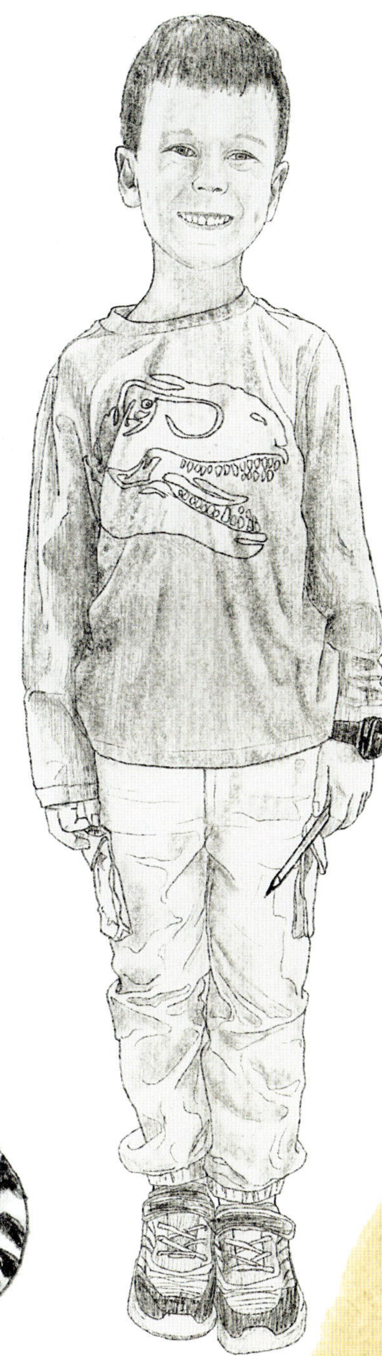

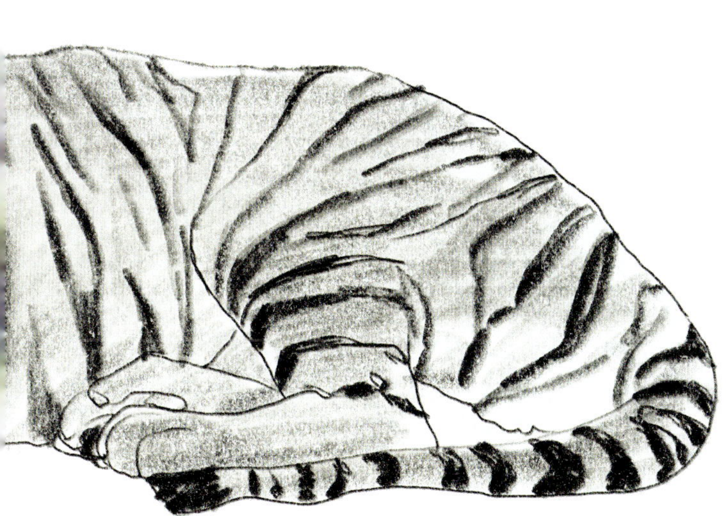

DRAWING MATERIALS

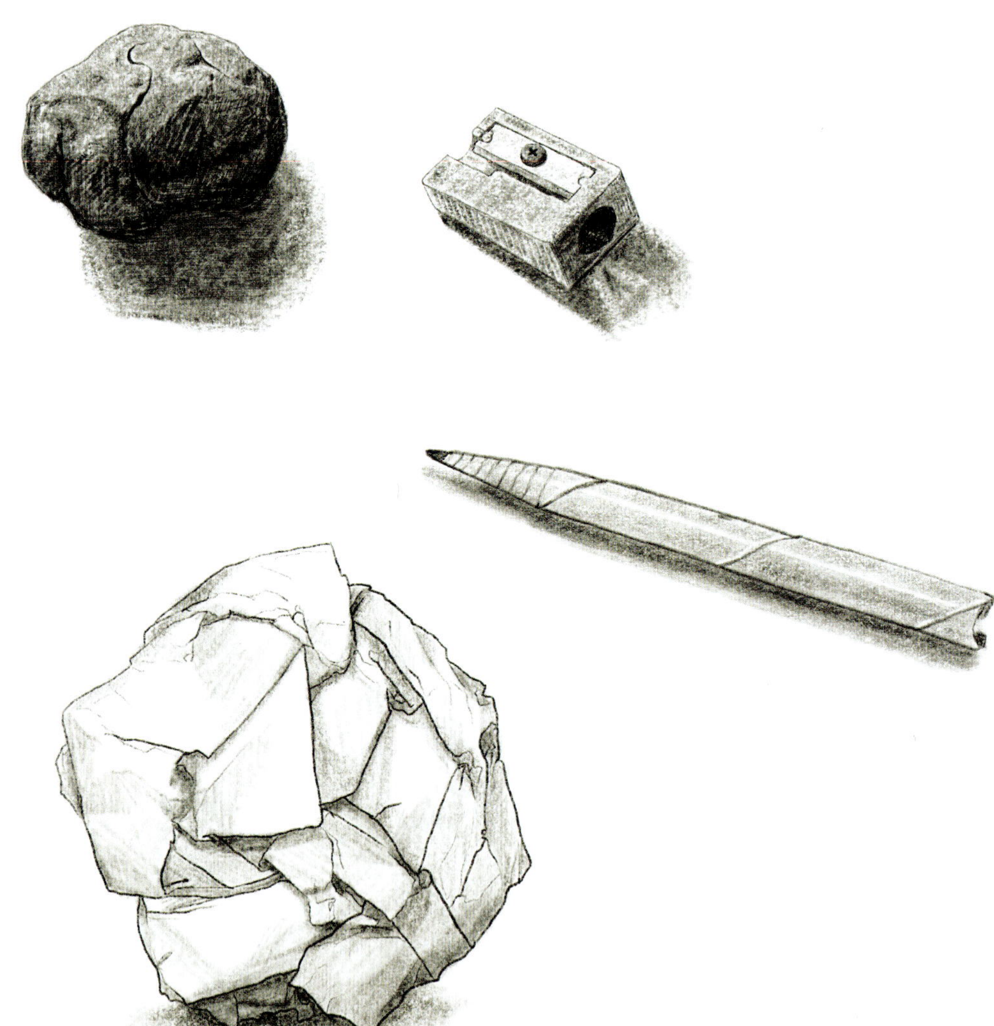

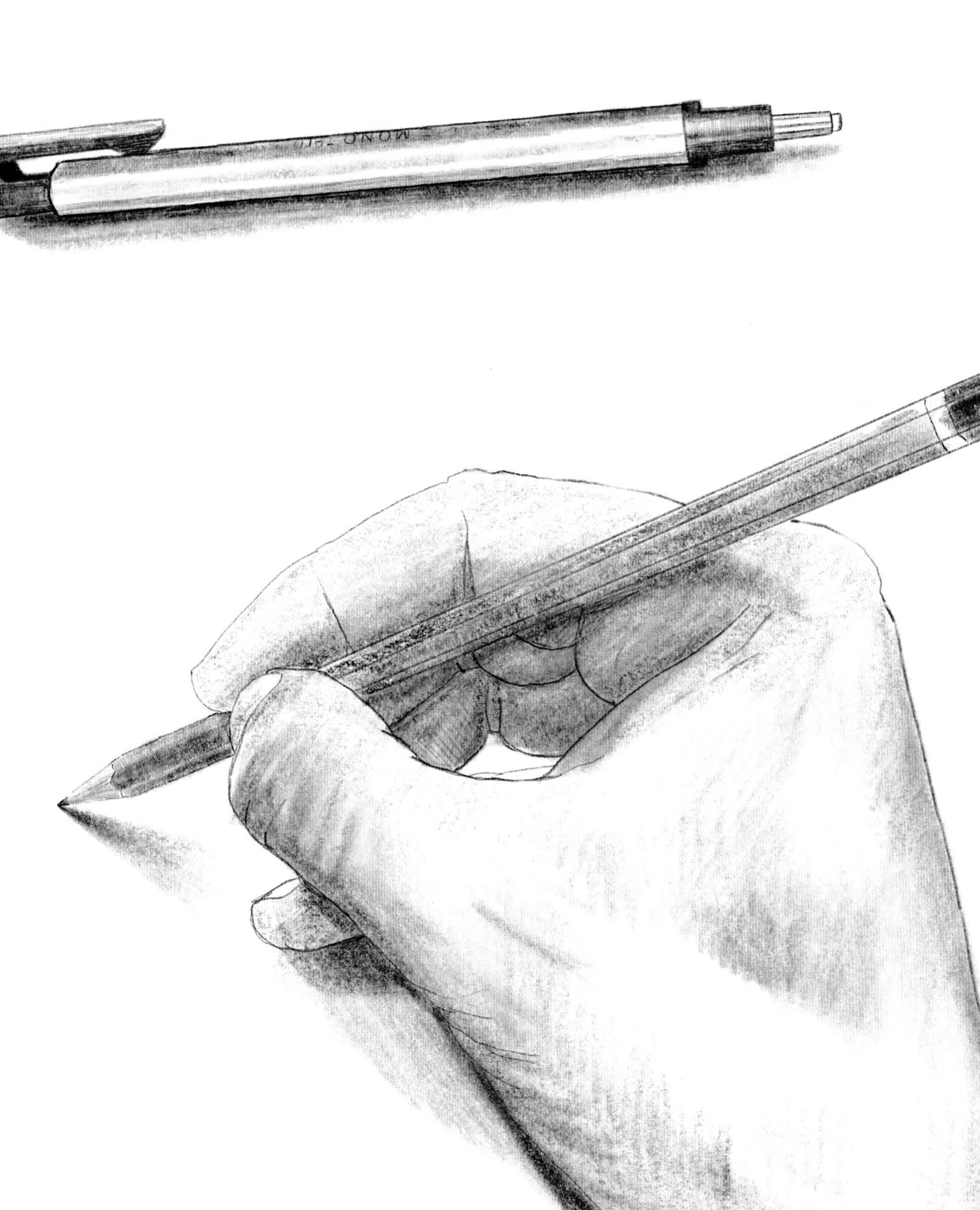

PAPER

There are lots of surfaces you can draw on—canvas, cardboard, leather, wood—but the most popular support for drawing is good old-fashioned paper.

Loose Leaf

If you're new to art, try to use loose sheets of printer paper or other relatively inexpensive paper. When you're getting started, you should be focused on learning, not on perfection. There's no need for fancy paper.

Sketchbook

Once you feel like you're ready, pick a sketchbook and start filling it up. The nice thing about keeping your drawings all in one place is that you'll get to see your progress over time.

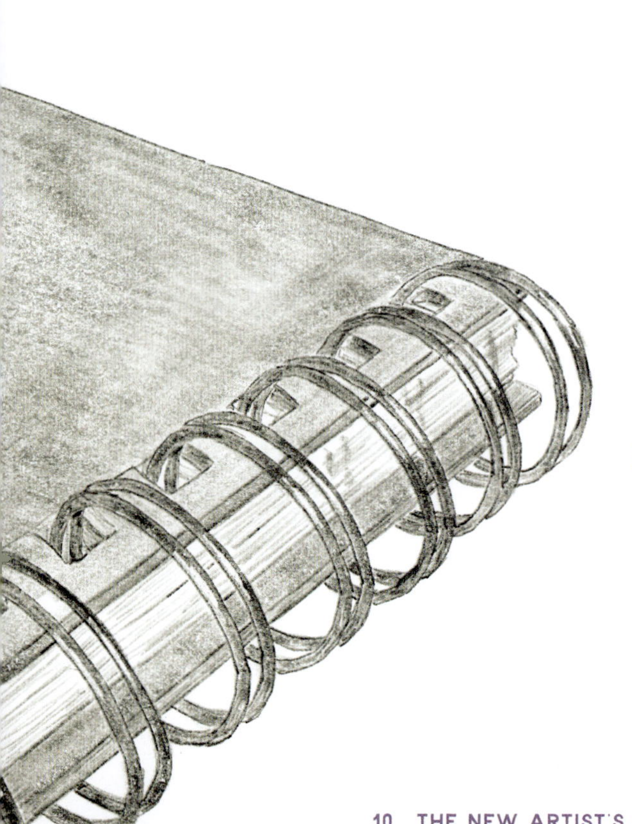

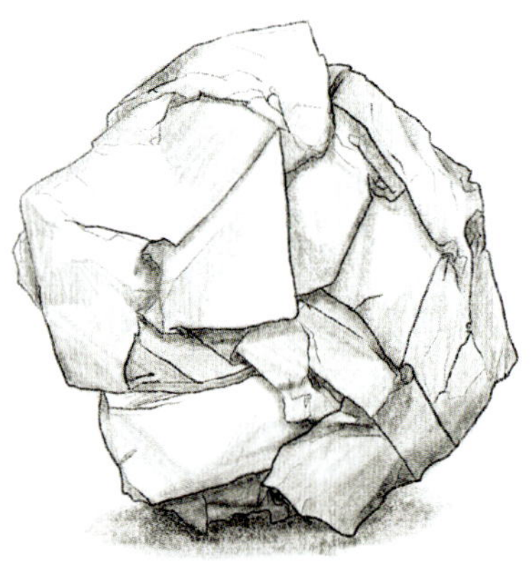

Experiment and play with ideas, techniques and materials. If you don't like what you've made, simply flip the page over. And if you don't like that, grab a fresh sheet and try, try again.

At some point, you'll want to create a drawing that you'll keep, give away or even sell. When the time comes, it's definitely worth swapping your printer paper for one of the three types of fine art paper below.

Hot-Pressed Paper

The smoothest of the set, hot-pressed paper is typically used for drawing with graphite and ink.

- ✔ **Ideal for realism**
- ✘ **Not good for showing texture**

Cold-Pressed Paper

Its textured surface makes cold-pressed paper a great choice for charcoal, pastels and watercolor paint.

- ✔ **Results in a unique, textured look that appeals to some artists**
- ✘ **Its texture can be hard on pencils**

Rough Paper

As the name suggests, rough paper is coarse and highly textured. It's used for watercolor paintings and ink drawings.

- ✔ **A work of art in and of itself**
- ✘ **Difficult to work on**
- ✘ **Has noticeable fibers**
- ✘ **Expensive**

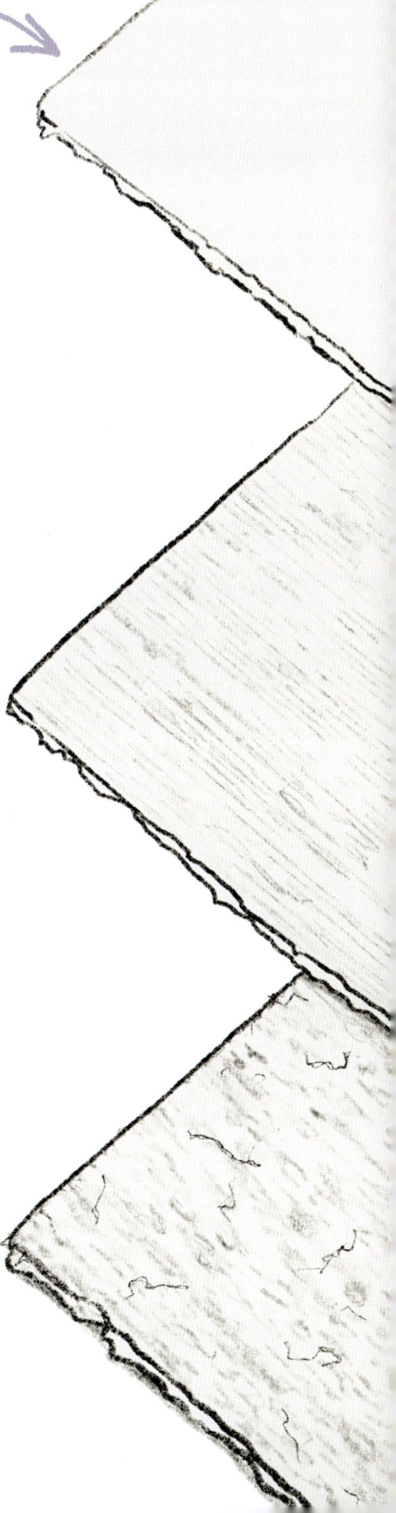

PENCILS

Figuring out which pencil is right for you starts with understanding the different characteristics of this universal drawing tool. To keep things simple, let's look at the main characteristics of a standard graphite pencil. These characteristics can also be applied to the various other types of pencils, as we'll see on the next page.

Grade

Pencils are made of a mixture of graphite and clay, a filler. The grade, or hardness, of a pencil is a measure of how much clay it contains: hard pencils (graded H) contain a lot of clay and little graphite, while soft pencils (graded B) contain little clay and a lot of graphite. That means if you draw with a soft B pencil, your lines will be darker and more likely to smudge, and if you draw with a hard H pencil, your lines will be lighter and less likely to smudge.

Value

Sometimes called tone, value is how light or dark an area is on a scale from black to white. Soft pencils can be used to make light or dark lines, but hard pencils can *only* be used for light lines. For a full list of different pencil numbers (e.g., HB, 2B, 4H) and their values, see page 23.

Tip Quality

You might already know that the sharper the tip, or point, of your pencil, the finer your details. Hard pencils can be sharpened to a fine point, making them great for drawing details and realism. Soft pencils, on the other hand, cannot easily be sharpened to a fine point.

Shine

In drawing, we call lines that are shiny *glossy* and lines that aren't shiny *matte*. All graphite pencils are glossy, regardless of their grade.

Graphite and mechanical pencils are glossy, while charcoal and black carbon pencils are matte.

Most people think the H on a pencil is short for Hard and the B is short for Black, but that's not the case. The letters actually come from the French words for high ("haut") and low ("bas"), in reference to the pencil's clay content.

Types of Pencils

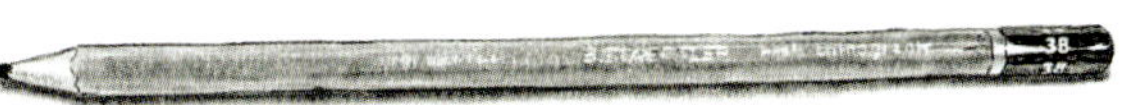

Graphite

- ✓ **Least expensive**
- ✓ **Most commonly available**
- ✓ **22 grades to choose from, ranging from 12B (softest) to 10H (hardest)**
- ✗ Glossy, which isn't great for realism
- ✗ Doesn't get as dark as black

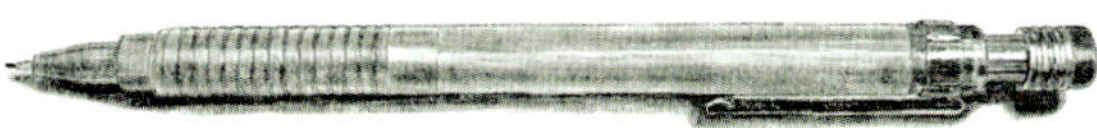

Mechanical

- ✓ **Lots of control**
- ✓ **Tip is always sharp**
- ✓ **Yields clean lines**
- ✗ Can only make one type of line width
- ✗ Breaks easily
- ✗ Glossy, which isn't great for realism

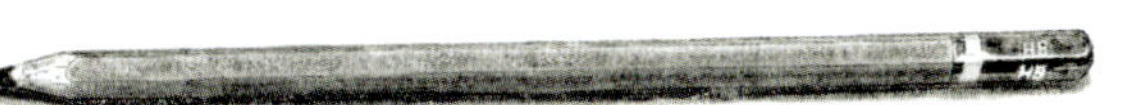

Black Carbon

- ✓ **Darker than regular graphite pencils**
- ✓ **Doesn't smudge like charcoal**
- ✓ **Matte, which is great for realism**
- ✗ Limited range of grades, with only soft (B) options
- ✗ Harder to find than graphite

Digital

- ✓ **Offers a range of characteristics: varying line width, tip quality, etc.**
- ✓ **Full range of dark to light lines**
- ✓ **Produces digital work that's easy to share**
- ✗ Expensive
- ✗ Feels different in your hand than standard pencils
- ✗ Can't be used on paper; requires a tablet or computer

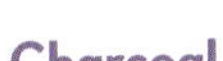

Charcoal

- ✓ **Makes the darkest lines**
- ✓ **Matte, which is great for realism**
- ✗ Smudges a lot, making it hard to work with
- ✗ Hard to sharpen

Charcoal pencils are softer and messier than graphite ones, which means they're great for smudging (but not ideal for details).

ERASERS

Erasers aren't just for fixing mistakes. In addition to removing a pencil mark or marks entirely, you can use them to simply lighten areas to varying degrees within a drawing. And, as you'll see on page 150, you can sometimes even use erasers to create drawings when starting from a shaded area.

Here are a few erasers you'll want to have on hand (and one you won't) as you dive into drawing.

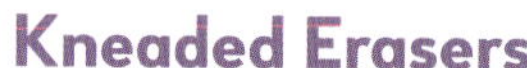

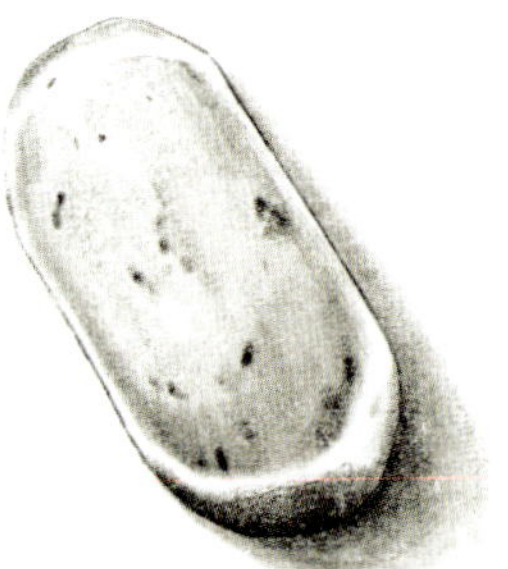

White Erasers

This classic eraser is most definitely a must-have. It's gentle on your paper and removes pencil marks very effectively.

Kneaded Erasers

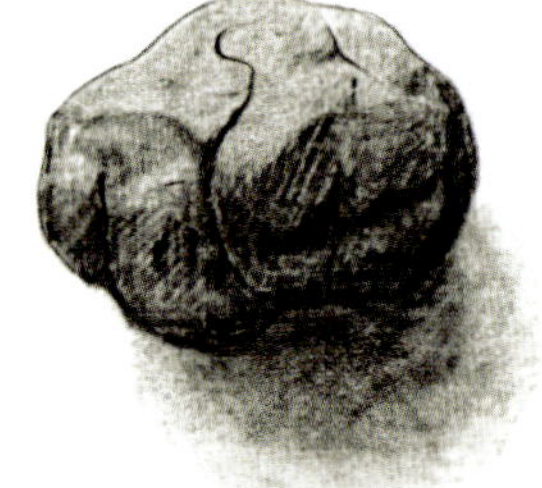

Kneaded erasers, also known as putty rubber, are gentle on paper, but they don't erase that well. That means they're not great for getting back to the white of your paper (if you're working on white). That also means they *are* great for making areas lighter without completely erasing them.

Stick Erasers

Stick erasers, pen erasers, click erasers. Whichever you use, you'll find them as easy to hold as a pencil. Stick erasers are great for precision erasing, so if you're working on details, this is your choice.

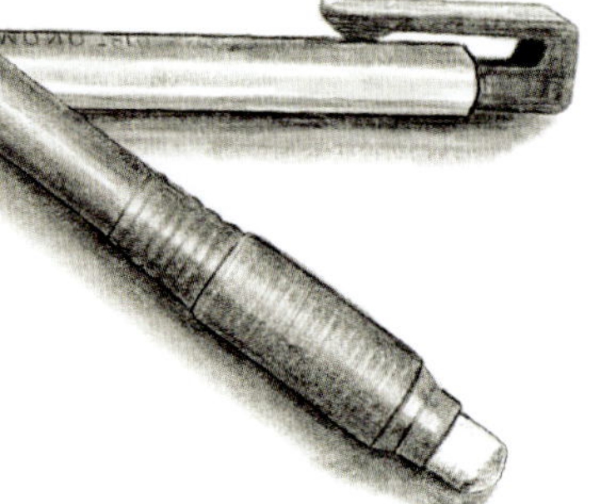

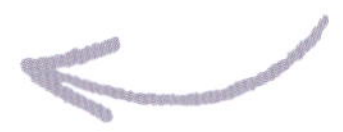

Stick eraser refills can get pricey, so try to use them for details only, and use a white eraser for larger areas.

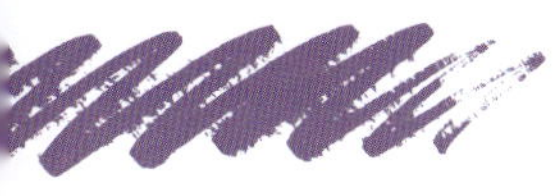

Pink Erasers

Try not to use these if you can help it. It's tempting, as they're often literally at the tip of your pencil, but they erase very poorly—and they often damage your paper in the process.

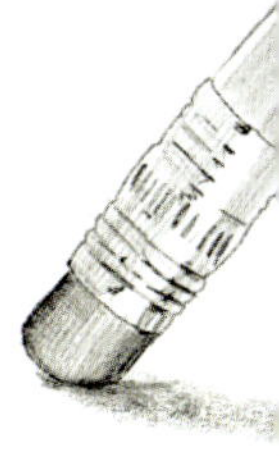

SHARPENERS

Unless you're using exclusively mechanical or digital pencils to draw, you're going to need a sharpener. Beyond extending the life of your pencil, sharpeners help you control the sharpness of your pencil—and therefore the lines in your drawing.

The following sharpeners are ideal for all artists, from beginner to advanced.

Single-Hole Metal Sharpeners

Typically made of stainless steel, metal sharpeners are inexpensive and virtually indestructible. The single hole is a great fit for most graphite pencils.

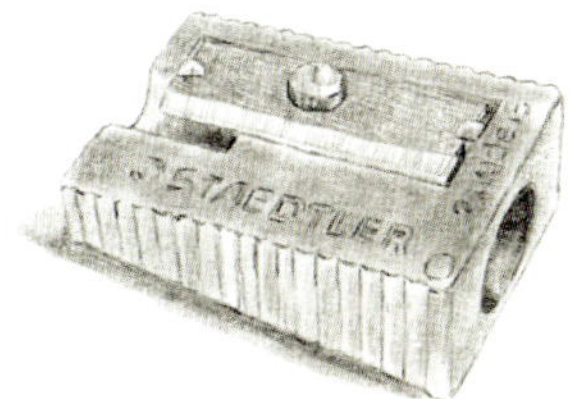

Double-Hole Metal Sharpeners

Double-hole sharpeners have the same advantages as their single-hole cousins, plus an added benefit: a second, larger hole for sharpening very soft pencils, like charcoal pencils or pastels.

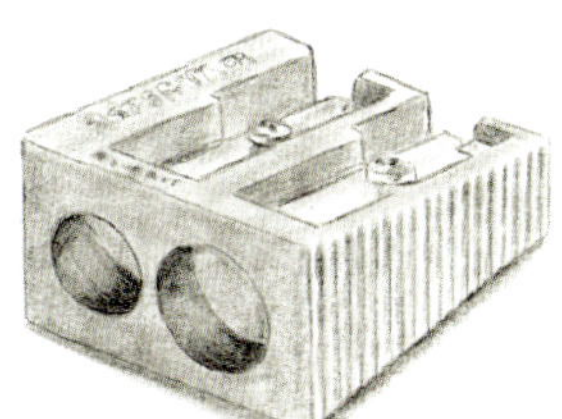

Metal Sharpeners with Reservoir

These are identical to metal sharpeners, except they come with a tub designed to collect pencil shavings. Pick one of these if you prefer a clean work surface.

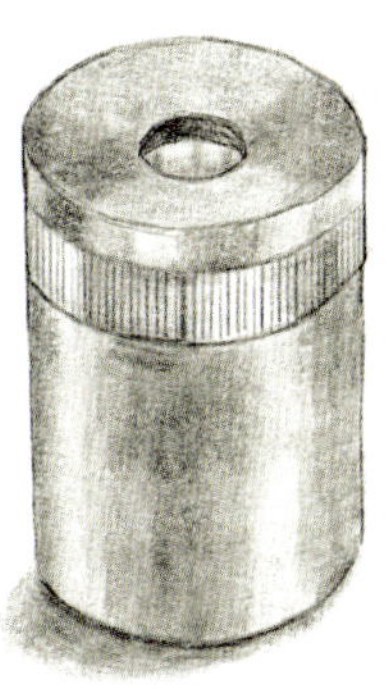

BLENDING TOOLS

Blending is one of the best ways to create smooth transitions between dark and light areas of your drawing for a realistic look. Below are a handful of blending tools you can use to help you blend the pencil marks in your drawings.

Blending Stumps

Made from tightly rolled or twisted paper, blending stumps are cylindrical tools used for smudging or blending graphite and charcoal (and pastels, if you use those). They have two tips.

- ✓ **Inexpensive**
- ✓ **Come in a variety of sizes**
- ✓ **Excellent for subtle blending**
- ✗ **Not great for use in small or detailed areas**

Tortillons

Similar to blending stumps, tortillons are made from rolled paper and are great for smudging and blending. Unlike blending stumps, they have only one tip, and it's a finer one, making it ideal for blending details.

- ✓ **Inexpensive**
- ✓ **Come in a variety of sizes**
- ✓ **Excellent for subtle blending**
- ✓ **Great for use in small or detailed areas**
- ✗ **Not great for use over large areas**

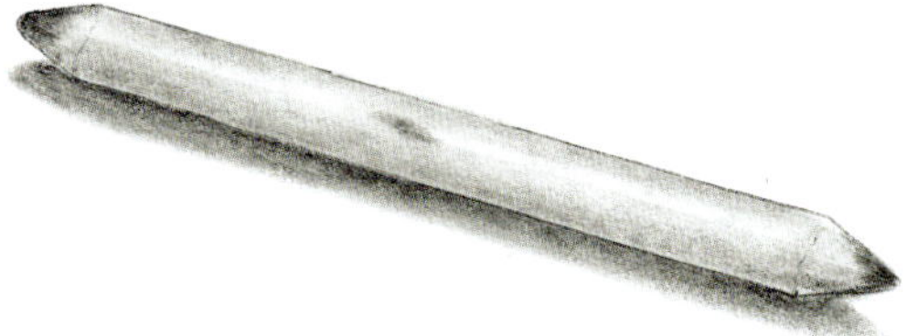

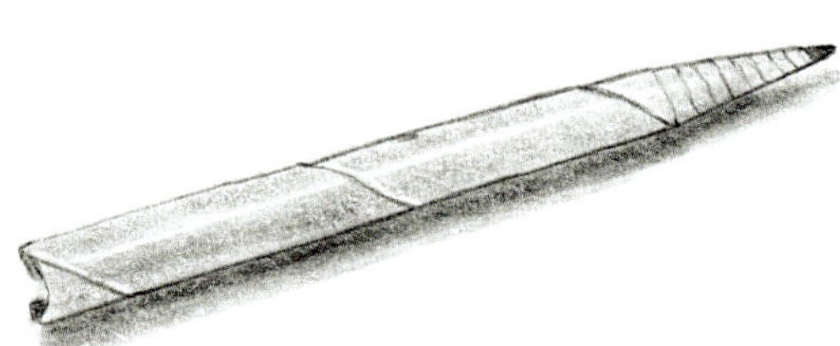

Blending is one of several ways to shade. See page 29 to learn how to use these tools to shade your drawings.

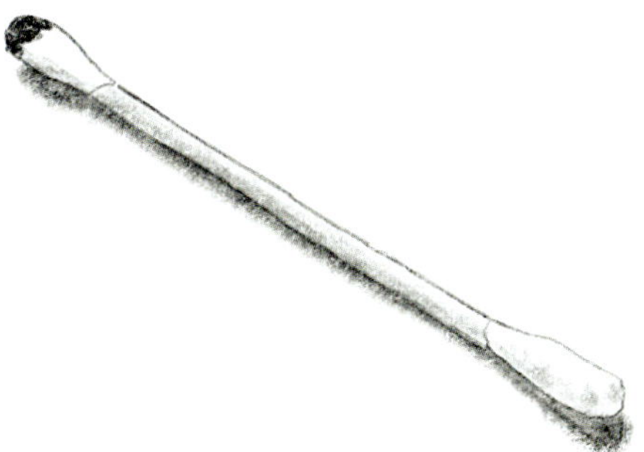

Cotton Swabs

Add one more use to this everyday household item. Because they have such fine tips, cotton swabs enable you to easily blend small areas. They work especially well with very soft graphite and charcoal pencils.

- ✔ **Inexpensive**
- ✔ **Easy to find**
- ✔ **Great for use in small or detailed areas**
- ✗ **Can leave behind cotton fibers**
- ✗ **Wear out quickly**

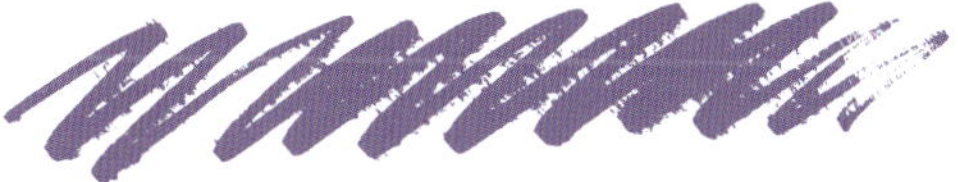

Your Fingers

As a last resort, and *only* as a last resort, you can use one of your fingers to blend. It's not ideal, because the skin on your finger contains oil, which can destroy your paper and your drawing. If you're going to do it, be sure to wash—and dry—your hands thoroughly beforehand.

- ✔ **Free**
- ✔ **Always available**
- ✗ **Risky, as the oils can ruin your paper and your drawing**

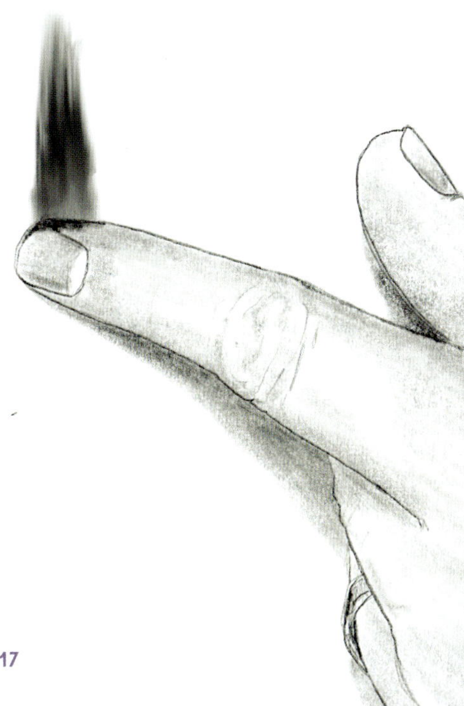

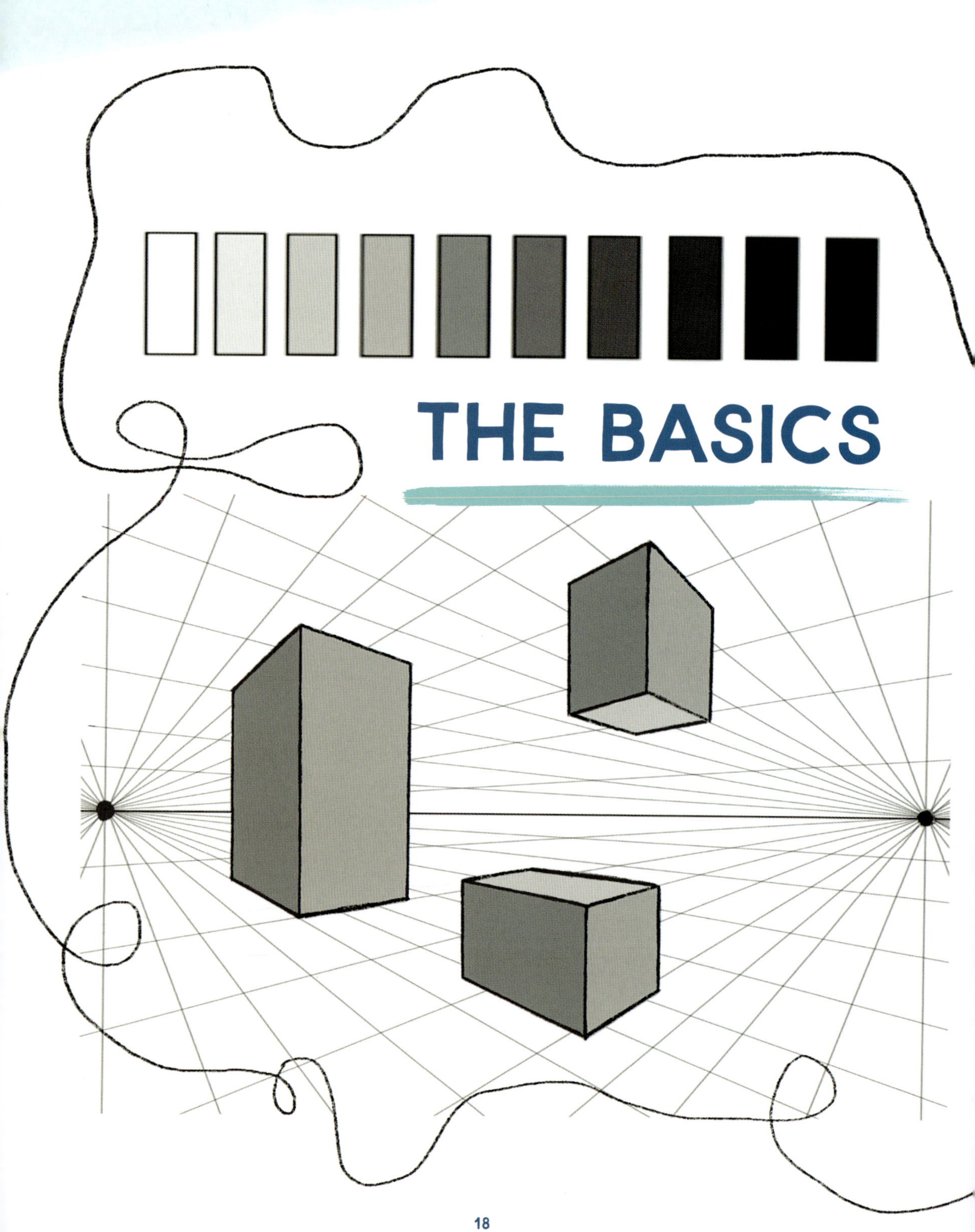

THE BASICS

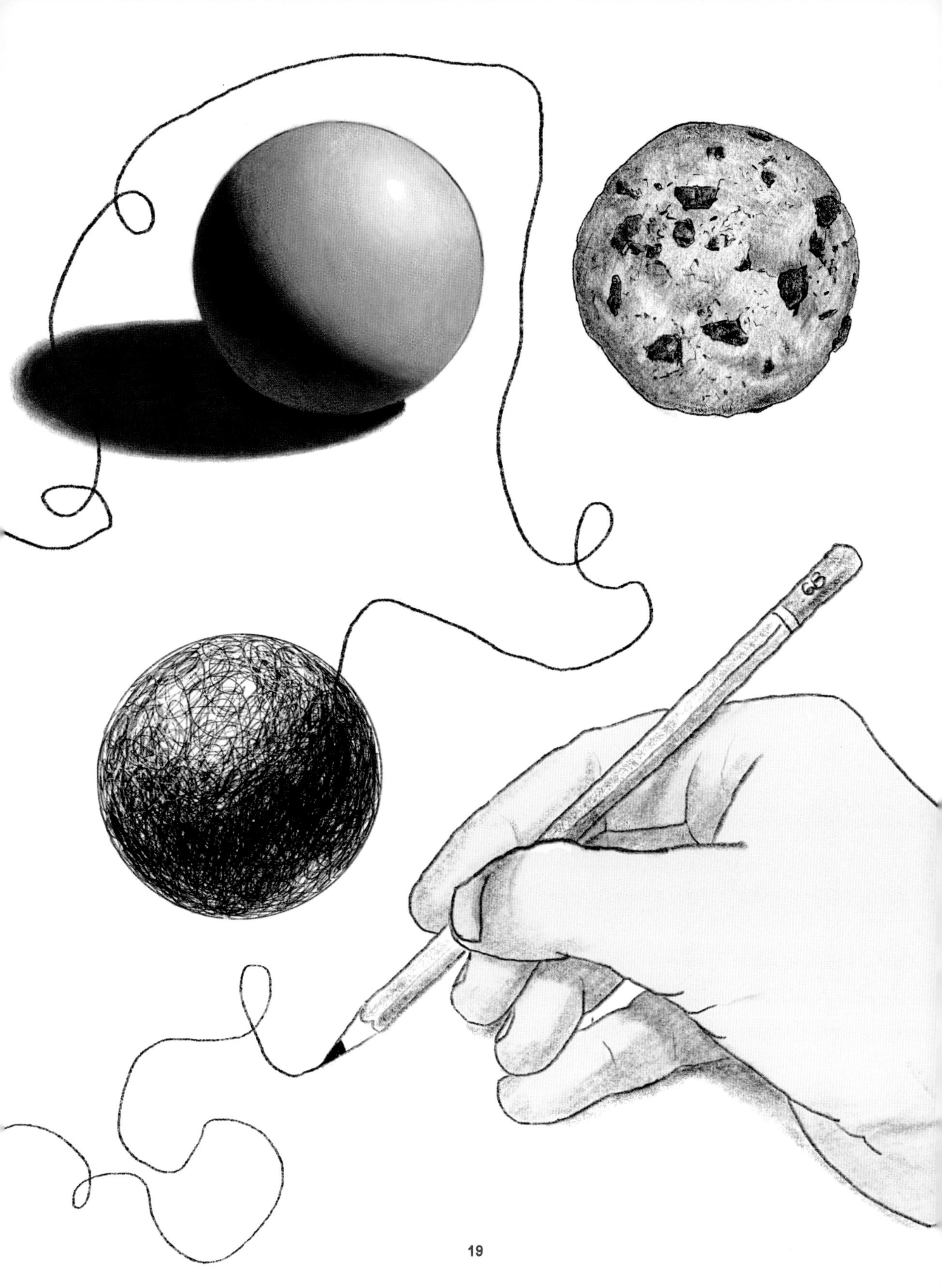

LINES

A line is just a line, right? Not really. The world is filled with lines—short and long, light and heavy, thin and thick and everything in between. Thankfully for those of us who like drawing realistically, it's fairly easy to manipulate your pencil to create as many different kinds of lines as you need to depict your environment.

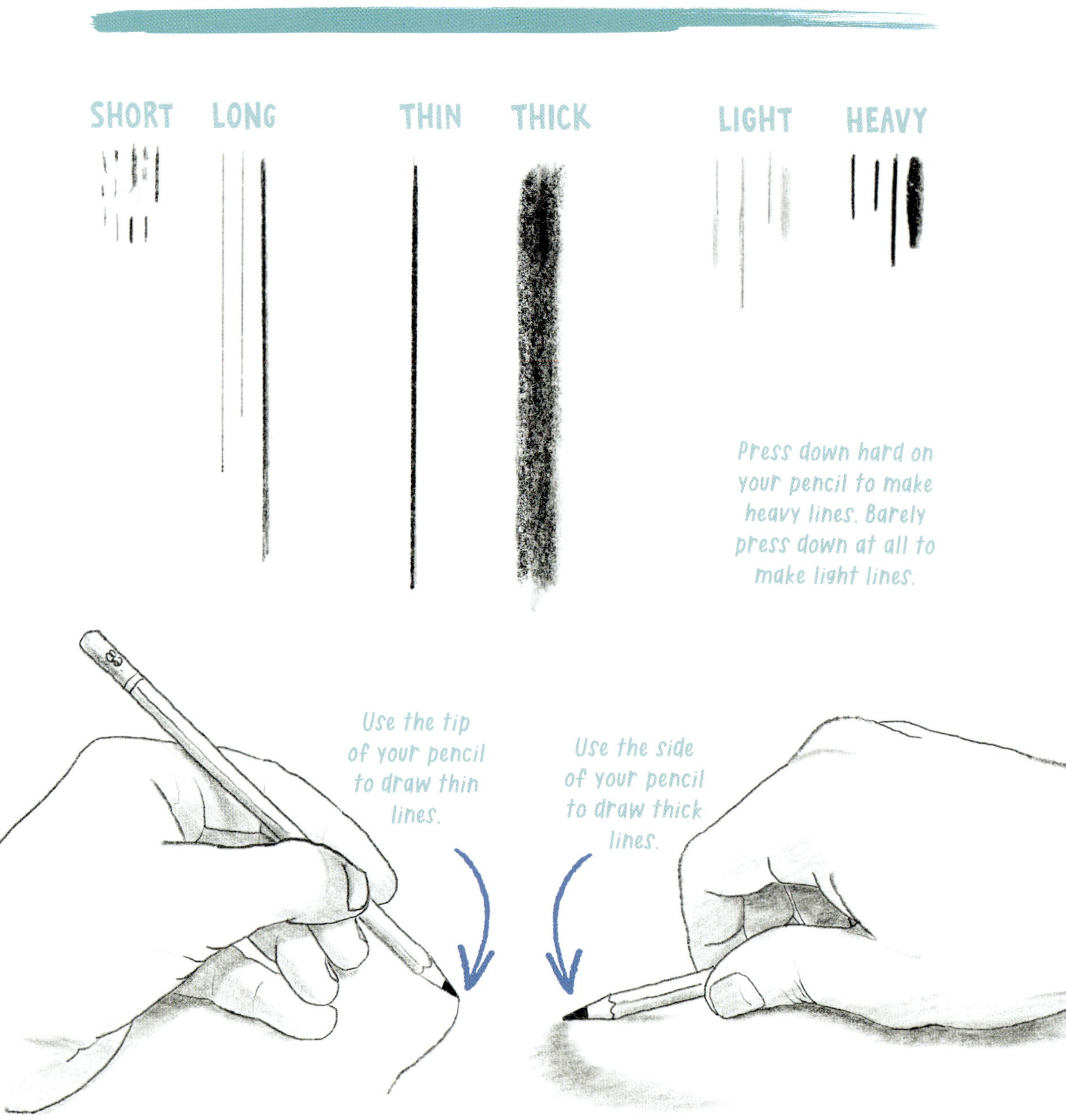

The drawing below uses a good range of different kinds of lines. See if you can name some of the lines that aren't called out.

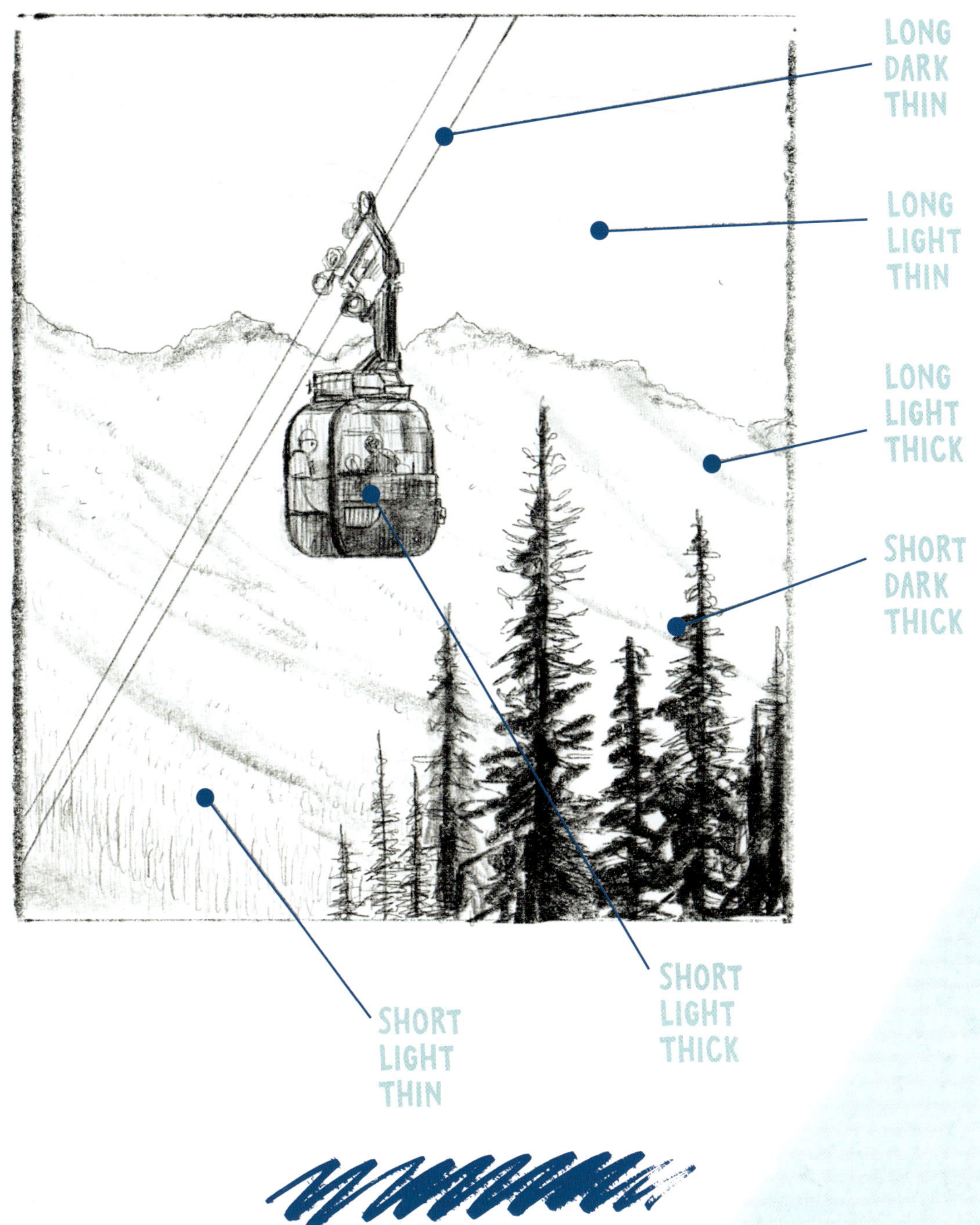

VALUE

Value is how light or dark something is. In art, we usually measure value on a scale from 1 to 10, with 1 representing the whitest white, 10 the blackest black and everything in between a shade of gray.

Understanding value is essential to creating the appearance of three-dimensionality in your drawings. Once you understand value, you can transform the simplest of line drawings into realistic drawings through a technique called shading (see page 26).

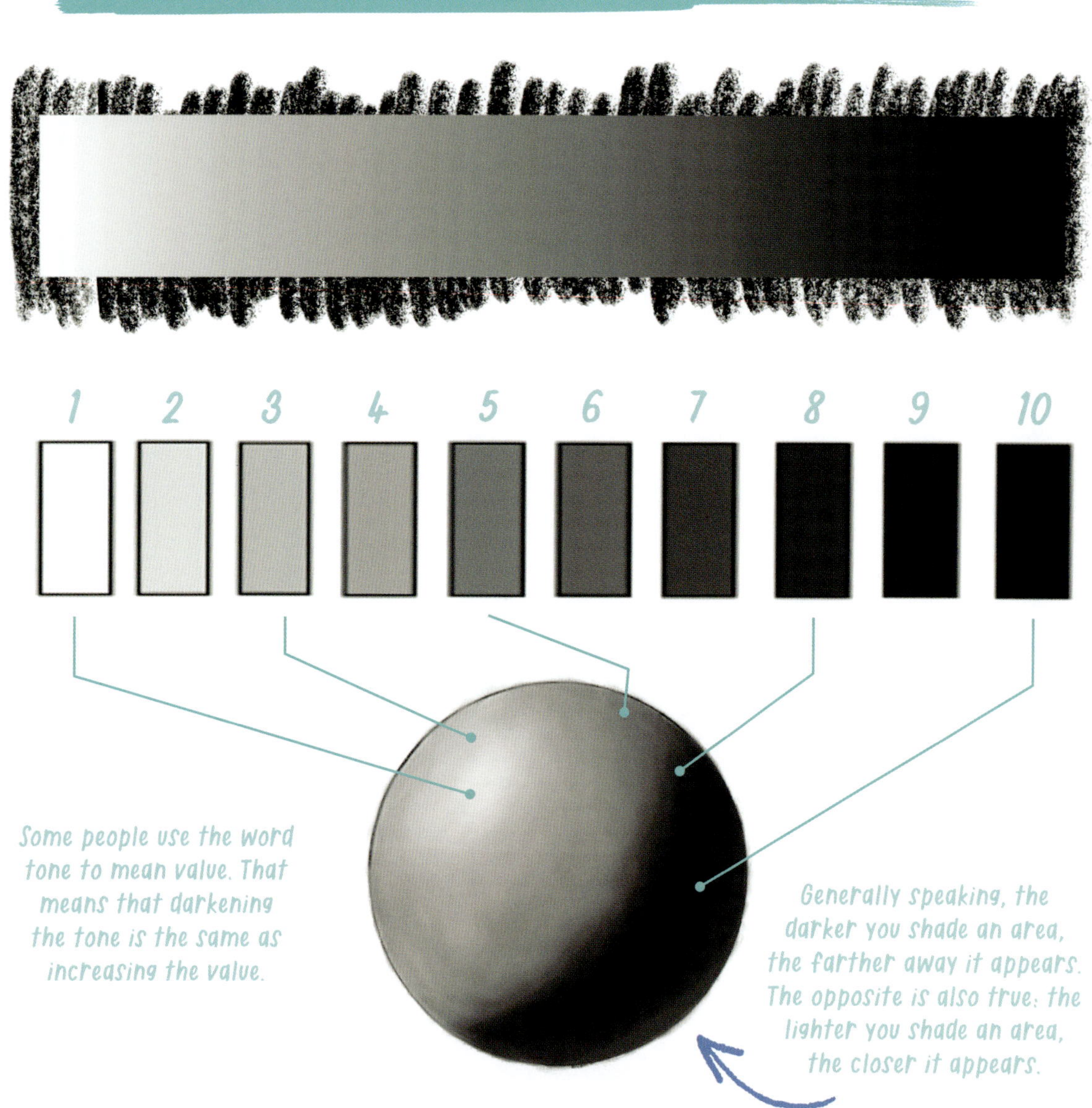

Different pencils make it possible to create different ranges of value. The 6H pencil, for example, only allows you to go up to 3 or 4 in value, while the 8B gets as dark as a 9 or so. That doesn't mean the 8B pencil is better: you can produce a range of values (light and dark lines) with an 8B, but it's more difficult to achieve those lower values than it is with harder pencils.

If you can only pick one pencil, reach for an HB, which will give you a wide enough range to create the 3D effect you're after.

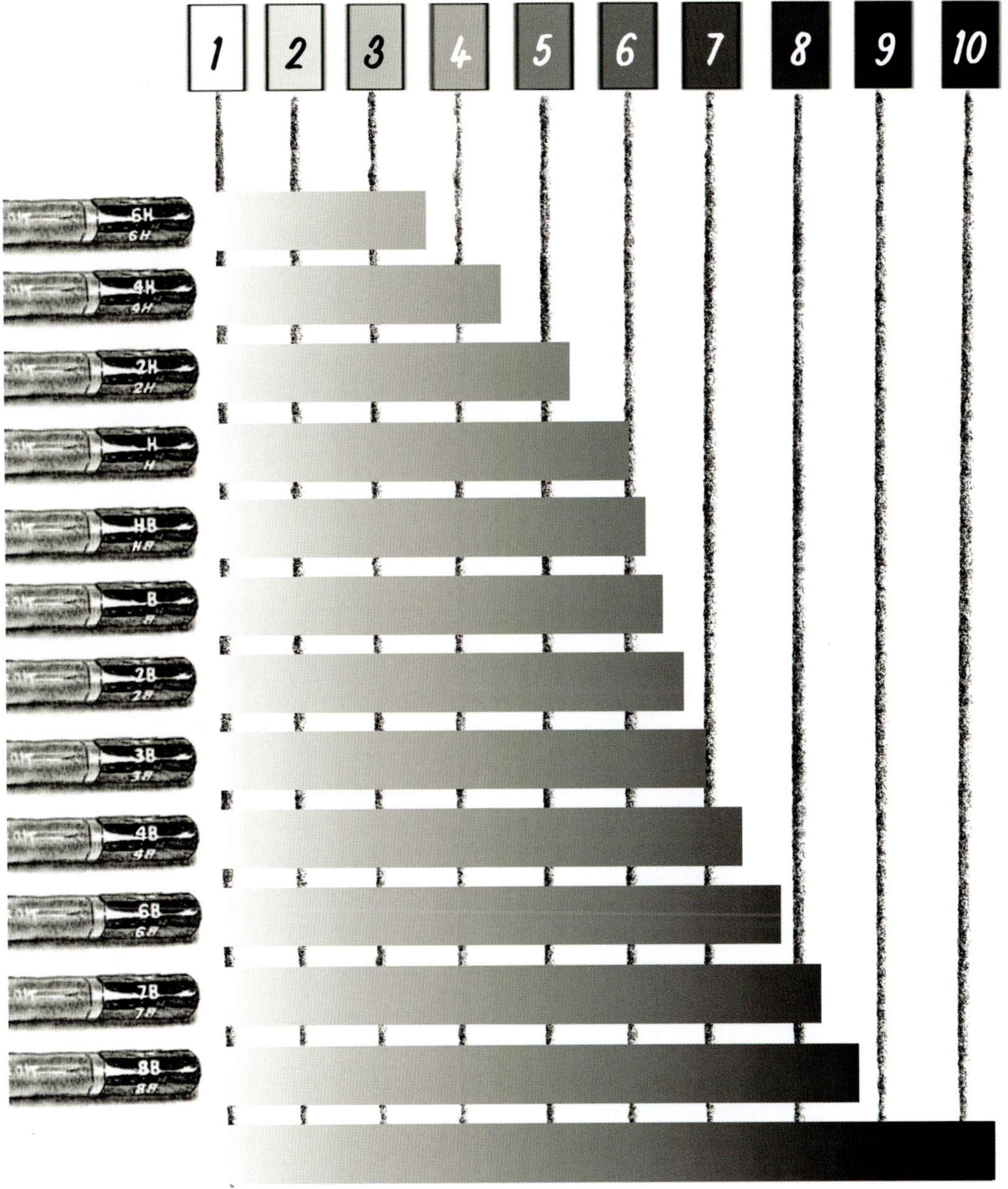

LIGHTING

If you've ever held a flashlight under your chin, you know just how drastically lighting can affect appearance. Most of the drawing exercises in this book assume neutral lighting, which means there is no particular light source—the same amount of light is coming from all sides to light the object.

 In reality, though, there can be multiple light sources that affect how something appears. Once you've identified which areas of your drawing should be lighter and darker, you can shade those areas accordingly to create the appearance of three dimensions.

Can you see the subtle differences in lighting in these two drawings? See what each area is called on the next page.

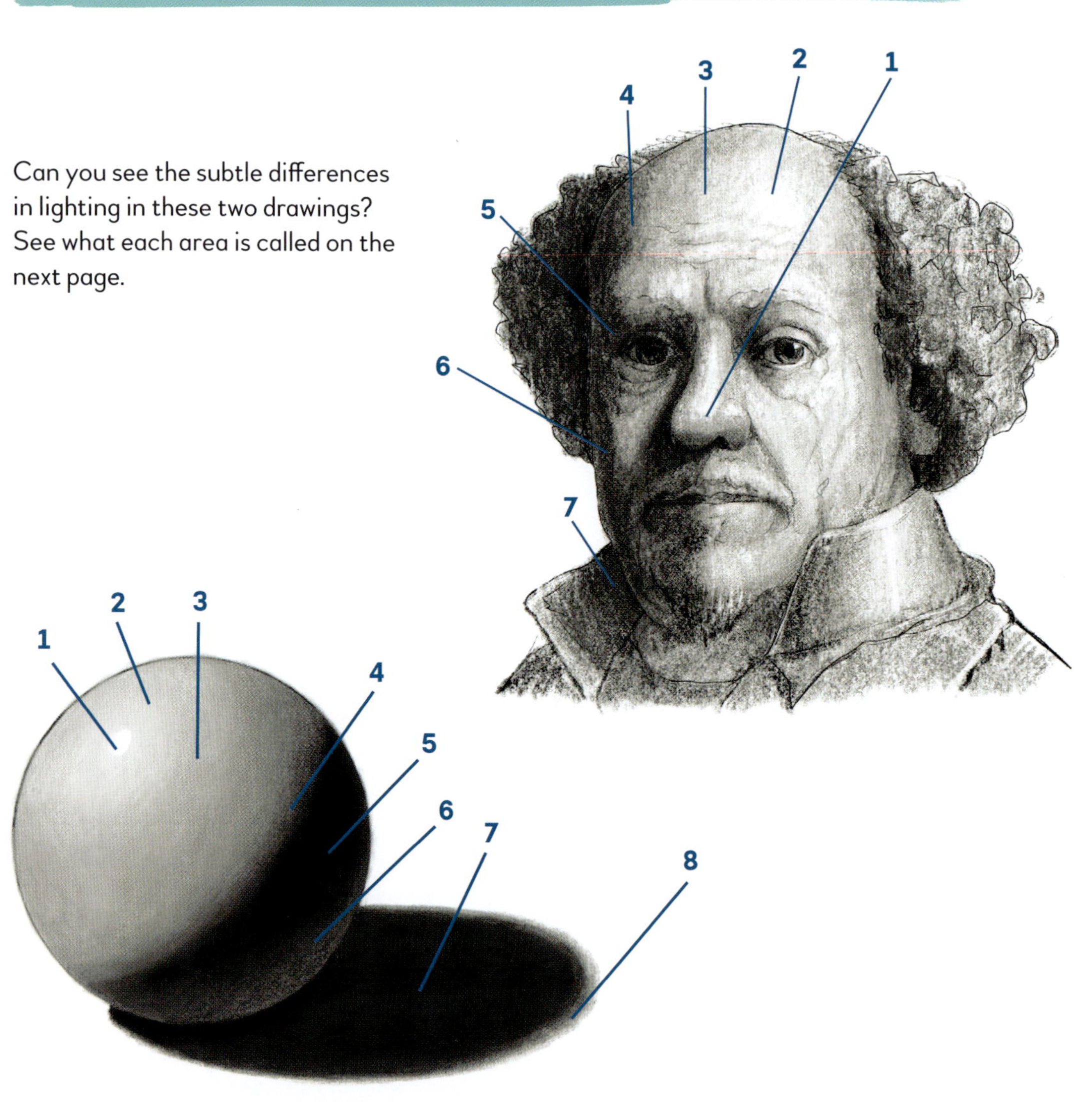

Types of Lighting

You don't need to memorize these terms and definitions, but they can be helpful to you as you take your drawing to the next level.

1

Highlight

The lightest area of a drawing is called the *highlight*.

2

Direct Light

If an area is in *direct light*, that means it is facing the light source straight on.

3

Halftone

A *halftone* is an area that is only partially facing the light source, so it's somewhere between direct light and shadow.

4

Terminator Line

The *terminator line* is where the light terminates, or stops illuminating an object. It marks the beginning of a transition to a shadow.

5

Core Shadow

The darkest part of the shadow side of an object is called the *core shadow*.

6

Reflected Light

If light bounces off one object and strikes another, that's called *reflected light*.

7

Cast Shadow

A *cast shadow* is a shadow that's created by something blocking the light source.

8

Penumbra

The area where a portion of light reaches the shadow is called the *penumbra*.

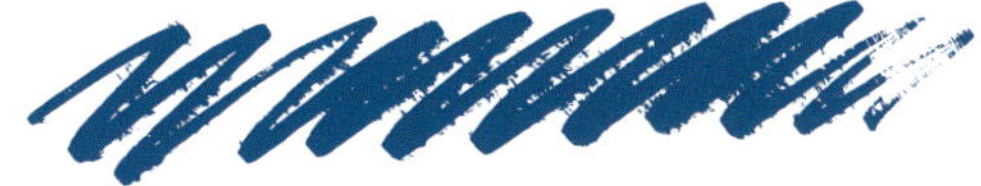

SHADING

Some people think shading is simply coloring something in. It's not. It's the act of creating lighter and darker areas in your drawings to make them seem three dimensional (3D) and, in turn, more realistic.

There are many types of shading. Here are the seven most common.

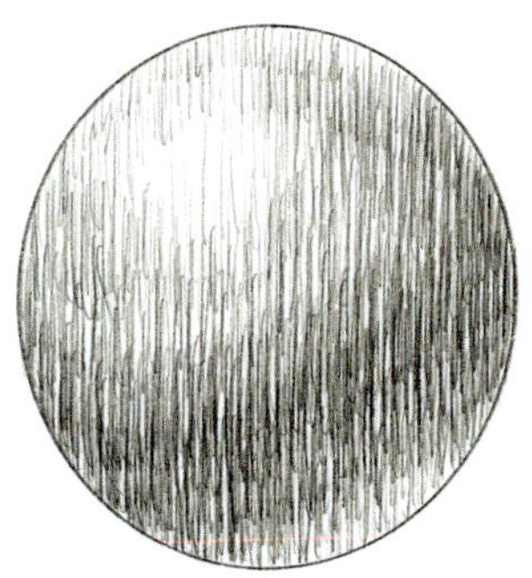

Hatching

Draw parallel lines in the same direction. Include more lines in the areas of the object that are farther away from the light source, and fewer lines in the areas that are closest to the light source.

- ✔ **Great for beginners**
- ✔ **Easy to master**
- X **Not very quick—it takes a while to build up form**
- X **Not recommended for realism**
- X **Because you're drawing many lines, the repetition can hurt your wrist**

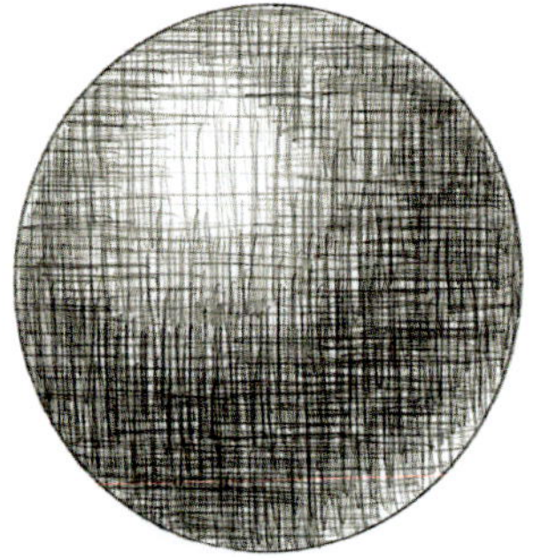

Cross-Hatching

Start by hatching, then add a set of lines that are perpendicular to, or cross, the first set. The more crossing lines you have on your object, the more 3D your object will appear.

- ✔ **Great for beginners**
- ✔ **Fairly easy to master**
- ✔ **Gives your drawings a stylized look**
- X **Takes a long time to build up form**
- X **Even harder on your wrist than hatching**

In drawing, when an object looks 3D, we say that object has something called form.

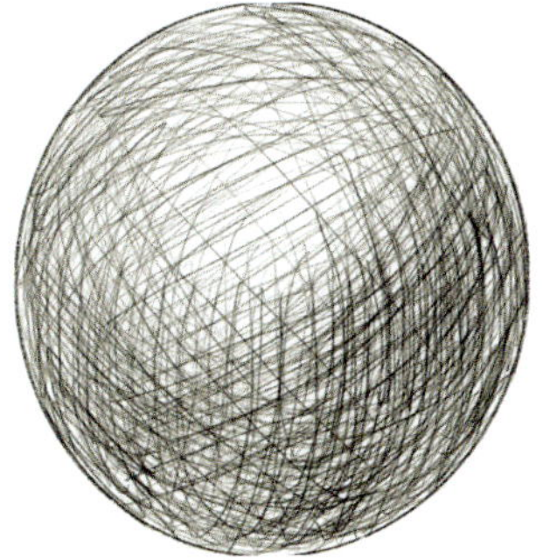

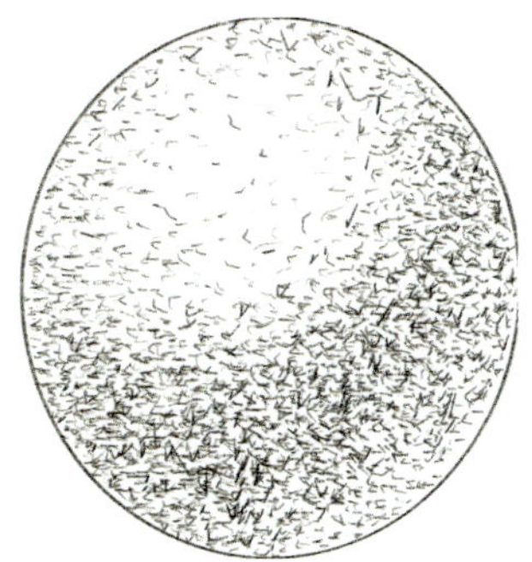

Contour Hatching

Imagine the object is in front of you. Now, draw lines that look like elastic bands wrapped around the object—they can be straight or curved. In the areas closest to the light source, draw fewer lines and draw them farther apart. The areas farther from the light source will be darker, so draw *more* lines and draw them closer together.

✔ **Great for showing form**

✔ **The most fun way to hatch**

X **Most difficult form of hatching to master**

X **Requires an understanding of the shape of the object**

Stippling

Draw hundreds or even thousands of small dots across your object. The more dots you have in an area, the darker it will appear, so make many dots and make them close together in the areas farthest from your light source, and draw fewer dots spaced farther apart in areas closest to your light source.

✔ **Not used by many artists, so your art will stand out**

X **Time-consuming**

X **Repetitive**

X **Requires a lot of dedication, patience and control**

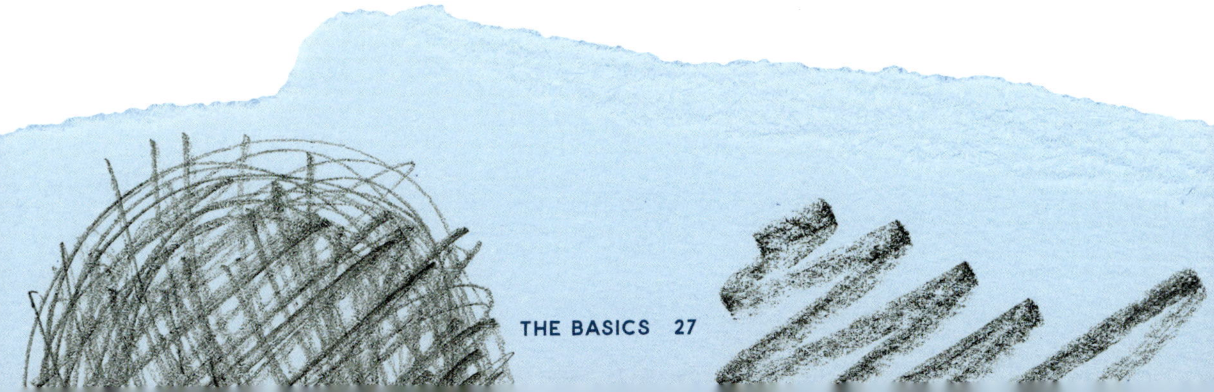

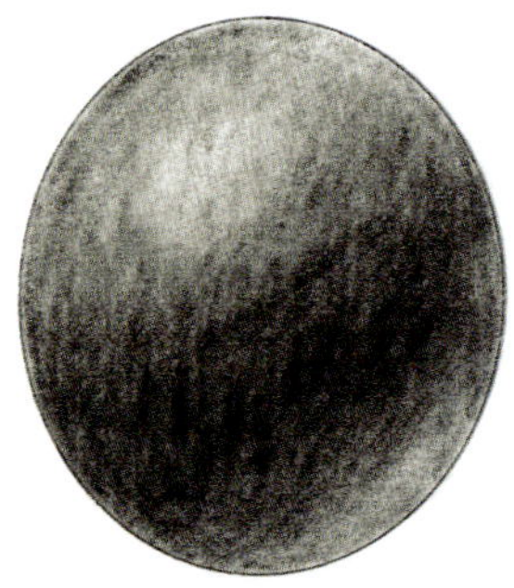

Blending

The goal is to avoid showing individual lines, so use only the side of your pencil. Make more marks in the areas that are farthest from your light source, taking your time to build up the darkness, and make fewer ones in the areas that are closest. Take your time creating smooth transitions between the light areas and dark ones.

- ✓ **Best for achieving realism**
- ✓ **Offers a lot of control**
- X **Most difficult to master**
- X **Hard to correct mistakes**

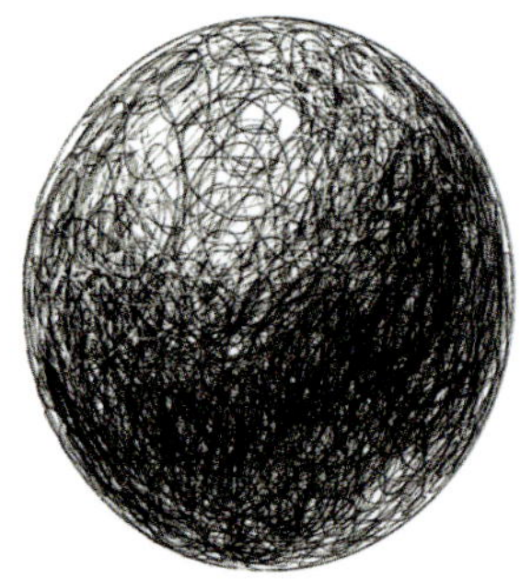

Scribbling

As the name suggests, to scribble is to create small circles and other random strokes with the tip of your pencil. Keep the marks irregular and chaotic, and avoid any patterns. Make more scribbles in areas that are darker, and fewer scribbles in areas that are lighter.

- ✓ **Great for beginners**
- ✓ **Requires little control**
- ✓ **Quick and, importantly, fun!**
- X **Can look messy**
- X **Not great for realism**

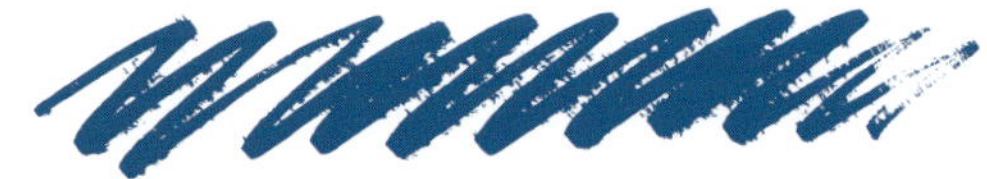

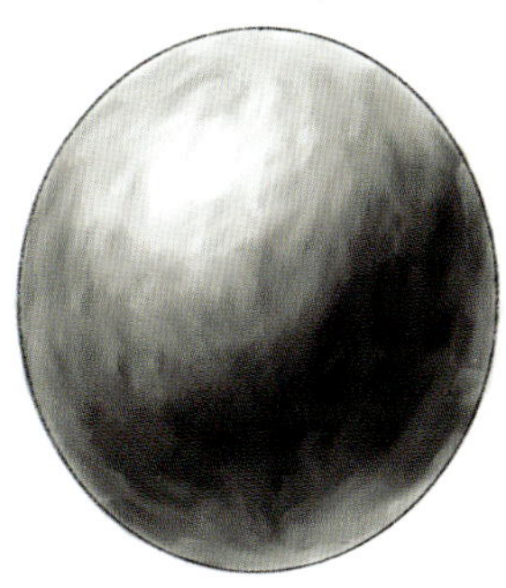

Smudging

Use the side of a soft pencil to lightly darken the dark areas of your object. Then, using a blending stump, press down firmly to smudge the parts of your object that are farther from your light source, and press down lightly to smudge the areas of your object that are lighter. Smudge between the areas to create smooth transitions from light to dark.

✔ **Very quick**

✔ **Great for realism**

✗ **Messy process**

✗ **Hard to correct mistakes**

If you don't have a blending stump or tortillon, don't worry. You can use a cotton swab instead (or even your finger, if you must).

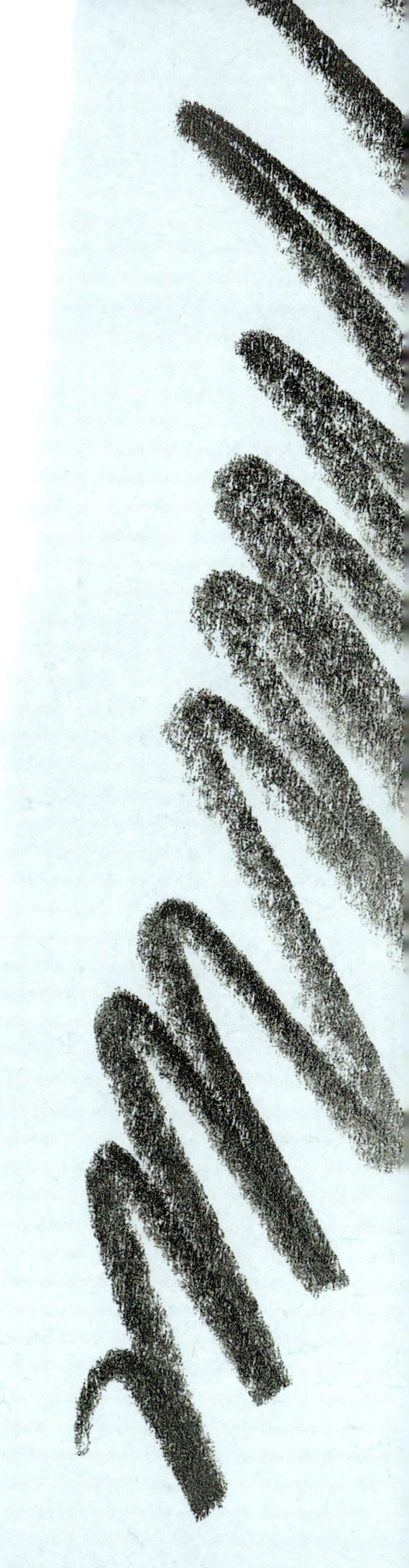

TEXTURE

In everyday life, the surface texture of an object is how it feels to the touch: bumpy, smooth, gritty, shiny, rough, dull, fuzzy, to name a few. If you want to be able to "see" a texture in your drawings, you'll need to use the range of lines available to you (short and long, light and heavy, thin and thick).

Dull objects, like the ones below, have a limited value range. That means the value doesn't go from very light to very dark—it doesn't vary much. But when the value does change, those transitions are smooth and slow, which means you'll want to show all the grays that fall in between your lighter and darker values.

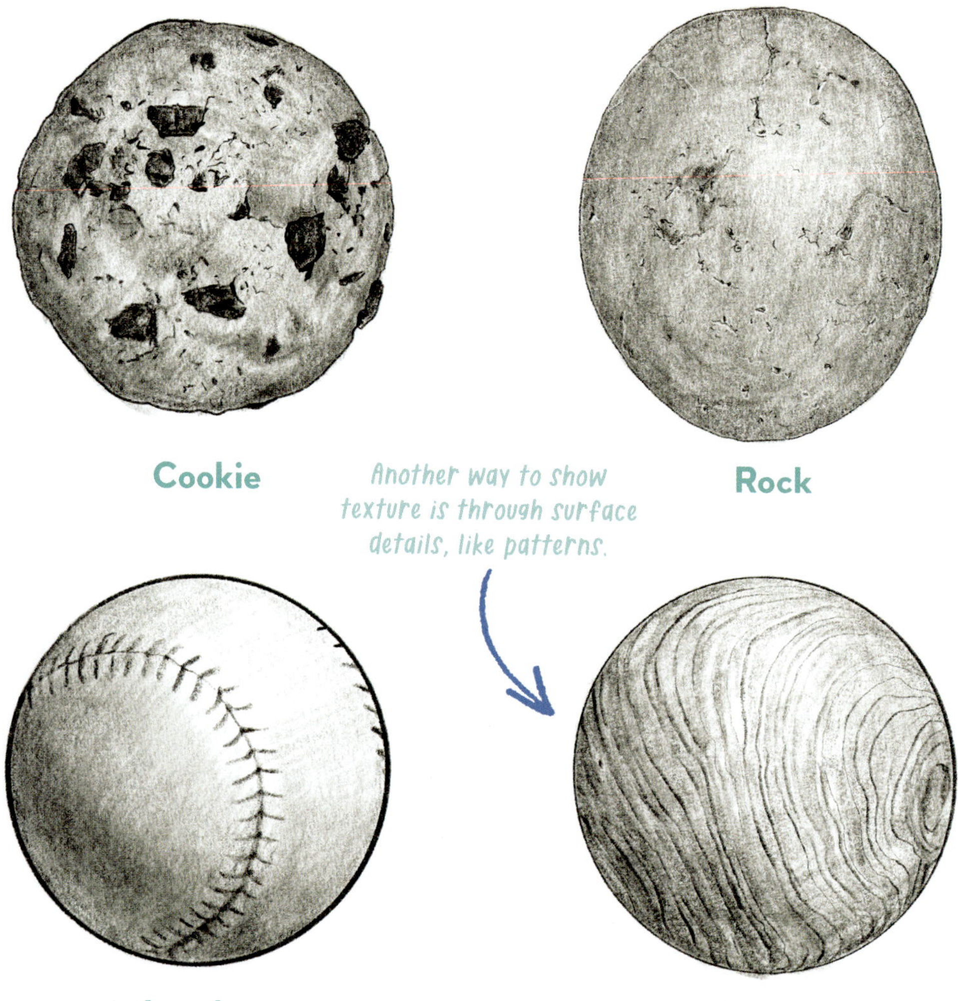

Below are some shiny objects. As you can see, shiny objects have a wide value range—areas can range from very light to very dark. And those transitions happen quickly, which means you don't need to show the values in between.

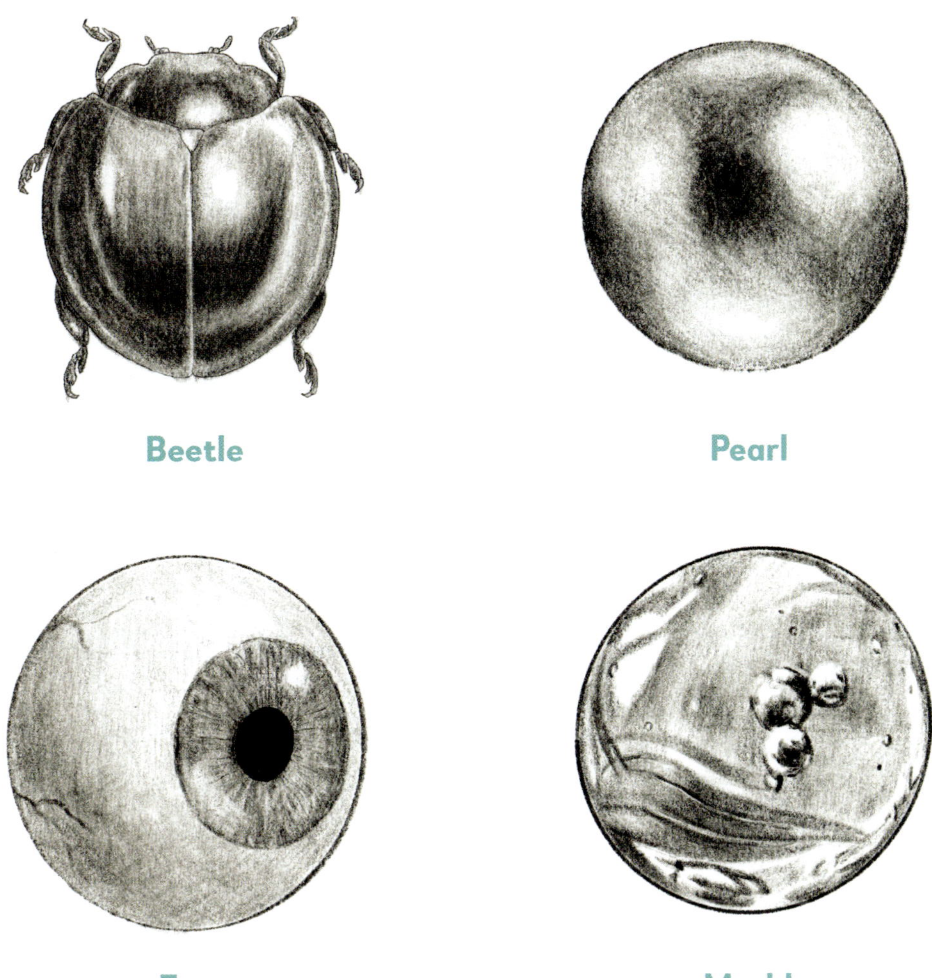

Beetle

Pearl

Eye

Marble

PERSPECTIVE

A flat piece of paper has two dimensions—height and width. That makes drawing in two dimensions quite straightforward: use vertical lines to show height, and horizontal lines to show width.

But to draw realistically, you're going to want to show the appearance of *three* dimensions: height, width and *depth*.

Enter 1-point, 2-point and 3-point perspective, three different ways of making your drawings look 3D. The easiest one to master is 1-point perspective, so start there and work your way up to 3-point perspective.

1-Point Perspective

1-point perspective is the easiest one to wrap your head around because you show height with vertical lines and width with horizontal lines, as you might expect. To show depth, however, you make all your depth lines point toward an imaginary vanishing point in the center of your drawing.

In 1-point perspective, there is *one* vanishing point, that is, a point where all the lines of a given dimension come together. Drawings in 1-point perspective look somewhat realistic.

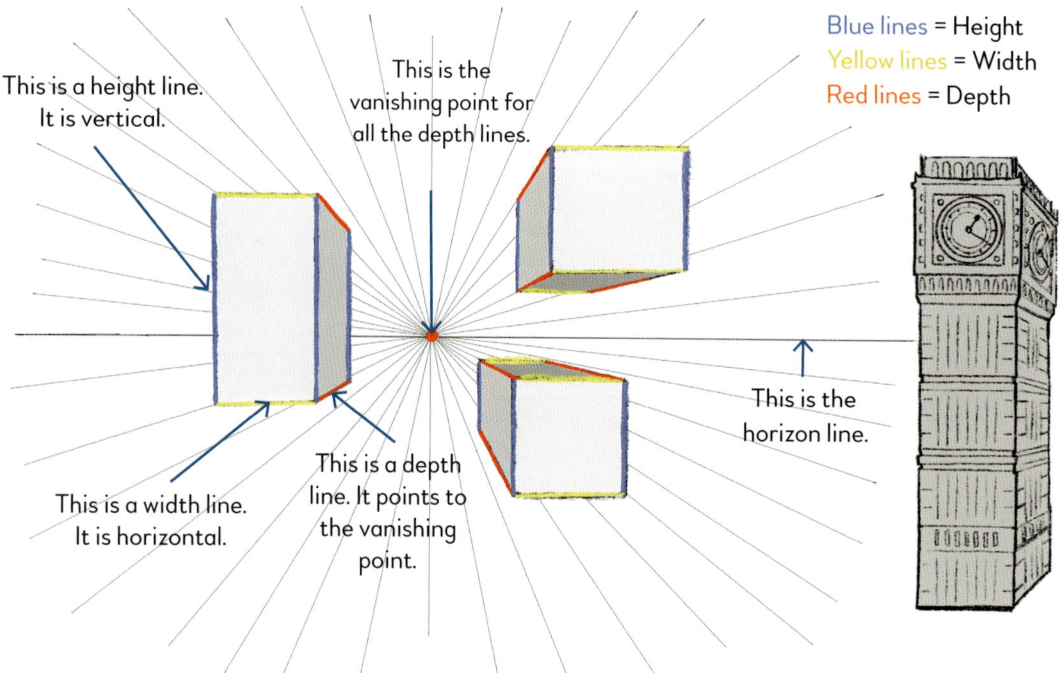

2-Point Perspective

As with 1-point perspective, 2-point perspective uses vertical lines to show height.

Unlike 1-point perspective, though, a 2-point perspective has—you guessed it—two vanishing points: one for your width lines, and another for your depth lines. Drawings in 2-point perspective look quite realistic.

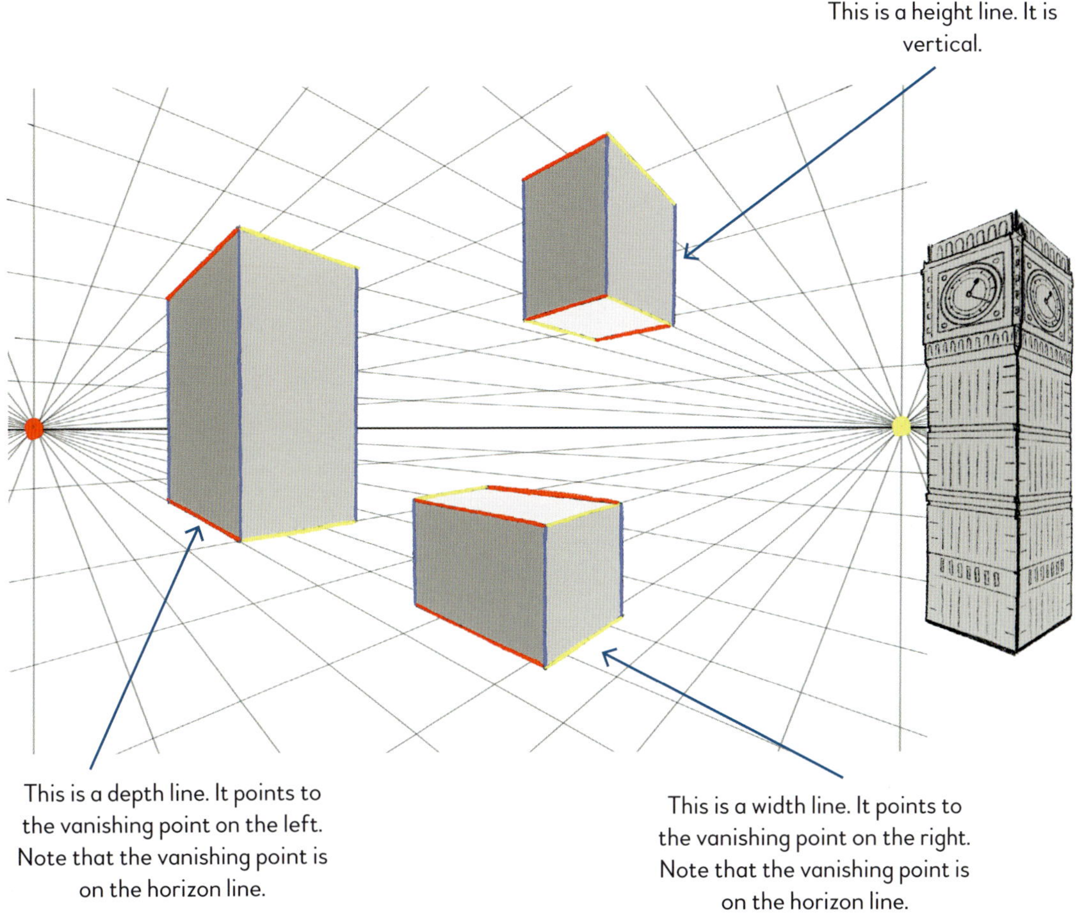

3-Point Perspective: Bird's-Eye View

In 3-point perspective, your height, width and depth lines all point to different vanishing points. Thankfully, your width and depth vanishing points are the same as in 2-point perspective: on either side of the horizon line.

There are two kinds of 3-point perspective: bird's-eye view and worm's-eye view. When you use a bird's-eye view, your height lines will all vanish to an imaginary point at the bottom of your drawing.

In 3-point perspective, there are *three* vanishing points. Objects in your drawing will look as though you're a bird in the sky looking down at them with a bird's-eye view.

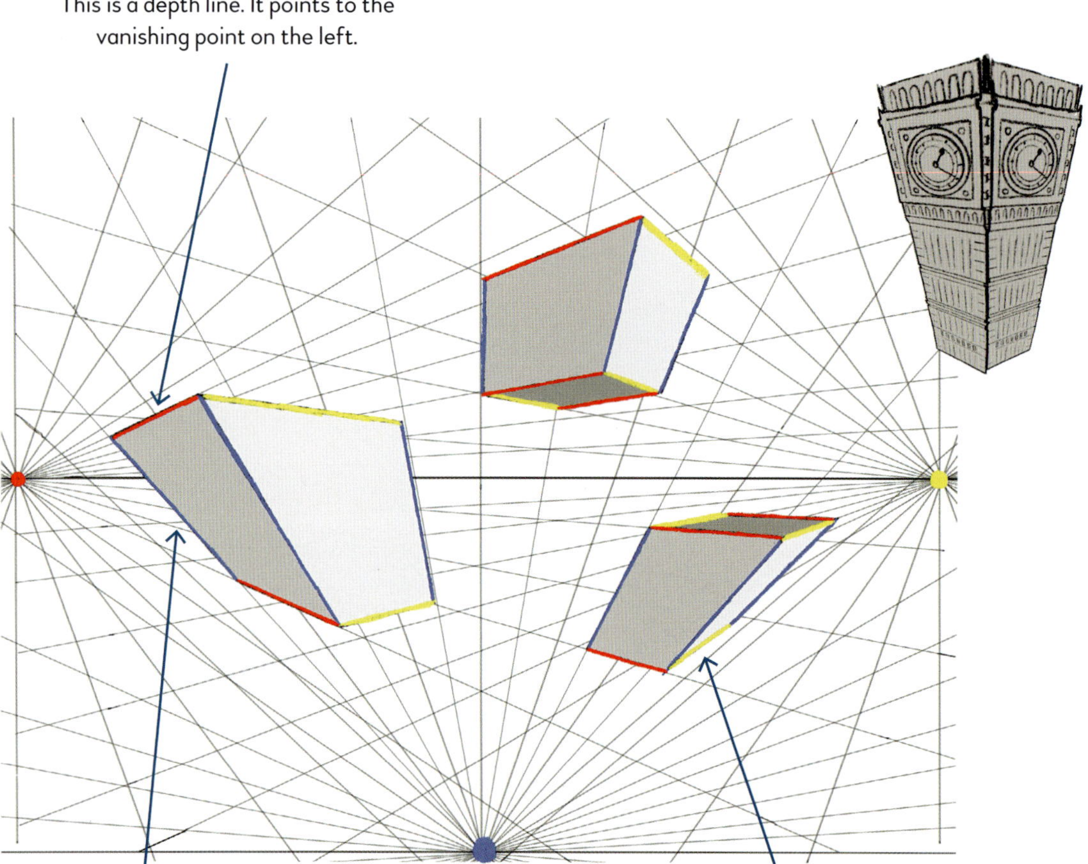

3-Point Perspective: Worm's-Eye View

Again, in 3-point perspective, your height, width and depth lines all point to different vanishing points, with your width and depth vanishing points on either side of the horizon lines.

To draw using a worm's-eye view, your height lines will all vanish to an imaginary point at the top of your drawing.

Objects in your drawing will look as though you're a worm on the ground looking up at the sky in a worm's-eye view.

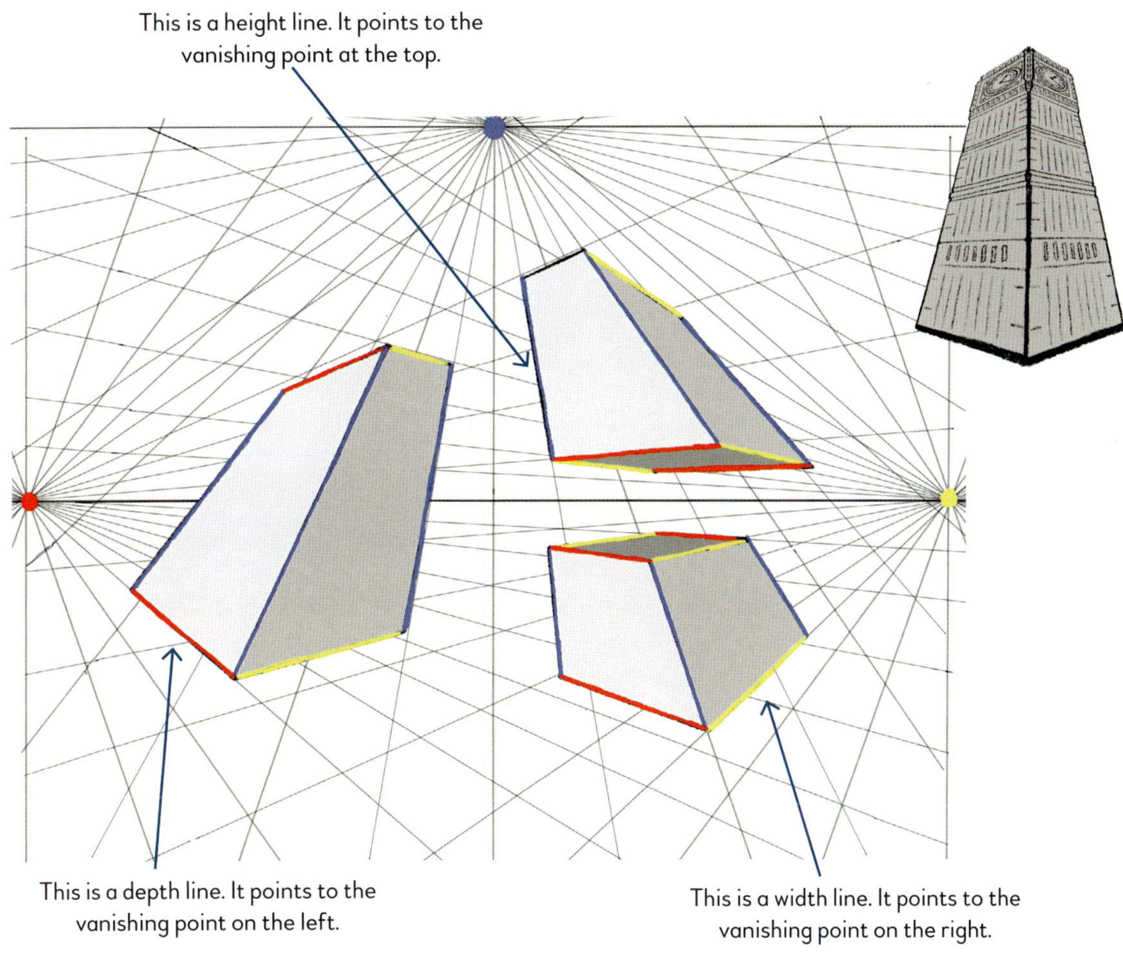

This is a height line. It points to the vanishing point at the top.

This is a depth line. It points to the vanishing point on the left.

This is a width line. It points to the vanishing point on the right.

DRAPERY

In art, drapery is how you show folds of fabric—anything from a tablecloth in a still life to clothing in a portrait. There are six kinds of folds you should learn to identify and draw as part of your realism journey.

1. Pipe Folds

Shaped like a series of cylindrical waves, pipe folds are often seen in curtains, capes and dresses.

Notice the curves at the bottom alternate between convex (curving outward) and concave (curving inward).

Shade the areas in between the parallel lines more darkly to make them fall to the background.

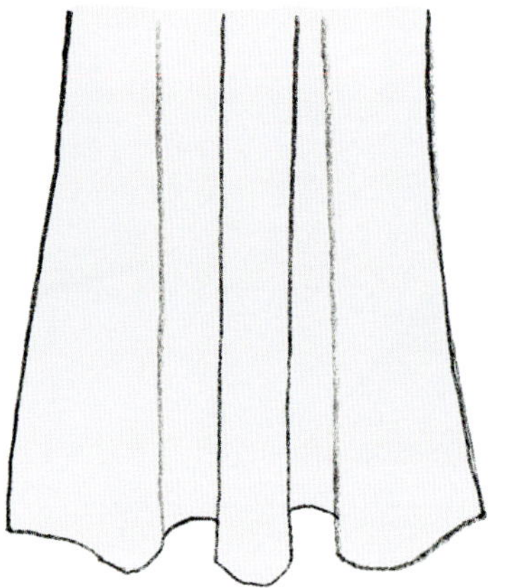
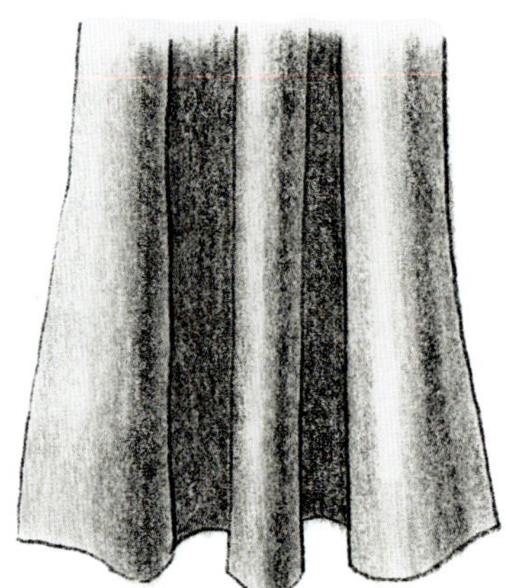

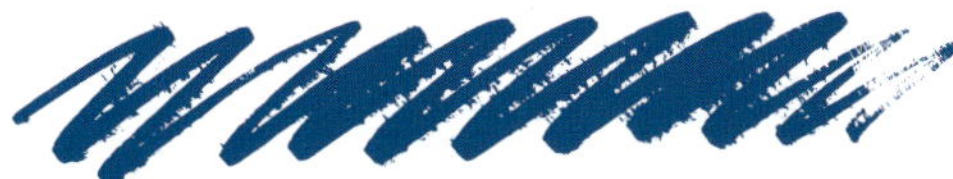

2. Zigzag Folds

Zigzag folds occur when fabric bunches up around a cylindrical shape—think pants bunching up around an ankle or behind a knee.

The little triangles can be used as guidelines to show you where to shade.

When shading each pair of triangles, note that the top one is dark, the bottom one a midtone, and the spaces between them light.

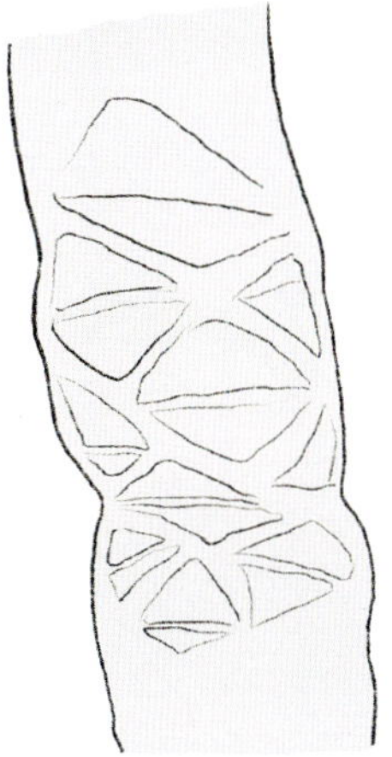

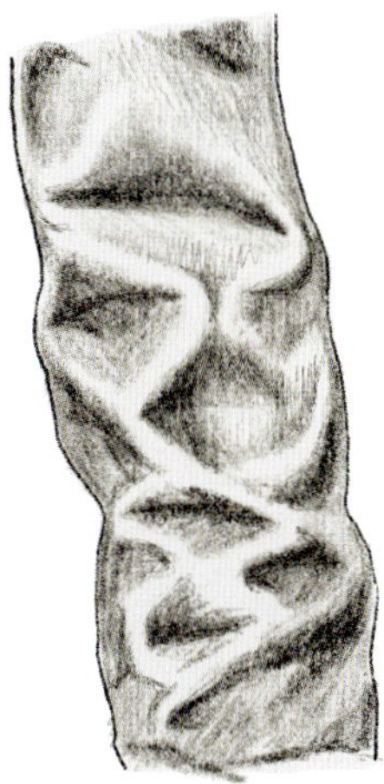

3. Spiral Folds

Spiral folds occur when fabric is loosely twisted around a cylindrical shape, like an arm or a leg.

These look like a series of curved lines that are nearly parallel to each other.

Focus your shading in the creases, that is, wherever you drew a curved line.

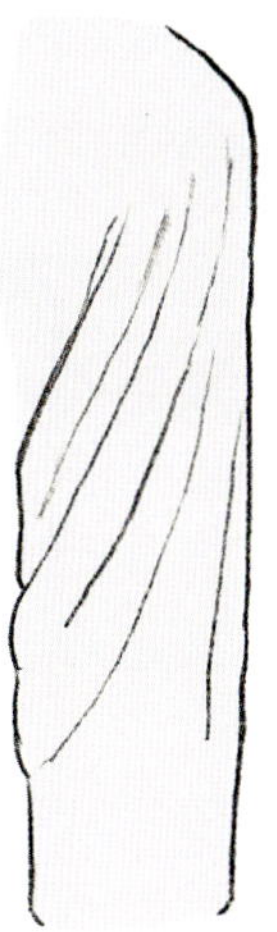

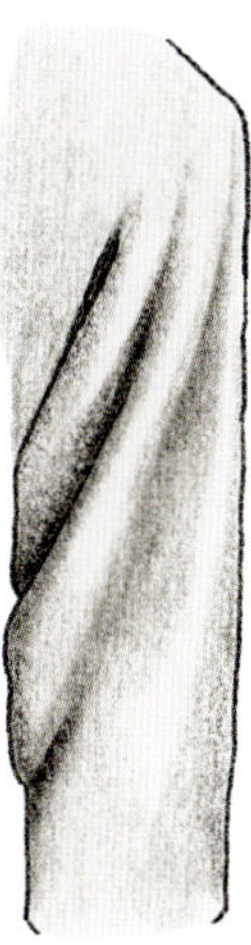

4. Half-Lock Folds

When a piece of fabric is pulled in different directions, it forms a half-lock fold. These are often found at the sides of the knees and at the elbows.

Think of the fold as a flattened oval with a C shape on each side.

Shade most darkly inside the C shapes, as that fabric is farther back.

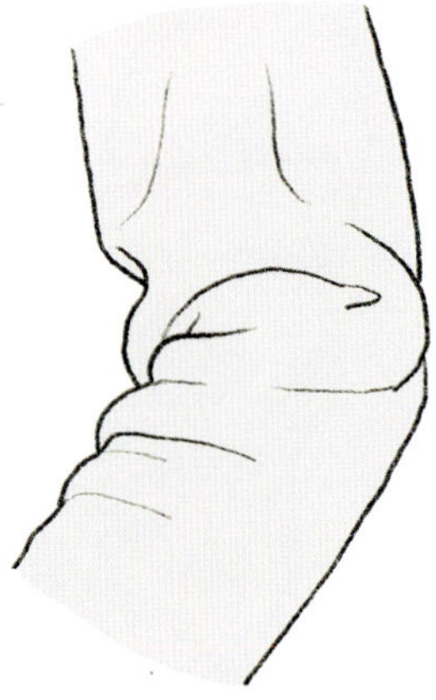

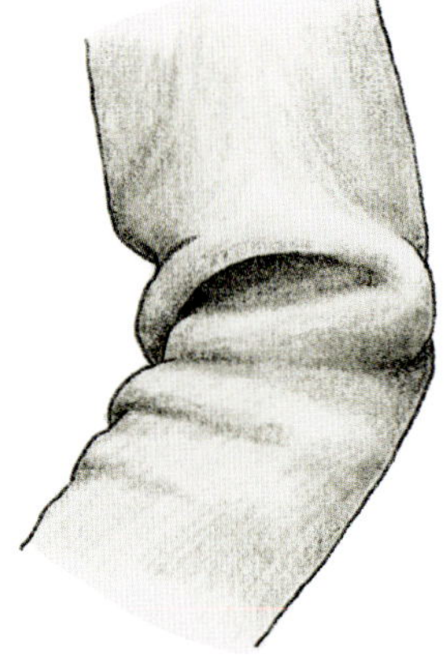

5. Diaper Folds

Drapes and curtains, handkerchiefs, and scarves all tend to create diaper folds, a sagging of fabric between two anchor points.

Diaper folds look like a series of U shapes cascading down between two anchor points.

The darkest shading is between the folds and on the underside of the U shapes.

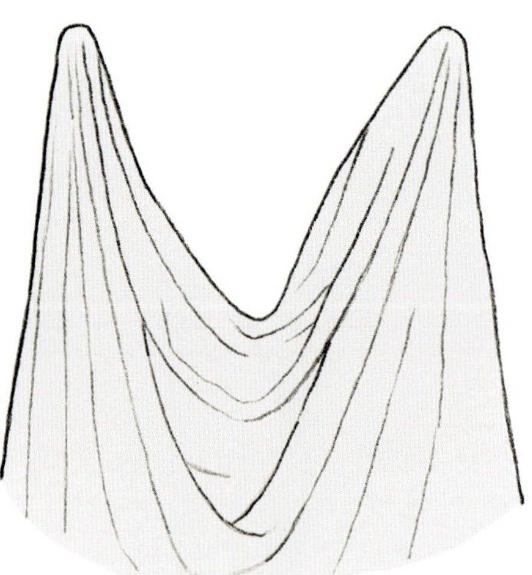

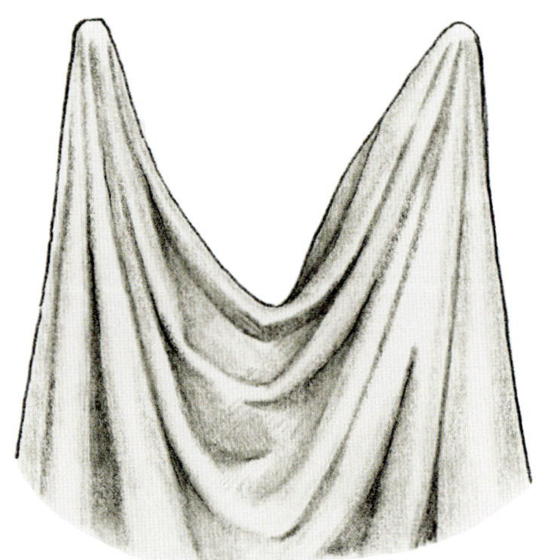

6. Drop Folds

Drop folds tend to show up when fabric hangs freely, like on dresses, skirts and flags.

Drop folds resemble pipe folds with S shapes at the bottom.

The darkest areas of shading are on the inside and along the lines.

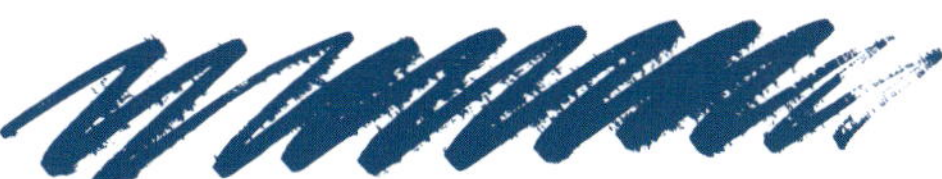

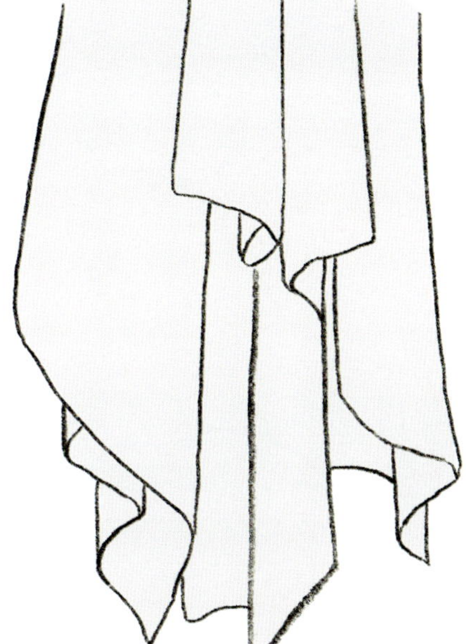

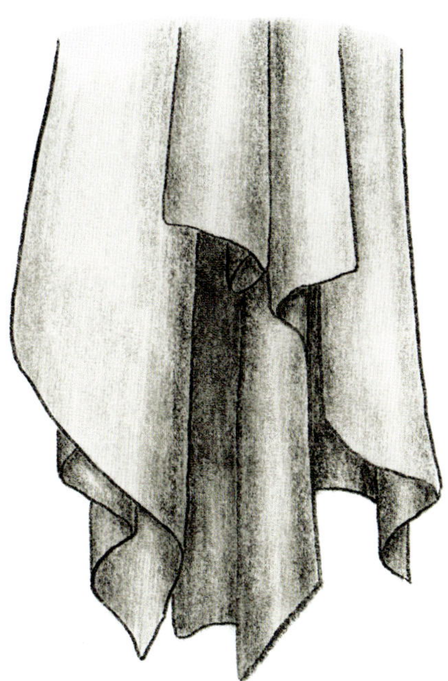

Notice how the different folds come to life in these drawings, and see if you can draw similar folds. Try to start noticing and identifying the folds in clothing and other fabric around you, too. After all, as you'll soon discover, learning to see like an artist is a crucial step in becoming an artist.

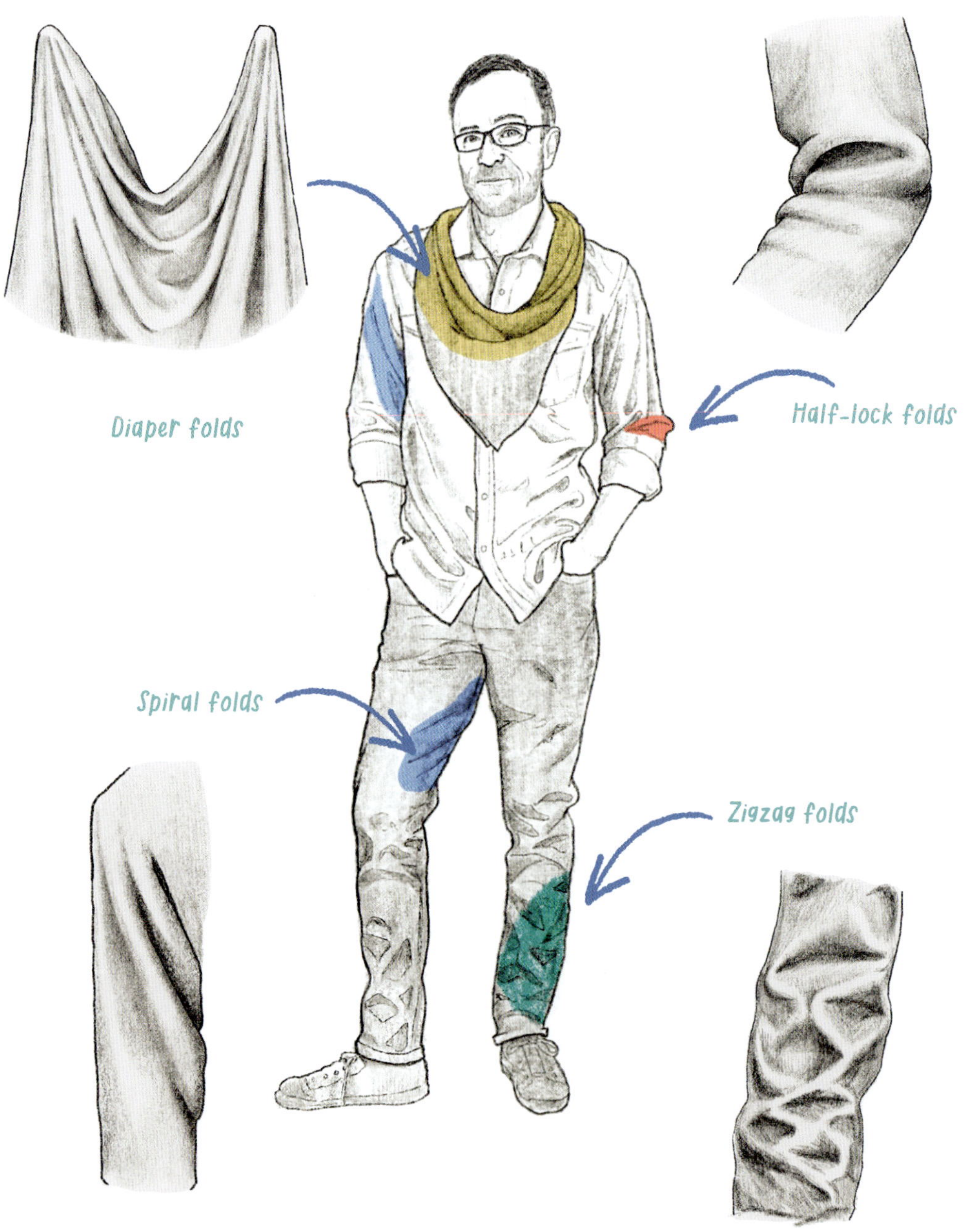

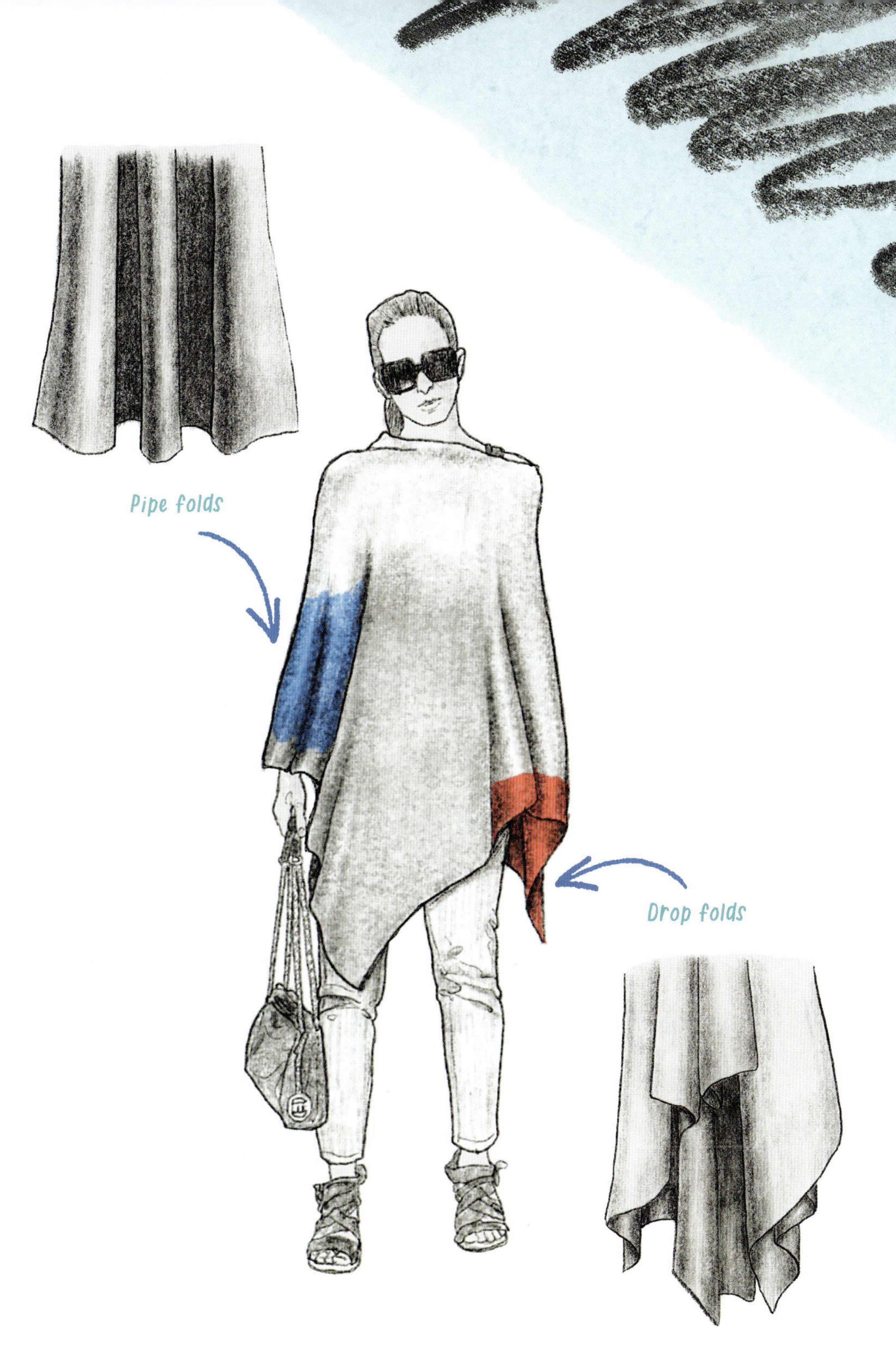
Pipe folds
Drop folds

TRAINING YOUR EYE

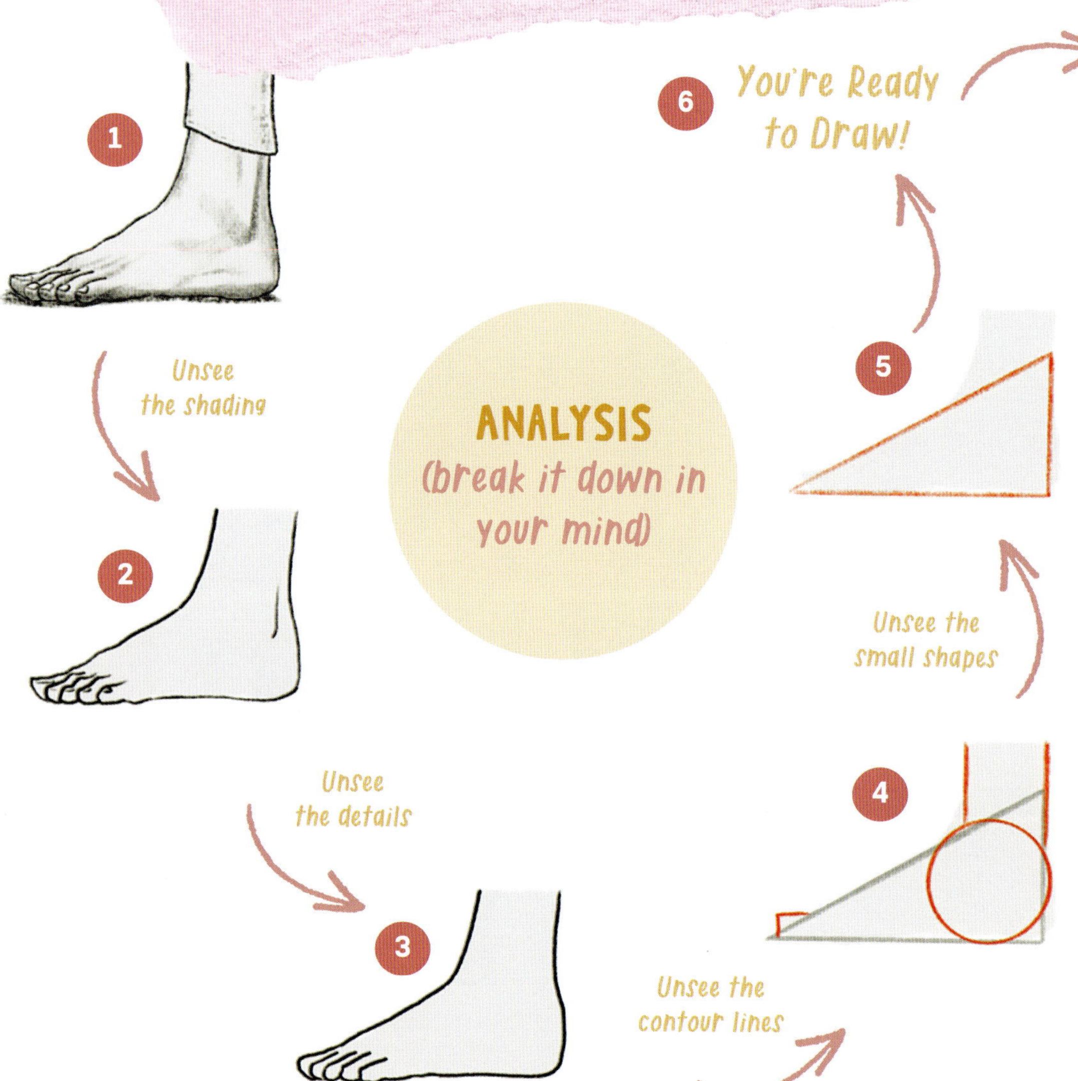

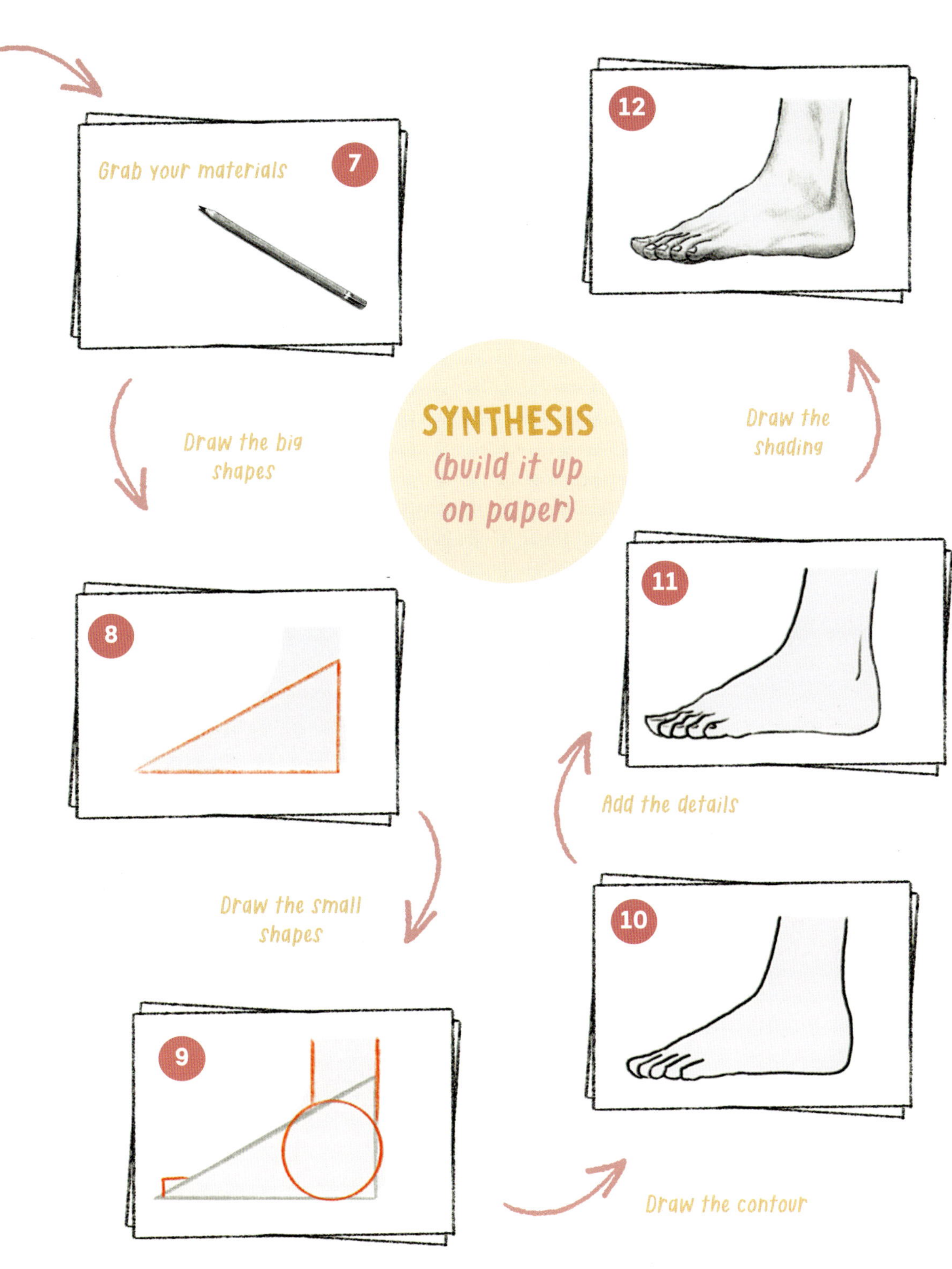

Grab your materials
7
SYNTHESIS
(build it up
on paper)
Draw the big
shapes
8
Draw the small
shapes
9
12
Draw the
shading
11
Add the details
10
Draw the contour

LEARN TO SEE THE WORLD LIKE AN ARTIST

In this book, you'll learn how to draw dozens of realistic facial features, body parts, animals, landscapes, objects and more.

That's exciting, but more exciting still is one of the other things you'll be learning along the way: how to break down complex shapes into simpler ones.

The drawing tutorials in this book are designed to help you see past surface details to the geometric shapes that make up the basic structure of the object you want to draw.

Because when you can learn to do that—to see the world like an artist—you can teach yourself to draw *anything you want.*

Over the next few pages, you'll start training your eye to see the underlying shapes, big and small, that make up the world around us. Once you learn how to see objects in this way, continue training your eye to see how light interacts with objects. How textures are shaded differently. How folds occur in clothing. How details appear from afar—and how they truly are from up close. The best part? While you're training your eye to know *what* to draw, you'll also be training your hands to know *how* to draw it.

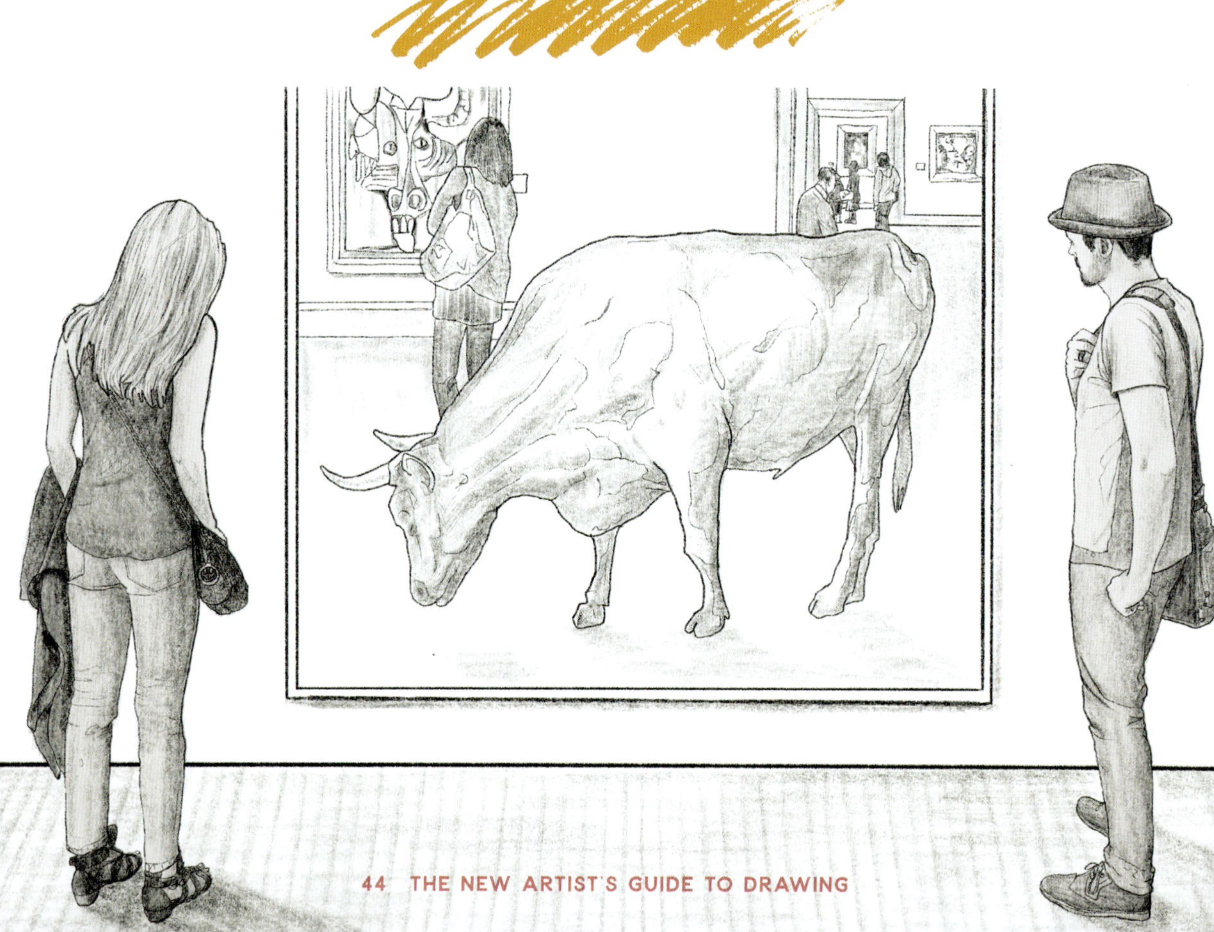

Let's see the steps in action—in reverse.
Imagine you want to draw an ice-cream cone,
a car or a house. Study the images below and
see if you can identify the underlying
geometric shapes in each one.

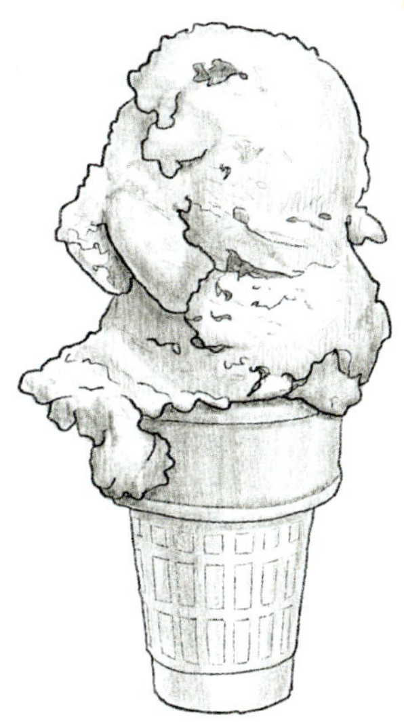

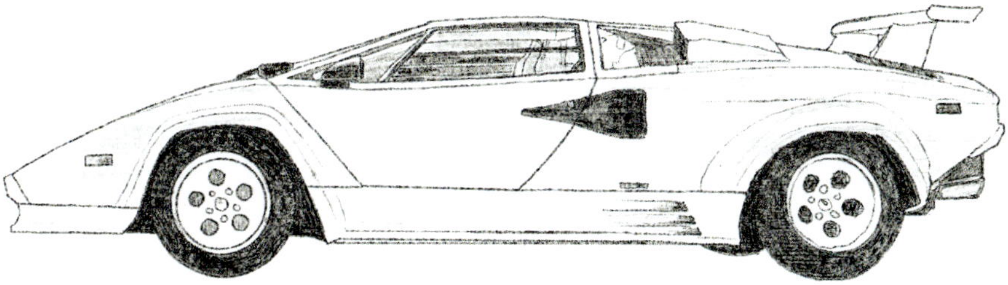

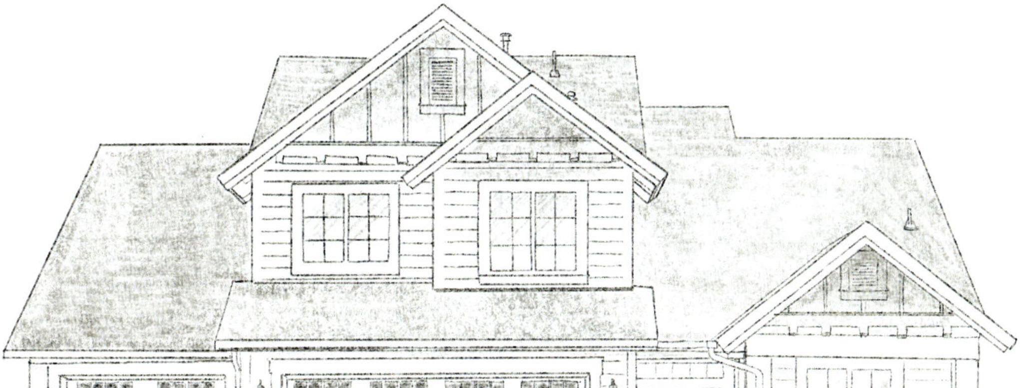

Primary Shapes

Below, you'll see those same images with their major underlying shapes identified in red. How did you do?

Step 1

Draw the primary shapes. That is, draw the major underlying geometric shapes.

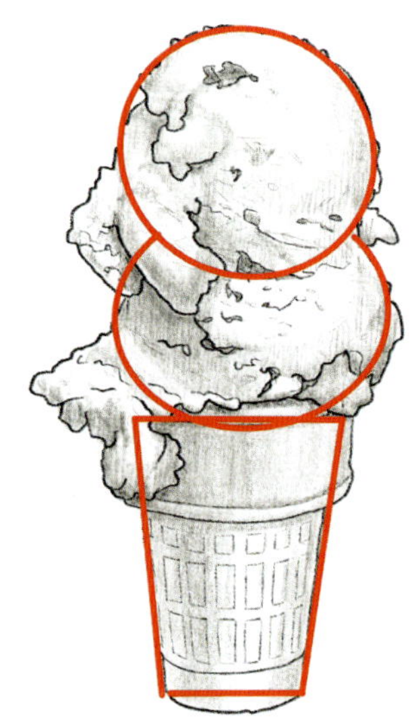

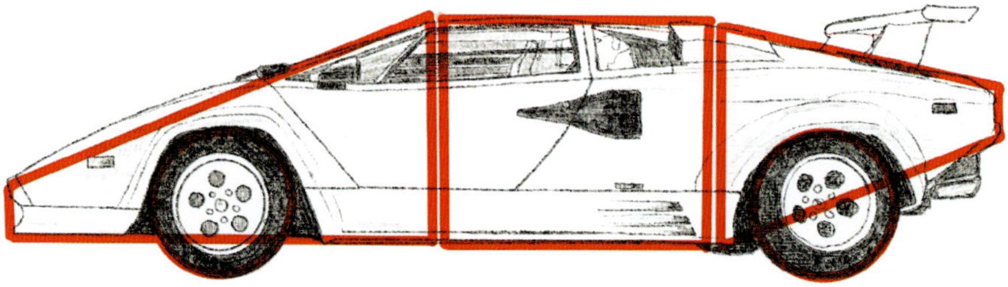

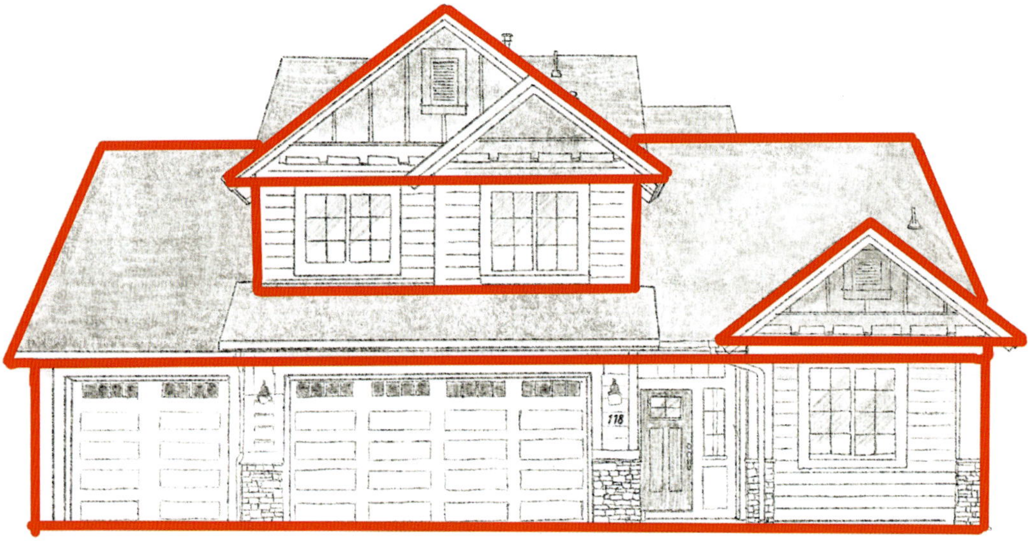

Secondary Shapes

Once you have the primary shapes, see if you can spot the smaller, supporting shapes and lines, shown here in blue.

Step 2

Identify and draw the secondary shapes and lines. Notice that you're not drawing any details yet.

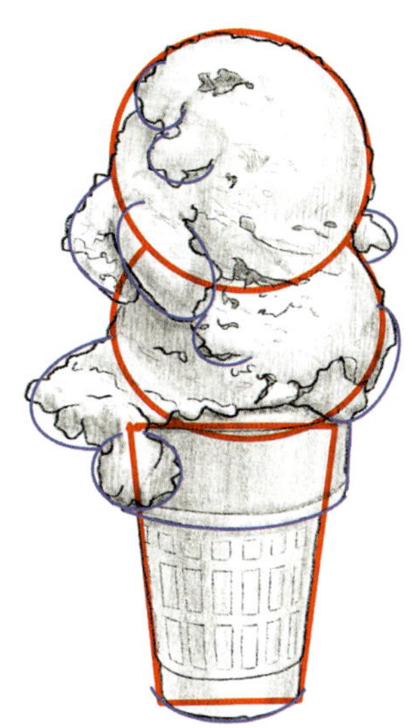

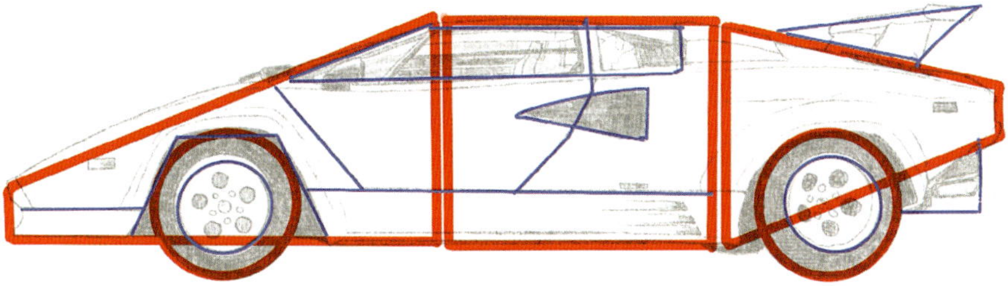

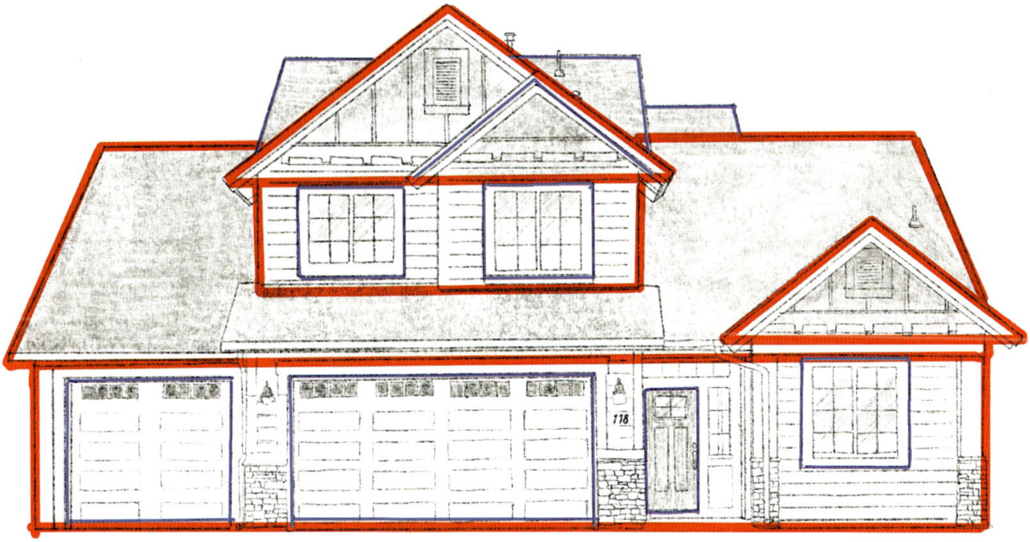

Details

Now focus on some of the finer details.

Step 3

Add in details. These details may connect primary and secondary shapes, or introduce textures or patterns.

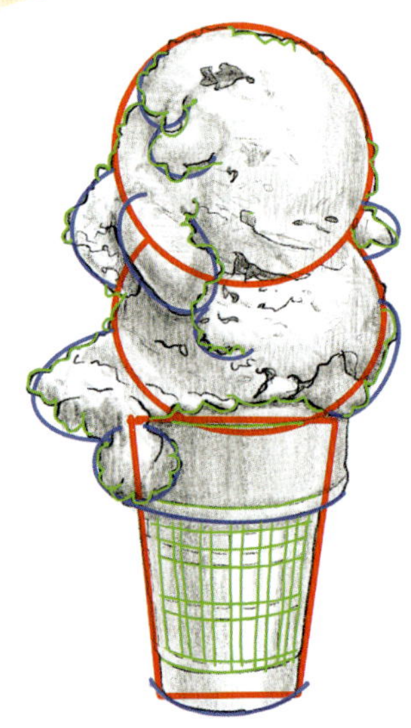

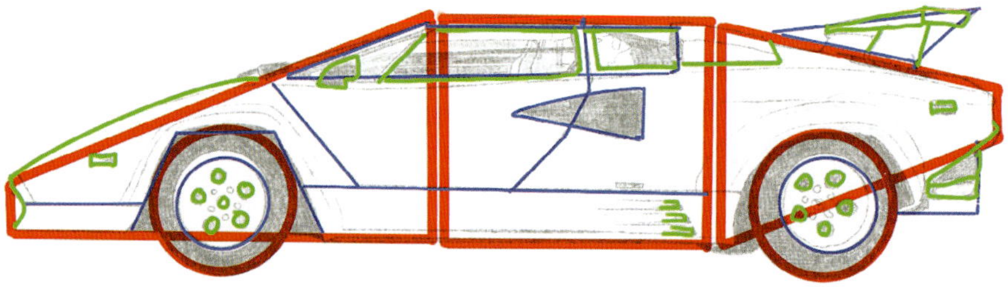

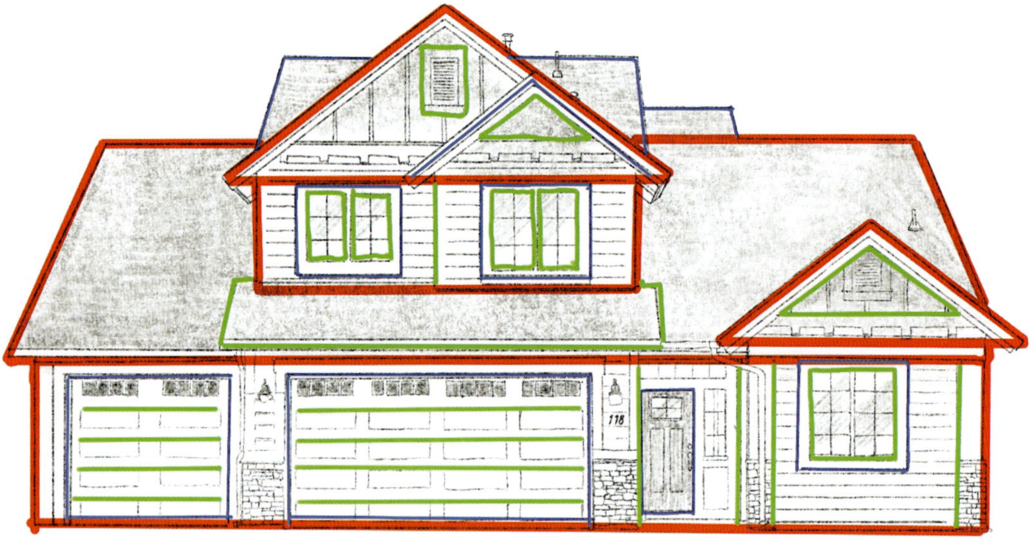

Shading

Lastly, create the illusion of three dimensions by shading your line drawing.

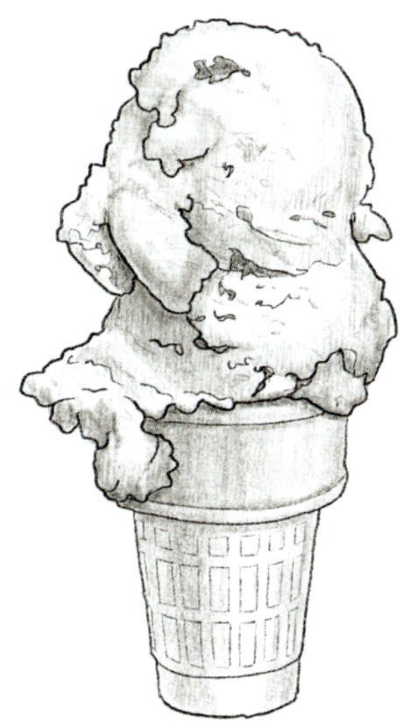

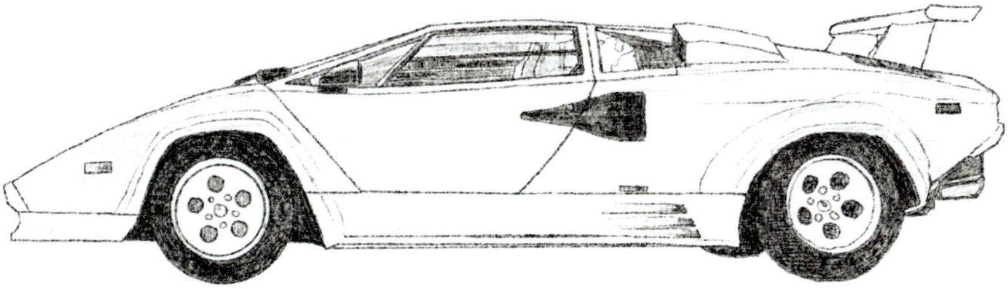

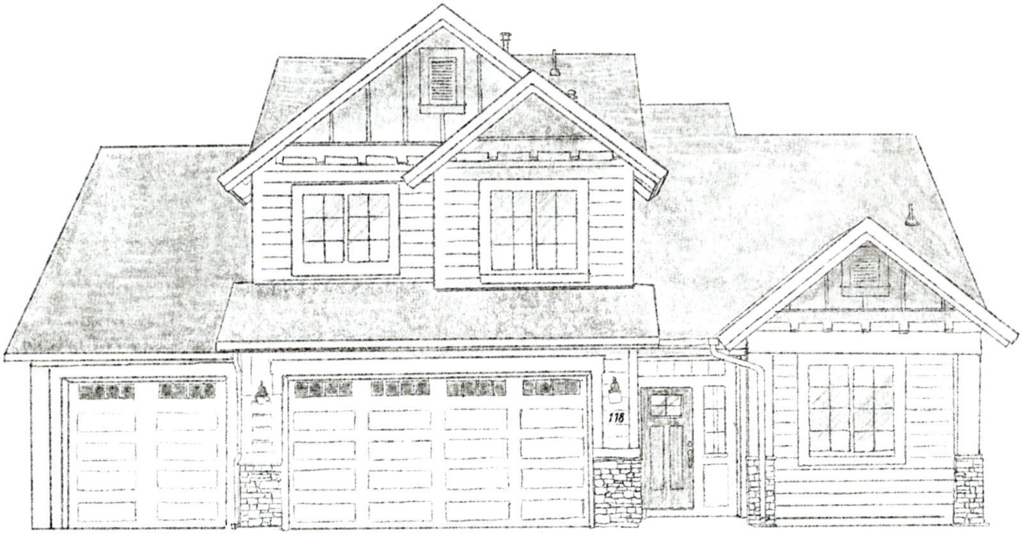

THE FACE

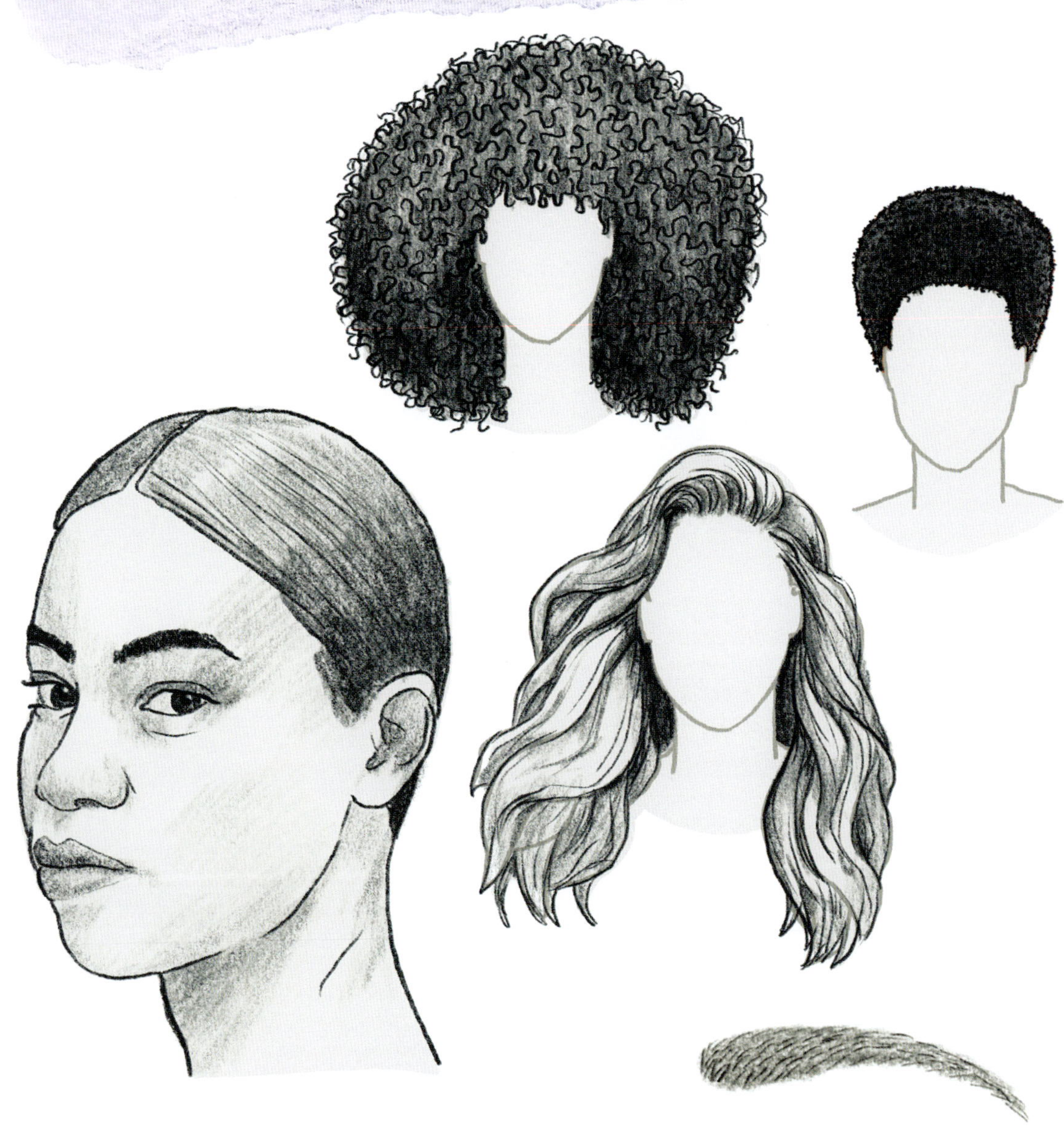

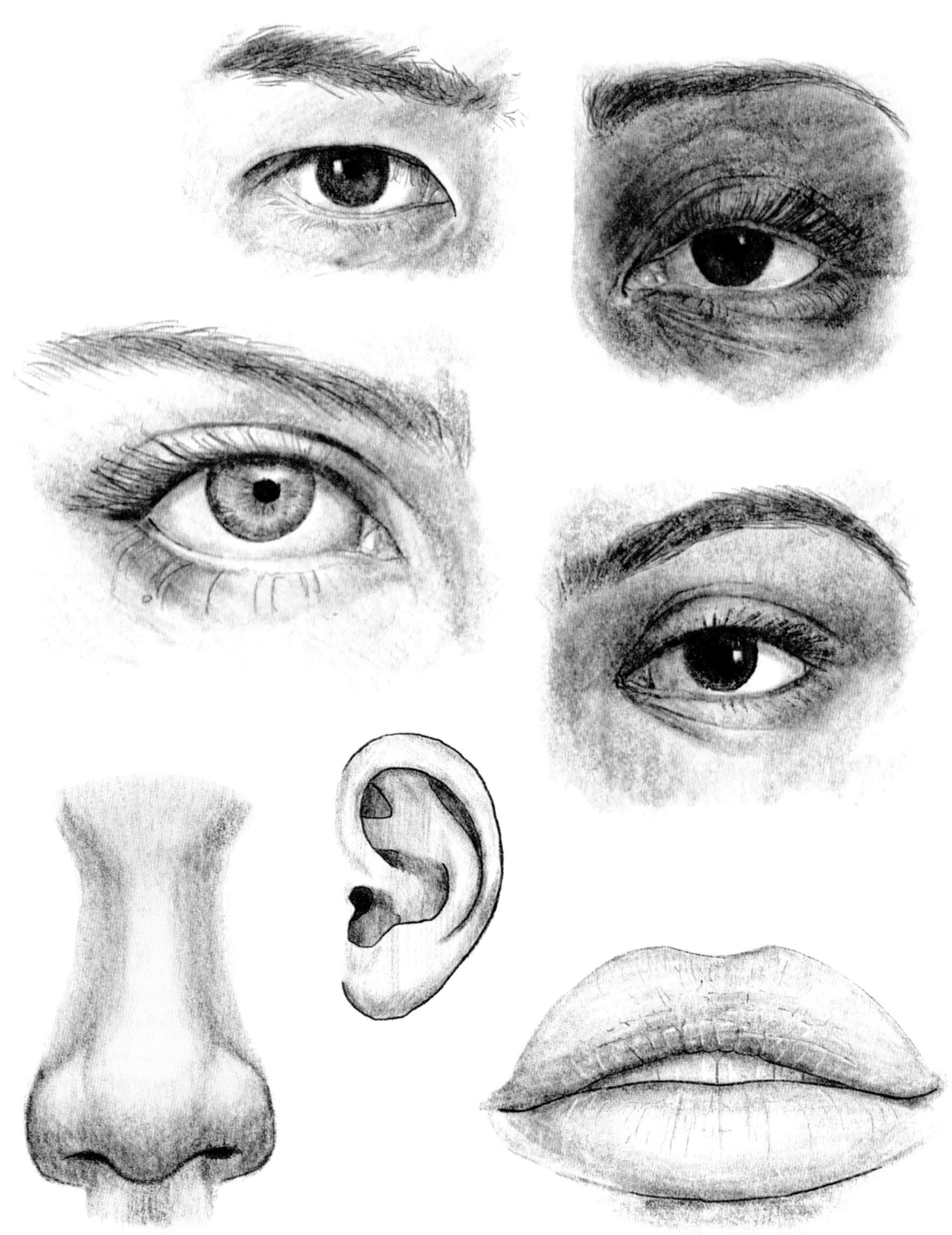

HEAD SHAPES

All of our facial features are framed by the shape of our face and, more broadly, our head. Below are some different things to look for when preparing to draw someone. On the next page, you'll see how combinations of these features come together to form the 12 most common head shapes. Note that only the defining features of a head shape are listed, not all of the possible features.

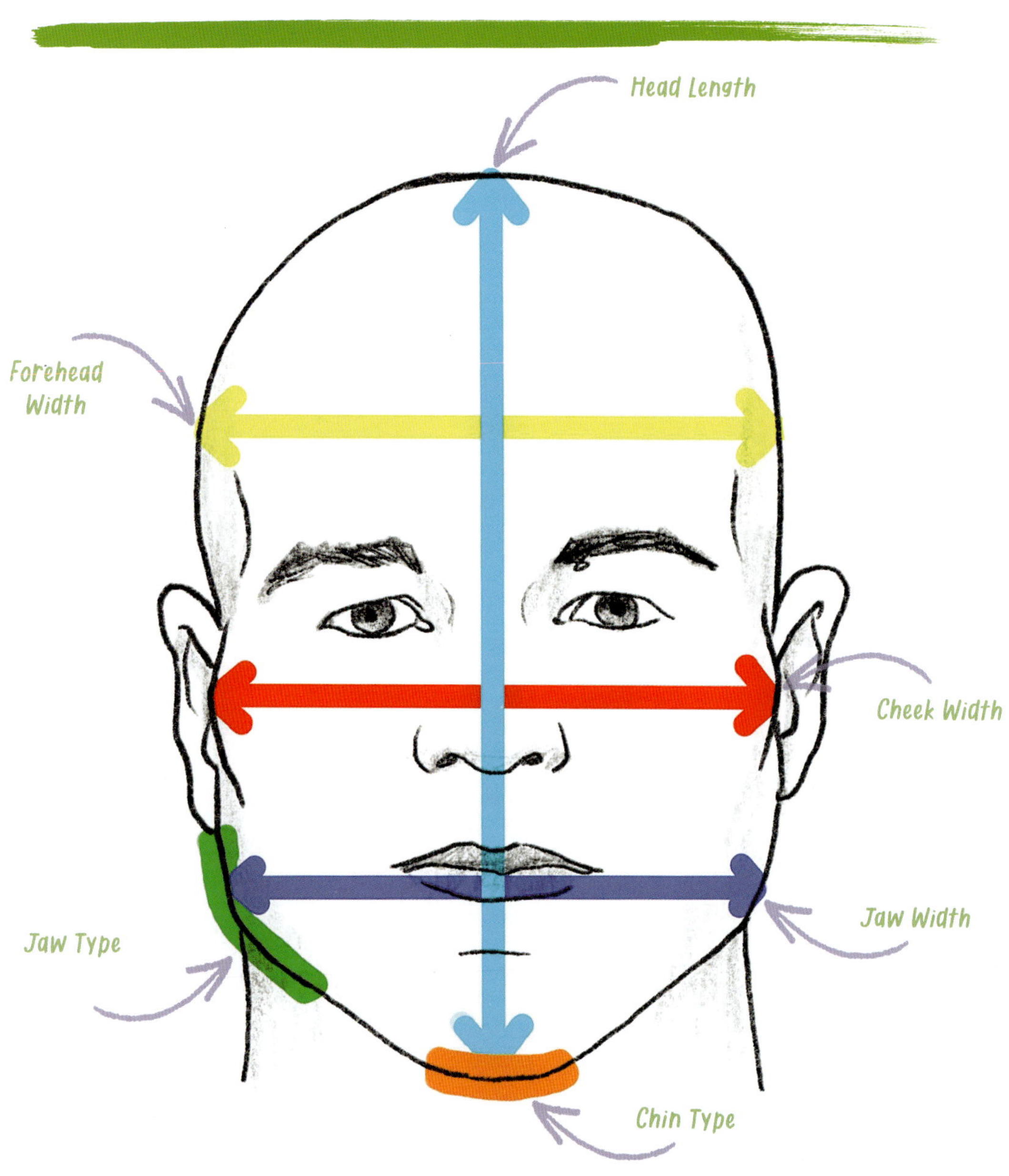

HEART

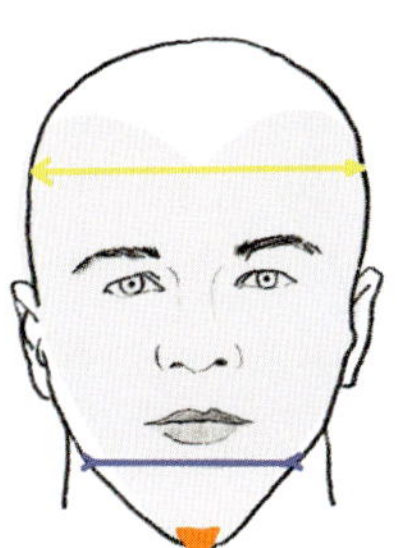

V-TRIANGLE

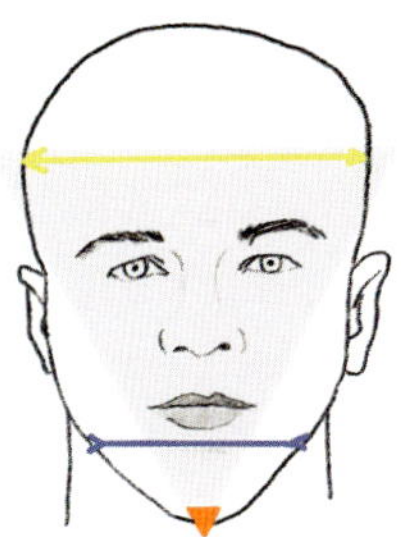

TRAPEZOID

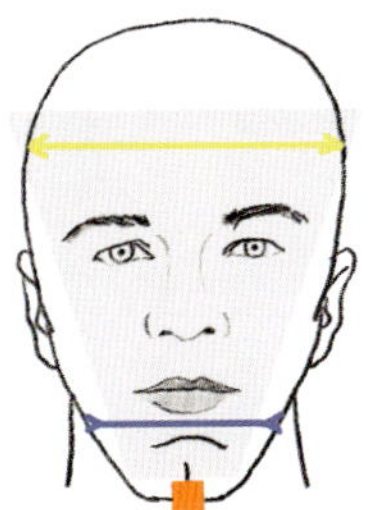

A-TRIANGLE

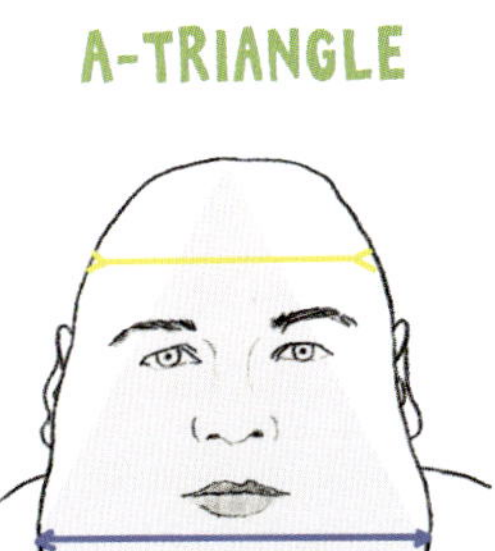

DIAMOND

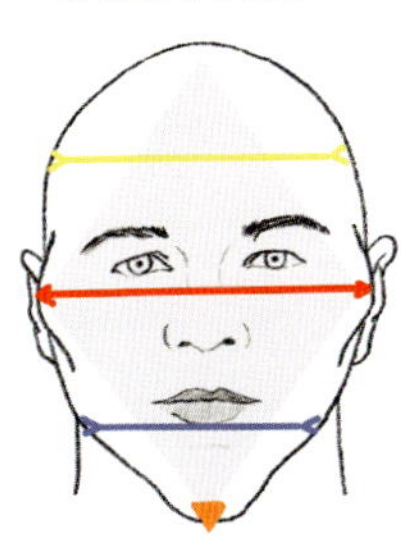

KITE

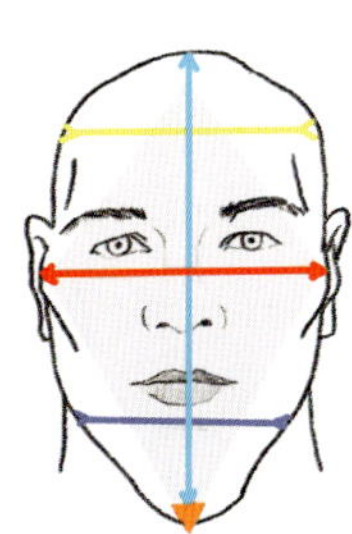

BLOCK

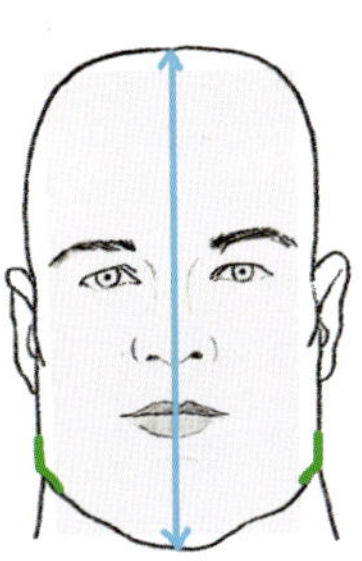

RECTANGLE

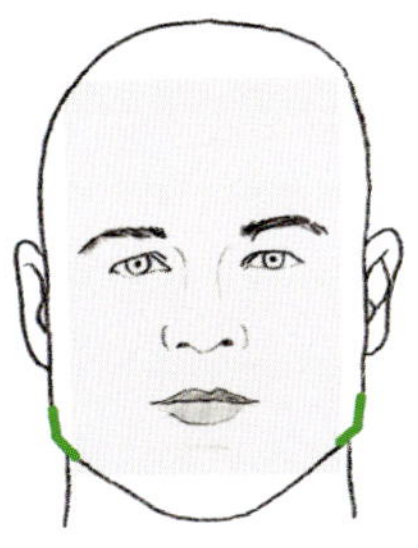

SQUARE

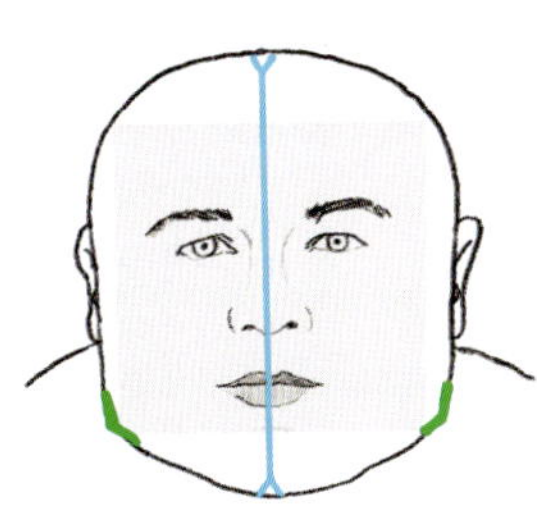

OBLONG

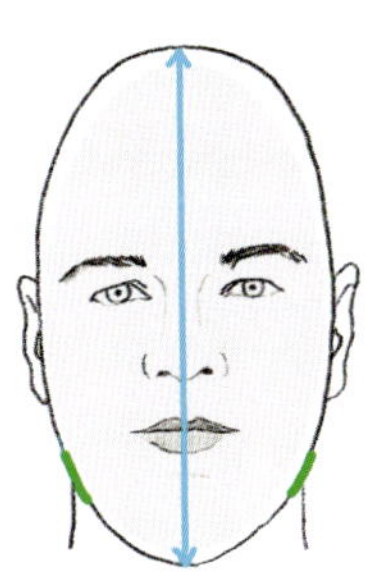

OVAL

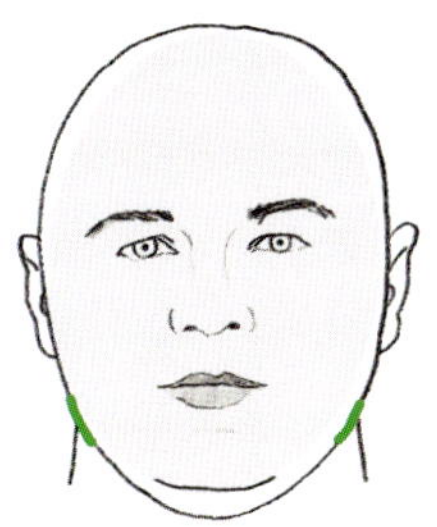

CIRCLE

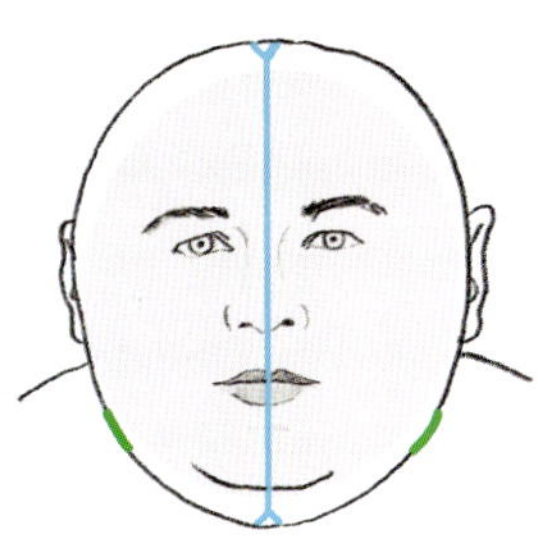

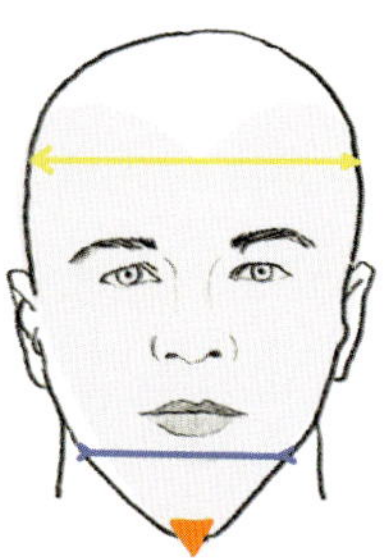

Heart

Forehead width: Wide
Jaw width: Narrow
Chin type: Pointed

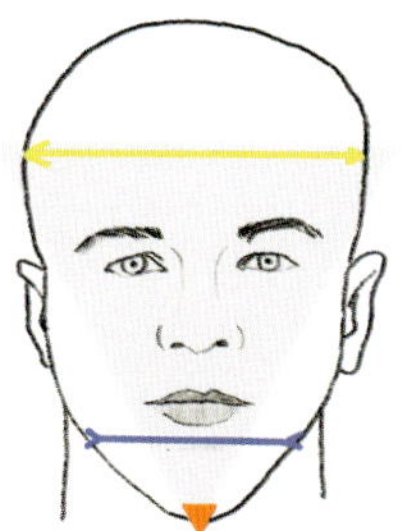

V-Triangle

Forehead width: Wide
Jaw width: Narrow
Chin type: Pointed

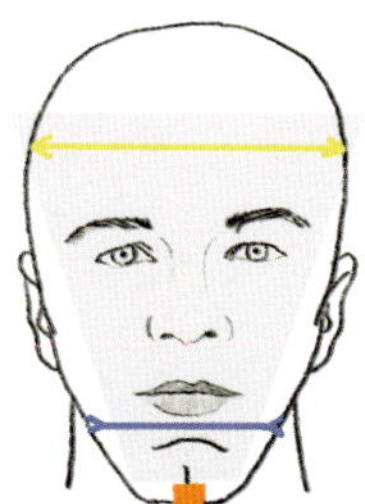

Trapezoid

Forehead width: Wide
Jaw width: Narrow
Chin type: Square

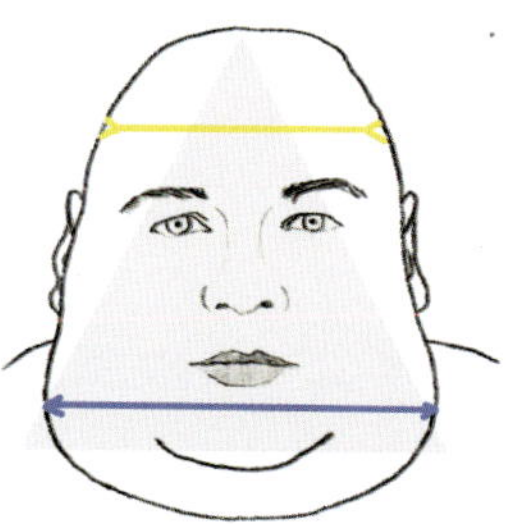

A-Triangle

Forehead width: Narrow
Jaw width: Wide

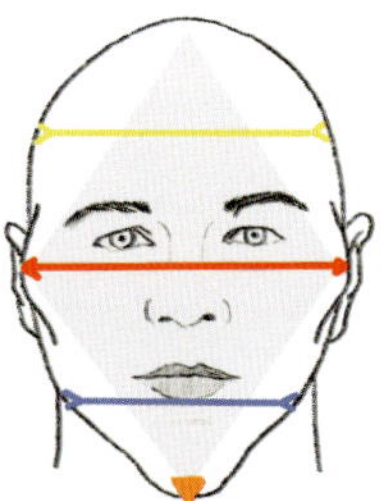

Diamond

Forehead width: Narrow
Cheek width: Wide
Jaw width: Narrow
Chin type: Pointed

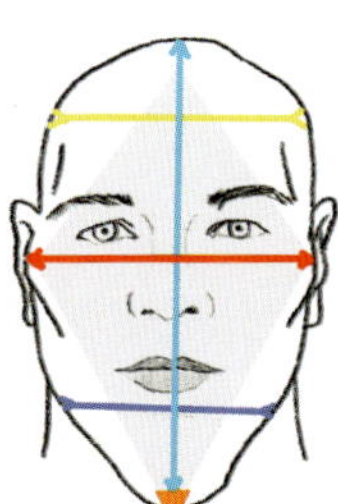

Kite

Forehead width: Narrow
Cheek width: Wide
Jaw width: Narrow
Chin type: Pointed
Head length: Long

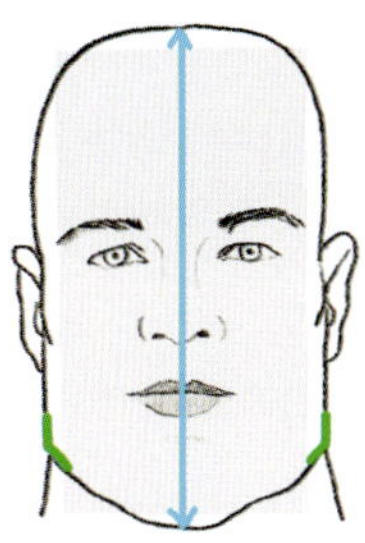

Block

Jaw type: Square
Head length: Long

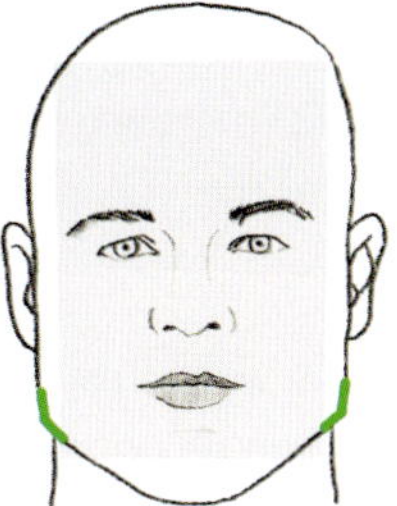

Rectangle

Jaw type: Square

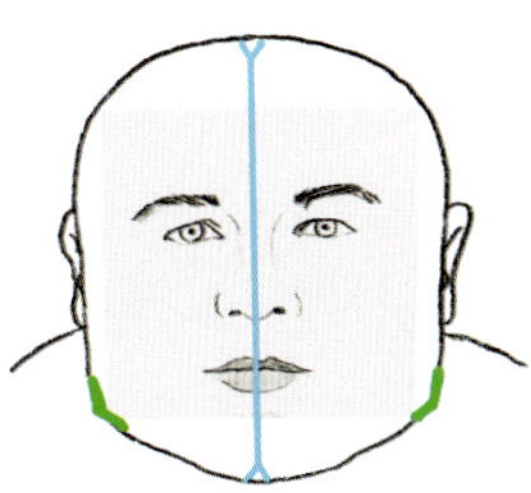

Square

Jaw type: Square
Head length: Short

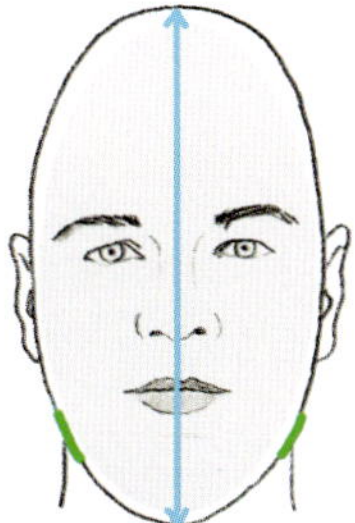

Oblong

Jaw type: Rounded
Head length: Long

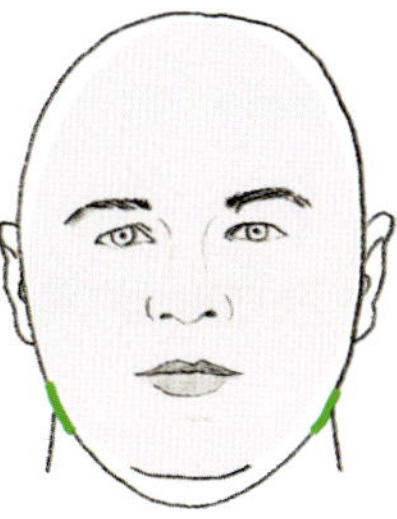

Oval

Jaw type: Rounded

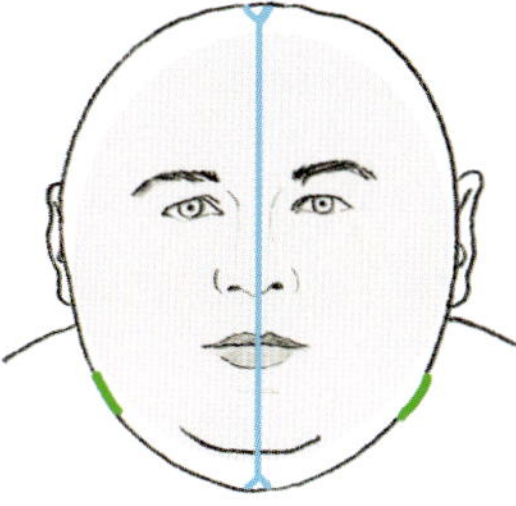

Circle

Jaw type: Rounded
Head length: Short

EYES

If you're trying to draw a specific person, getting a good likeness starts with capturing their eyes. That means paying close attention to eye shape—and other features. Eyes can be tricky, but with enough practice, you can become a pro.

In this exercise, we'll draw one type of eye, but keep in mind that eye shapes vary a good deal, as you'll see on page 58.

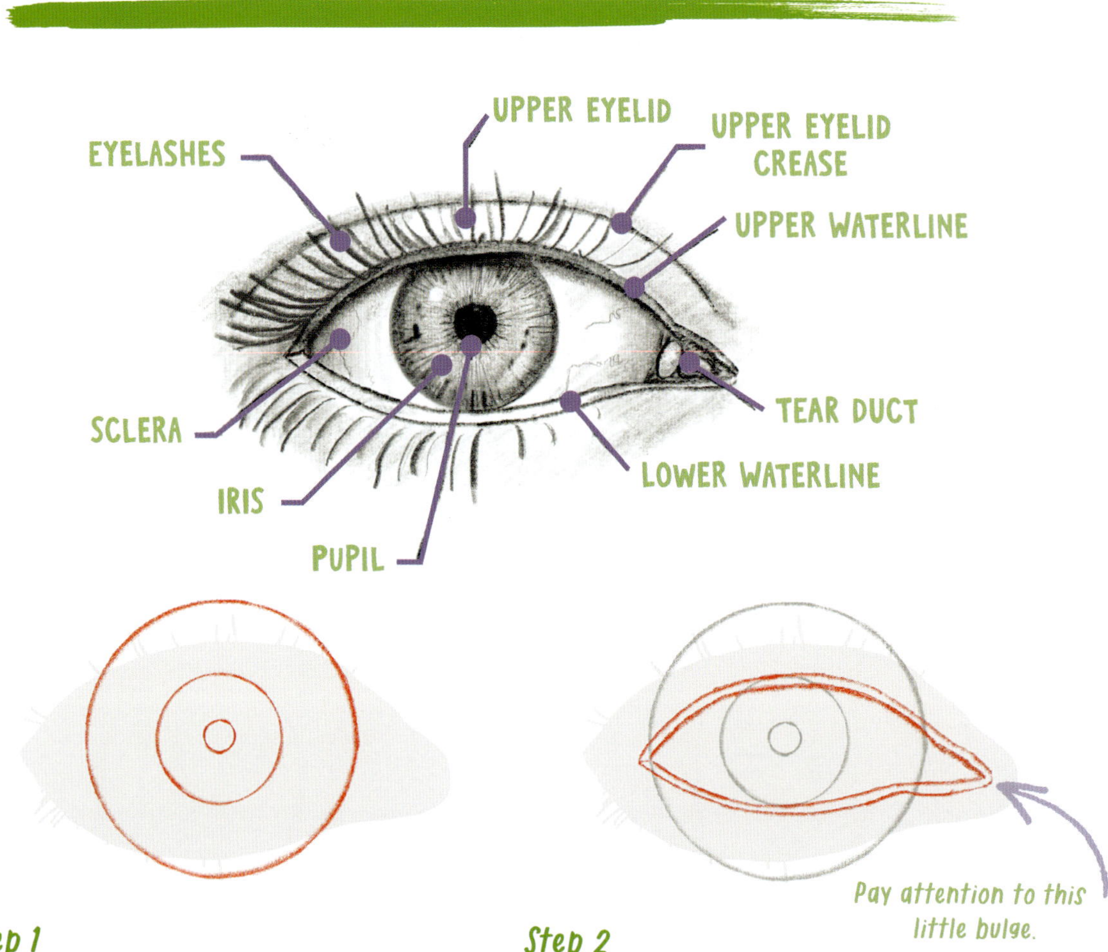

Step 1

Draw three circles: a small one for the pupil, a medium one for the iris, and a large one for the eyeball. Don't press down too hard on your pencil—we're going to erase these guidelines later.

Step 2

Draw an almond shape that extends past the eyeball, and then a second one around that. These shapes will be the waterlines. Try to maintain the same distance between the two lines throughout.

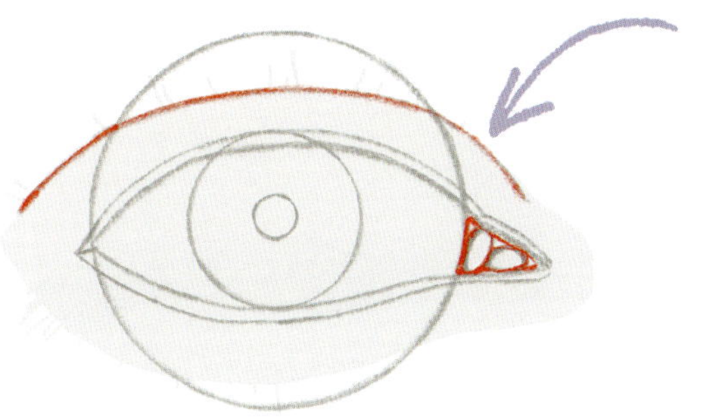

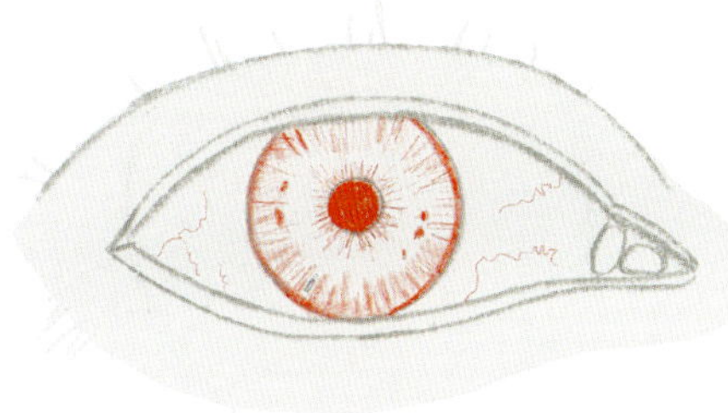

Step 3

Draw a curved line that follows the shape of the upper waterline. This will be the eyelid crease. Now draw two ovals in the inside corner of the eye for tear ducts.

Step 4

Color in the pupil. Now draw short, thin lines around the pupil, and longer, slightly thicker lines around the inside edge of the iris. Erase the guidelines.

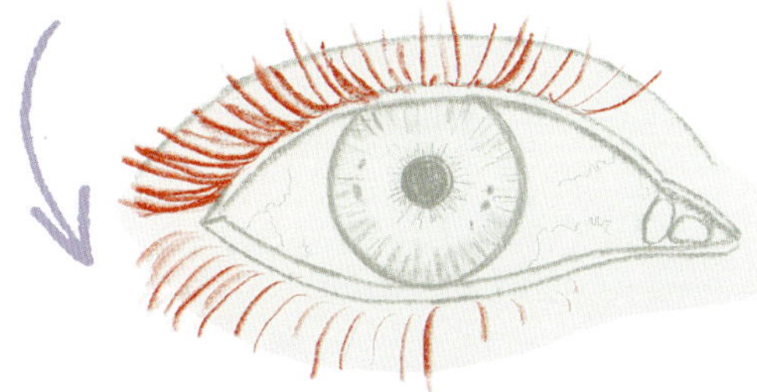

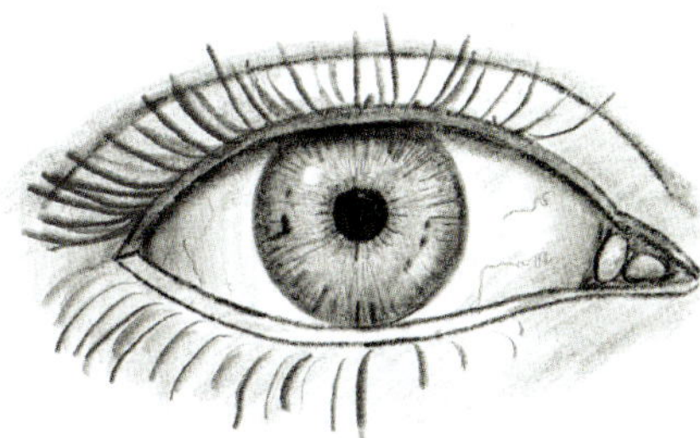

Step 5

For this example, we'll draw curved lines for the eyelashes. Draw thicker lashes at the outer edge of the eye, and fewer, thinner ones closer to the tear duct.

Step 6

Shade the corners of the eyeball to create the illusion of roundness. Add a shadow underneath the upper waterline. Darken the areas around the small ovals in the tear ducts. Now lightly shade the iris by drawing straight lines extending out from the pupil. Lastly, erase very small highlights at the top left and bottom right of the iris.

Reference: Eyes

Eye shapes can vary widely from person to person, and they can even shift as you age.
Here are a few different eye shapes. See if you can notice some differences.

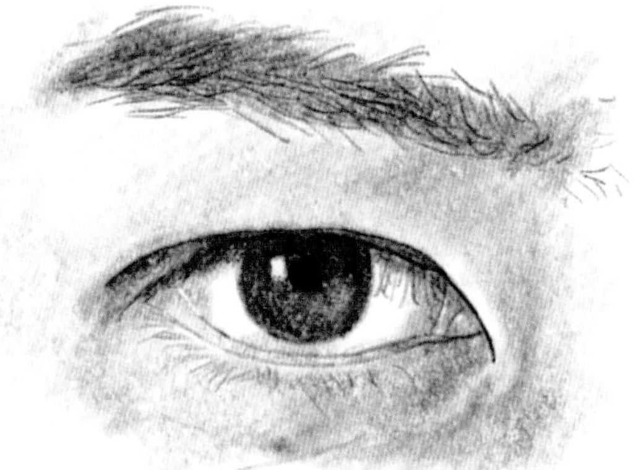

This eye has an epicanthal fold,
also known as a monolid.

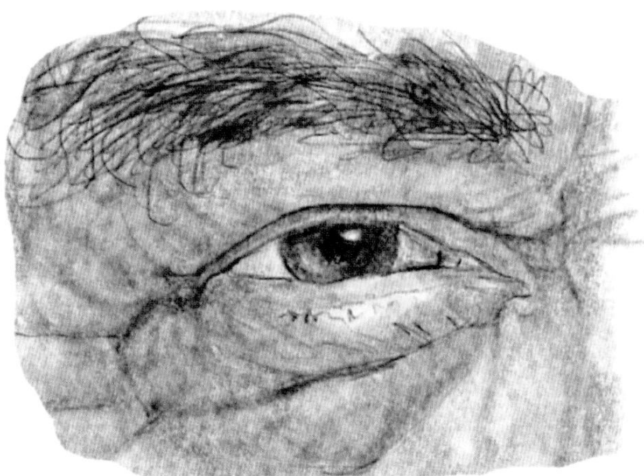

As wrinkles form, we tend to see less
of the eye itself.

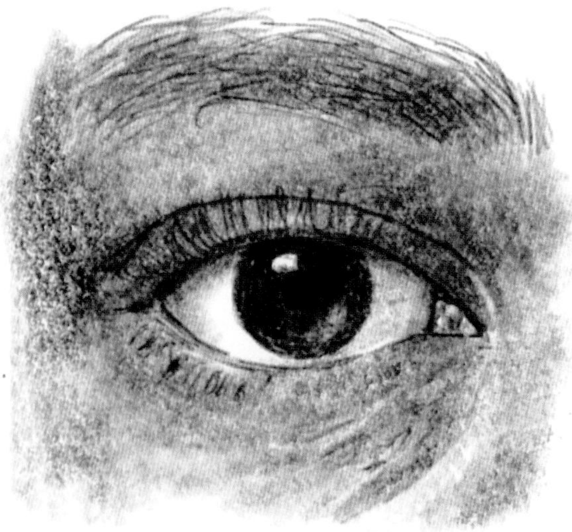

This is an almond-shaped eye.
Notice that the iris is quite dark.
This person has brown eyes.

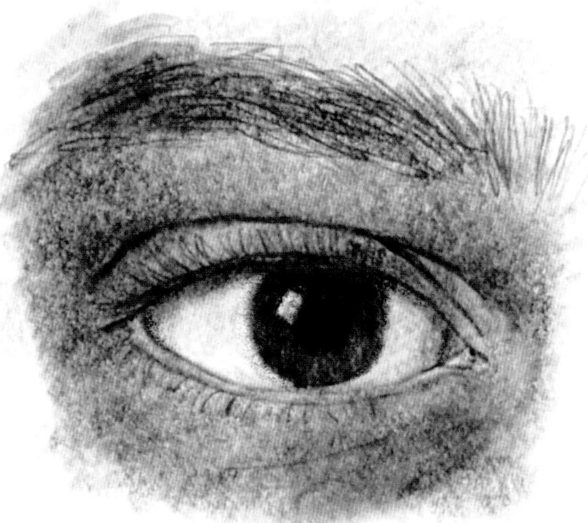

Irises are not always in the center of the eye.
They can turn outward or, as is the case
in this eye, inward.

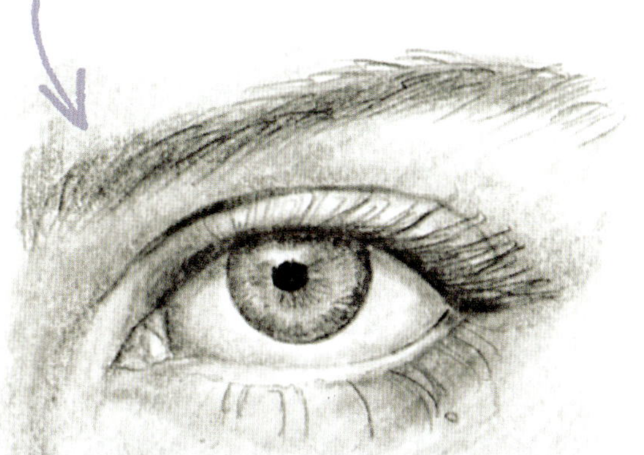

Some people, like this person, have a fair amount of white, or sclera, showing under the iris.

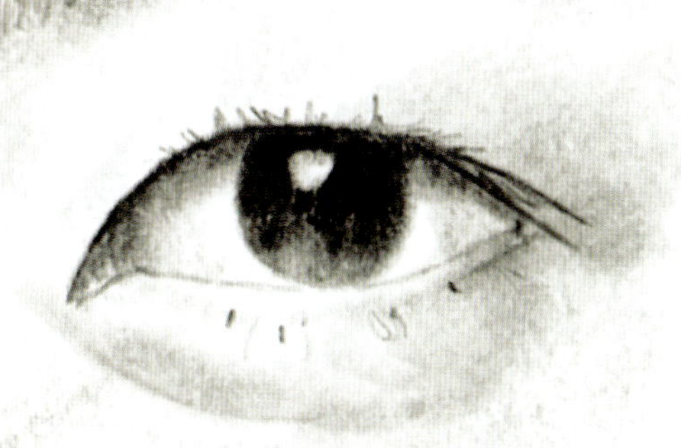

The eyelashes here are straight, sparse and point down.

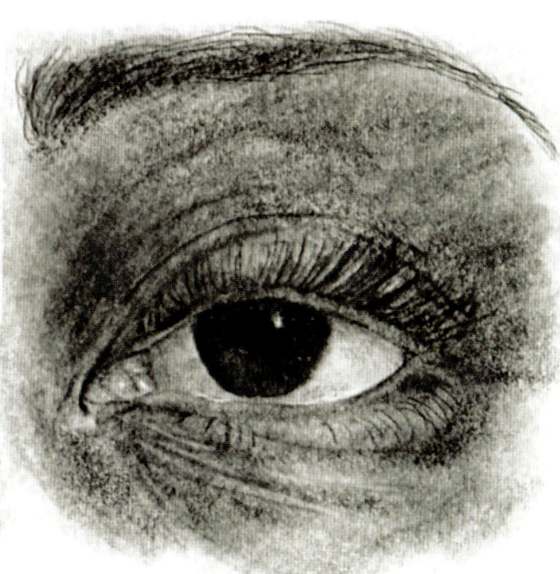

This eye has a heavier upper eyelid, as well as more wrinkles toward the inside corner of the eye.

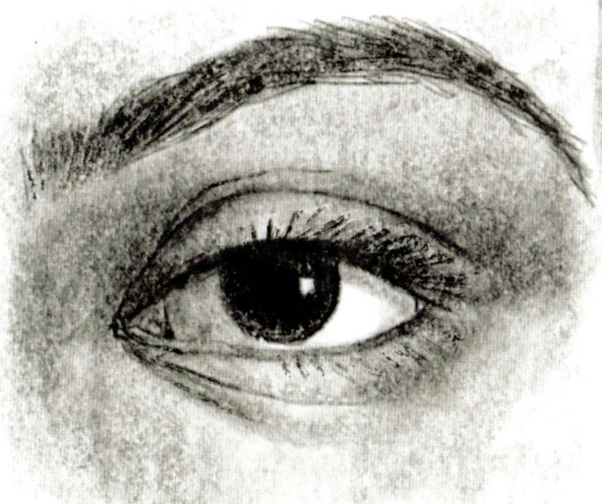

Eyebrow shape can vary as much as eye shape. Some eyes, like this one, are framed by a long, curved eyebrow.

EYEBROWS

Eyebrows may seem like a minor detail on the face, but they're quite important: they frame our eyes, communicate emotion and shape our appearance dramatically. Let's look at how to draw a soft-angled eyebrow.

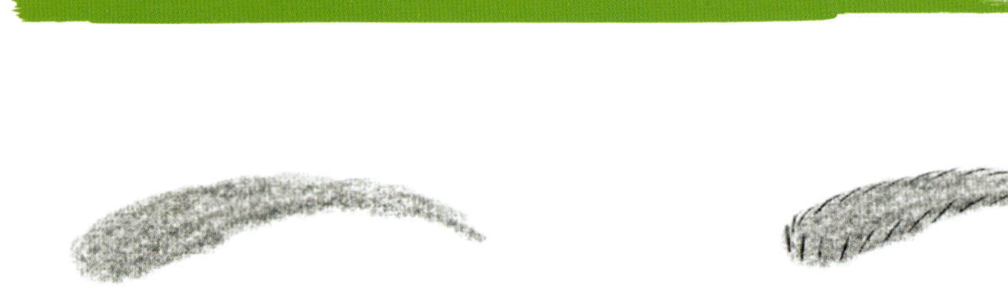

Step 1

Using the side of your pencil, evenly and lightly shade an area in the shape of a comet.

Step 2

Using the tip of your pencil, draw short lines around the outside of the eyebrow. Make the lines vertical on the nose side, then gradually angle them downward as you make your way to the ear side.

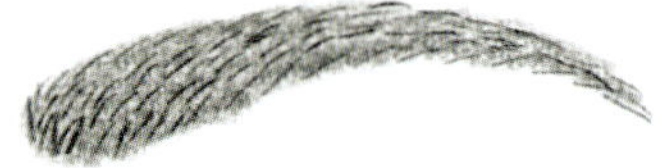

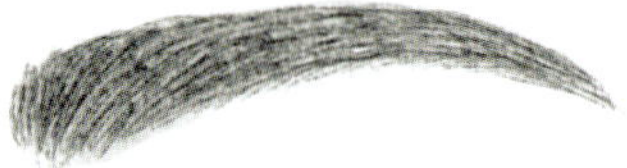

Step 3

Follow the angles of the lines drawn in Step 2 to fill in in the rest of the eyebrow with short lines.

Step 4

Keep adding lines, as in Step 3, to darken the eyebrow and give it an appearance of fullness.

This is a groomed eyebrow. In ungroomed eyebrows, hairs tend to be longer and may not be uniform in thickness or direction.

Reference: Eyebrows

Below, let's look at four common eyebrow shapes. Although these are drawn with medium thickness, keep in mind that each of these—and all the eyebrow shapes in between—can be drawn in thin, medium and thick styles.

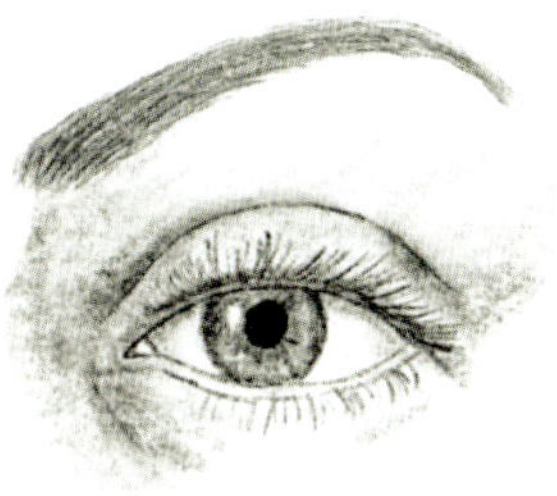

Rounded

Rounded eyebrows are characterized by a curved shape. The peak of the curve is above the white of the eye on the ear side.

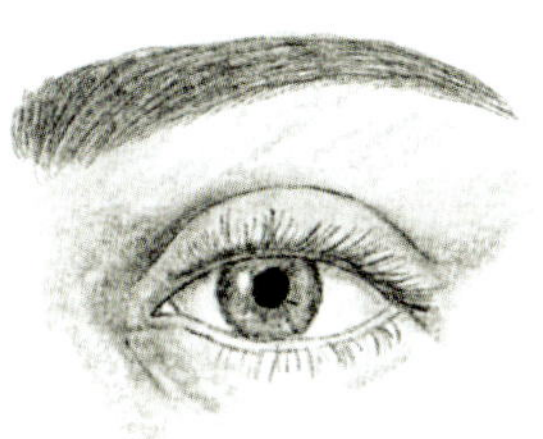

Soft-Angled

Soft-angled eyebrows are very similar to rounded ones, except the brow line is not as curved—it's nearly straight.

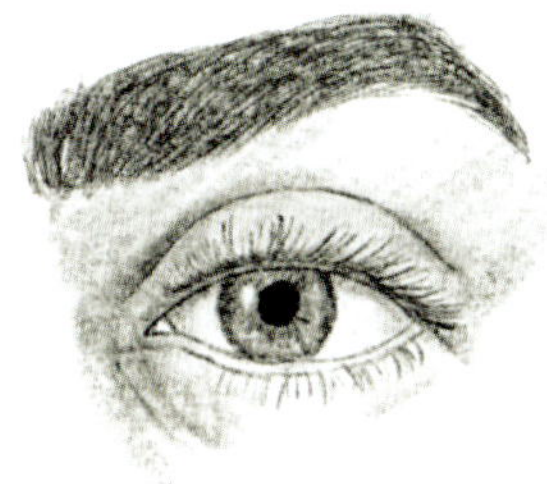

Hard-Angled

The hard-angled eyebrow has a distinctive peak and abrupt change of direction downward. The peak of the curve is above the white of the eye on the ear side.

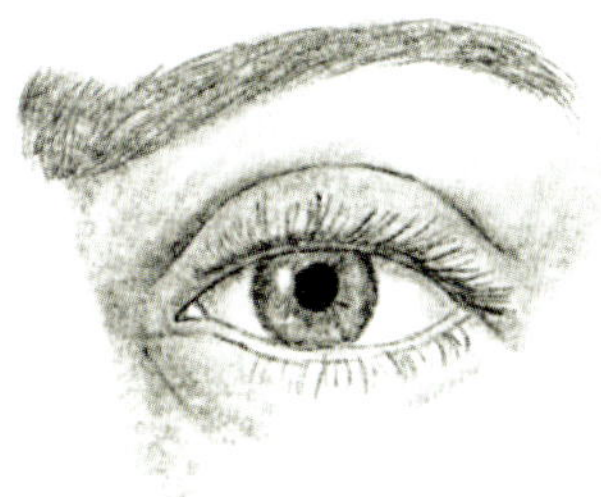

S-Shaped

The S shape refers to eyebrows that have an additional upward curve in the eyebrow on the nose side. The rest of the eyebrow can be curved or angled.

NOSE

Drawing a nose can feel intimidating to beginners, but it's actually one of the easiest facial features to draw. That's because although noses can look different from one person to another, they're all made up of just a few simple shapes.

Here you'll learn to draw one nose, but flip to page 64 to see some more shapes and sizes.

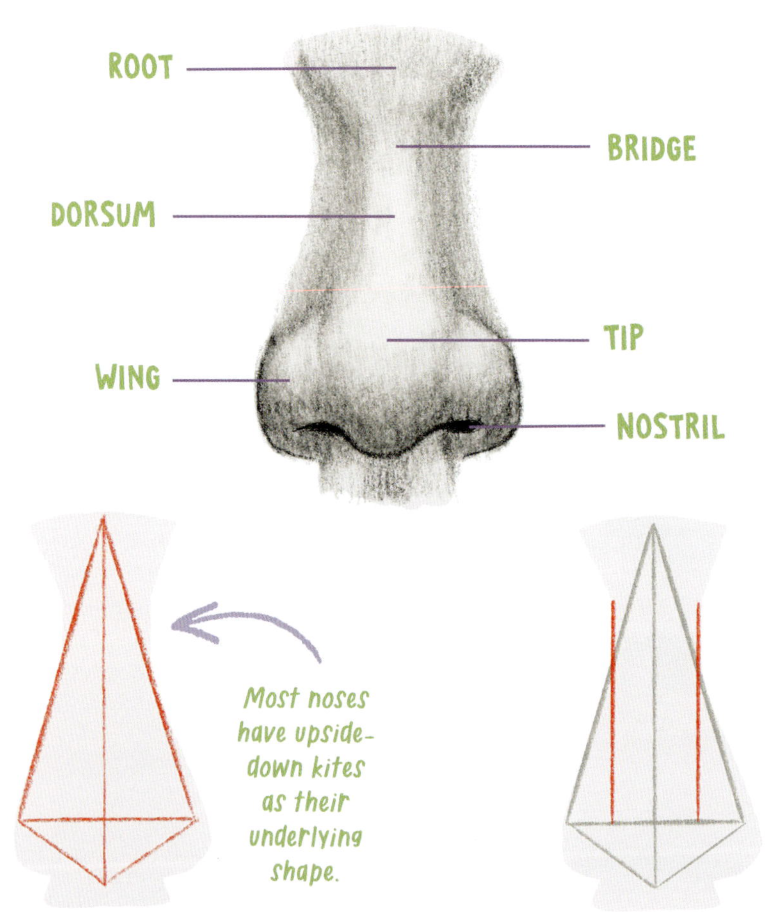

Step 1

Draw an upside-down kite. Connect the top and bottom points with a vertical line. Draw a horizontal line connecting the left and right points.

Step 2

On each side of the midline, draw a straight vertical line that extends from just under the top of the triangle down to the horizontal line.

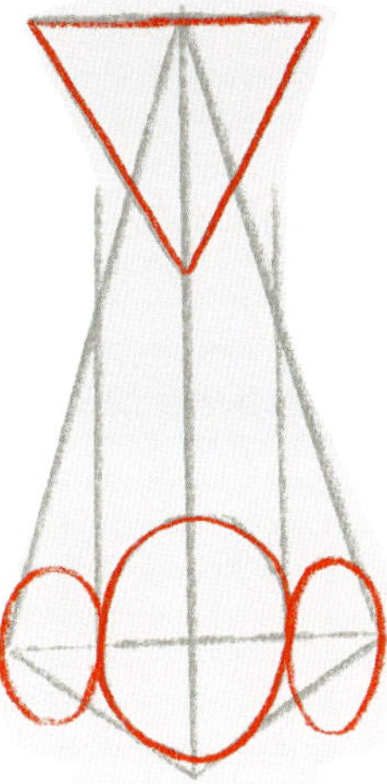

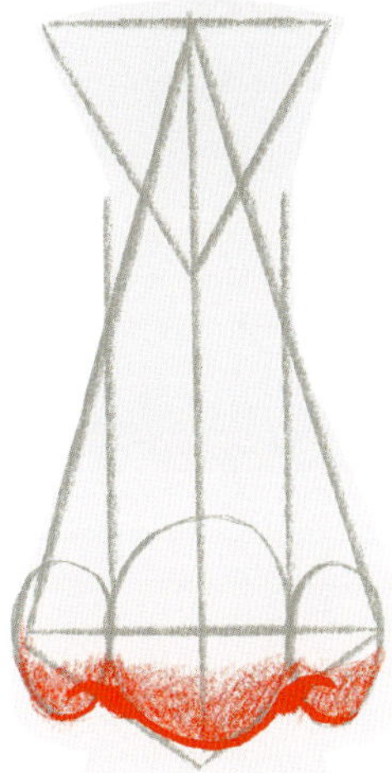

Step 3

Draw an upside-down triangle at the top of the nose. Draw an oval over the intersecting lines at the bottom of the kite—this will be the tip of the nose. Add a smaller oval on each side.

Step 4

Color in the nostrils by darkly outlining and shading the area where the small ovals intersect with the large one. Outline the bottom of the center oval, and lightly shade across the bottom of all three ovals.

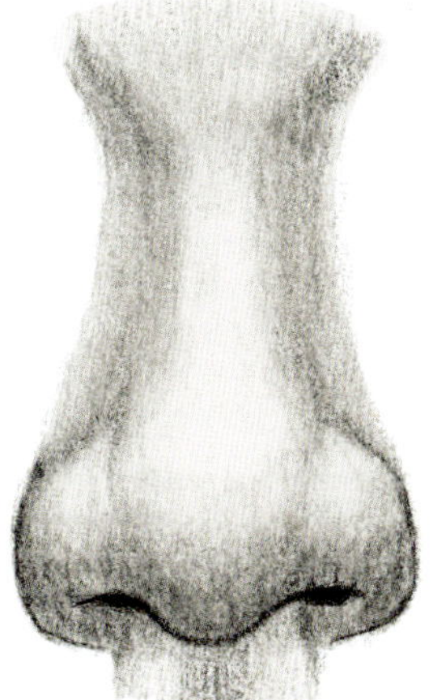

Step 5

Erase your guidelines and get shading. Shade more darkly in the areas where the external guidelines were, and follow the shapes of the ovals to create depth around the nostrils.

Reference: Nose

There are nearly as many nose shapes as there are people. You've just seen one—here are a few more.

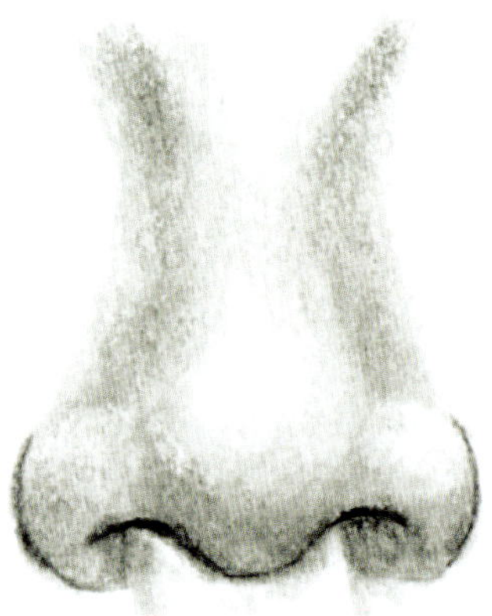

Some people have wings of their nose that are quite rounded, making the bottom of the nose appear wider in relation to the dorsum.

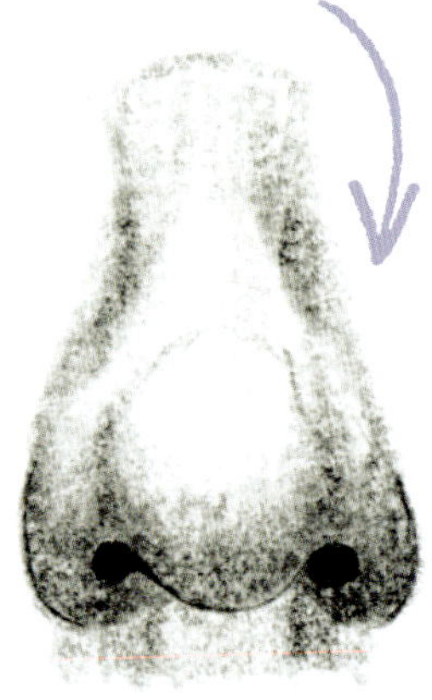

The wings of this nose are a bit rounded.

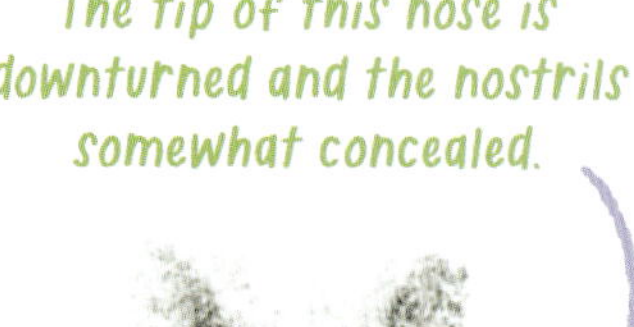

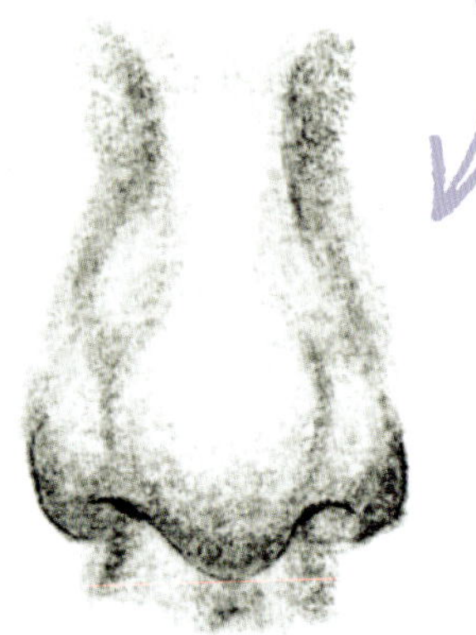

The bridge of this nose is pinched.

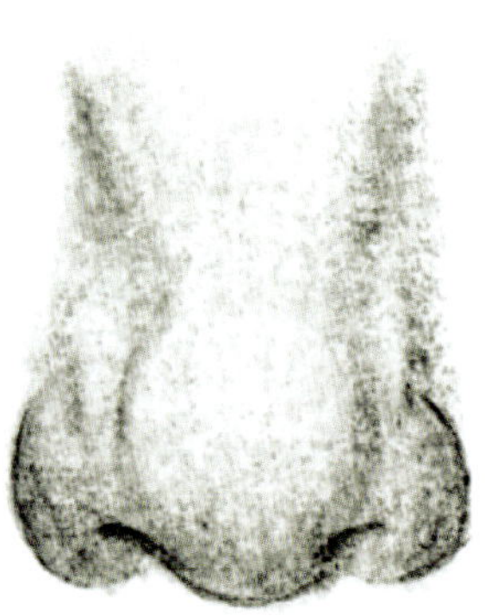

The dorsum of this nose is short.

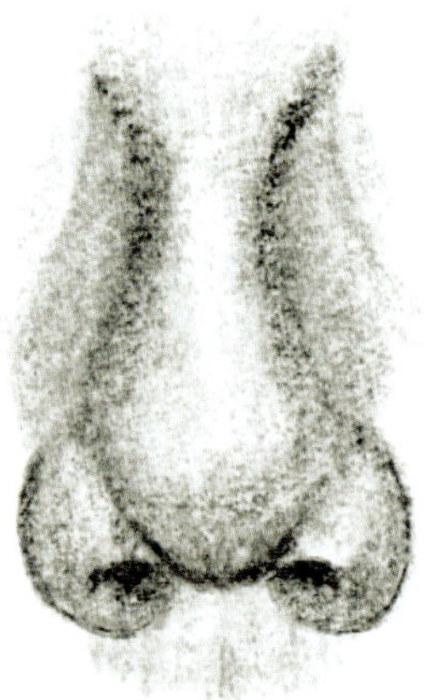

The bridge of the nose here is narrow in relation to the dorsum.

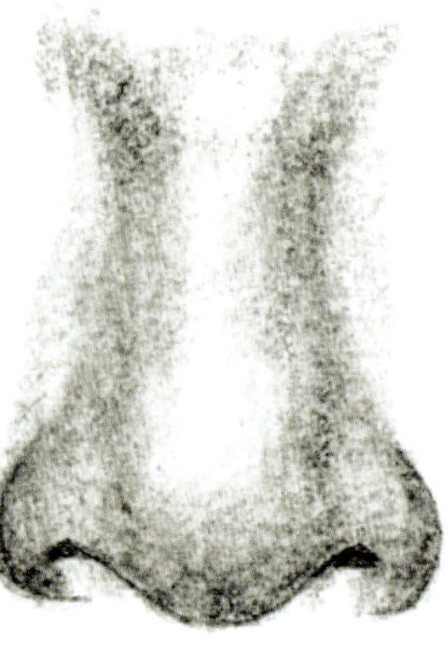

These nostrils, though small, are far apart from each other.

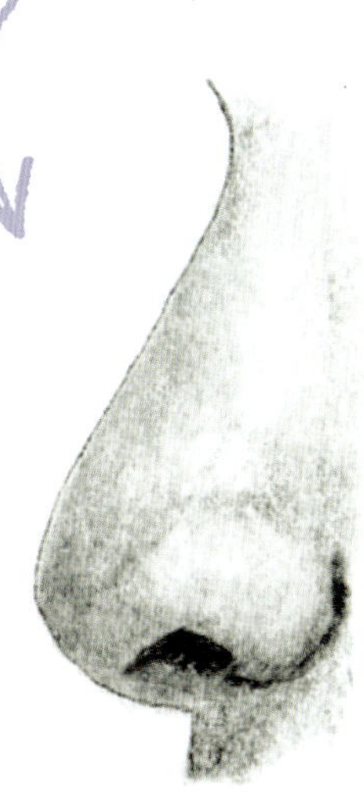

The nostrils are visible in the profile view of this nose.

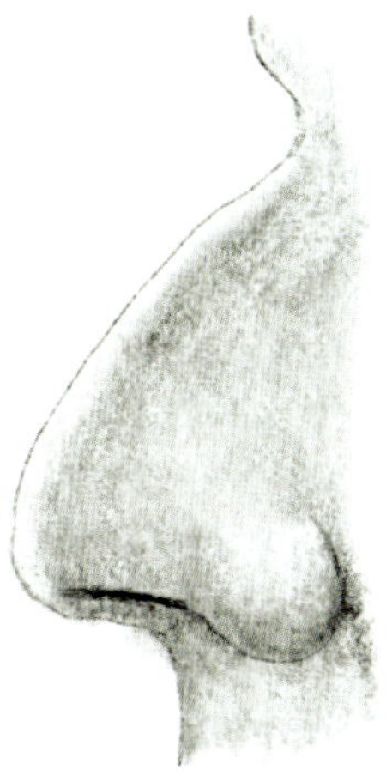

The dorsum of this nose is slightly curved.

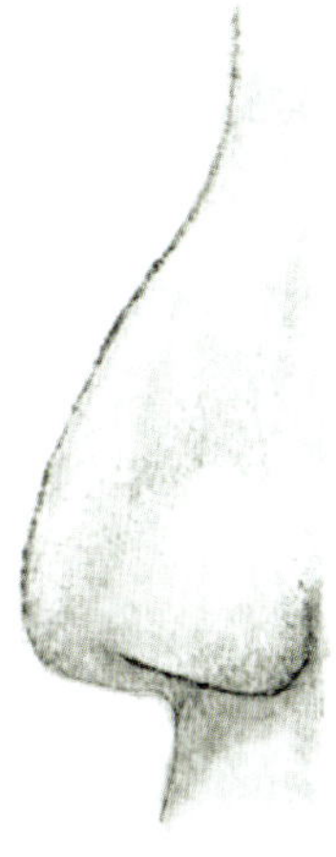

The nostrils are not visible in the profile view of this nose.

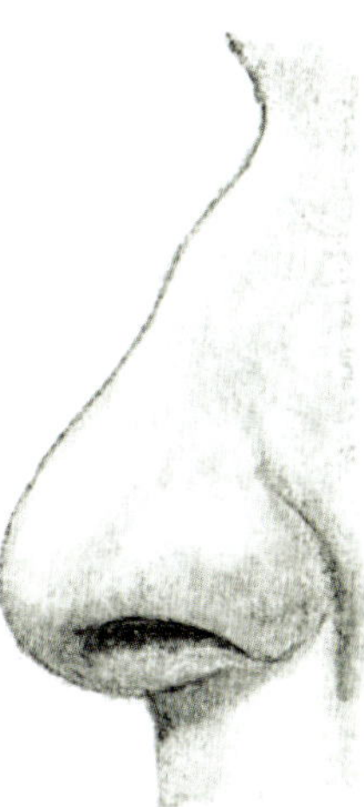

In some noses, we see a bump in the dorsum where the nasal bone ends.

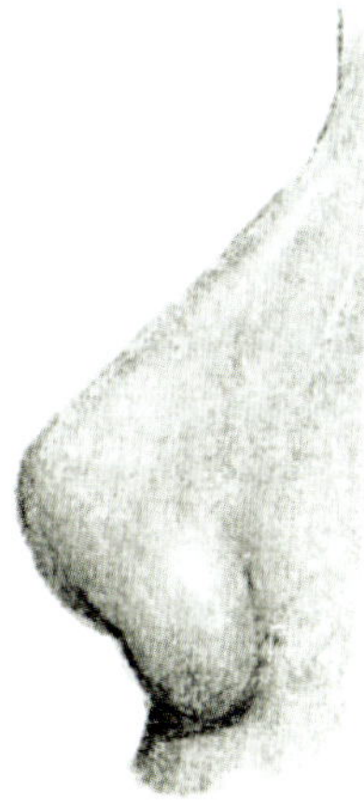

Some noses feature an upturned tip.

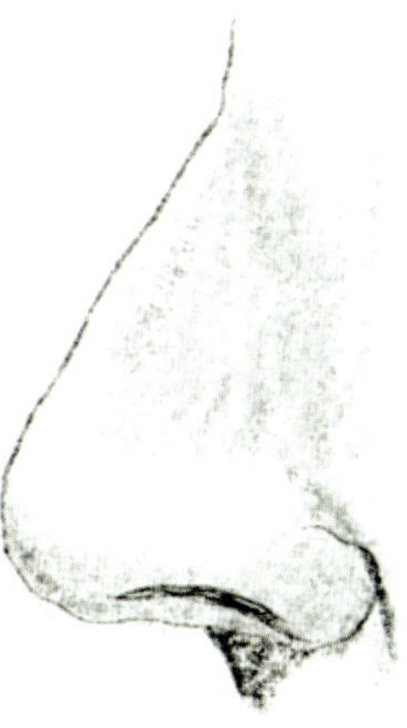

The wings of this nose are not prominent.

MOUTH

As kids, we learn to draw simplified mouths as U shapes, upside-down U shapes or straight lines. Realistic mouths aren't that different: a few basic shapes, some fine details and shading will do the trick.

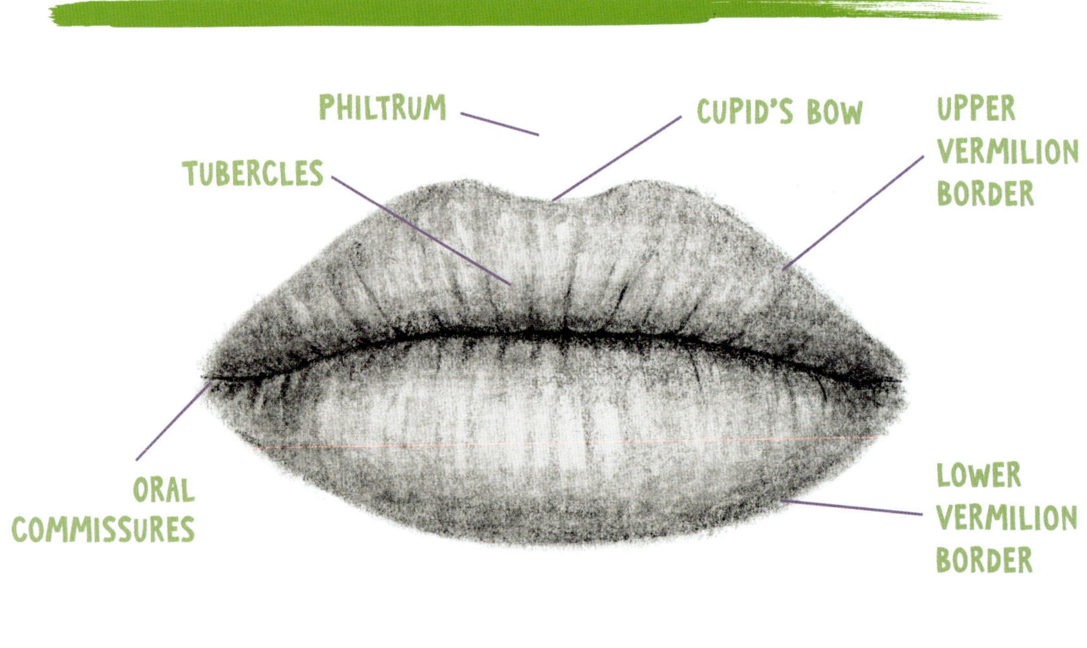

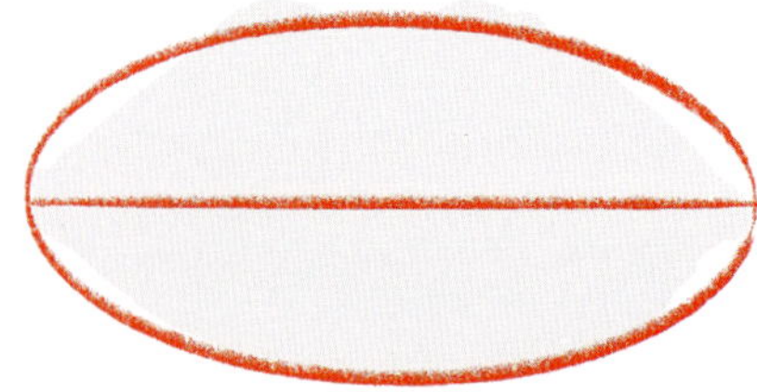

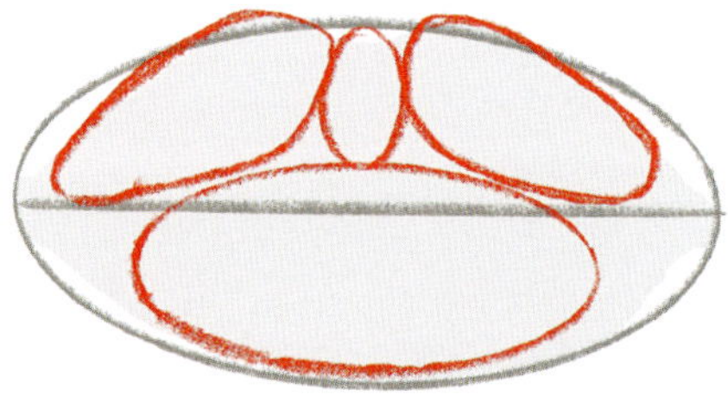

Step 1

Very lightly, draw an oval and split it in half with a straight line. Everything above the line is the top lip; everything below it, the bottom lip.

Step 2

For the top lip, draw a small oval in the middle and two larger bean shapes on either side of it. For the bottom lip, draw a large oval.

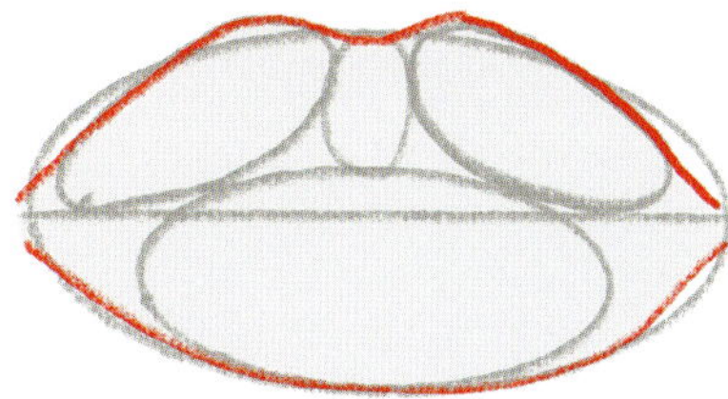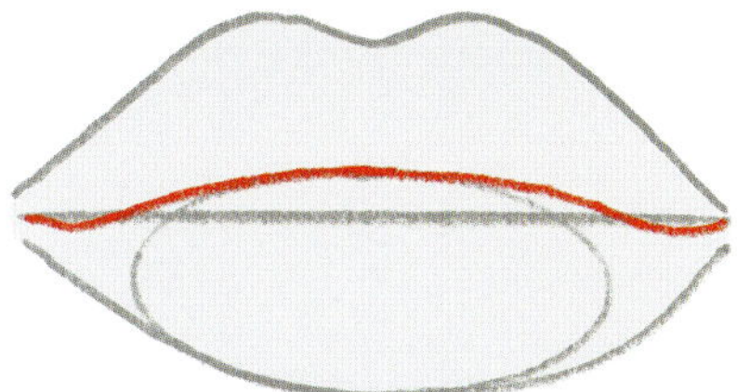

Step 3

Using your guidelines, draw a curved line across the top. This line is the Cupid's bow and the vermilion border. It separates the lips from the skin of the face. Now draw a curved line across the bottom.

Step 4

Replace the horizontal guideline splitting the top and bottom lips with a curved line that bends down at the corners and up at the middle.

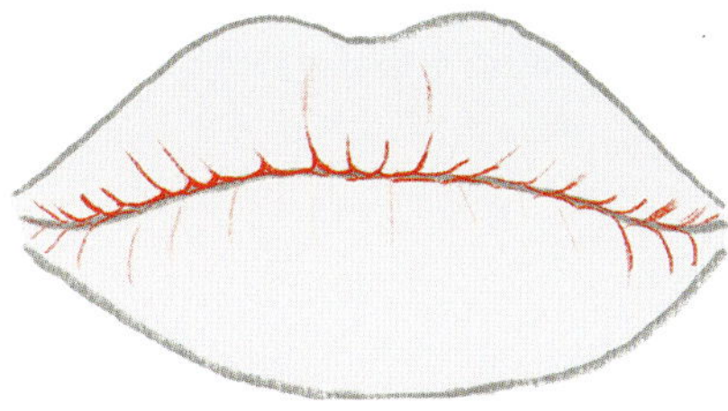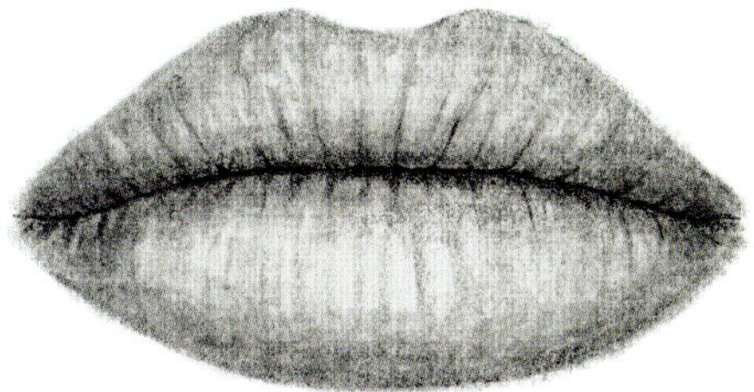

Step 5

To draw the tubercles, or small bumps, in the top lip, draw a small U shape in the center, followed by a series of small, curved lines pointing toward the corners of the mouth. For the bottom lip, concentrate the curved lines in the corners of the mouth.

Step 6

Shade the lips. The shading should be darker at the corners of the mouth and between the top and bottom lips. Erase some of the shading between the creases to make the tubercles appear three dimensional.

Reference: Mouth

The shape of the mouth and fullness of the lips can vary from person to person. Let's take a look at some more forms that the mouth can take.

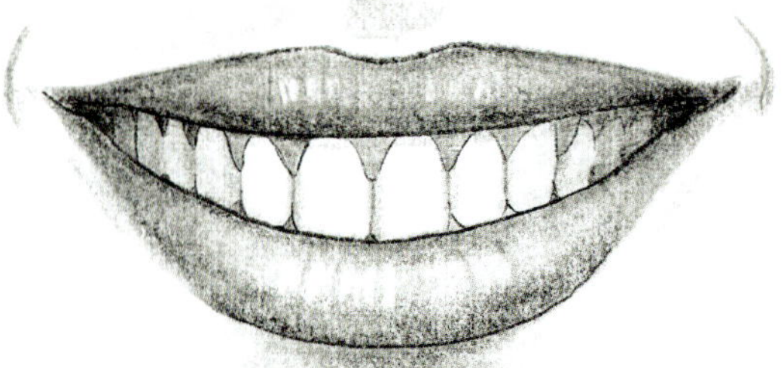

In this kind of smile, we only see the top teeth.

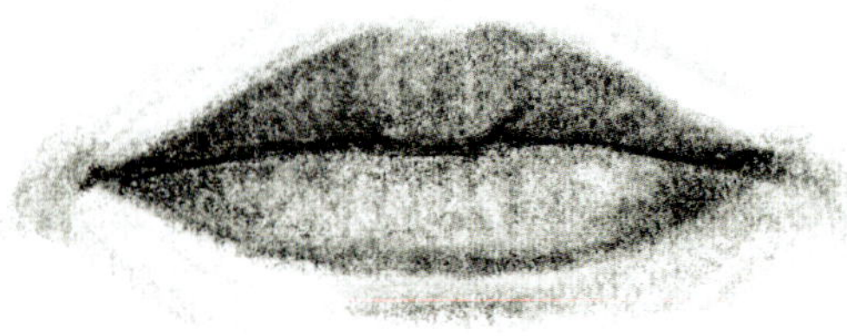

The Cupid's bow is not pronounced, making this mouth look oval in shape.

Note that the top lip is quite a bit smaller than the bottom lip here.

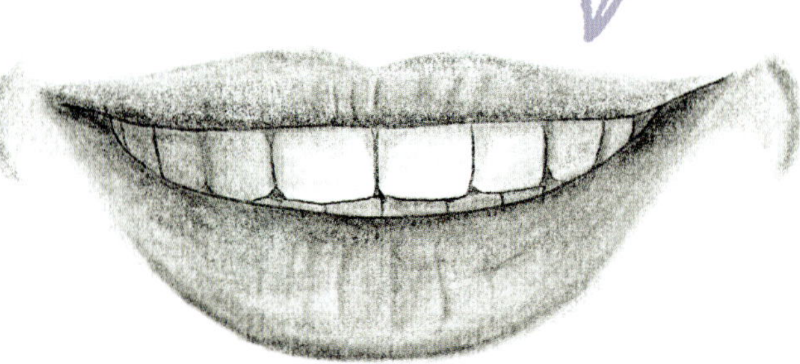

In this smile, we see both the top and bottom teeth.

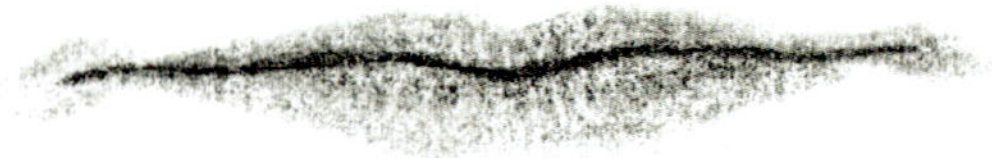

These are classic thin lips.

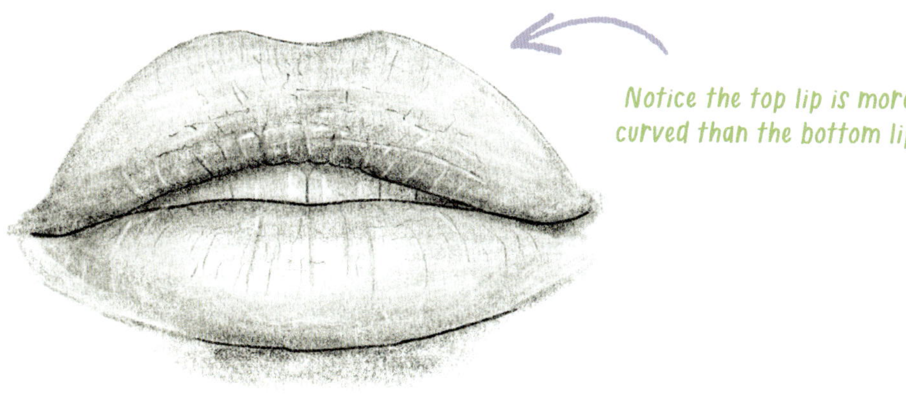

These are full lips.

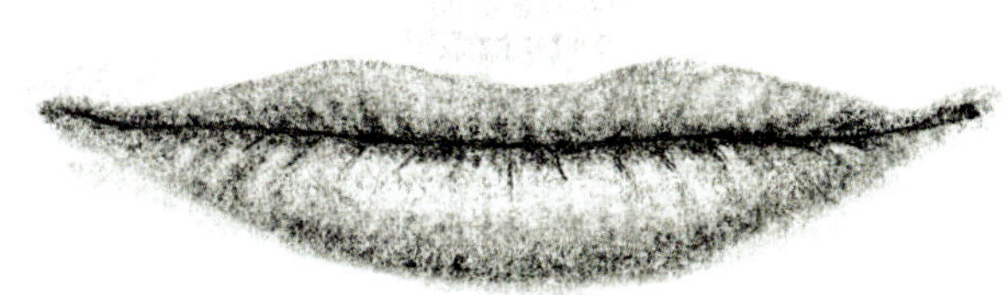

The Cupid's bow is wide in these lips.

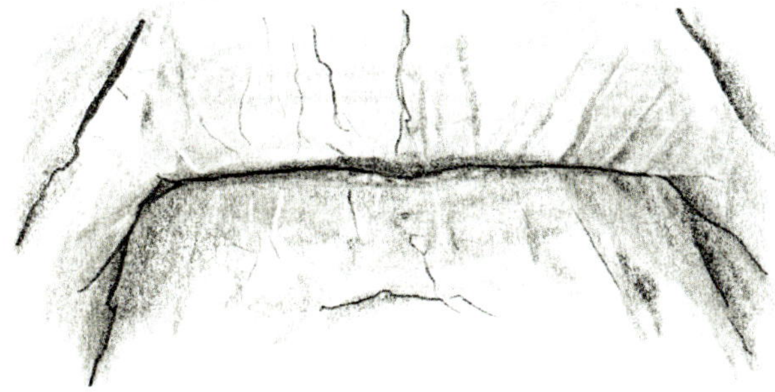

As we age, our lips tend to become thinner, and wrinkles develop at the corners of the mouth.

FACIAL HAIR

There are four areas that define facial hair types: hair on the upper lip creates types of mustaches, hair on the lower lip creates types of soul patches, hair on the chin creates types of goatees, and hair along the jawline creates types of sideburns. Let's combine all of these together to draw a full beard.

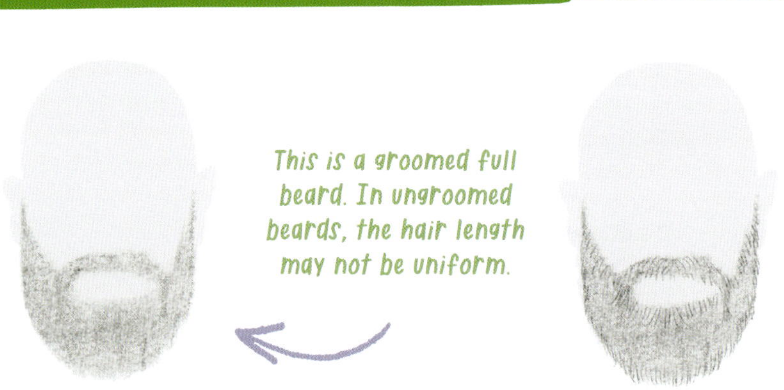

This is a groomed full beard. In ungroomed beards, the hair length may not be uniform.

Step 1

Using the side of your pencil, lightly shade in a crescent shape extending from ear to ear, up to the mouth. Shade the area above the upper lip as well. This will define the shape of your beard.

Step 2

Using the tip of your pencil, draw short lines around the outside of the beard. Make the lines slightly angled, following the shape of the face.

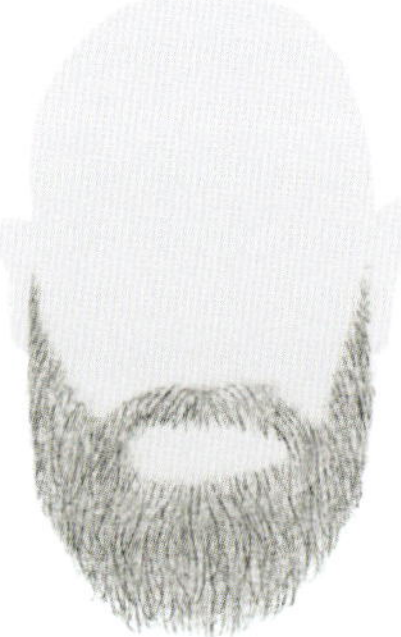

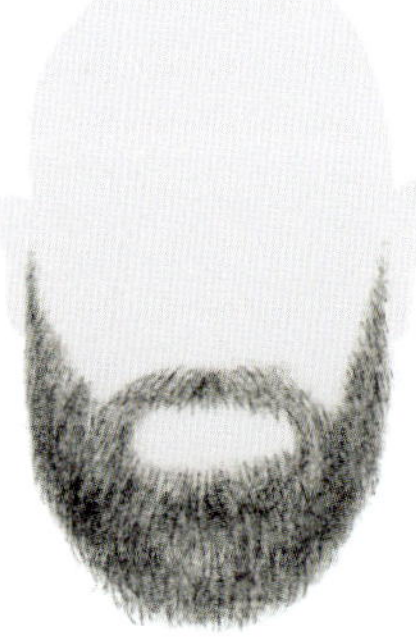

Step 3

Continue making short lines to fill in the entire shaded area. Remember to follow the shape of the face.

Step 4

Continue darkening the entire beard, making the area around the jawline the most dense and the area under the lower lip the most sparse.

Reference: Facial Hair

There are enough styles of facial hair to fill an entire drawing book. Thankfully, most styles are variations on the following common ones.

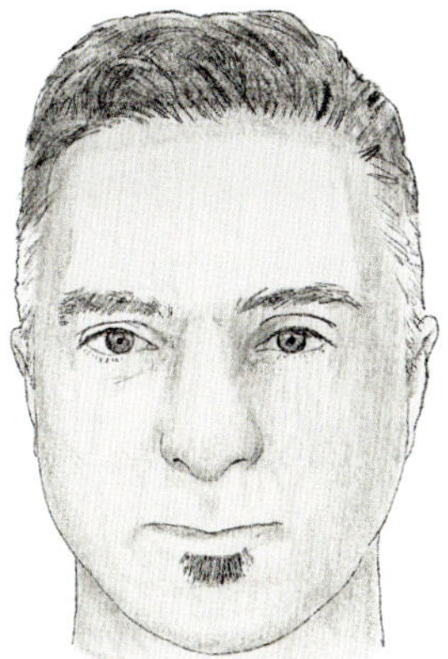

Soul Patch

The smallest of the facial hairstyles, the soul patch is contained to the area under the lower lip and above the chin. Use short, vertical pencil strokes to draw the hairs.

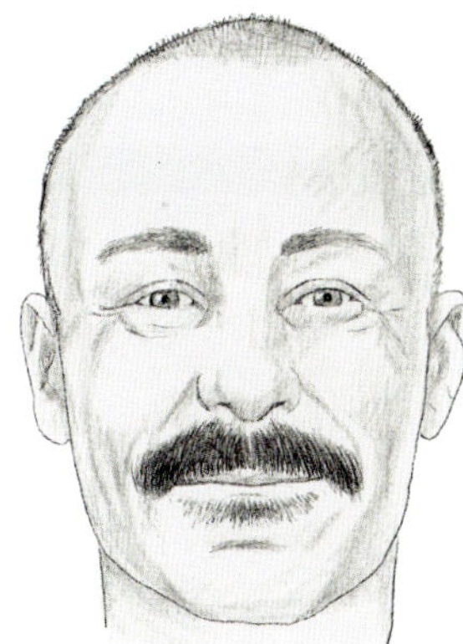

Mustache

Mustaches are made up of the facial hair between the upper lip and the nose. Usually, the hairs are slightly angled toward the corners of the mouth.

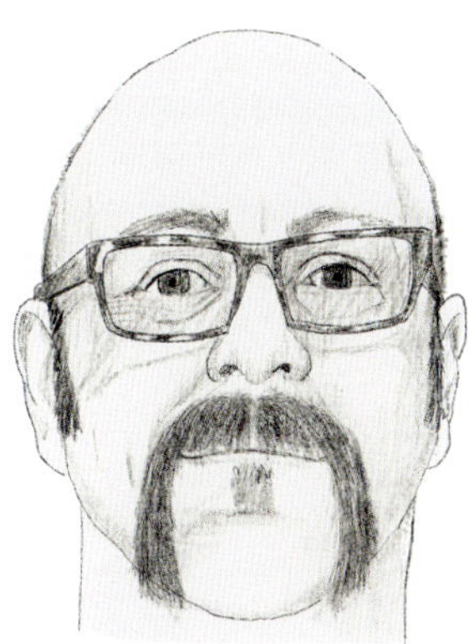

Handlebar Mustache

The handlebar mustache is a regular mustache that extends down both sides of the mouth and stops at the jawline. Use short lines to show individual hairs.

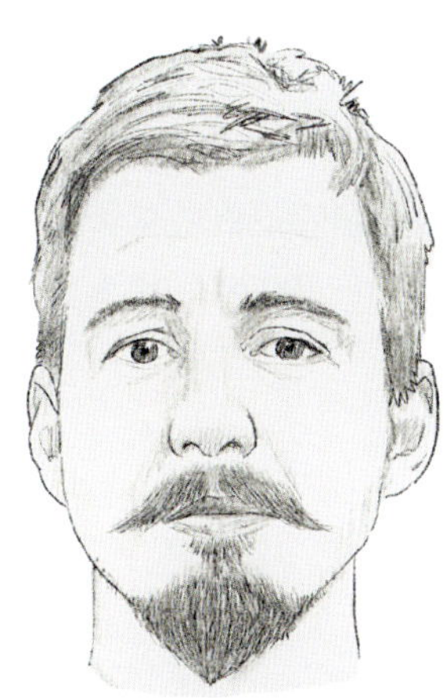

Vandyke

The Vandyke pairs a goatee (chin-only facial hair) with a soul patch and mustache. Note that the hairs at the corners of the mouth should be longer and curled upward slightly. Also, the goatee should be pointed.

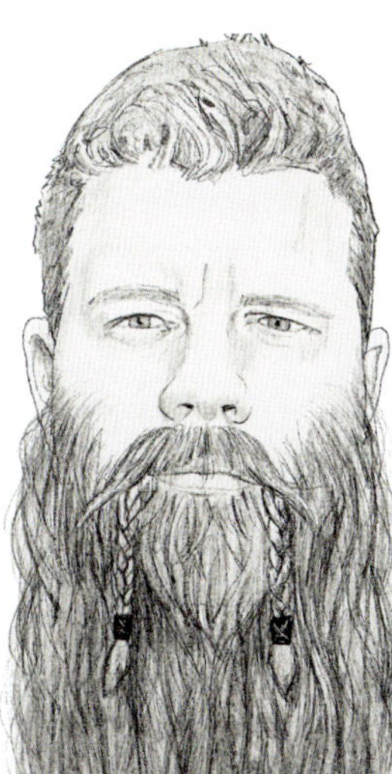

Viking Beard

The Viking beard is nearly the same as a full beard, but it is trimmed to create a strong jawline. The braided hairs are an optional feature.

For how to draw braided hair, flip to page 82.

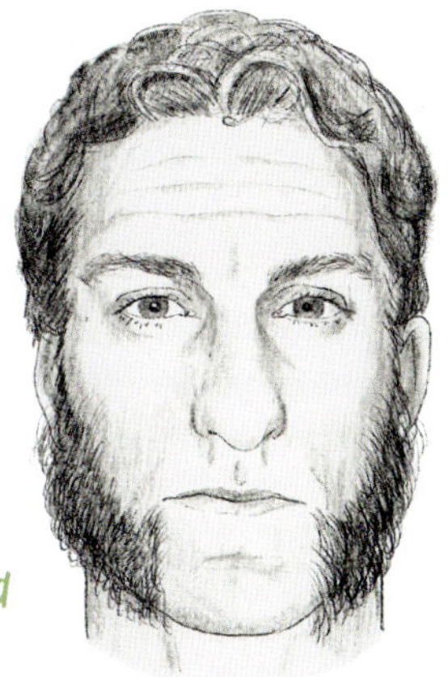

Sideburns

Sideburns begin at the front of the ear, extend down along the jawline and stop short of the chin. Sideburns can vary in length.

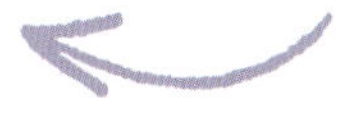

EARS

Ears may not be fully visible when drawing someone from straight on, but they become more important when drawing someone from a three-quarter or side view. Ears have a lot of little bumps and turns, but, as with almost everything, they can be broken down into some basic shapes.

Step 1

Draw a curved line for the outline of the ear. It should resemble a backward C shape, with a bottom that is narrower than the top.

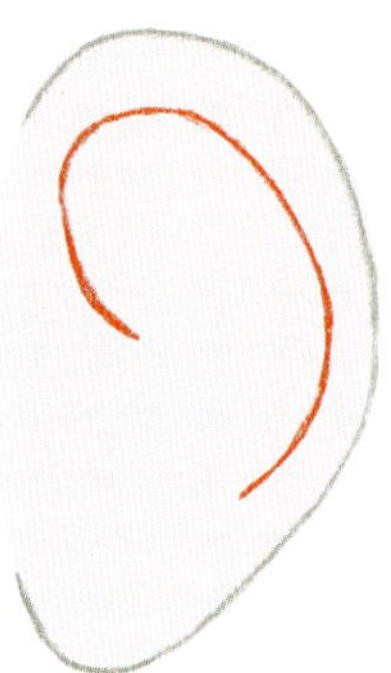

Step 2

Draw a shorter curved line inside the first one. Draw lightly, as you may want to adjust the line later.

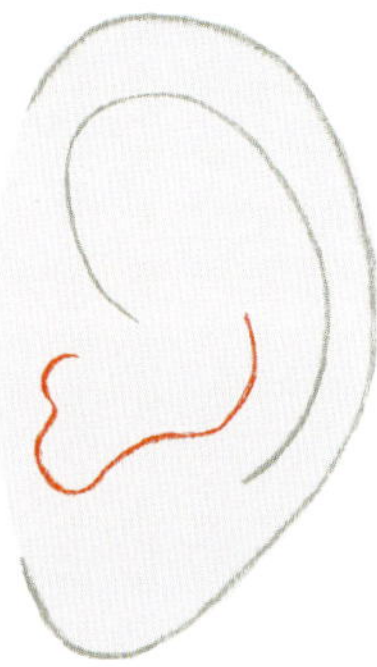

Step 3

Starting on the left side, draw a curved line that looks like a backward 3 followed by a reverse S shape. This will be the major inside line for the ear. It does not overlap with the lines you've already drawn.

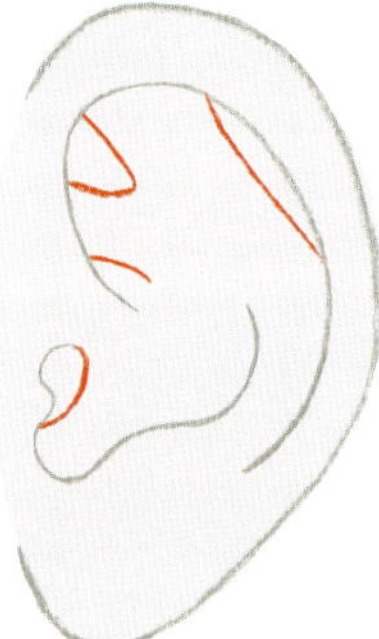

Step 4

Now, let's draw guidelines for the interior part of the ear. Inside the lines you've already made, draw a short, curved line connecting the top part of the backward 3 shape to itself, a short line a bit higher up, a U shape and a longer line.

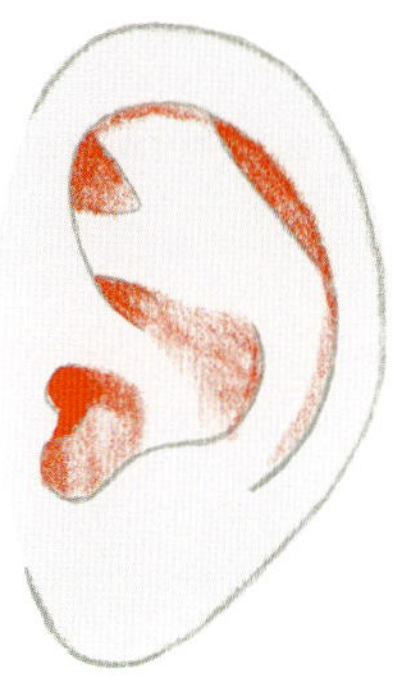

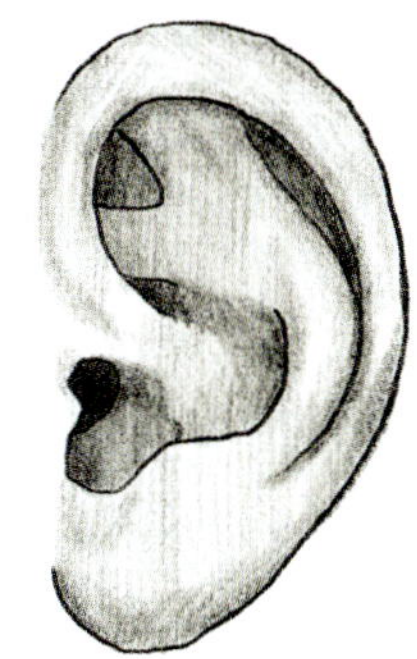

Step 5

Darkly shade the areas immediately surrounding the guidelines you've just drawn. Lightly shade the rest of the ear. Contrasting dark and light shading gives the ear depth.

Step 6

Finish the shading by darkening the sides and leaving the middle light. This creates a rounded look. This is especially important at the bottom of the ear and around the ear folds.

Back and Front Views

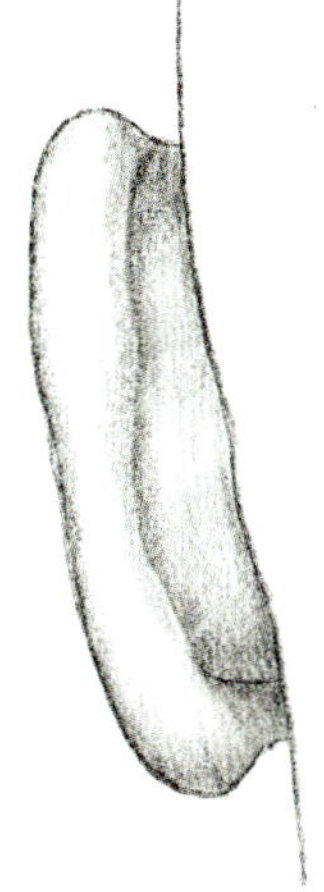

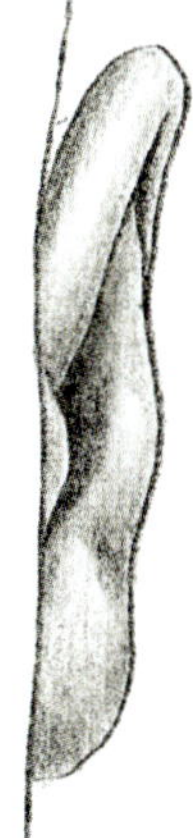

There are only a few lines to draw when depicting the ear from the back. Most of the structure is achieved by shading the top and bottom of the ears.

The front view of the ear is much simpler to draw than the side. Note the shading at the center and at the folds creates a rounded effect.

Reference: Ears

From small lobes to bigger ones and flatter ears to ears that stick out, here are just some of the many shapes an ear can take.

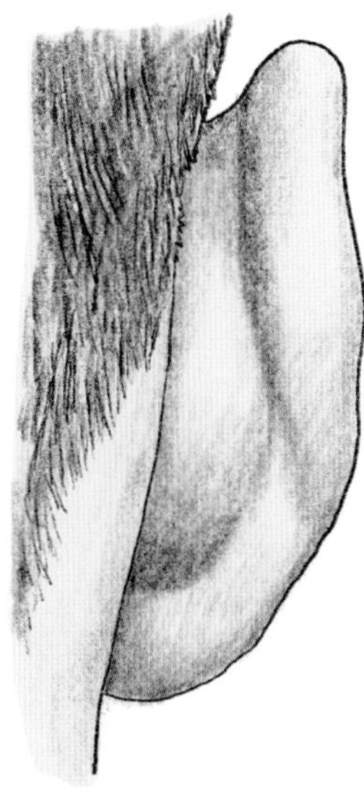

In ears that protrude, or stick out, notice that the contour of the ear creates a J shape from the back.

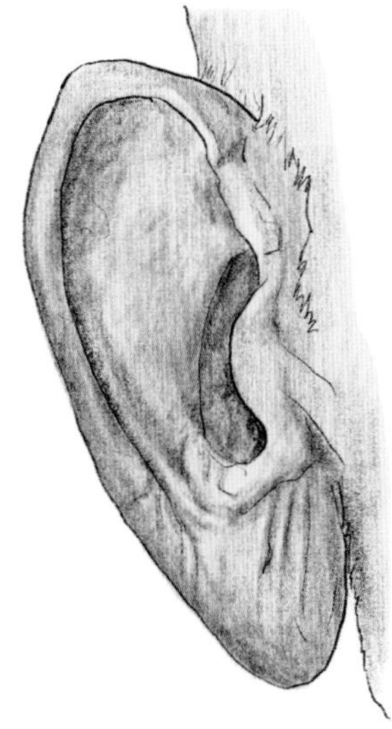

Elderly people often have wrinkles that form in the area where the lobe attaches to the face.

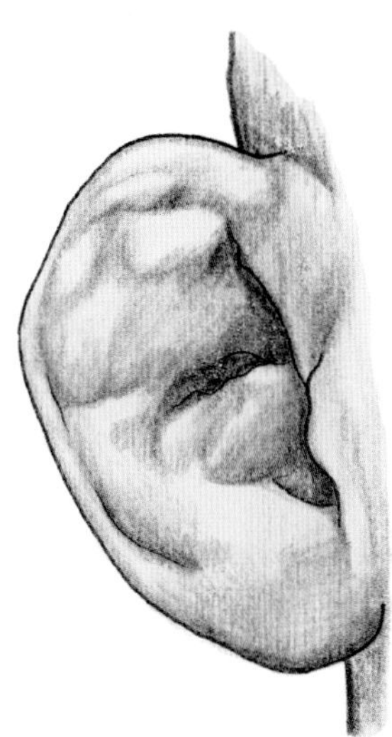

Sometimes seen in boxers, wrestlers and other fighters, the scar tissue buildup that defines cauliflower ear can be drawn by adding bumpy areas in the upper ear.

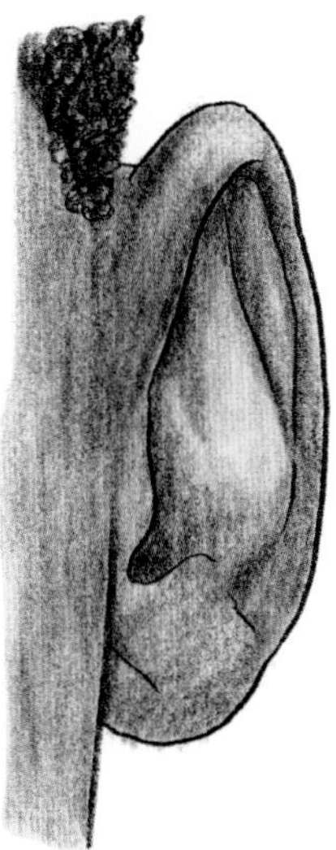

Some ears have attached lobes, which means the bottom part of the lobe is attached to the face. This gives the ear a smaller appearance.

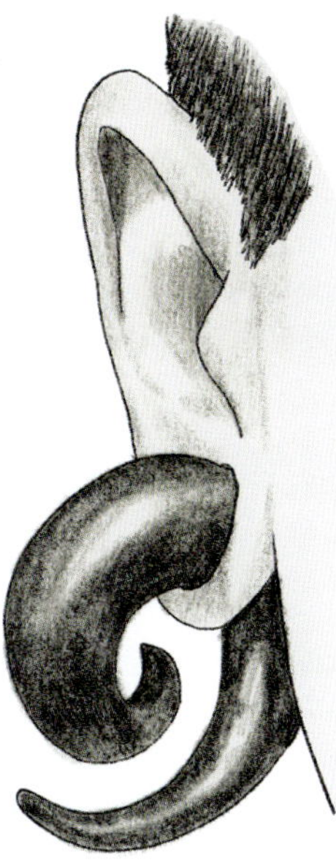

The earlobe can be stretched to accommodate varying styles and sizes of ear jewelry.

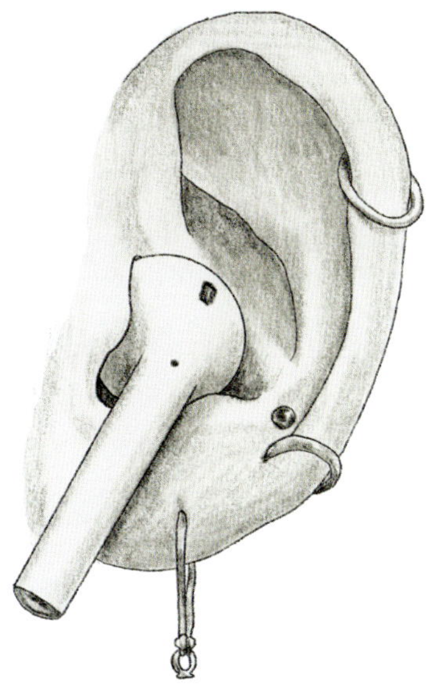

When drawing an ear with Airpods or piercings, add a light shadow around each object.

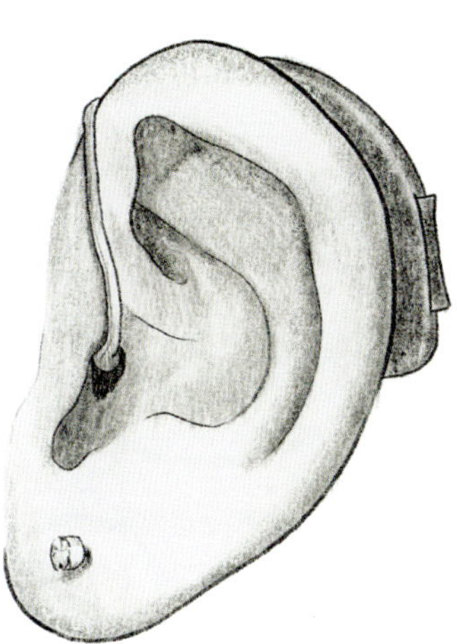

Some hearing aids follow the contour of the ear, while others are contained within the ear canal and are barely visible.

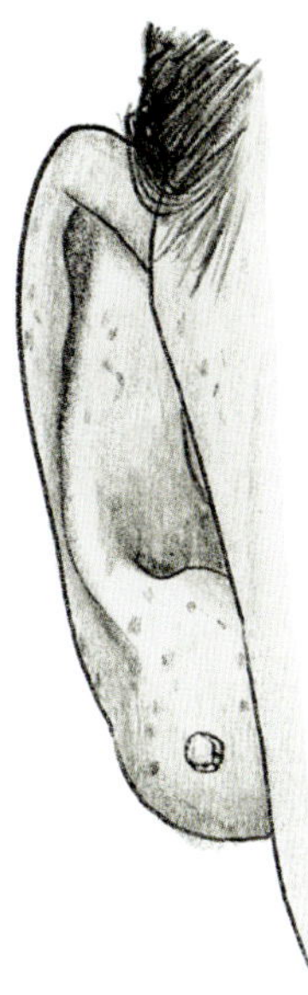

Ears, like all external parts of the body, are subject to moles, beauty marks, freckles and other skin features.

HAIR

Some people think you need to draw individual hairs to create a realistic effect. Unless you're creating an extremely detailed or close-up drawing, that's simply not true. In fact, in realism, we *don't* draw individual strands of hair. Rather, we draw what we tend to see when we look at people: clumps of hair and the general shape of their hair.

Although we won't be drawing individual strands of hair, it is important to know the structure of those strands, because the structure is what determines how the hair clumps together—and what we'll draw.

There are four major types of hair: straight, wavy, curly and coily. Three of those major hair types can be further divided into subtypes.

Type 1: Straight

There is only one type of straight hair.

Type 2: Wavy

There are three types of wavy hair, ranging from loose waves to tight waves.

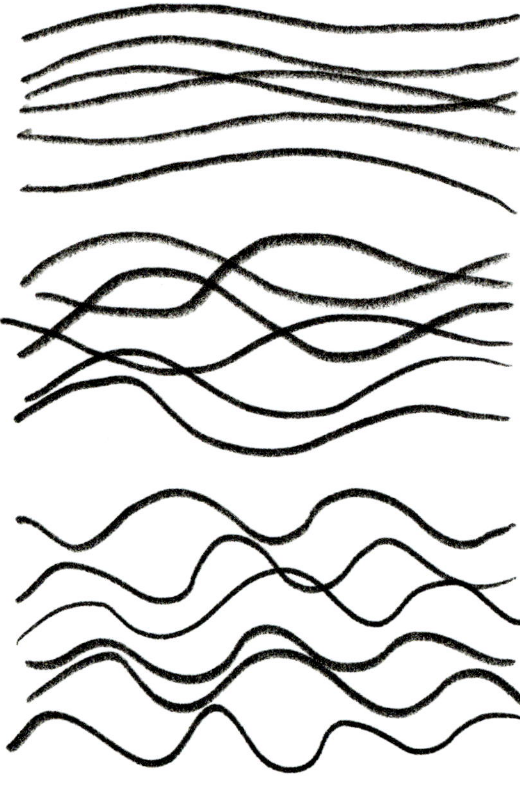

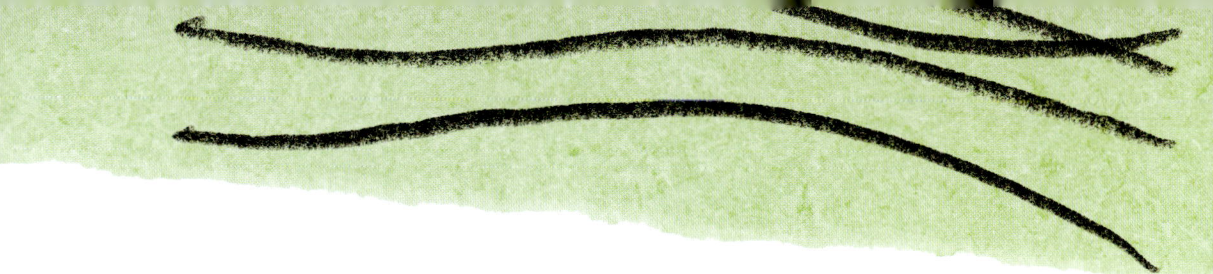

Type 3: Curly

There are three types of curly hair, ranging from loose curls to tight curls.

Type 4: Coily

There are three types of coily hair, ranging from loose coils to tight coils.

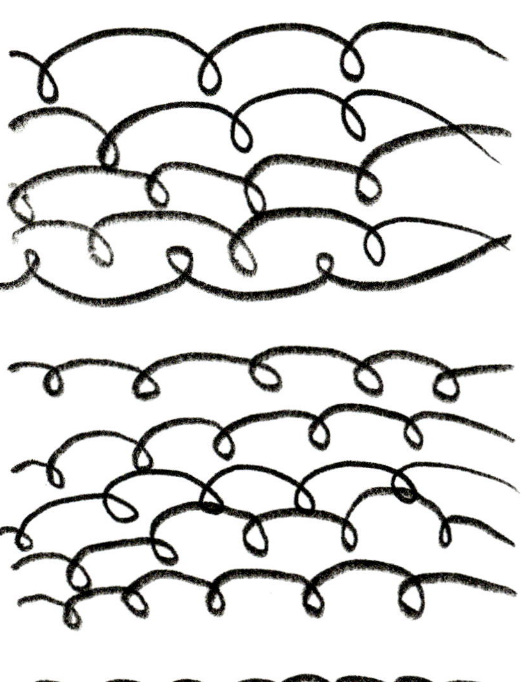

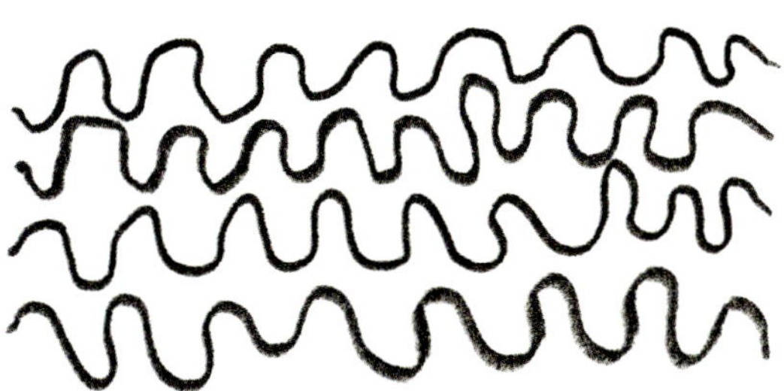

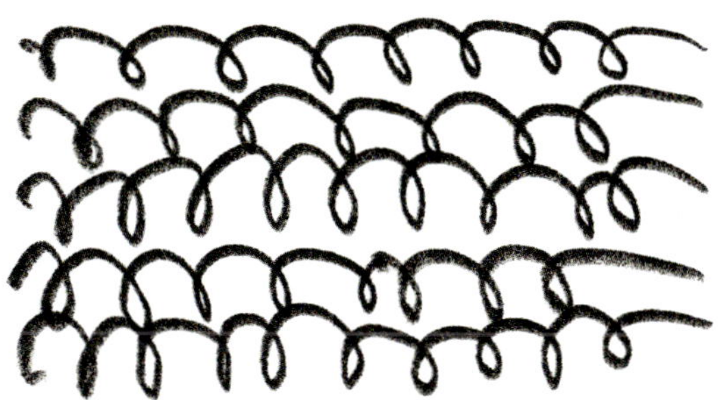

Straight Hair

Straight hair may seem fairly straightforward, but it can take on different appearances based on length and volume. Here's how to draw one example of straight hair worn down.

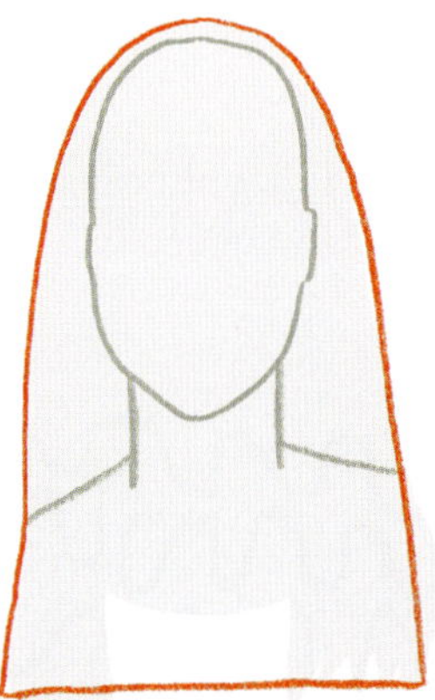

Step 1

Draw an upside-down U shape. Leave a little bit of space above the head for the thickness of the hair. Draw a straight line across the bottom to indicate the length of the hair.

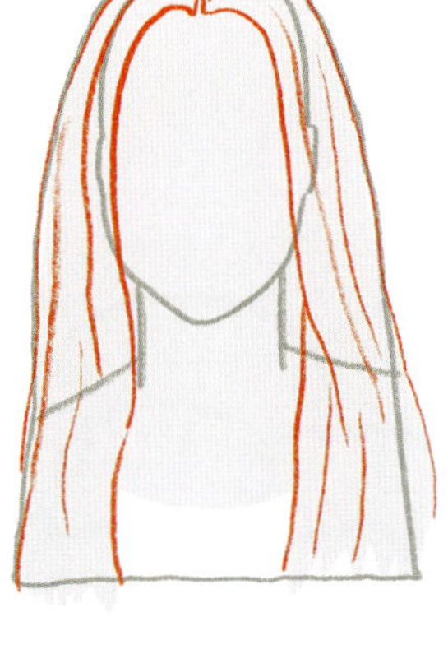

Step 2

Draw a few nearly straight long lines along the sides of the head and some very short lines where the hair is parted.

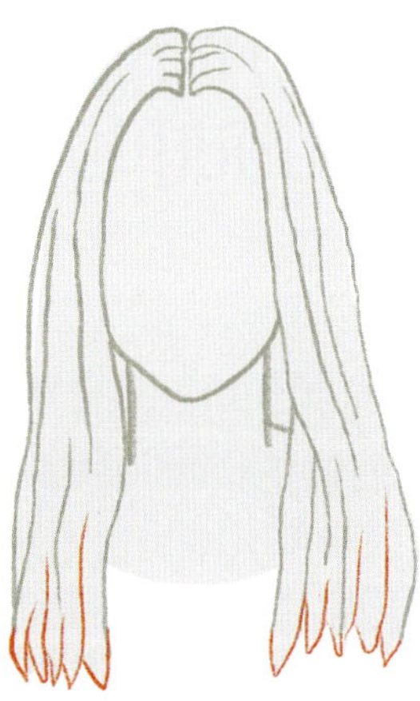

Step 3

Draw the tips of the hair. Don't draw single hairs here; instead, draw the bottoms of clumps of hair. Use rounded V shapes.

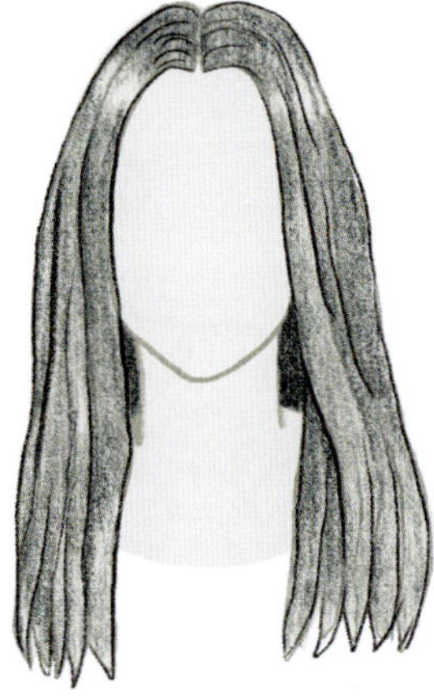

Step 4

Add shading. Shade the areas between the clumps a bit darker than the rest to separate the clumps. Also, leave the hair quite light just above the temples of the head. This will create the illusion of shine.

Wavy Hair

Not all wavy hair looks the same. Genetics, styling and other factors make for a range of variations. Below let's draw one example of wavy hair.

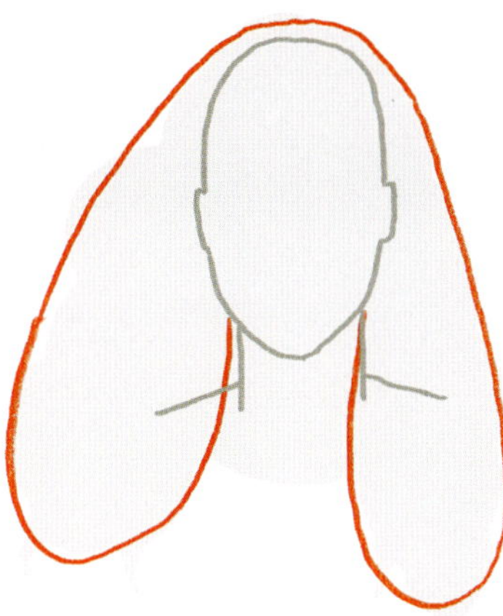

Very lightly draw a U shape on each side of the head, extending down below the shoulders. Connect them with an upside-down U shape that goes over and around the head. The hair will mostly be drawn in this area.

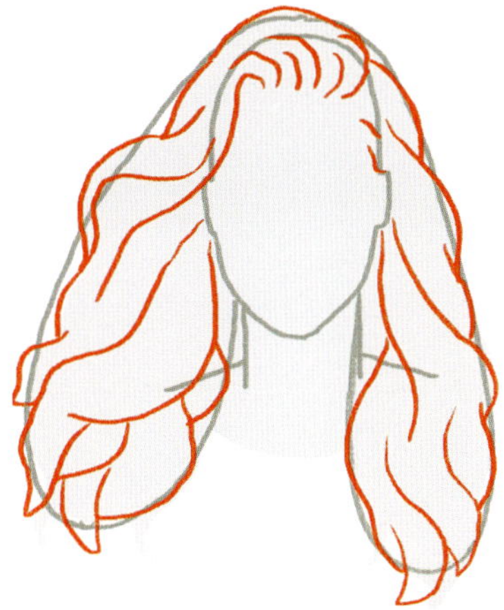

Draw multiple S shapes reaching from the head to the edge of the guidelines for clumps of hair. Space them more or less equally apart. Make backward C shapes along the forehead for the hairline.

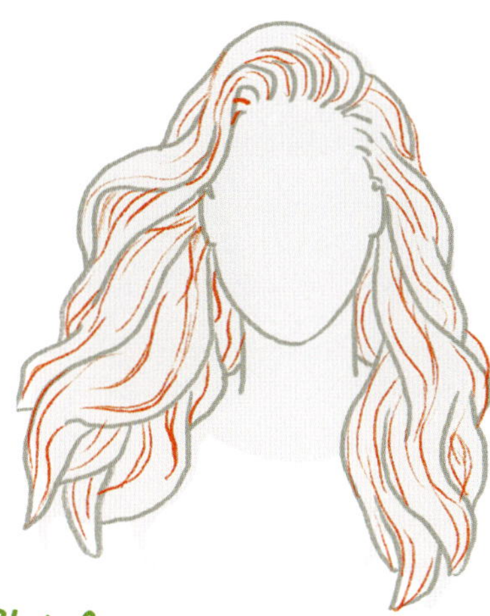

Now divide those large clumps of hair into smaller ones by drawing smaller S shapes. Follow the same curves as you did in the last step.

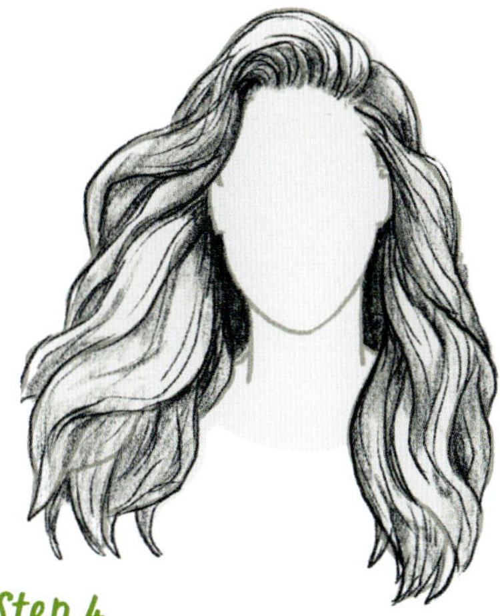

Time to shade. The darkest areas of the hair will be below the ears and in the places where one clump of hair falls behind another one.

Curly Hair

Curly hair can take on many different shapes depending on hair length and volume. Here's one shape that curly hair can take.

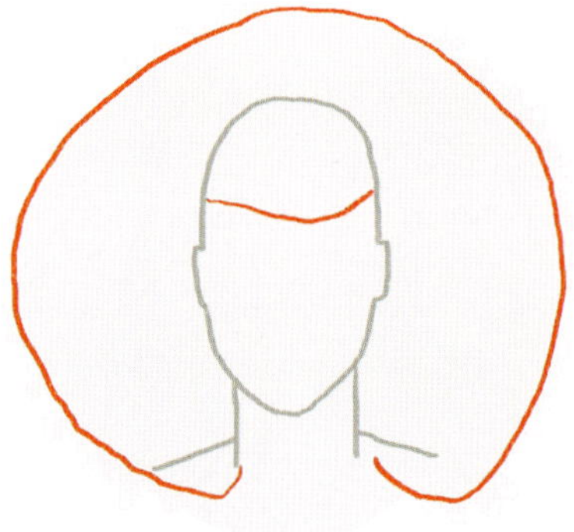

Step 1

Start with a light guideline circle around the head. Draw a curved line across the forehead for bangs.

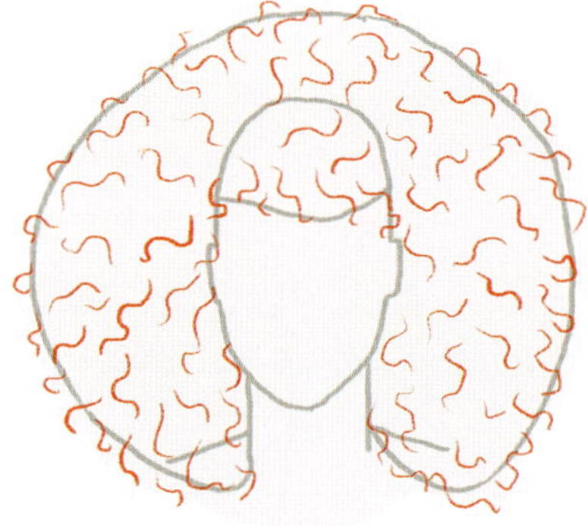

Step 2

Draw very short squiggles throughout the circle. The squiggles should be S shapes or loose 3 shapes.

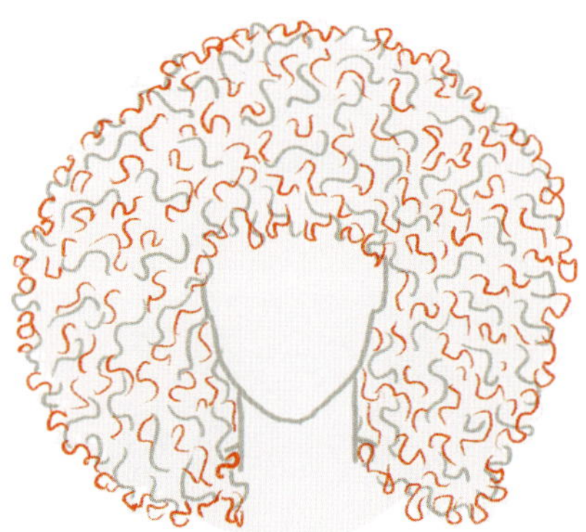

Step 3

Fill the circle with more of the same. The shapes should not point in any one direction. Try not to overlap the squiggles too much.

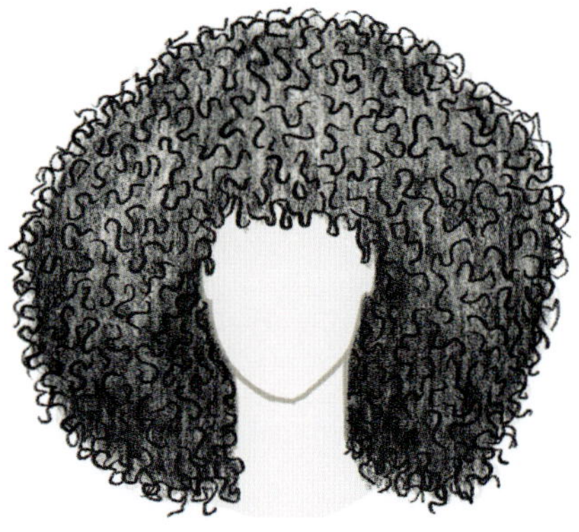

Step 4

Shade the entire head of hair, making it darkest at the bottom and the sides. This will give an overall rounded effect.

Coily Hair

Like all hair types, coily hair can be long or short, thick or thin, tight or loose.
Let's draw one example of coily hair.

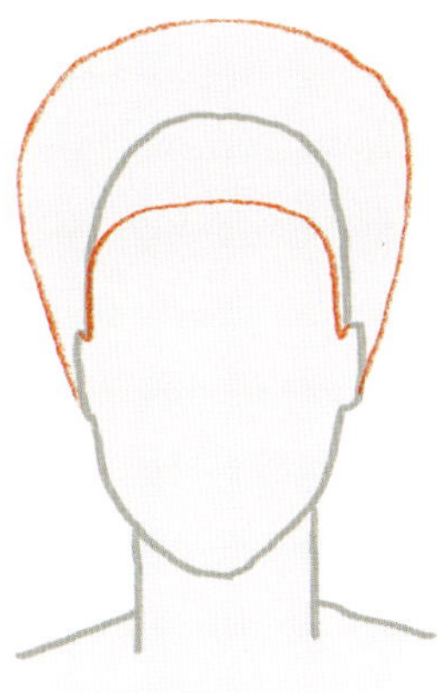

Step 1

Lightly draw the guidelines for the hair. Draw one curved line for the outside of the hair and another line across the forehead for the hairline.

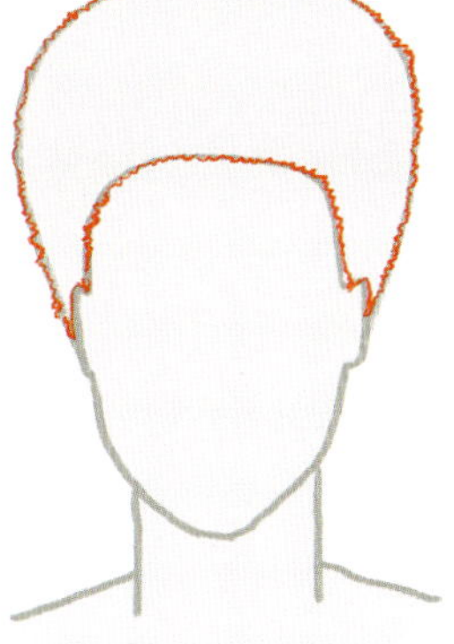

Step 2

Go over the line you just drew with very small, very tight zigzags. Make the zigzag points irregular and small enough so that they do not look like spikes.

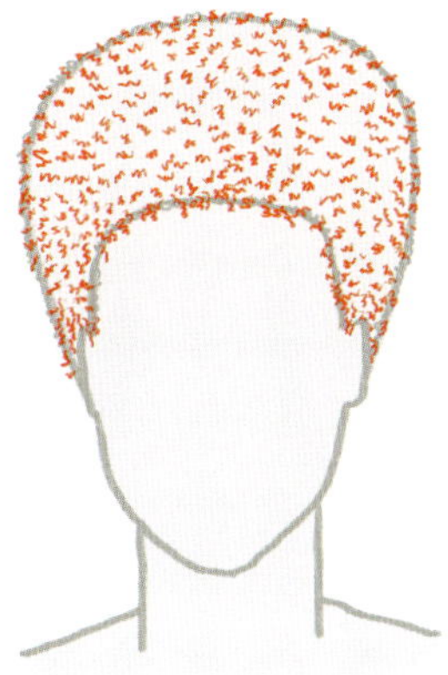

Step 3

Draw very small zigzags all throughout the hair. Space them out evenly and point them in random directions.

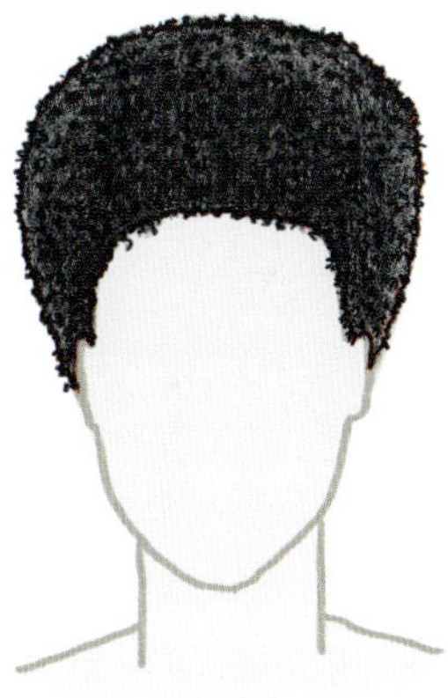

Step 4

Shade the hair quite darkly. It should be darker in the middle than the sides in order to show the thickness through the middle.

Braids

Braids are a type of hairstyle where three, or sometimes more, sections of hair are interlaced in a particular way. Here's how to draw one type of braid in pigtails.

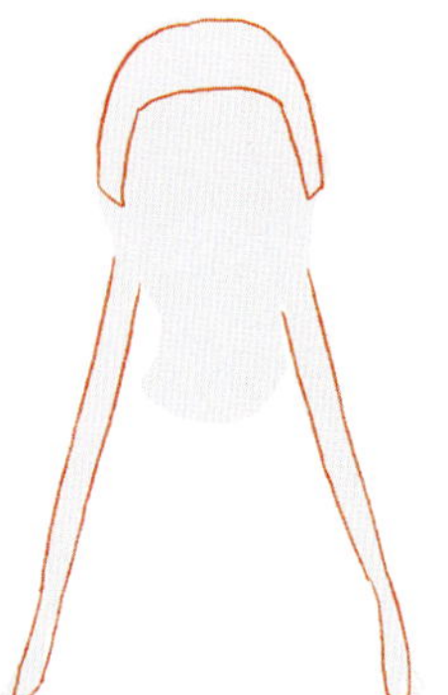

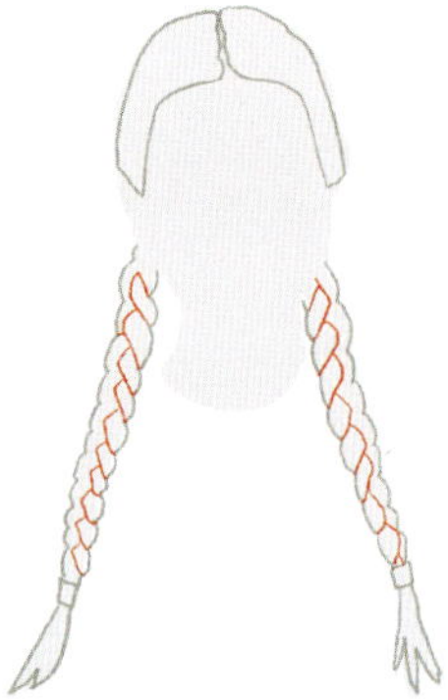

Step 1

Start with the crown. Lightly draw a crescent shape, making the hairline somewhat flatter. Draw a long, narrow U shape for each braid.

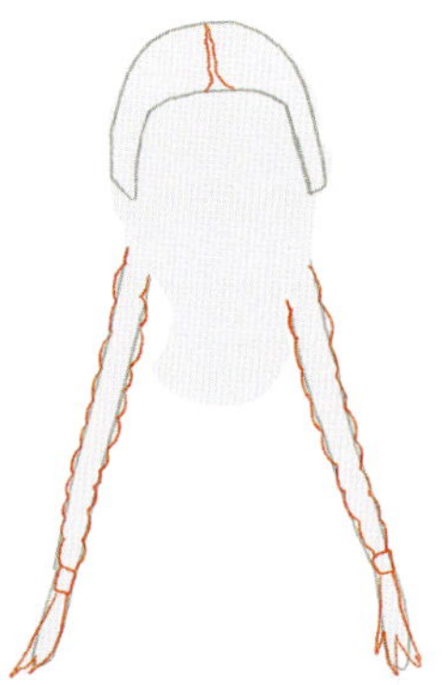

Step 2

Draw two lines to create a center part in the hair, distancing them slightly at the hairline. Along the outside of each braid, draw bumps. Add a small rectangle for the hair tie, then draw a jagged W shape to represent the loose hair at the bottom.

Step 3

Time to draw the interior of the braid. At the low points between each bump, draw a series of curved L shapes along both pigtails.

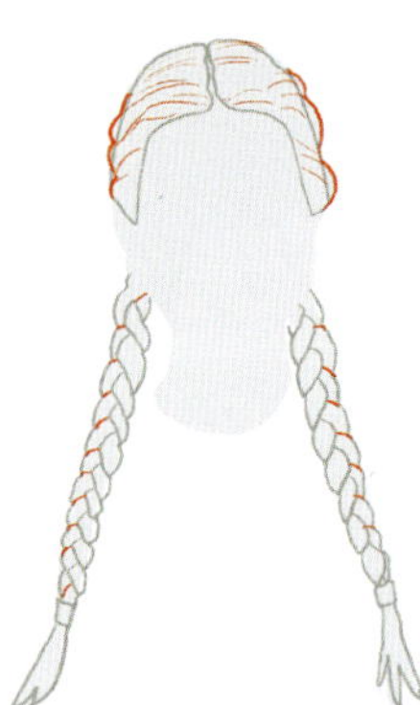

Step 4

At the crown of the head, add short, curved lines that extend out from the part. Add bumpy lines along the sides of the head. Now, at the low points between each bump on the other side of the pigtail, add a series of short lines connecting to the L shapes.

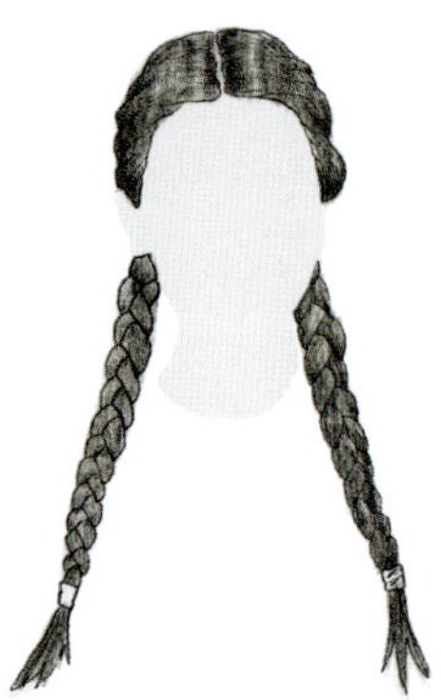

Step 5

Shade the areas around the center part and the sides of the head darkly. Lightly shade all the hair. Shade the braids darkest on the sides and along the lines you drew in Steps 3 and 4.

Reference: Hair

Hair can be pulled back and styled in many ways. Here are a few examples.

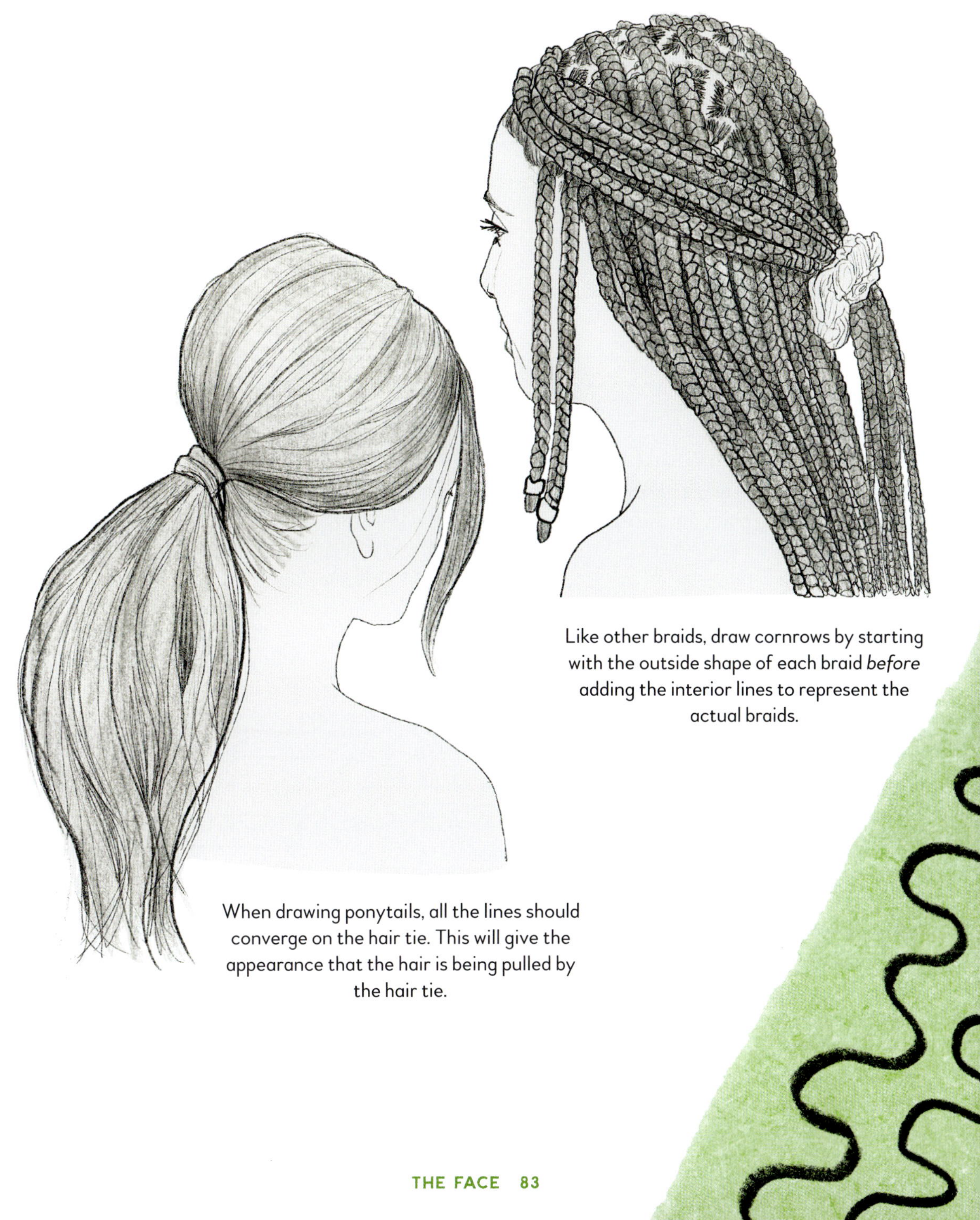

Like other braids, draw cornrows by starting with the outside shape of each braid *before* adding the interior lines to represent the actual braids.

When drawing ponytails, all the lines should converge on the hair tie. This will give the appearance that the hair is being pulled by the hair tie.

THE FACE: FRONT VIEW

Now that you can draw each of the individual features of the face—eyes, ears, nose, mouth and hair—let's try to put it all together. The front view of the face is the most common one, so let's start there.

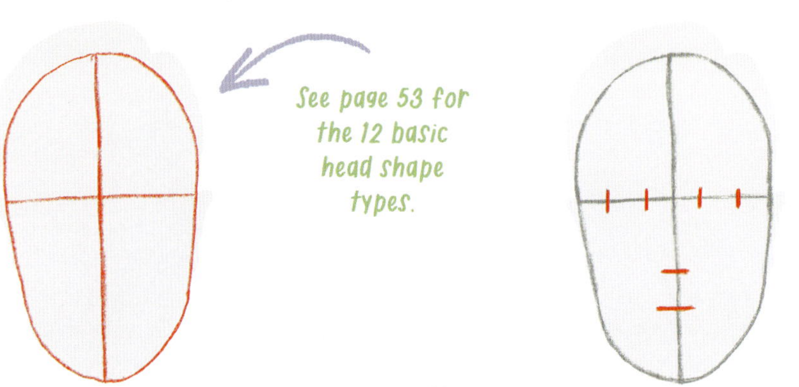

Step 1

Draw an oval shape for the head. Add a vertical line down the middle and a horizontal line just above the halfway point for the eyeline.

Step 2

Make four ticks along the horizontal line to divide it into five roughly even spaces. Draw a small line where the bottom of the nose will sit, and another one where the bottom of the mouth will go.

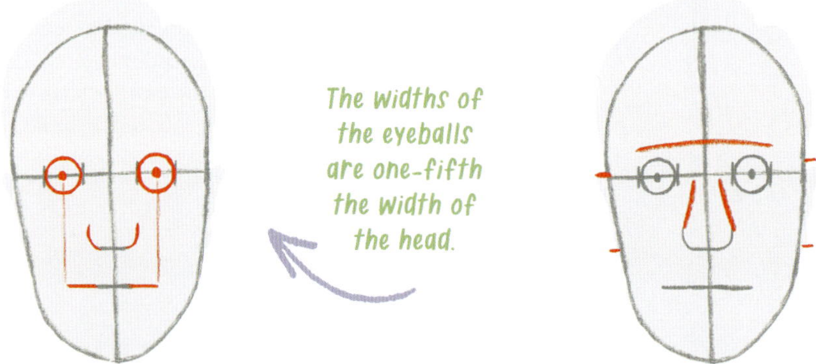

Step 3

In the second space, between the first and second ticks, lightly draw a circle for the left eye. Between the third and fourth ticks, draw another circle for the right eye. Draw the mouth. It is the same width as the distance between the centers of the eyes. Draw a small U shape for the bottom of the nose.

Step 4

Draw angled lines for the sides of the nose. Draw a light guideline for the top of the eyebrows. Make indications for the ears at the eye line and the bottom of the nose.

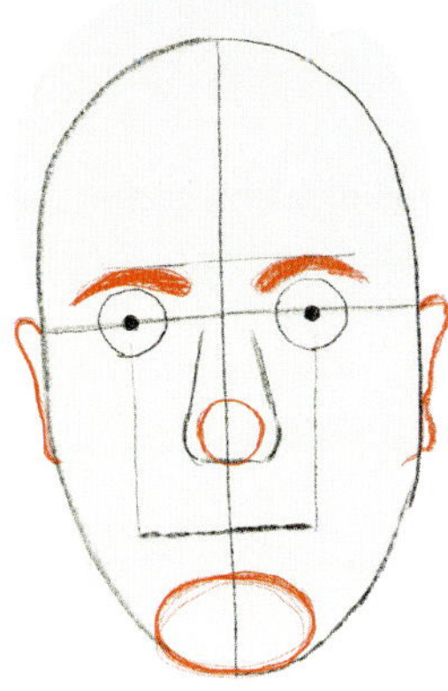

Step 5

Draw curved lines for the eyebrows. Very lightly draw an oval for the chin. The top of this oval will indicate the chin line.

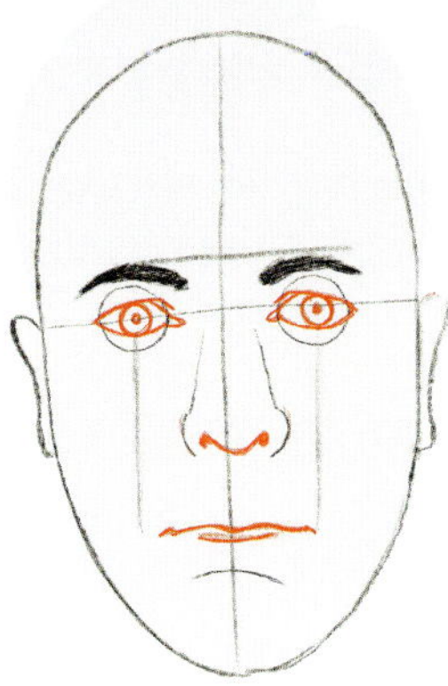

Step 6

Using the eye, nose and mouth tutorials, replace your guidelines with the drawn features.

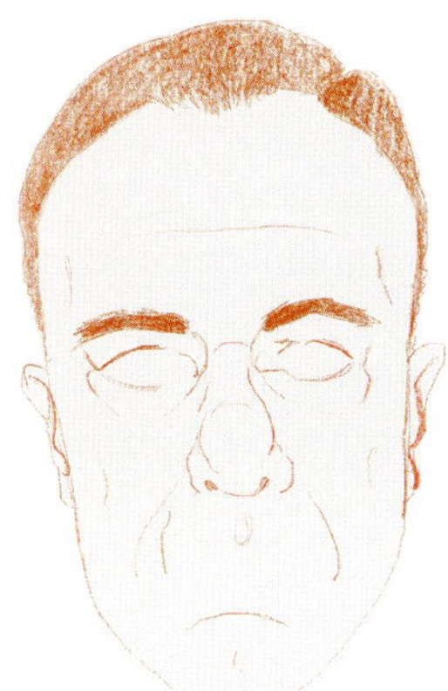

Step 7

Starting at the top, add hair on the head. Add light detail lines around the temples and forehead. Refine the details in the eyebrows. Add wrinkles, as needed, around the eyes, nose and mouth. Add lines to the inside of the ears.

Step 8

Using the side of your pencil, lightly shade the sides of the head around the temple and ears. Also shade the area between the nose and each eye, and just under the tip of the nose. Add facial hair, as needed.

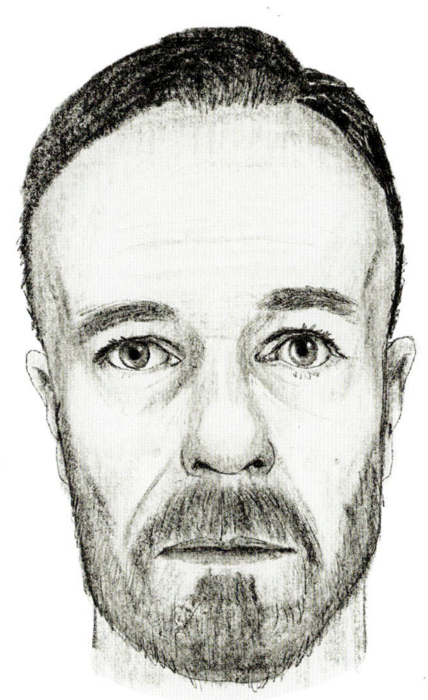

THE FACE: THREE-QUARTER VIEW

The three-quarter view is a classic view in the history of art. When drawing someone in a three-quarter pose, the far half of their face is smaller than the near half, making those facial features smaller as well.

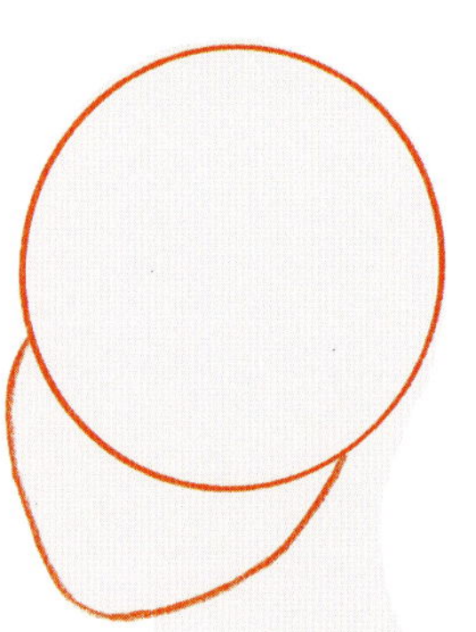

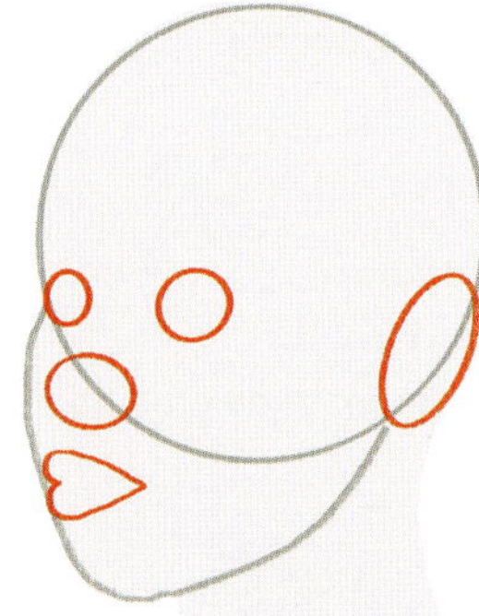

Step 1

Draw a circle. Attach a U shape to the bottom of it. That will become the far cheek, chin and near jawline.

Step 2

Draw some more guidelines: two circles for the eyes, making the far eye smaller than the near one; a circle where the end of the nose will go; a sideways heart shape for the lips; and an oval for the ear.

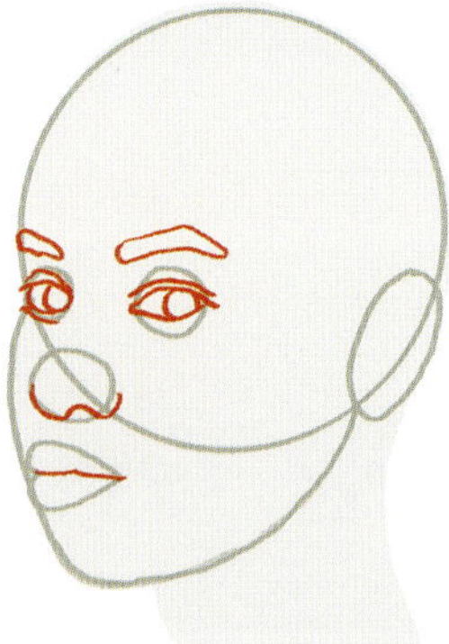

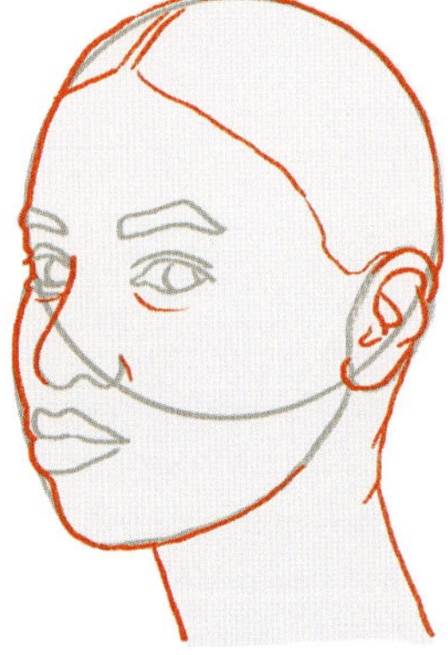

Step 3

Replace your guidelines with features, without going into too much detail. Most of the details of this view come from the shading.

Step 4

Draw the details for the ears and hairline. Add a curved line for the dorsum of the nose. Refine your guideline to sculpt the cheek, chin and jawline. Draw two lines for the neck.

Add shading. Make the far side of the face slightly darker than the near side so that it appears farther back. Shade under the nose, on the neck along the jawline and in the middle of the ear.

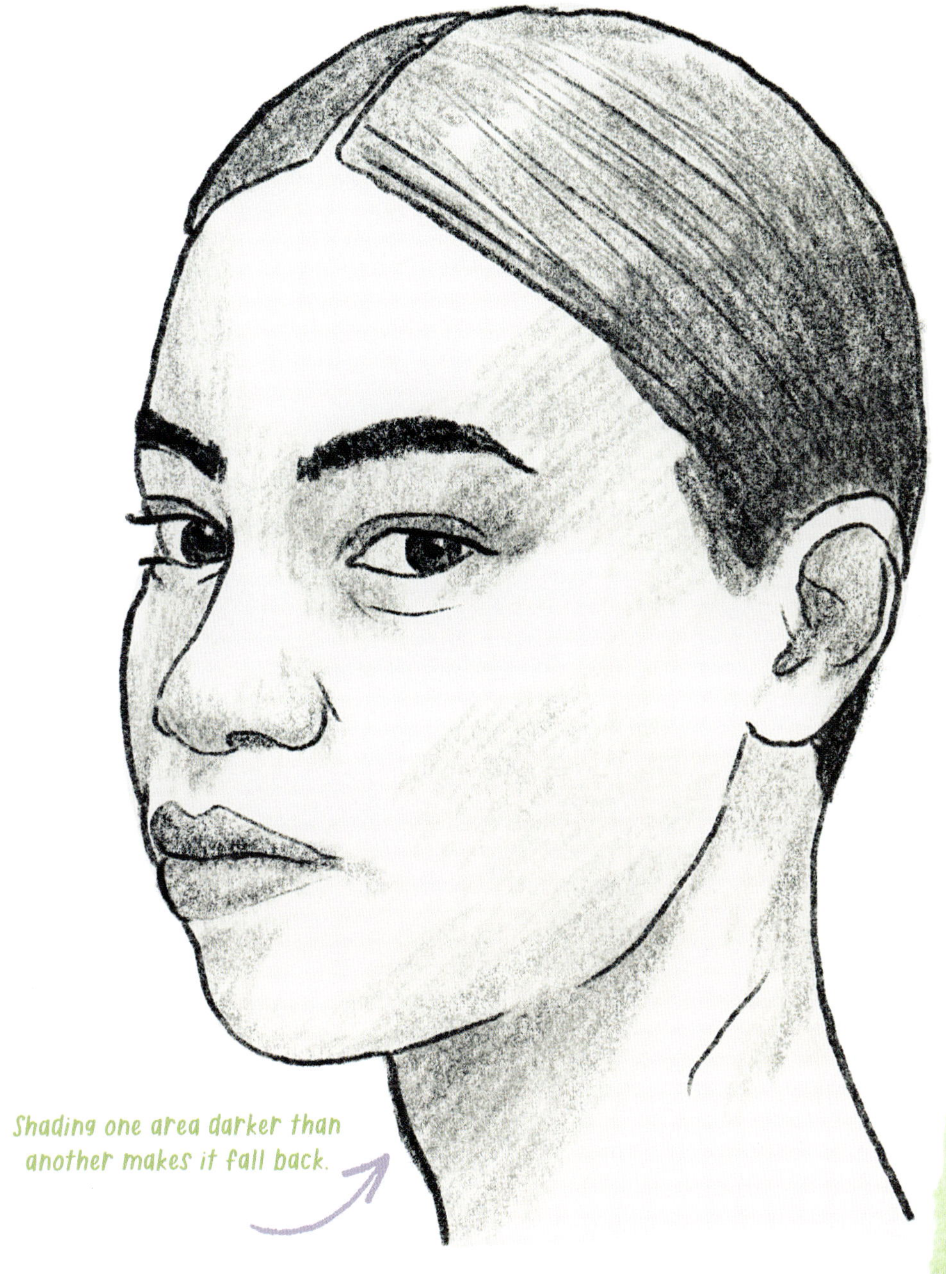

Shading one area darker than another makes it fall back.

THE FACE: SIDE VIEW

The side view, otherwise known as the profile, is a view of only one half of a person's face. Although it's probably the least drawn view of the head, it's an opportunity to learn the facial features from new angles.

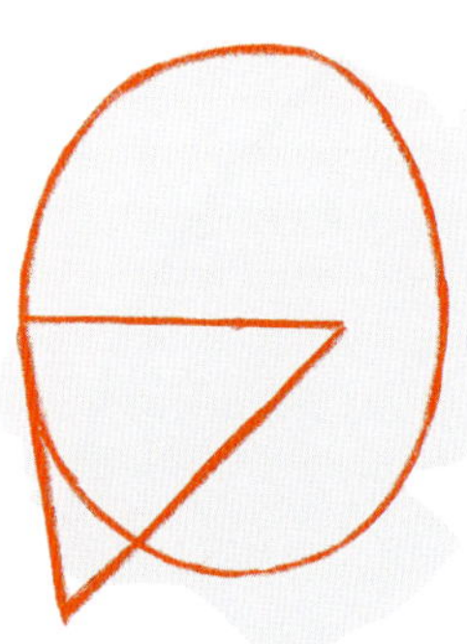

Step 1

Draw a circle that is slightly pinched into an oval. Halfway up, add a triangle, extending one of its points outside the oval. That will be the chin.

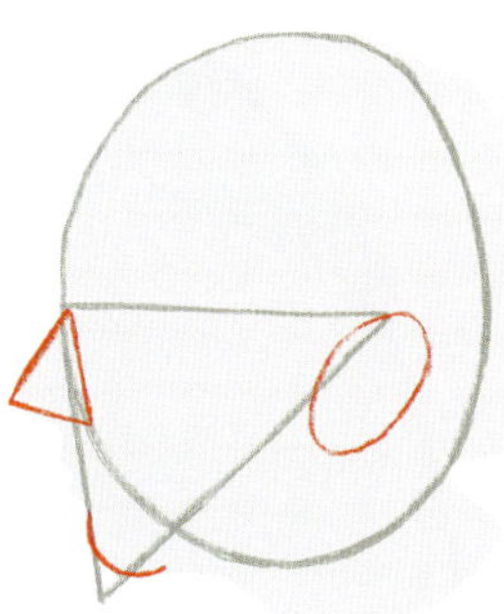

Step 2

On one point of the triangle, draw a smaller triangle where the nose will go. Across from that, draw a small oval. This will be the ear. Add a small curved line for the chin.

Make sure to leave space in front of the eye for the bridge of the nose.

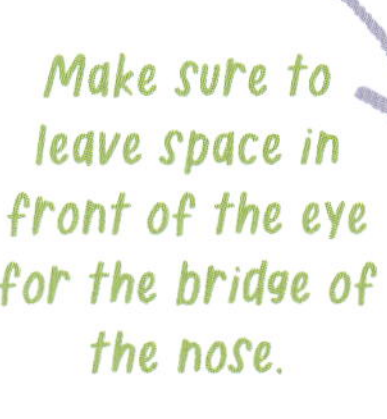

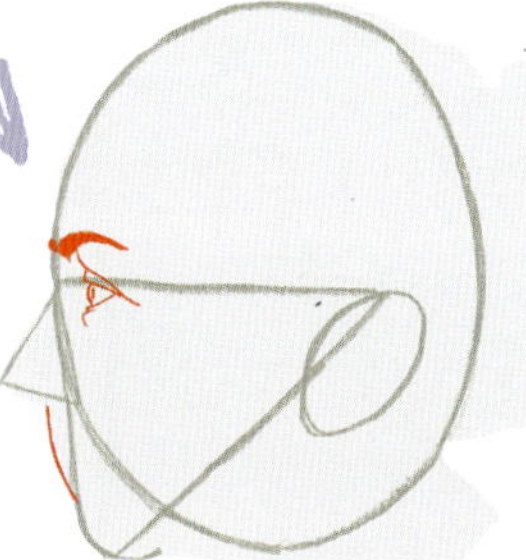

See page 65 for examples of different nose profiles.

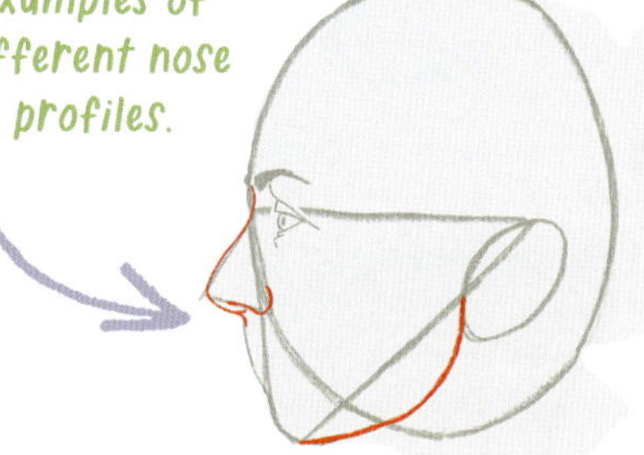

Step 3

Add the shape of the eye, placing it inside the initial triangle. Add a curved line for the eyebrow. Add another curved line that runs from the bottom of the nose to the top of the chin. We'll add the mouth to this line later.

Step 4

Draw the final lines for the nose. From this angle, the nostril is just a line. Draw a curved line for the jaw. It should go from the bottom of the chin to just below the bottom of the ear.

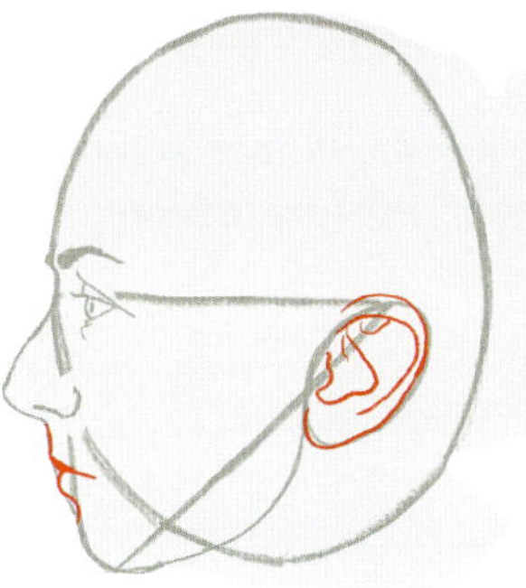

Step 5

Draw the details of the mouth. The line between the top and bottom lips isn't usually straight, but rather angled down slightly. Draw the ear. See page 72 for a detailed tutorial on this.

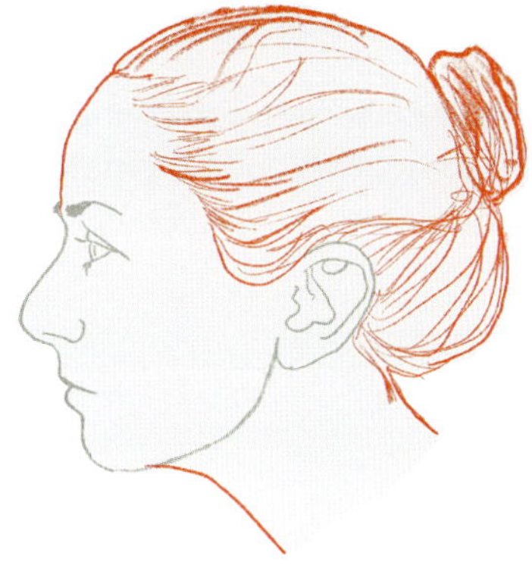

Step 6

Add the hair. Pay attention to the direction of the hair. Draw the neck with two curved lines.

Step 7

Add shading between the eye and the bridge of the nose, at the side of the nose, under the earlobe and in the place where the neck meets the head.

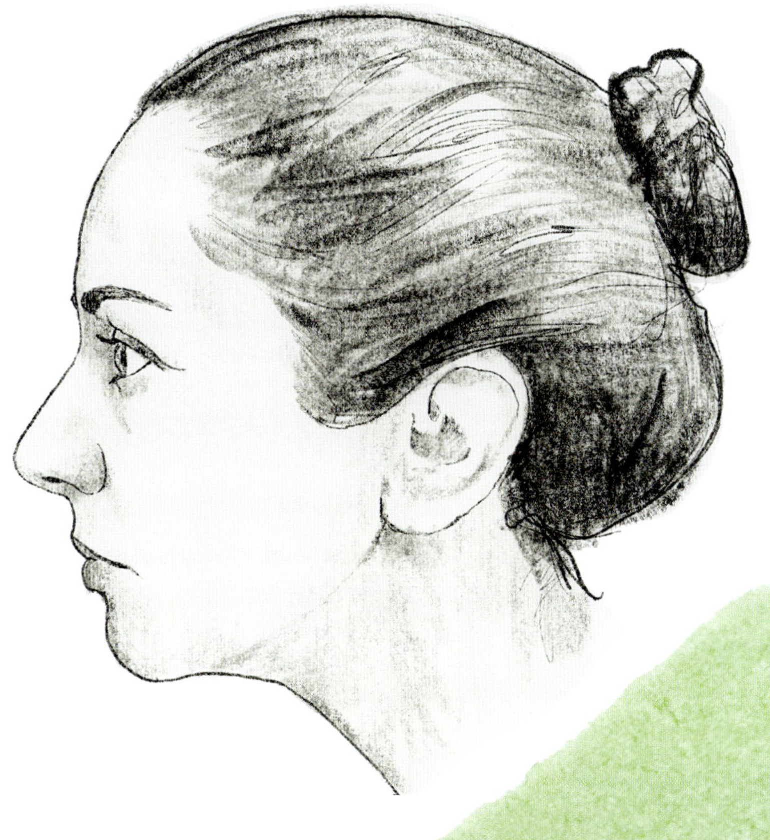

BONUS: FACIAL EXPRESSIONS

How someone is feeling can change the appearance of their face—sometimes in subtle ways, and sometimes quite dramatically. Here are some common facial expressions, along with some pointers on how you can capture them in your drawings.

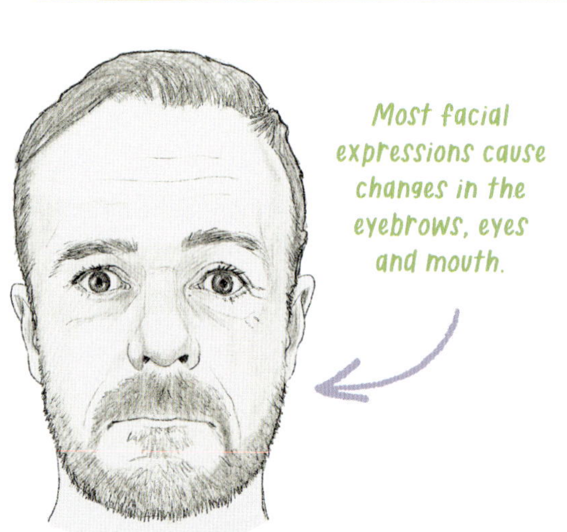

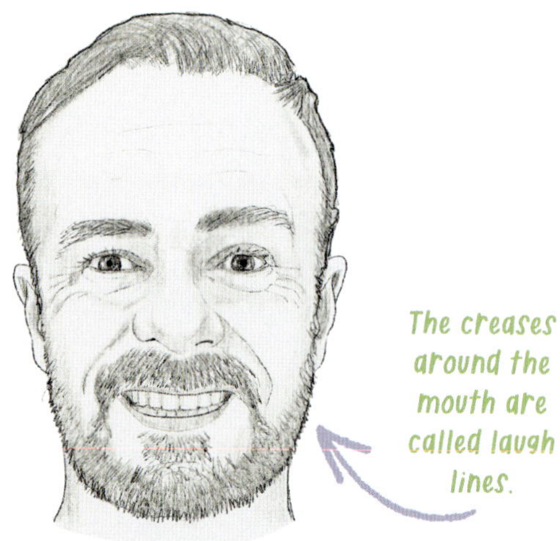

Neutral

Eyebrows: Straight
Eyes: Relaxed
Mouth: Closed, straight

Happy

Eyebrows: Slightly rounded
Eyes: Squinting slightly, with wrinkles below the lower eyelids and at corners of the eyes
Mouth: Upturned, lips may or may not be parted, laugh lines appear

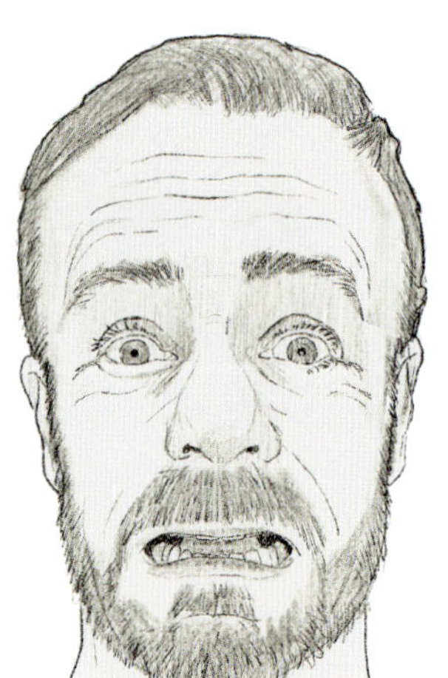

Scared

Forehead: Horizontal wrinkles
Eyebrows: Raised
Eyes: Widened
Mouth: Open, slightly downturned

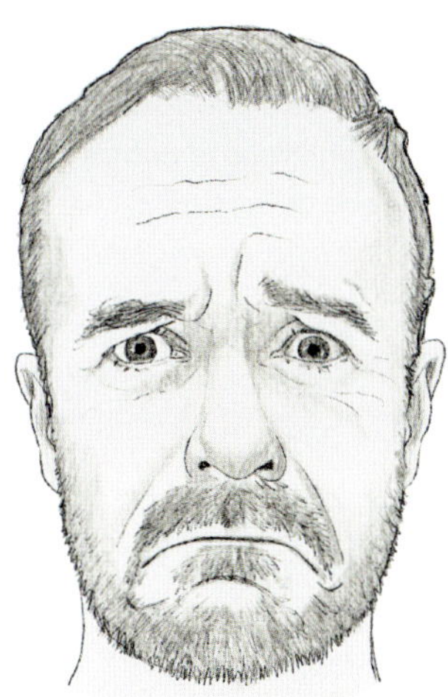

Sad

Eyebrows: Pinched up at inner corners
Eyes: Squinting slightly, with wrinkles below the lower eyelids and at corners of the eyes
Mouth: Downturned, lower lip sticking out slightly

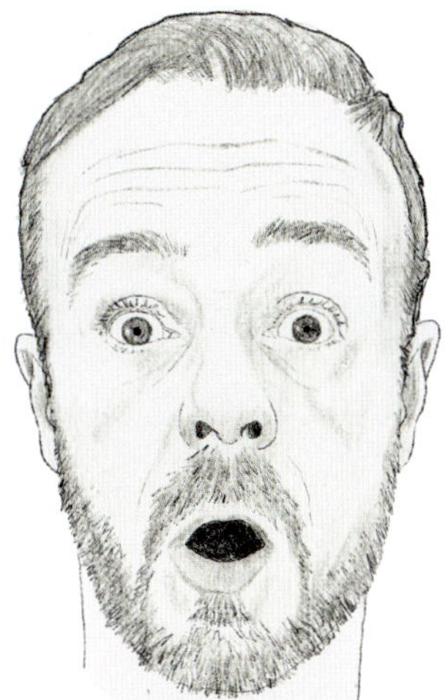

Surprised

Forehead: Horizontal wrinkles
Eyebrows: Raised
Eyes: Widened
Mouth: Opened in an O shape
Chin: Dropped

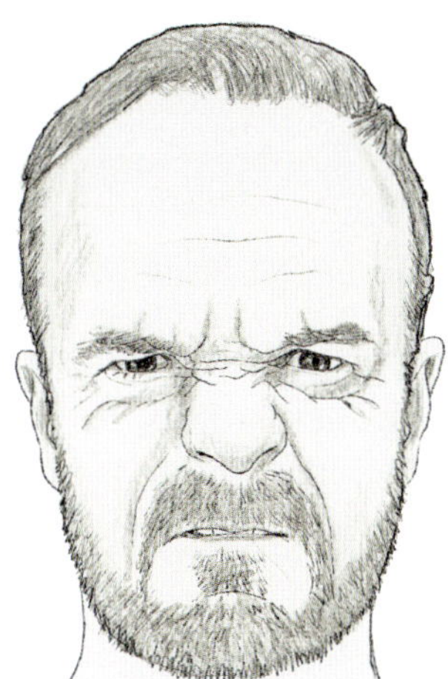

Angry

Forehead: Vertical wrinkles between the eyebrows
Eyebrows: Lowered and drawn inward
Eyes: Squinting
Nose: Nostrils flared
Mouth: Slightly downturned

BONUS: YOUNG AND OLD SUBJECTS

Our faces change quite a bit over our lifetimes. Our features become more pronounced as we enter adulthood and even more so as we get older. Even though each face is different, there are some commonalities that will help you draw faces at different stages of a person's life.

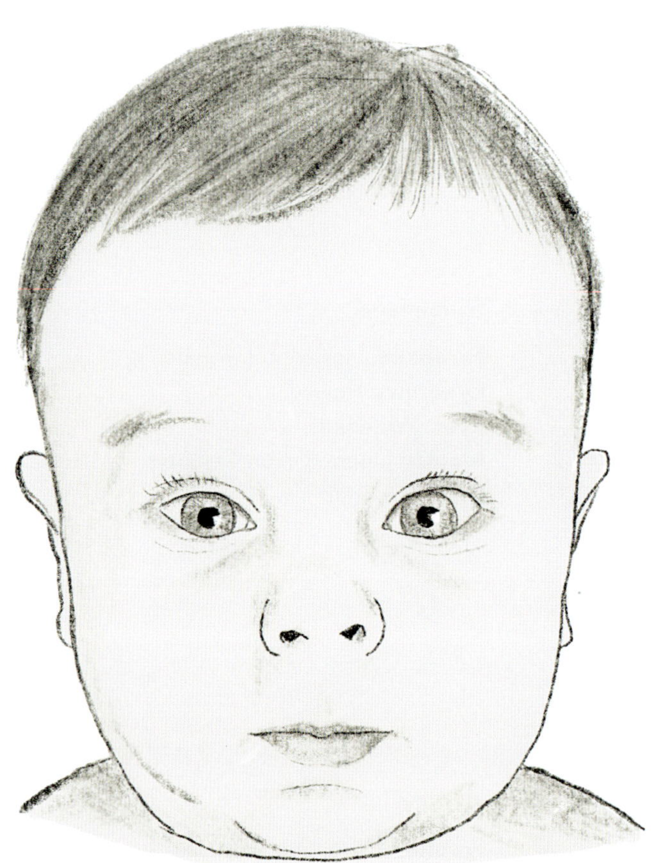

One of the most notable things about drawing young faces is the lack of lines. There are no wrinkles and very few lines on the skin—even the nose is not defined. In younger people, the head is typically rounder than that of adults. Also, the whites of their eyes are not as visible as they are in adults.

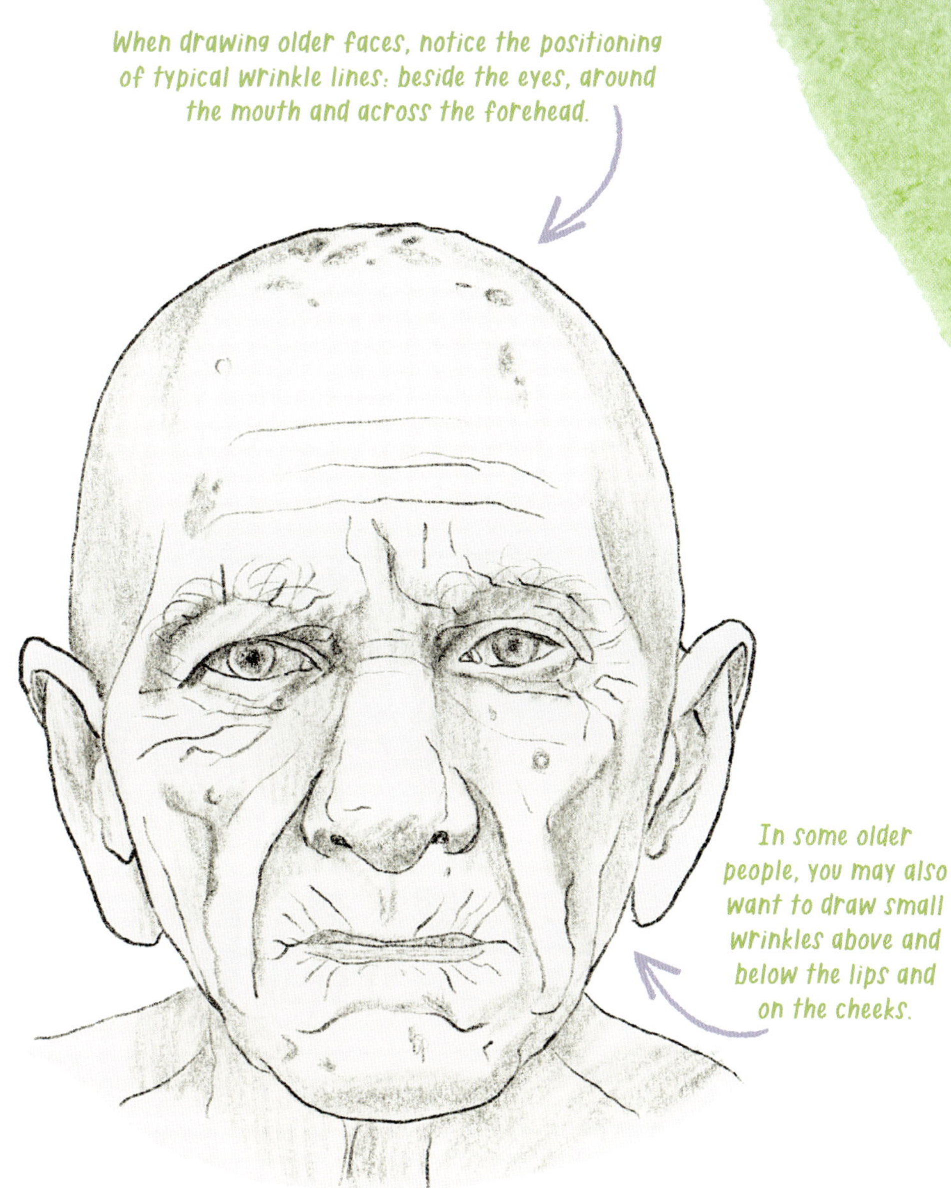

In contrast to younger faces, older ones have wrinkles, sunspots, moles, scars and other details. Eyes are typically highly wrinkled and appear sunken. Due to changes in the skin and cartilage, noses appear larger. Ears get bigger.

THE HUMAN BODY

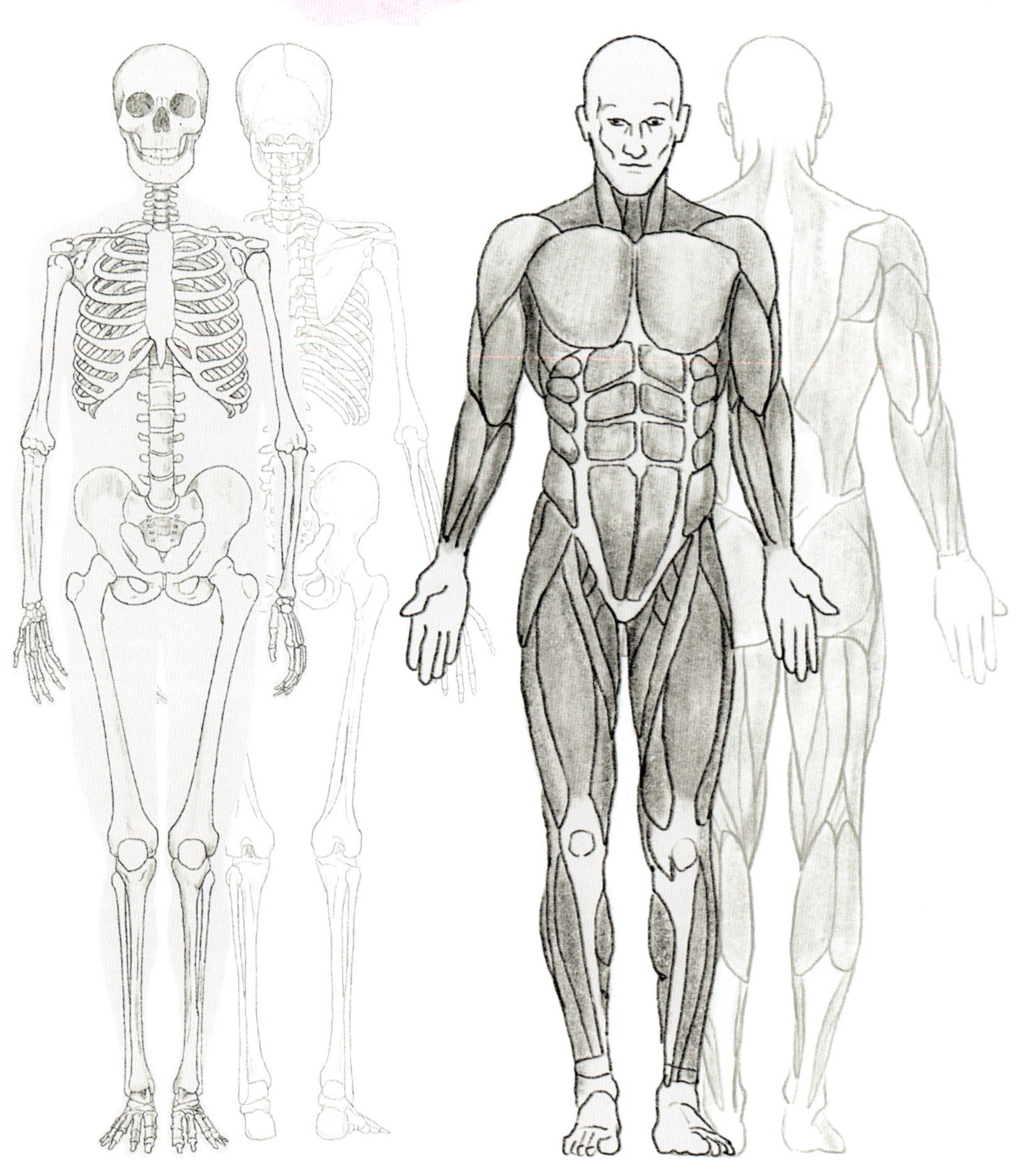

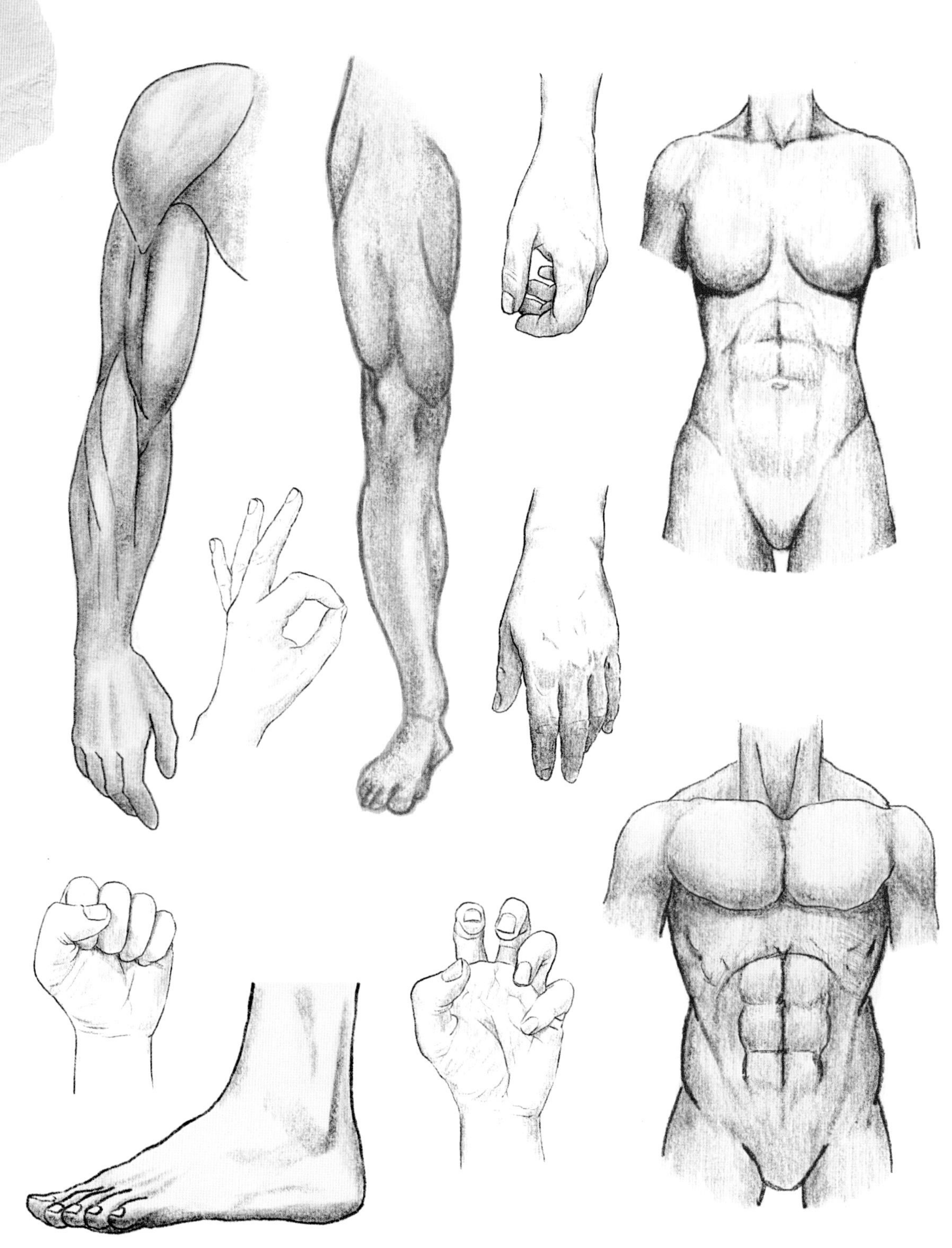

HANDS

The hand is often said to be the hardest part of the body to draw, likely because it can take so many different forms. Let's focus on the simplest form of the hand before looking at more complicated hand positions on page 98.

Step 1

Draw a rectangle. The top and bottom should be slightly shorter than the sides.

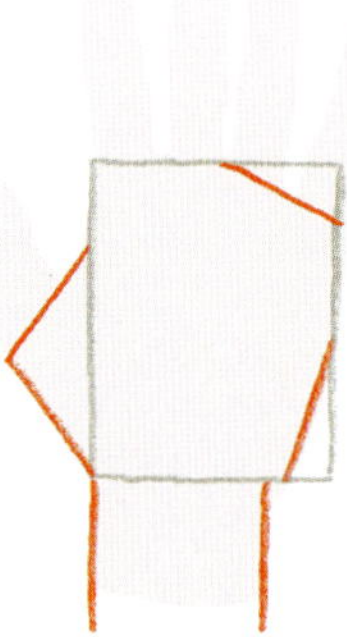

Step 2

Add a triangle to the outside of the rectangle, placing it on the left side. Draw two straight lines across the right inside corners of the rectangle, angling them slightly. Add two lines for the wrist.

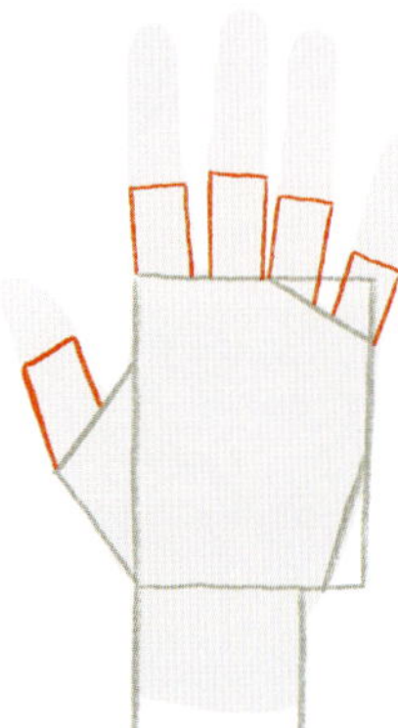

Step 3

Draw five small rectangles. They will be slightly different lengths depending on which finger they belong to: the middle finger is the longest, the index and ring fingers a bit shorter, and the pinky finger the shortest.

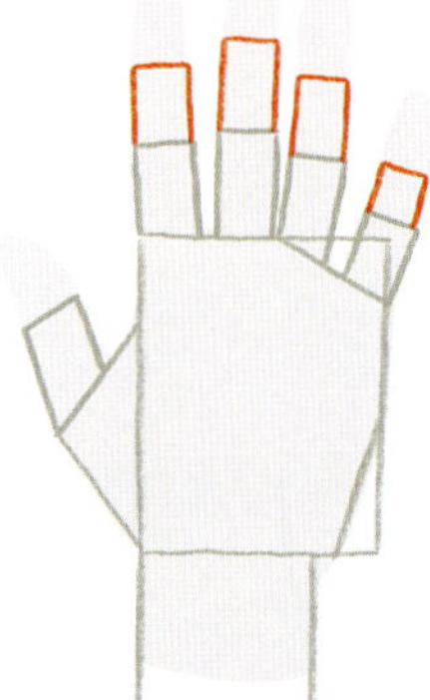

Step 4

On top of each of those rectangles, add another small rectangle. Make them shorter than the rectangles they attach to.

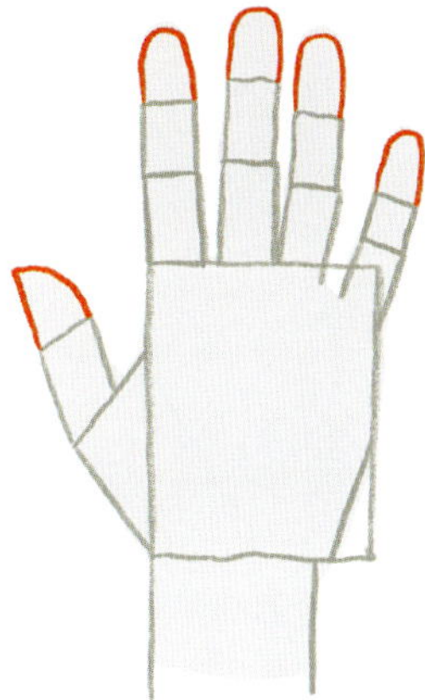

Step 5

Draw a quarter circle for the tip of the thumb.
Draw half ovals for the tips of the fingers.

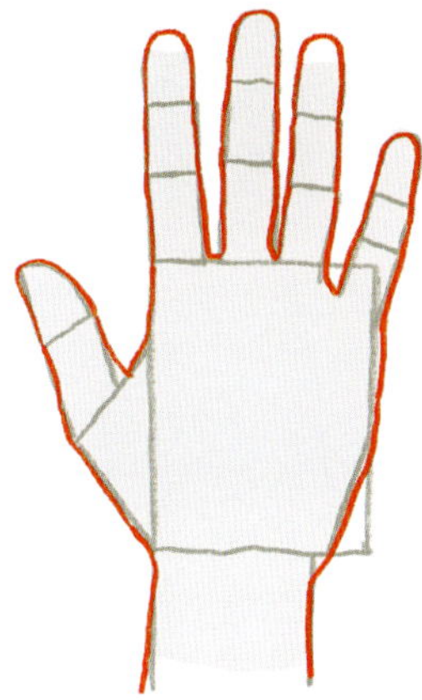

Step 6

Erase your guidelines, and draw a line around
the outside of the hand. Draw little bumps
where the smaller rectangles meet. Those will
be the knuckles.

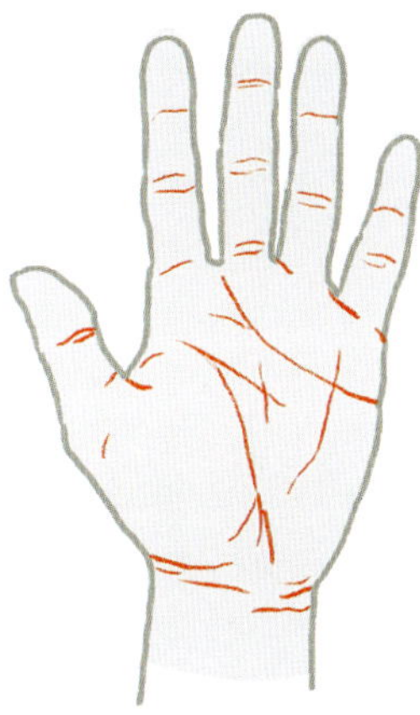

Step 7

Draw some wrinkles in the palm and on the
fingers. You can use your own hand for
reference if you'd like.

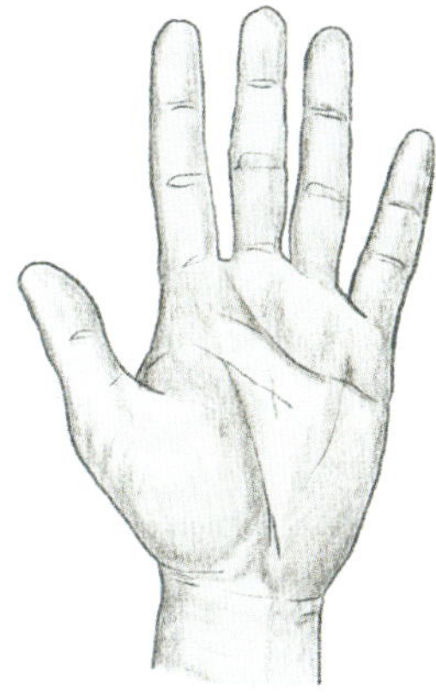

Step 8

With the side of your pencil, lightly shade the
outsides of the fingers and along the wrinkle
lines in the palm. This will give the fingers and
palm a more three-dimensional, rounded
appearance.

Reference: Hands

Now that you've drawn a hand from straight on, see if you can identify the underlying basic shapes in each of these different poses.

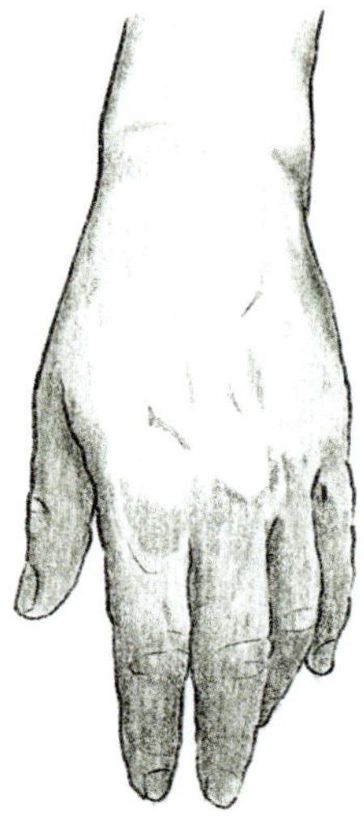

There are slight bends in the fingers even when the hand is relaxed.

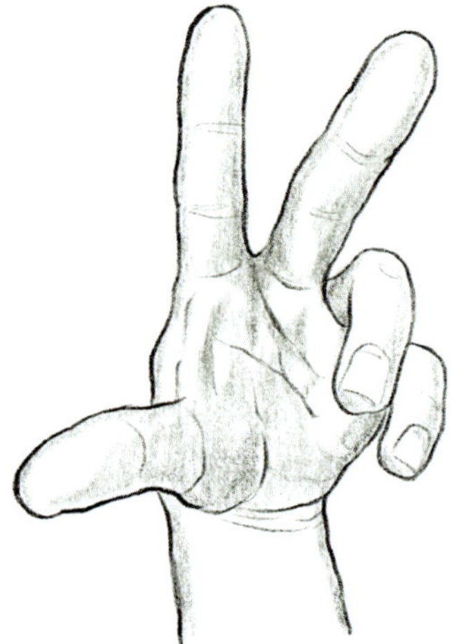

When fingers point toward the viewer, those fingers look bigger. This is called foreshortening.

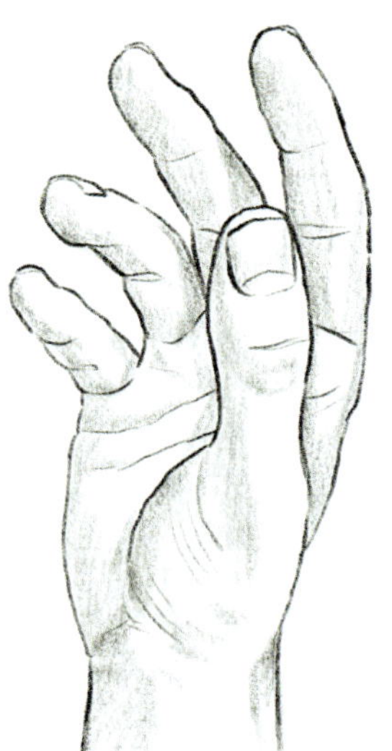

Here, an invisible curved line connects the tips of the fingers. This fan shape is quite common.

This easy-to-remember pose is one of the simplest to draw.

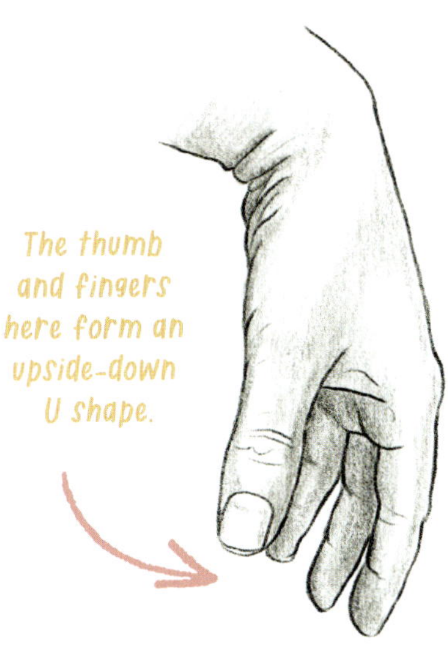

Remember that fan shape? This is what
it looks like turned upside down.

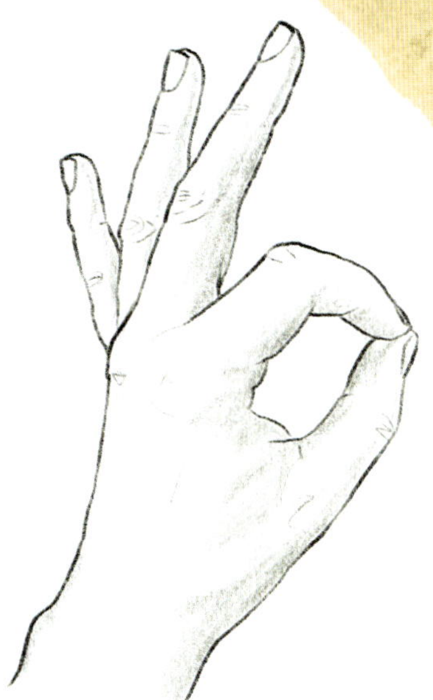

This pose is part fan shape
and part circle.

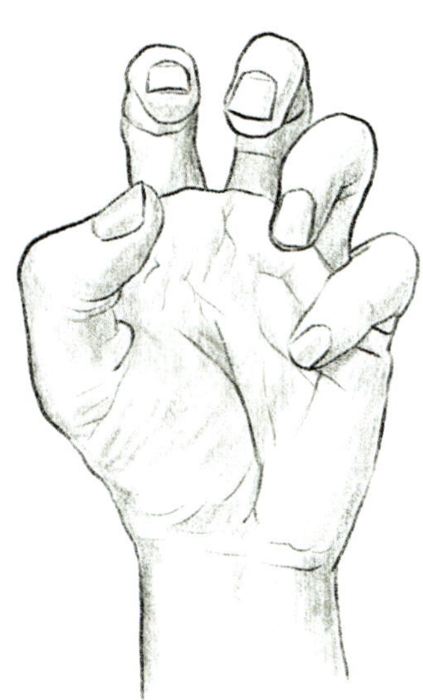

Notice that each finger looks different
in this gesture.

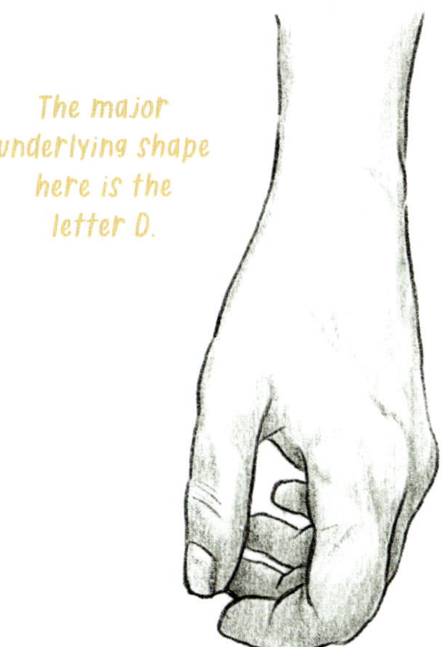

This is what the hand looks like
when it is at rest.

ARMS

Whether you're drawing superheroes or a mere mortal, you'll need to know how to draw an arm. Arms aren't made up of too many shapes—two cylinders and a ball—but the magic happens when you sort out how those shapes fit together.

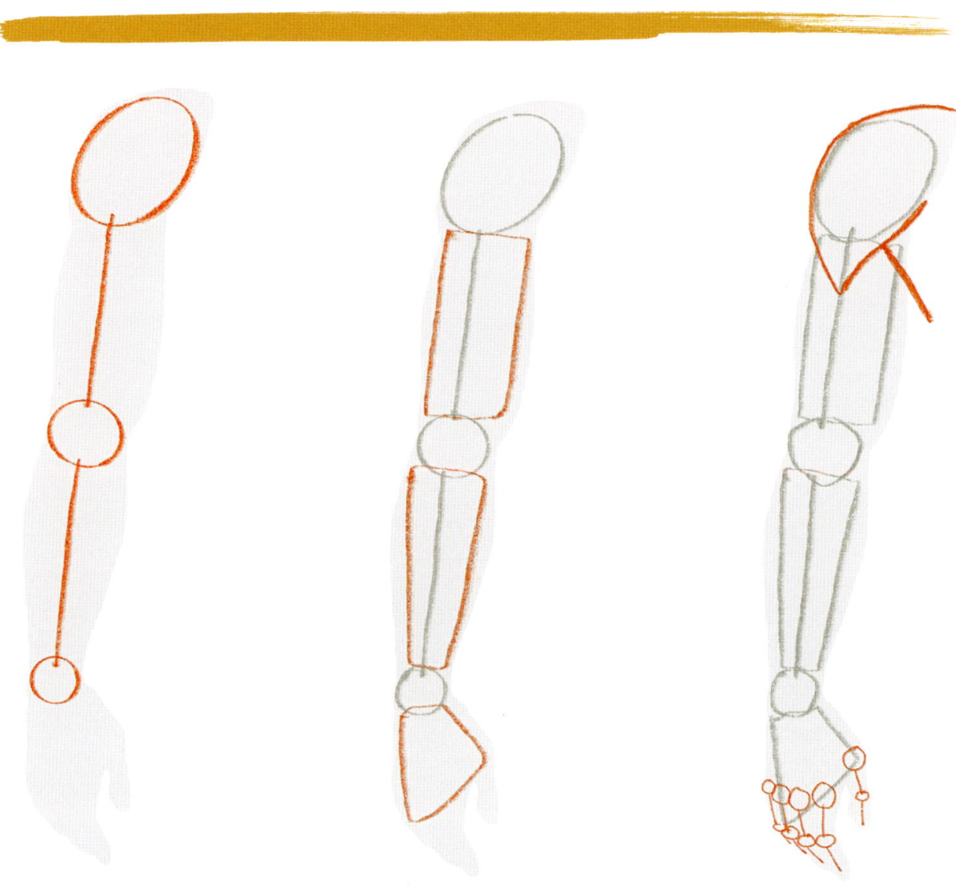

Step 1

Very lightly draw three ovals and connect them with two lines. The larger top oval is for the shoulder. The middle oval is for the space between the upper and lower arm. And the small oval is for the wrist.

Step 2

Draw a rectangle for the upper arm and a narrow trapezoid for the forearm. Notice it is narrower at the wrist than the elbow. Now draw another trapezoid for the hand.

Step 3

Outline the shoulder (deltoid) muscle. It is curved at the top and forms a V at the bottom. Draw circles for knuckles, and connect them with lines for each finger.

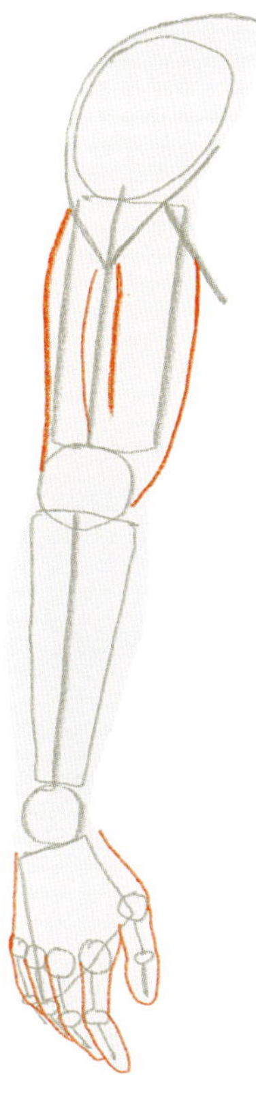

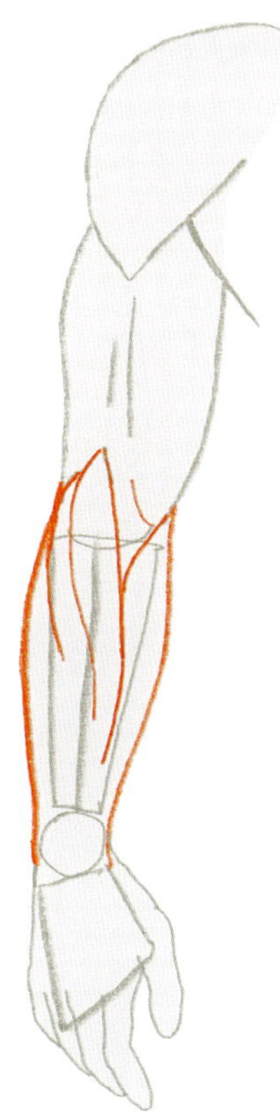

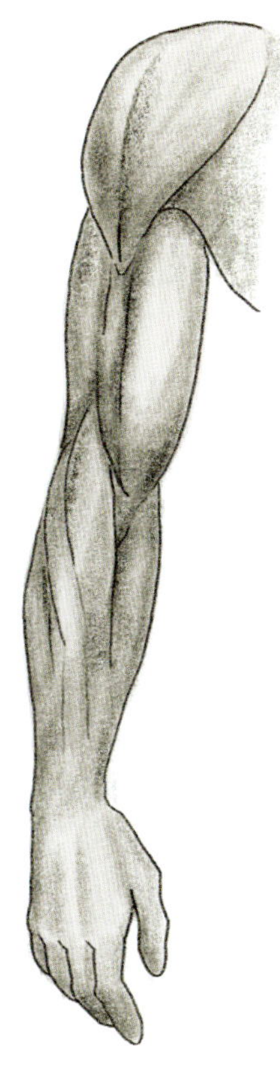

Step 4

Draw a curved line for the triceps on the outside of the arm and another curved line for the biceps on the inside of the arm. Draw two shorter lines between those. Outline the fingers and the hand.

Step 5

Draw leaf shapes for the forearm muscles. Pay attention to the location of these muscles. Note that they extend above the elbow joint.

Step 6

Add shading to the areas between muscle groups. The bottom of the shoulder muscle, the bottom of the biceps and the sides of the arm should all be darker than other areas. This will give the appearance of roundness.

Reference: Arms

As with facial features and other body parts, everybody's arms are different. That means you'll come across a range of shapes as you set out to draw a variety of people.

The arm and shoulder here form a sharp angle.

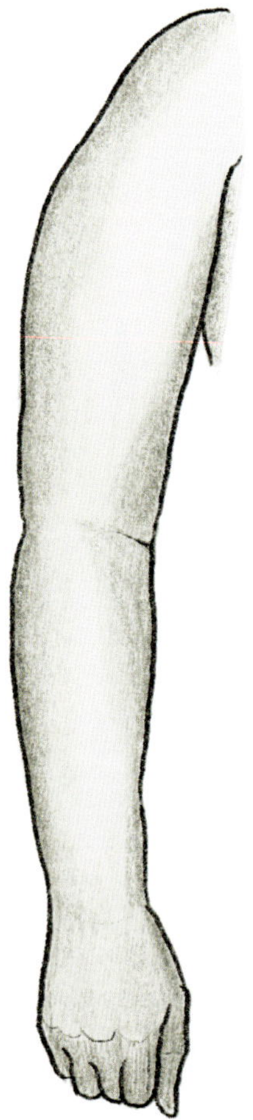

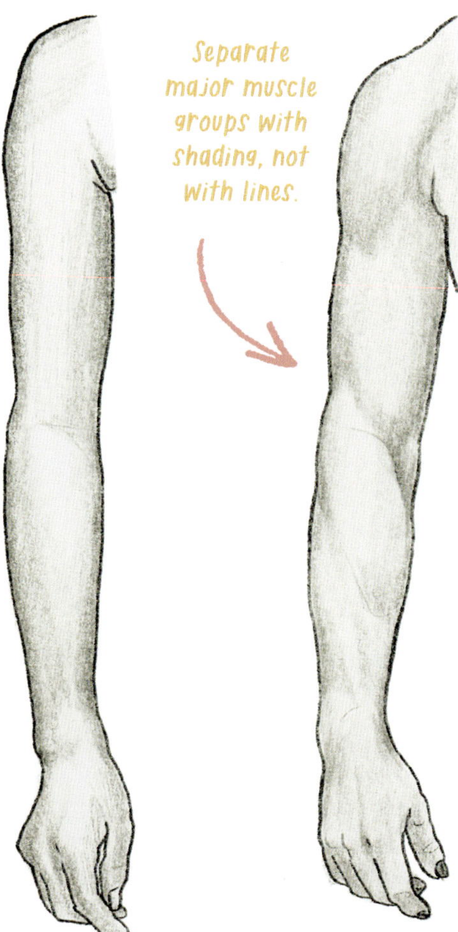

The width of the arm is fairly consistent from shoulder to wrist.

Notice that the forearm muscle extends above the elbow line.

Some arms are wider toward the top
and taper down at the wrist.

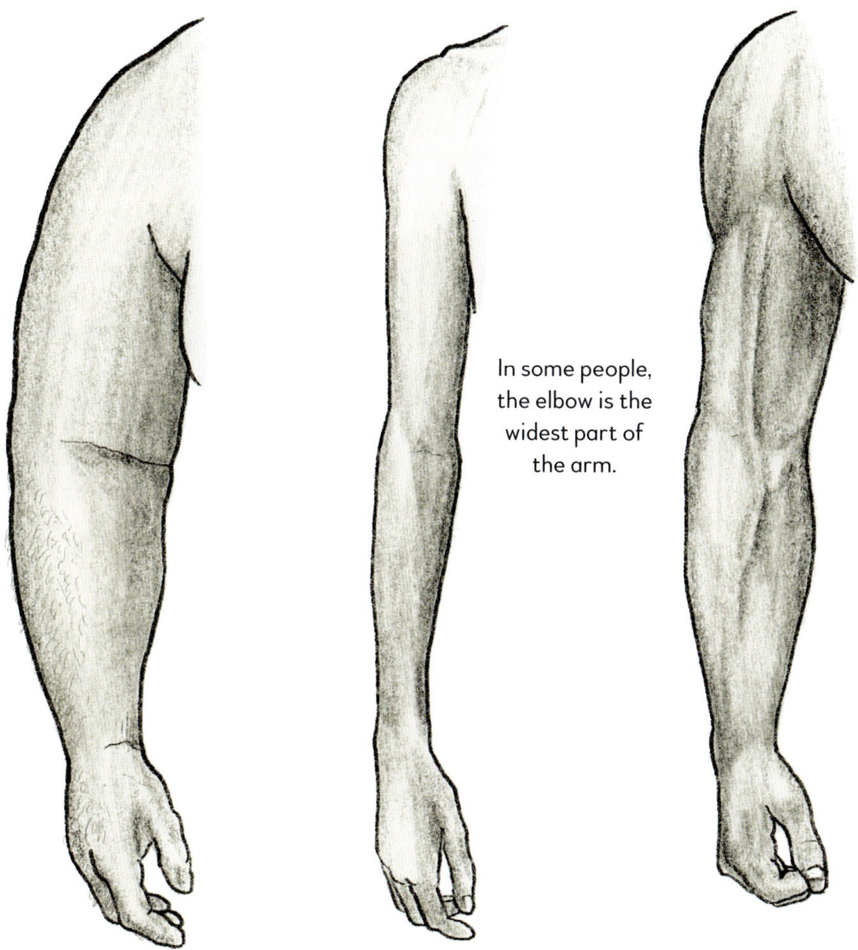

In some people,
the elbow is the
widest part of
the arm.

Veins tend to be more visible in
muscular arms.

TORSO

The torso, or trunk of the body, is the area of the body to which the head, arms and legs connect. There are as many different shapes as there are people on this earth. Let's take a look at one of them here, step-by-step.

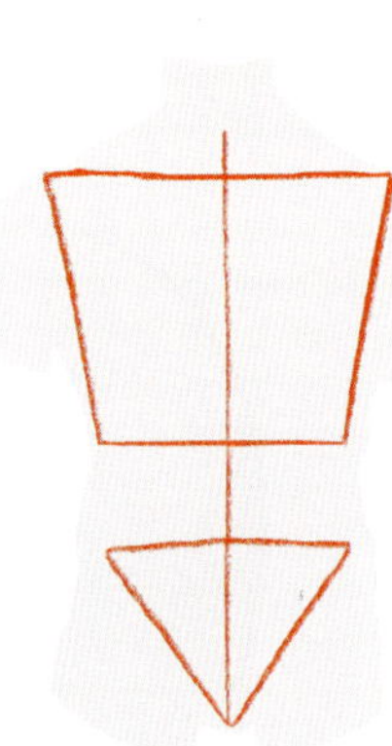

Step 1

Draw a trapezoid for the upper part of the torso and a smaller triangle for the hip area. Make sure to leave a little room between the upper shape and the lower shape. Now, draw a center line.

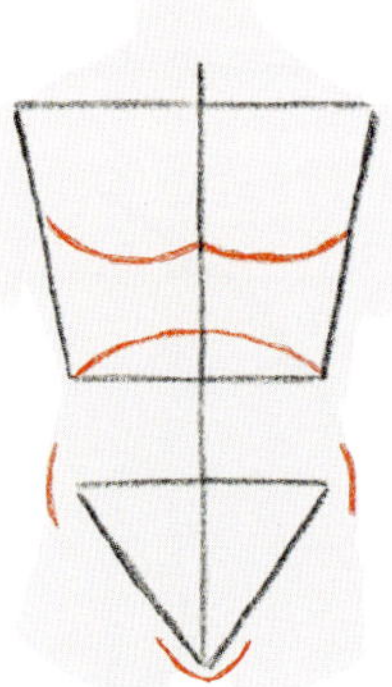

Step 2

Inside the trapezoid, draw two curved lines for the bottom of the chest (pectoralis muscles). Draw another curved line for the bottom of the rib cage. Around the triangle in the lower half, draw three guidelines to show the hips and groin area.

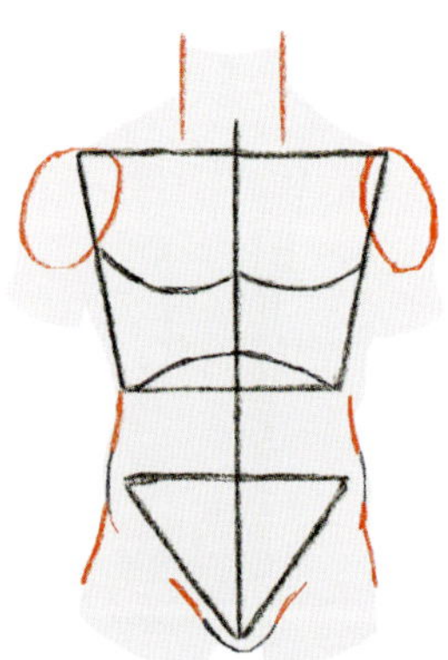

Step 3

Add two ovals for the shoulder (deltoid) muscles. See page 100 for a how-to on drawing arms. Follow your guidelines to connect the chest to the hips. These curved lines form the waist.

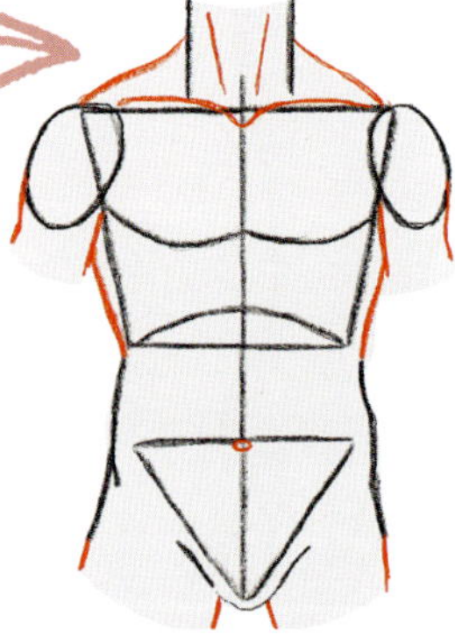

Step 4

Add two curved lines to connect the shoulders to the neck. Draw a curved line connecting the two shoulders. This is both the collarbone line and the top of the chest muscles.

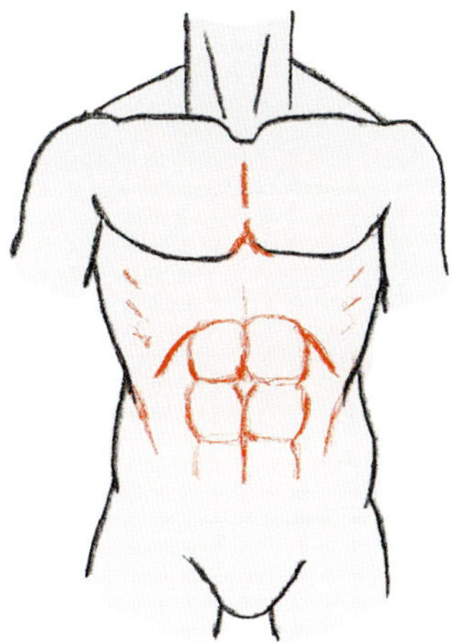 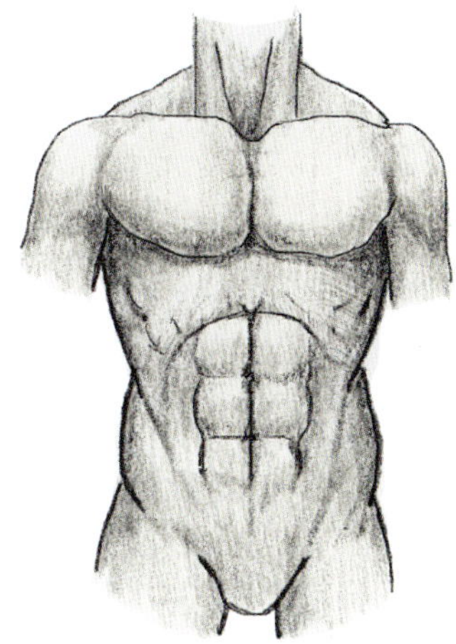

Step 5

Erase your guidelines, and draw six rounded squares in the belly area for the abdominal muscles. You can also indicate some muscles in the rib area with a few short lines.

Step 6

Time for shading. Round all of your muscles by shading the sides and bottom of each shape. Notice that the areas under the chest muscles and armpits are particularly dark.

Here are two more of many other torso shapes.

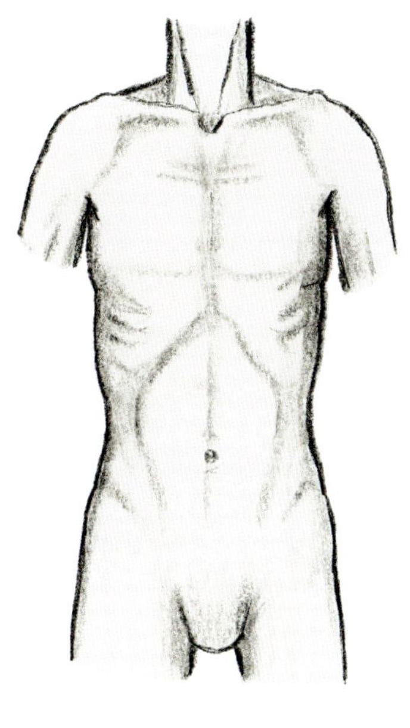 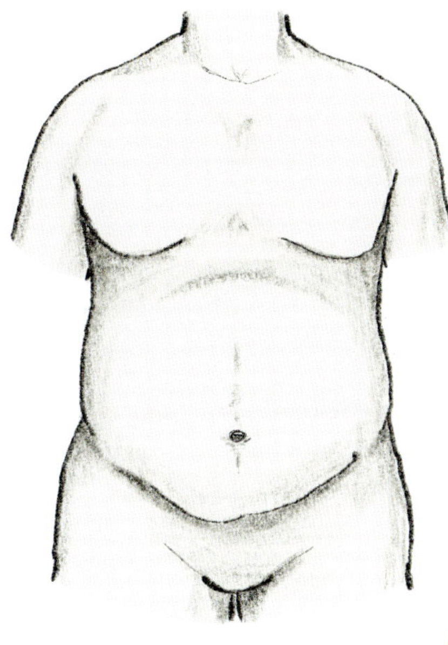

Remember that there are as many different torso types as there are people—no drawing book could cover them all. Here is another type to use as a starting point for your own creations.

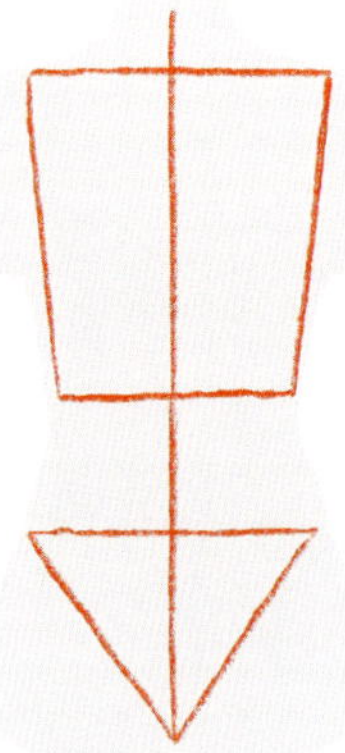

Step 1

Draw a trapezoid for the upper part of the torso and a triangle for the hip area. Make sure to leave a little room between the upper shape and the lower shape. Now, draw a center line.

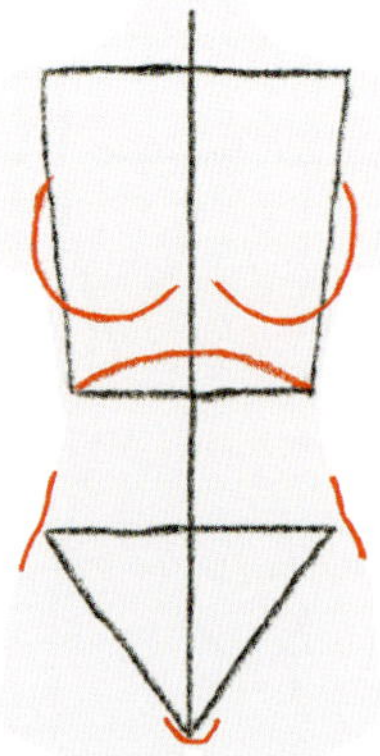

Step 2

For this torso, instead of drawing pectoralis muscles in the chest area, draw curved lines. Also draw a curved line for the bottom of the rib cage.

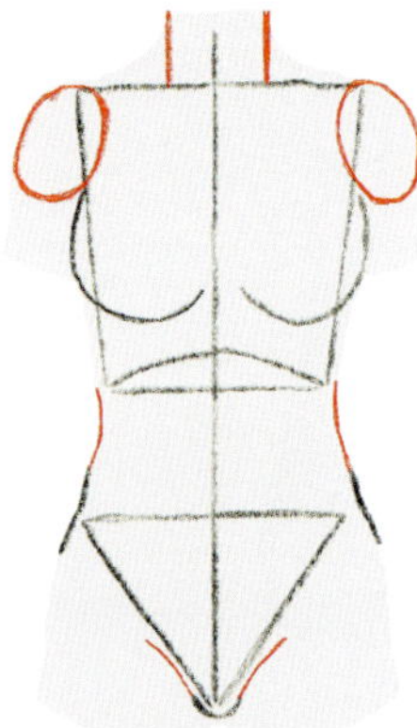

Step 3

Add two ovals for the shoulder (deltoid) muscles. Follow your guidelines to connect the chest to the hips. Notice that the waist is more angled with this torso type. Add a U-shaped line for the groin area.

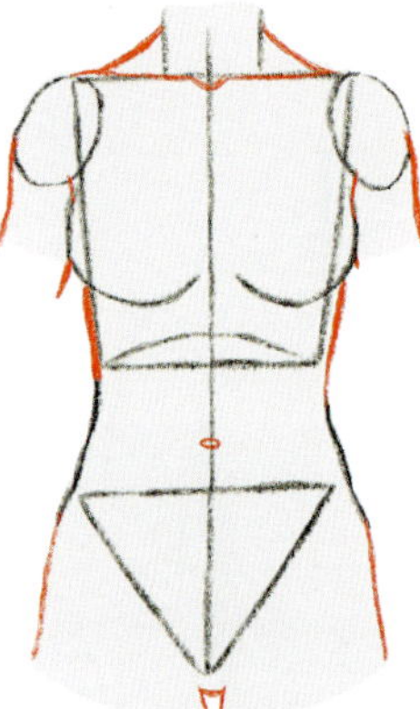

Step 4

Draw curved lines from the shoulder to the neck to indicate the trapezius muscles. Also add very slightly curved lines for the legs and rib cage.

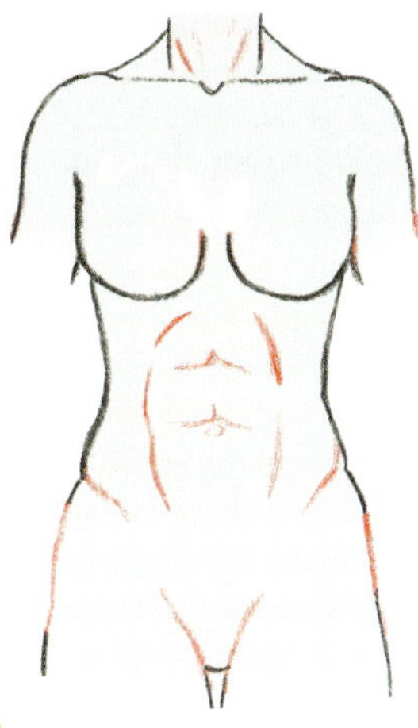 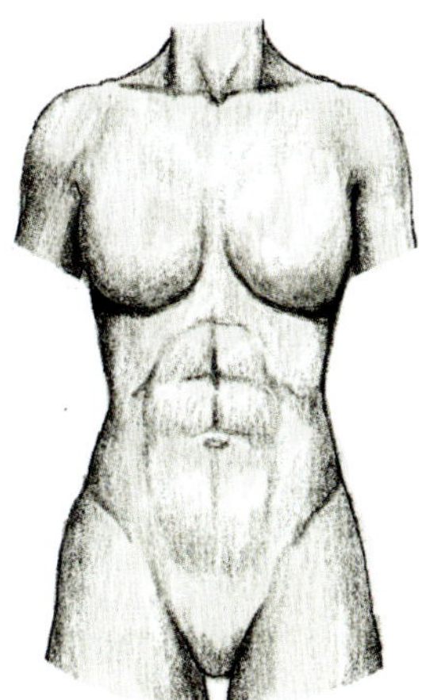

Step 5

Make some lines to separate the top of the thighs from the torso. Add a few indications of abdominal muscles in the mid-torso area.

Step 6

Time to shade. Shading should be darkest around the armpit region and under the chest area. Also, make the sides darker in order to create the illusion that the middle is coming forward.

This torso type can have many variations. Try playing with the initial trapezoid and triangle shapes in Step 1 to see how many different torsos you can come up with.

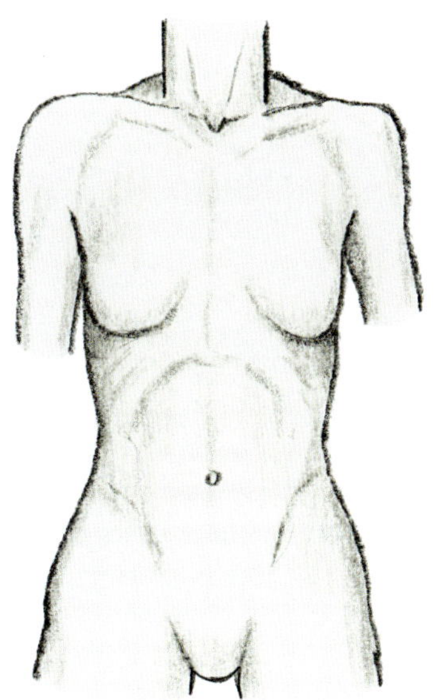 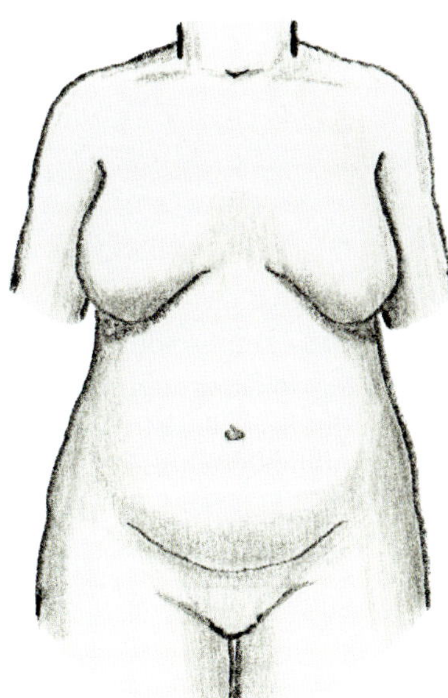

LEGS

Drawing the leg is very similar to drawing the arm in that it's made up of two cylinders and a ball shape. It differs in that the upper cylinder, or thigh, is much wider than the lower cylinder, or lower leg. Let's have a look at one leg shape.

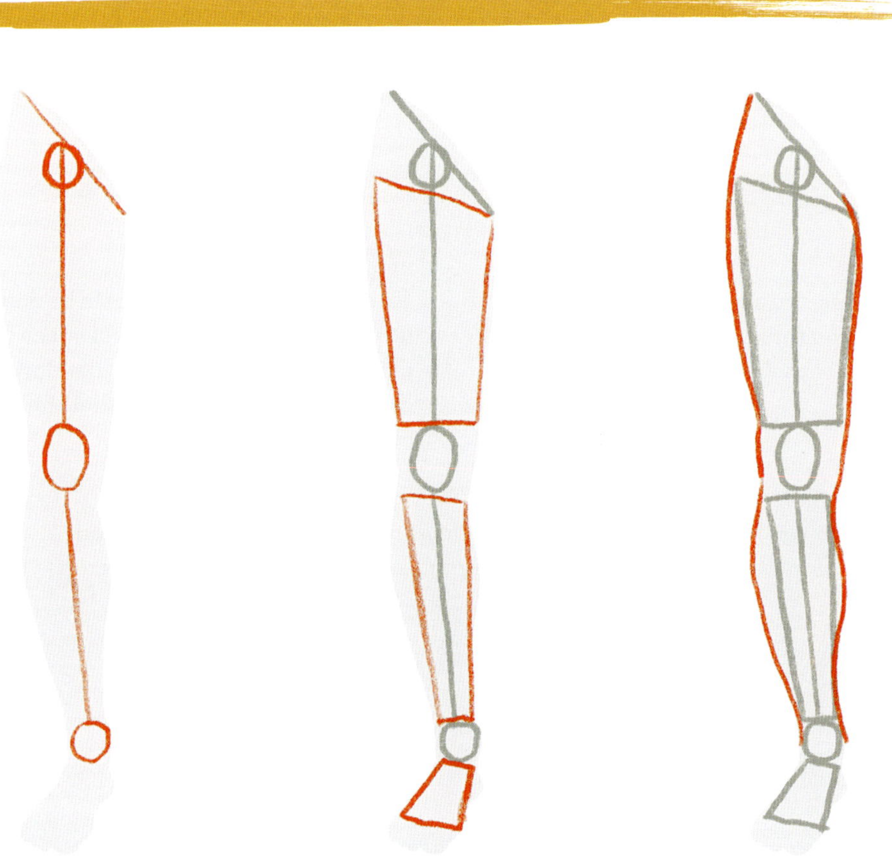

Step 1

With very light guidelines, draw three circles as placeholders for the parts of the leg that bend (the ankle, knee and hip). Connect those circles with straight lines.

Step 2

Draw trapezoids for the upper leg and lower leg, making them smaller at the bottom than the top. Also note the upper leg is about twice as wide as the lower leg. Draw another trapezoid for the foot.

Step 3

Draw curved lines around your guidelines. The inner side of the lower leg has a shorter curve than the outer side, and the inner side of the upper leg is almost a straight line.

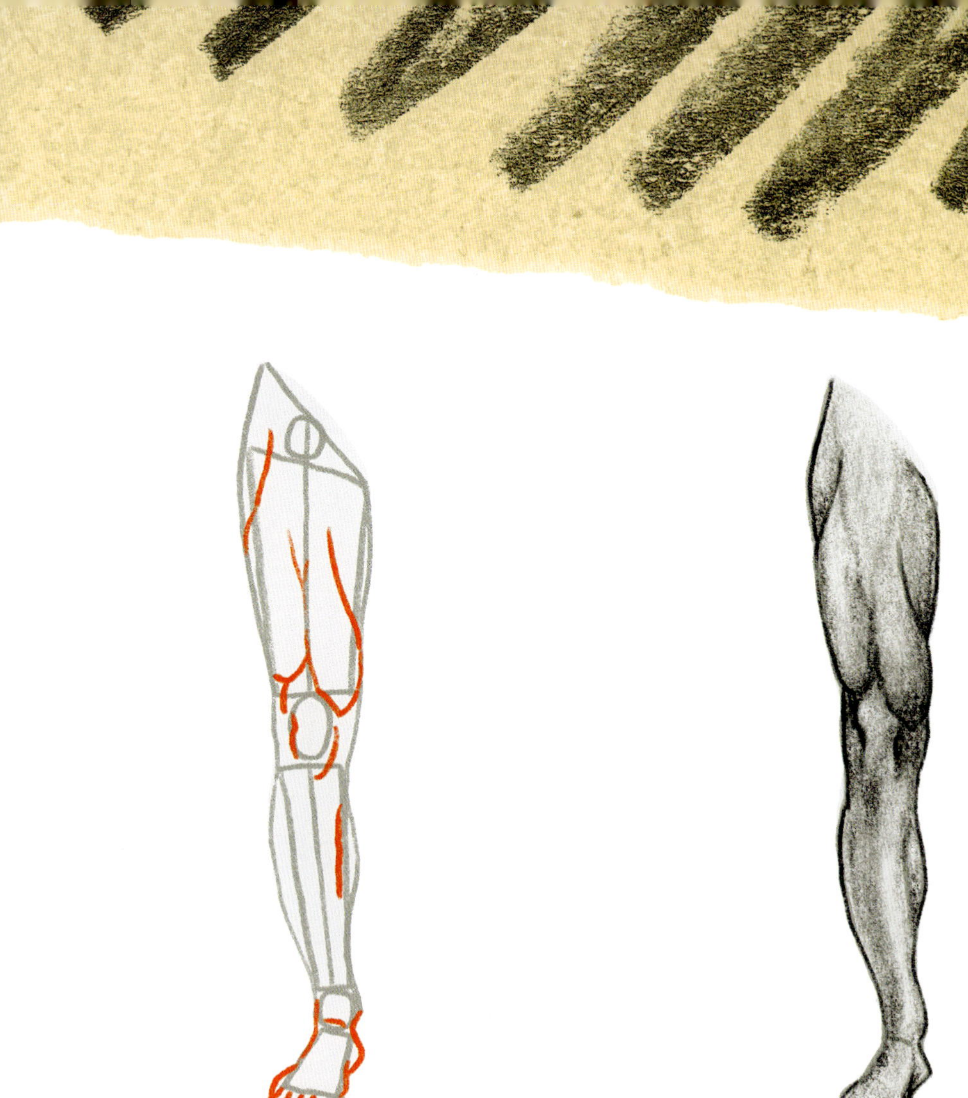

Step 4

Draw the inside lines. The upper leg has tear-shaped muscles called the quadriceps. You only need a couple of lines around the kneecap and a short line to separate the calf from the rest of the lower leg. See page 112 for how to draw the foot.

Step 5

Add shading. Shade darkest at the bottom of the muscles and at the sides to give your leg a rounded shape.

Reference: Legs

Again, everybody has a different body. From short to tall and everything in between, celebrate each shape you set out to draw.

Use very light shading instead of lines to render the shape of the knee.

In this leg, the knee is slightly turned in.

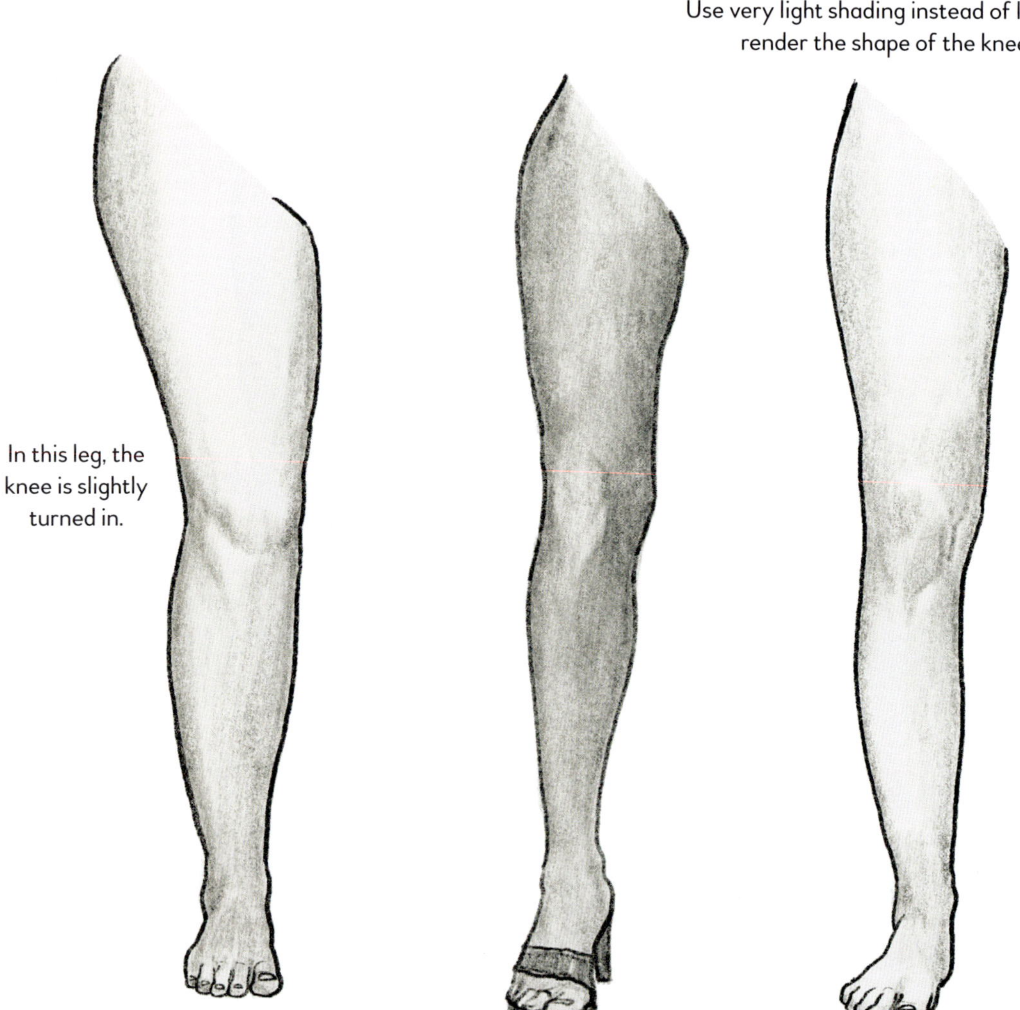

For legs in high heels, draw the calf muscles a little higher.

For very muscular legs, shade each
muscle group separately.

Notice the curve that is created when the
hips are wider than the upper thigh.

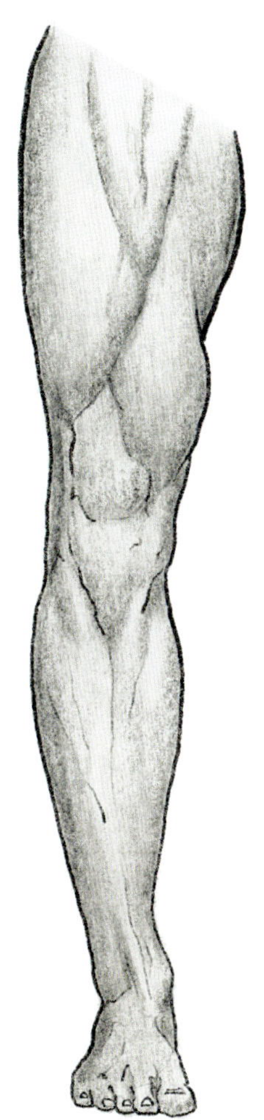

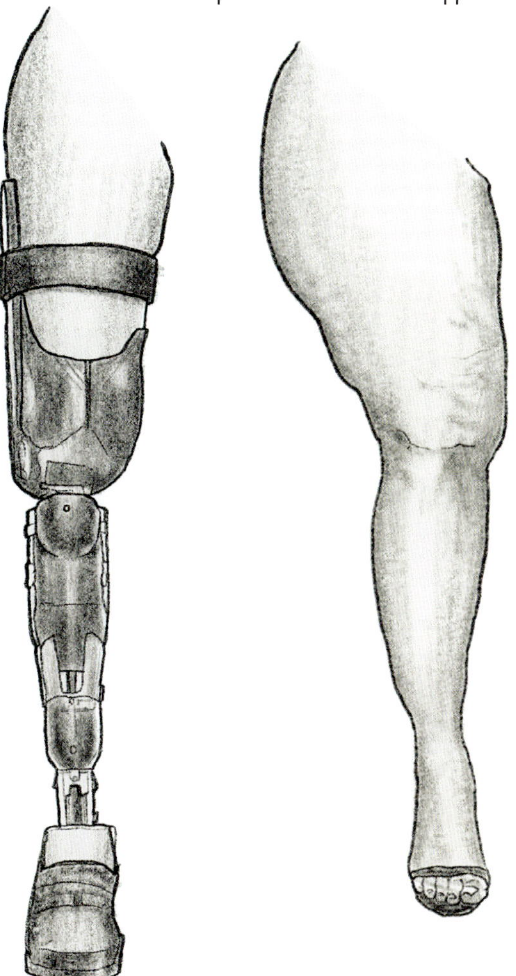

Not all legs are made of skin and bone, but they
still have the same underlying trapezoid shapes.

FEET

People avoid drawing feet almost as much as they avoid drawing hands. Feet really aren't as difficult to draw as they might seem, though. With a few well-placed guidelines, they can be drawn fairly easily.

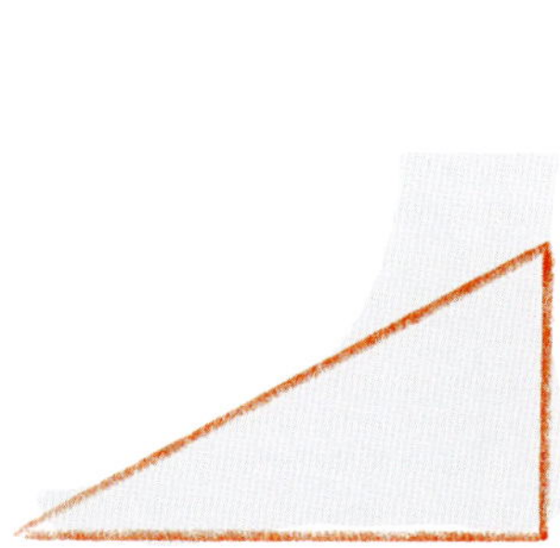

Step 1

Draw a triangle. It should be about twice as long as it is high.

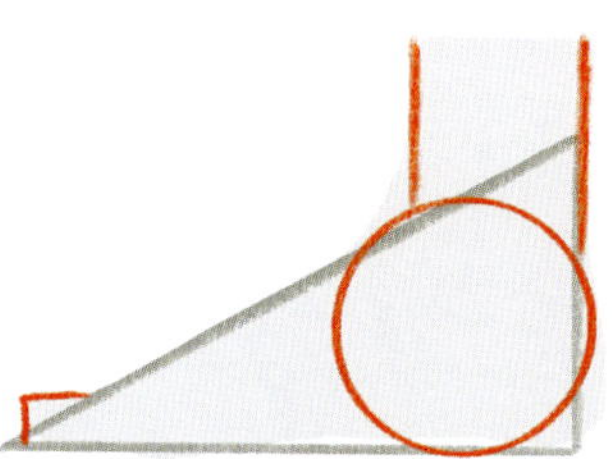

Step 2

Draw a large circle on the right side of the triangle. This will help you visualize where to contour the heel. Also draw a small triangle on the left side for the toes. Draw two vertical lines for the ankle.

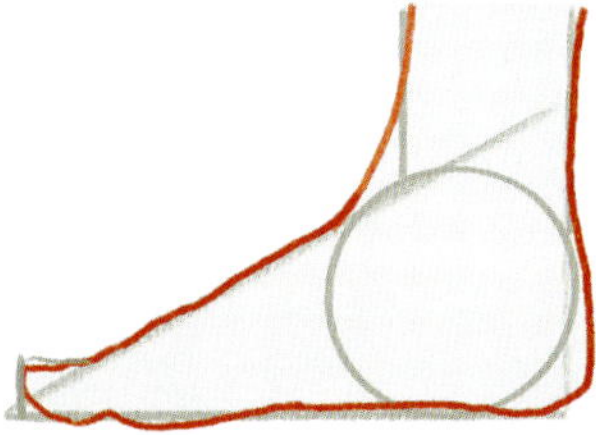

Step 3

Now draw the outline of the foot. Follow the guidelines closely, making two small curves by the toes: the first for the big toe and the second for the ball of the foot just behind the toes.

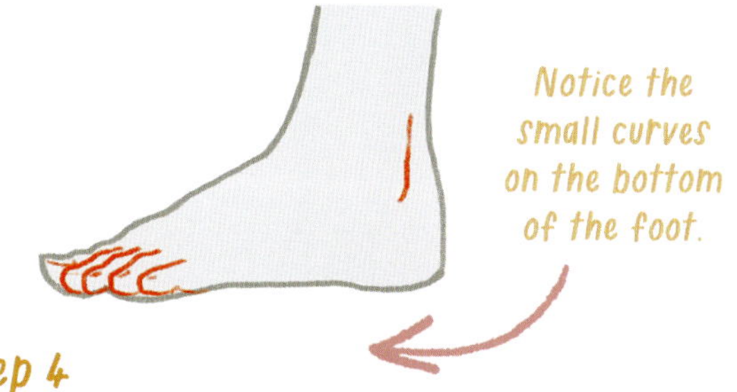

Step 4

Add four C shapes for the other four toes. You can even add little toenails with a small straight line for each toe. Now draw a line toward the back of the foot to show the ankle bone.

Time for shading. Most of the shading is on the bottom of the toes and foot. Add some very light shading on the top of the foot that looks like shaded lines extending each toe.

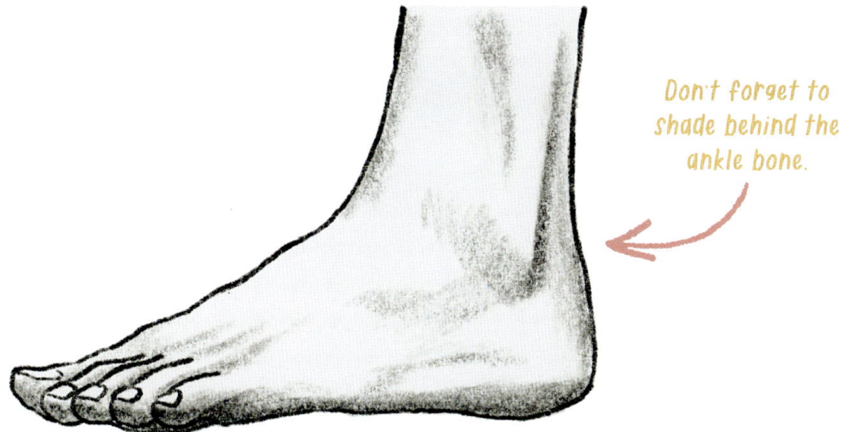

Here are some common foot positions. Can you see where you would draw triangles or circles as guidelines for these feet?

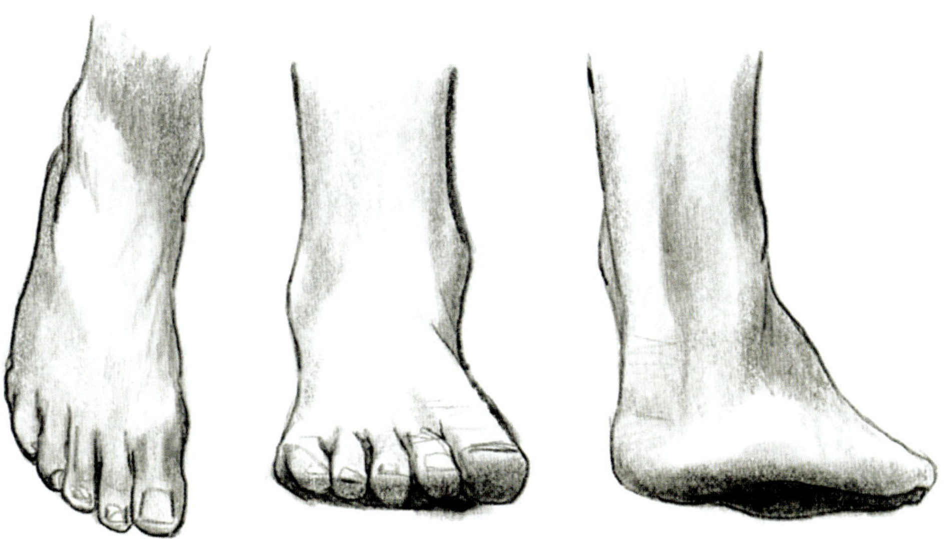

Reference: Skeleton

When you're learning to draw, you don't necessarily need to know which bones lie beneath the skin. But if you want to take your drawing to the next level, it helps to understand the underlying body structures and how they fit together.

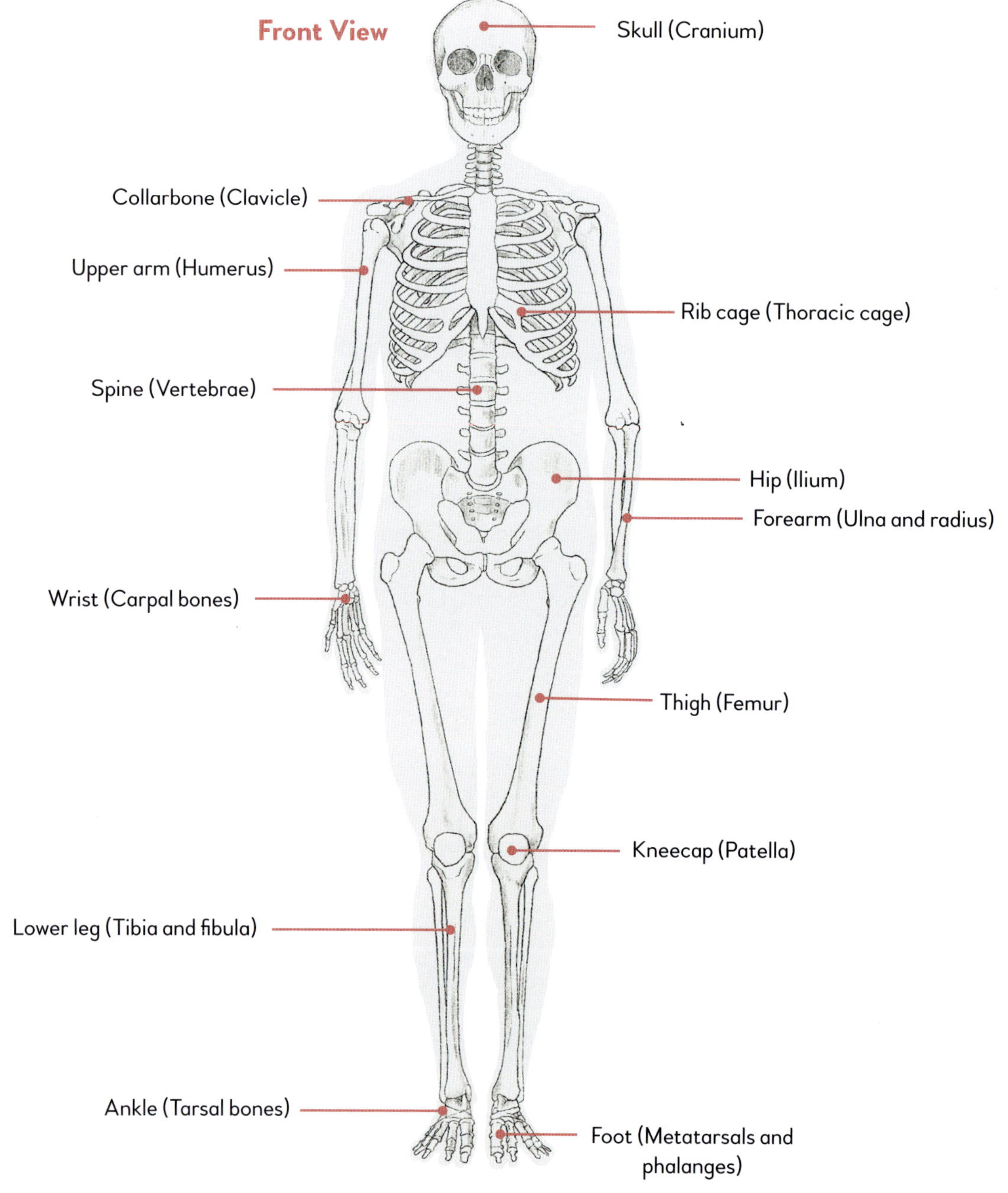

Back View

Skull (Cranium)
Shoulder blade (Scapula)
Upper arm (Humerus)
Rib cage (Thoracic cage)
Spine (Vertebrae)
Hip (Ilium)
Wrist (Carpal bones)
Hand (Metacarpals and phalanges)
Thigh (Femur)
Lower leg (Tibia and fibula)
Heel (Calcaneus)

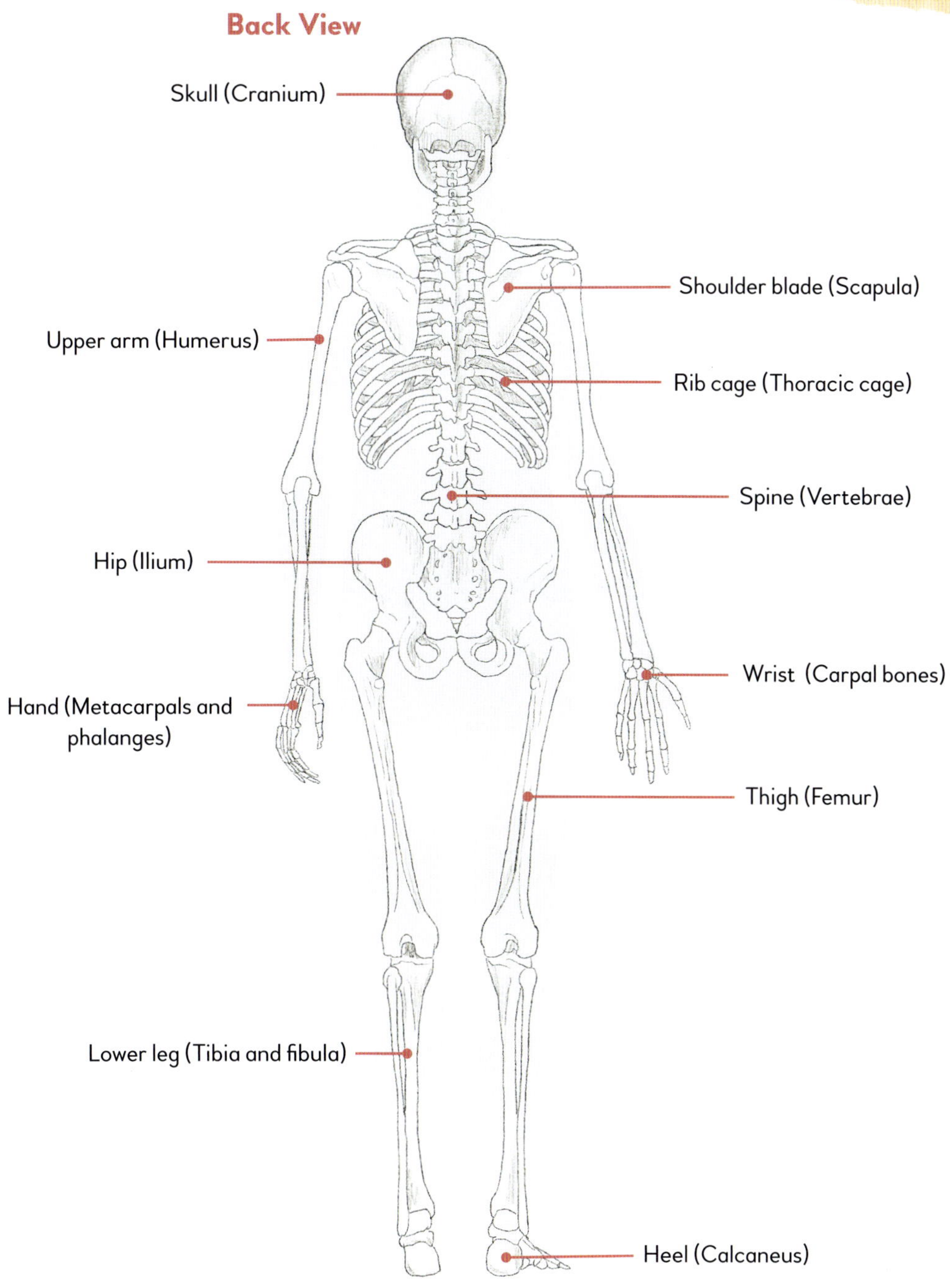

Reference: Muscles

Just as you don't *need* to know which bones lie beneath the skin, you don't *need* to know the muscles, either. However, familiarizing yourself with the muscles that move and shape our bodies will help you draw the body in any position.

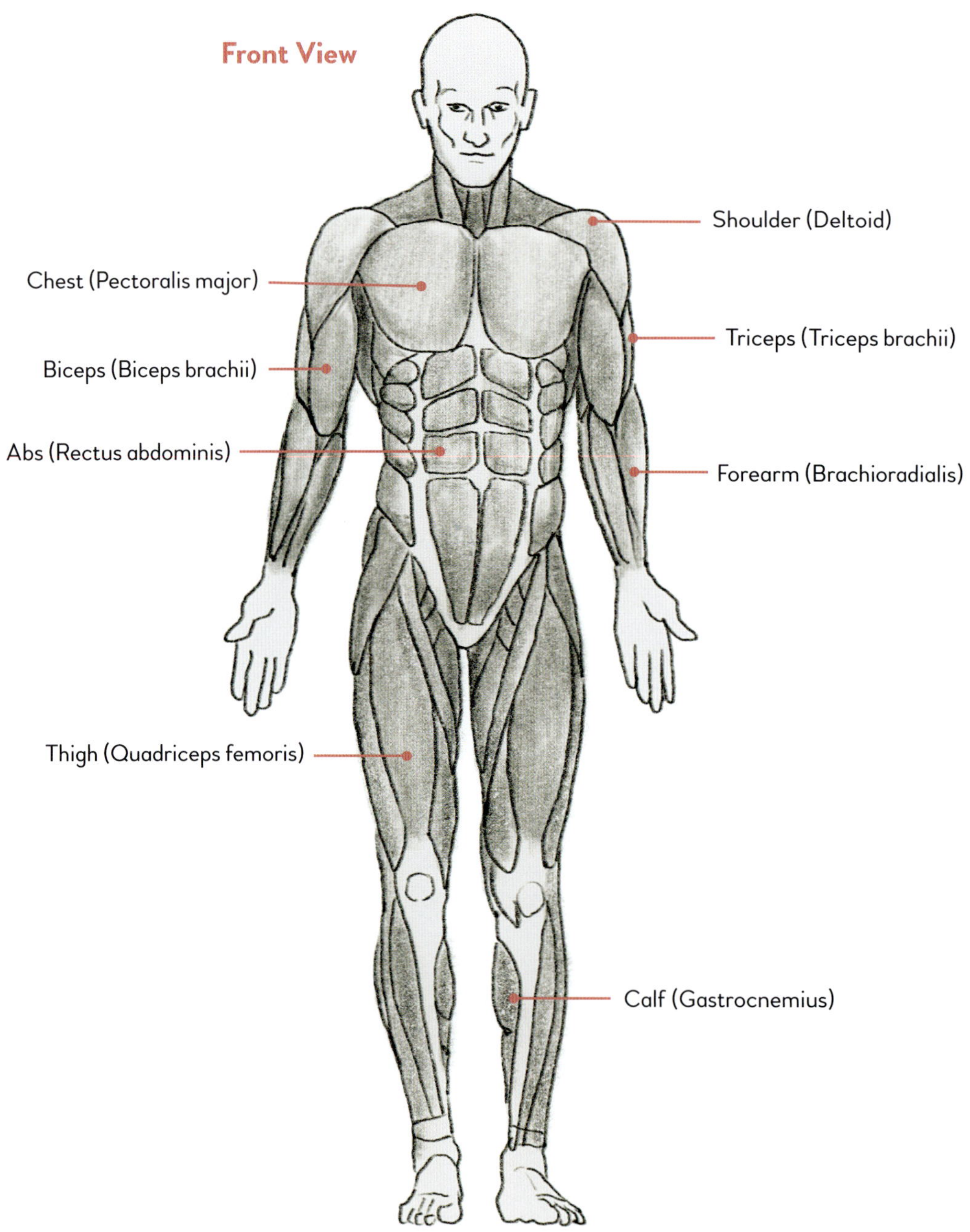

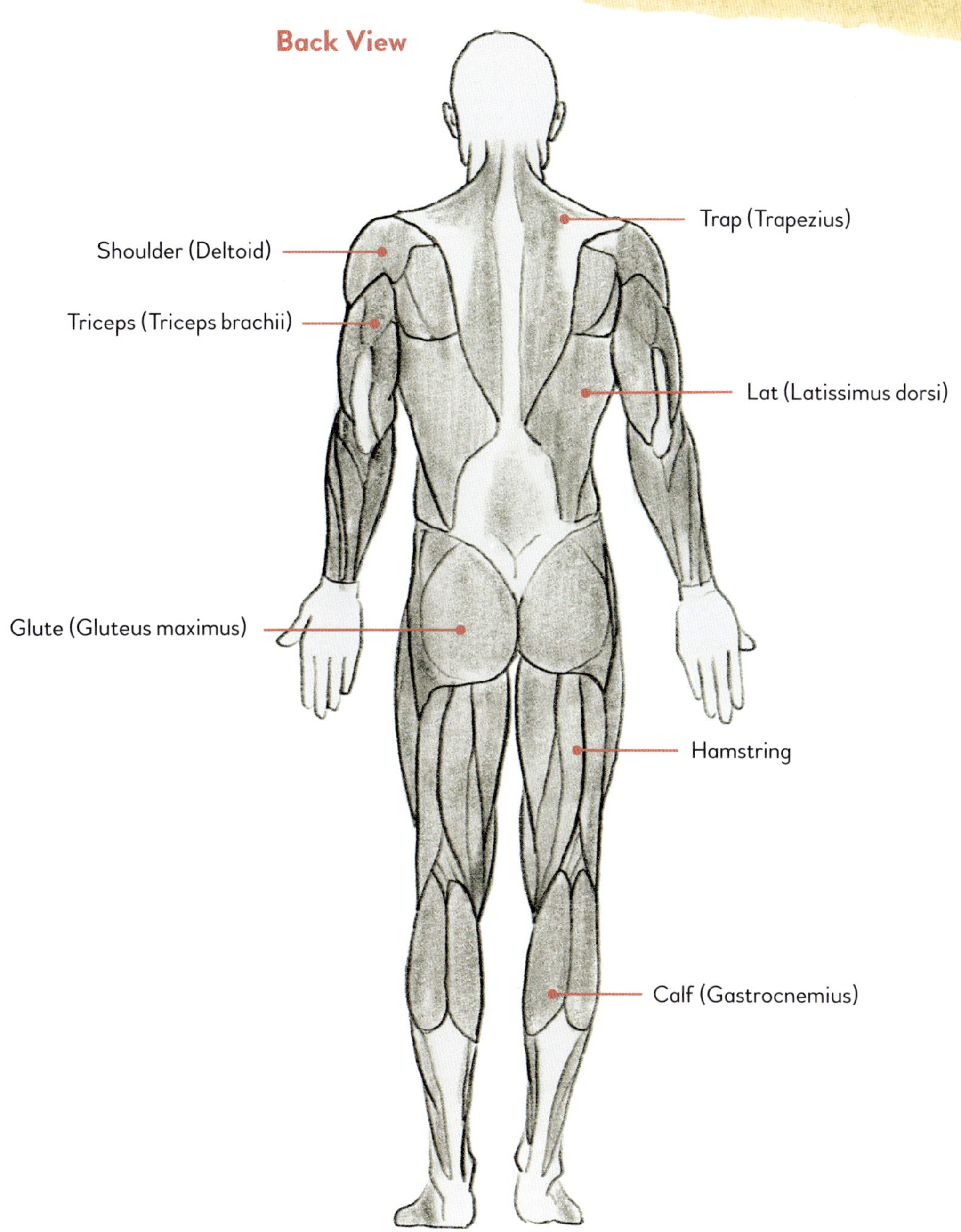

Back View
Shoulder (Deltoid)
Triceps (Triceps brachii)
Glute (Gluteus maximus)
Trap (Trapezius)
Lat (Latissimus dorsi)
Hamstring
Calf (Gastrocnemius)

ANIMALS

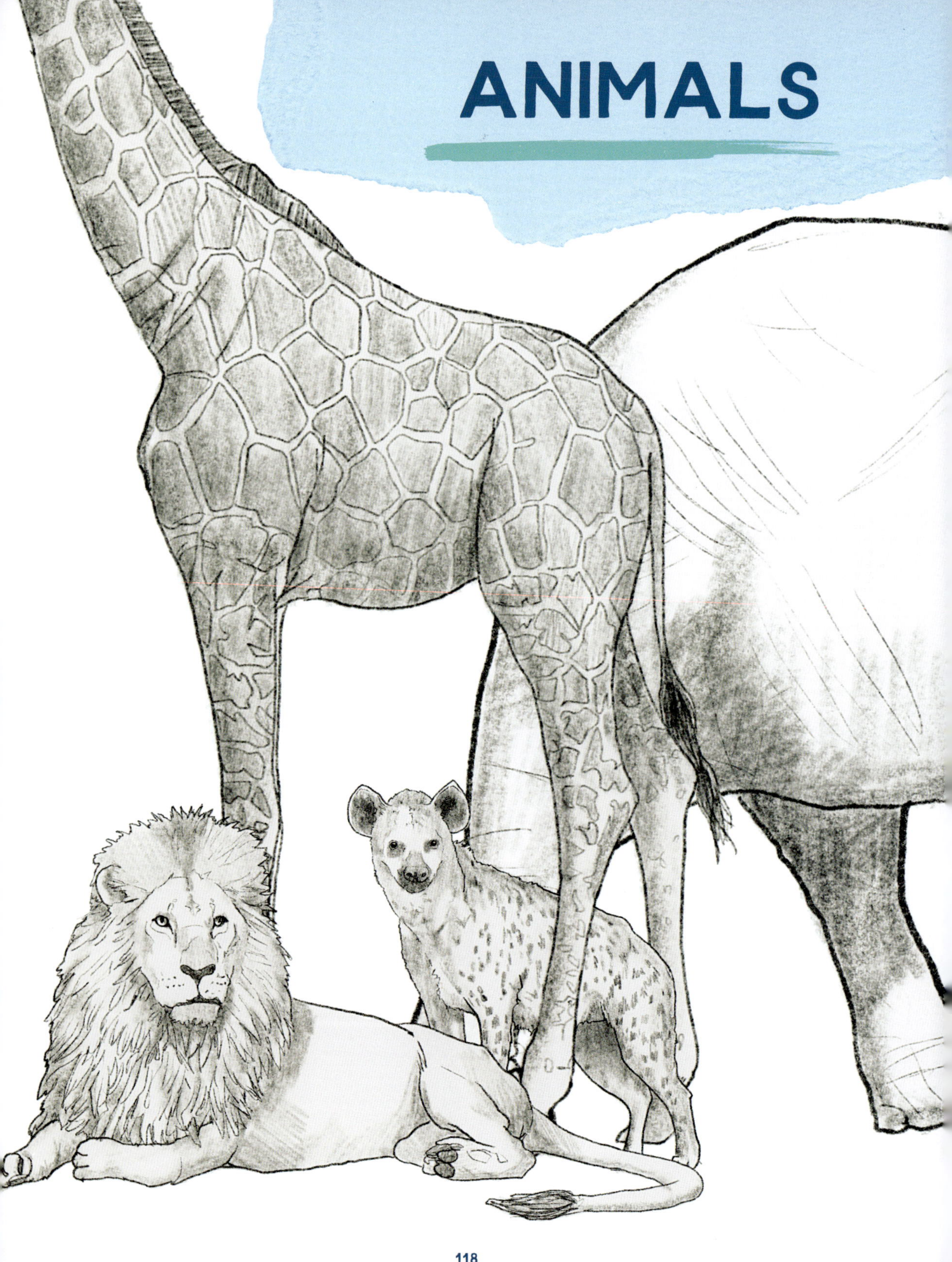

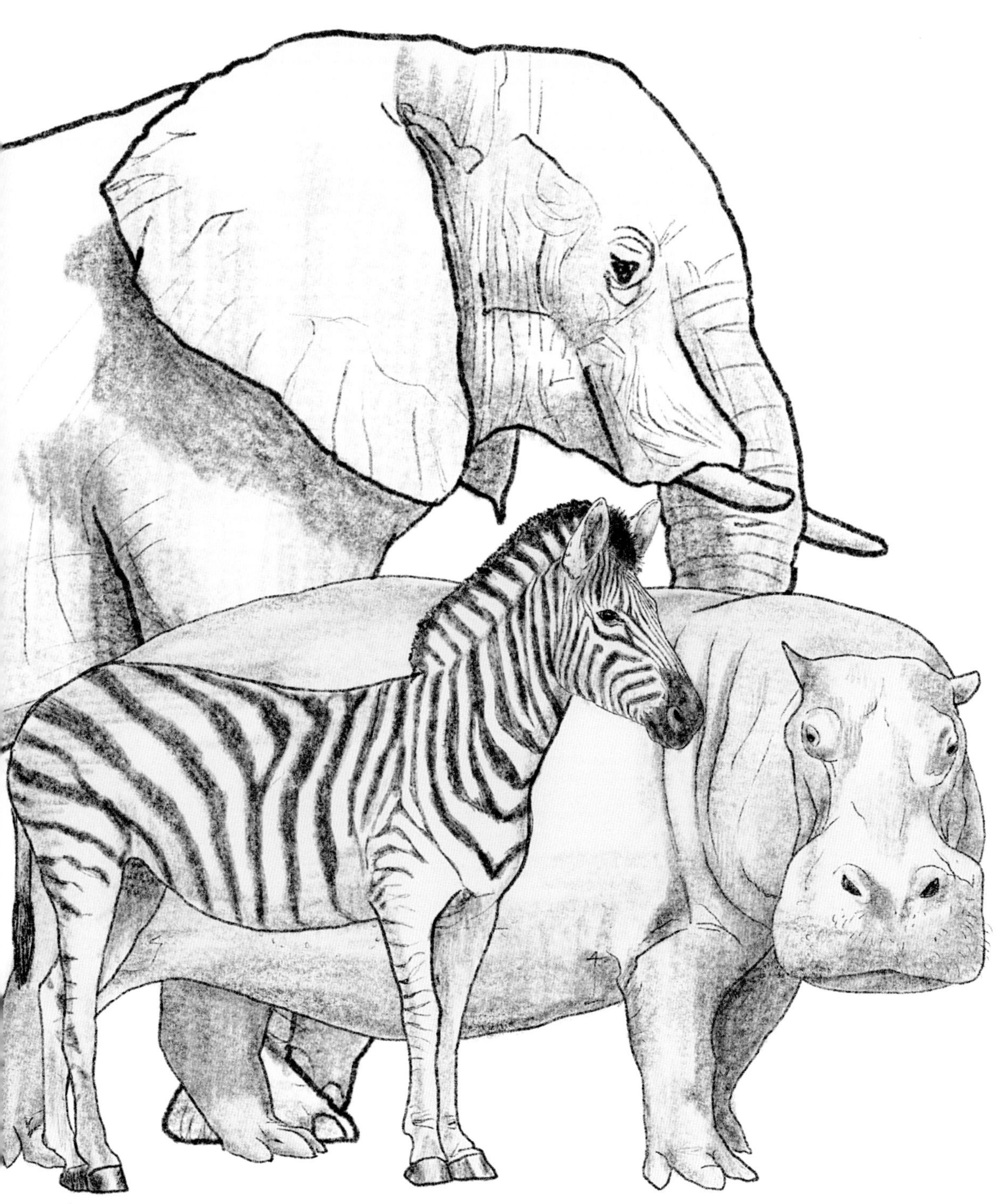

DOG

The first step in drawing a dog depends on which breed you're drawing: some dogs have cone-shaped heads (like German Shepherds), others round heads (like Pugs) and others still oval-shaped heads, like the French Bulldog you'll learn to draw below.

Step 1

Draw a large oval. Draw a smaller circle within the oval, starting from the lowest point of the oval. This will be the muzzle.

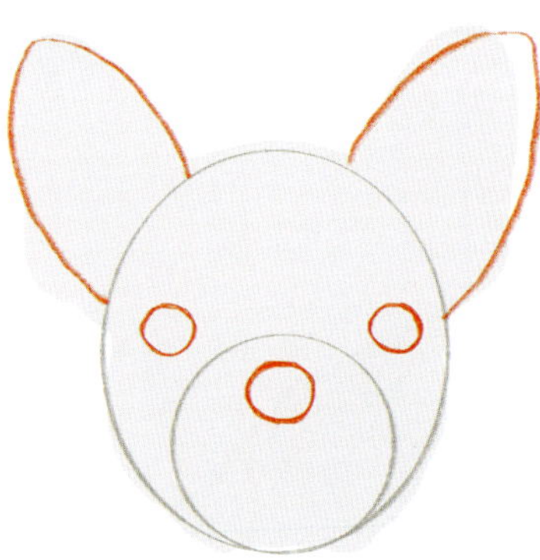

Step 2

Draw two circles for the eyes about halfway down the face. Next, draw a slightly larger circle toward the top of the muzzle for the nose. Add two arch shapes on either side of the head for ears.

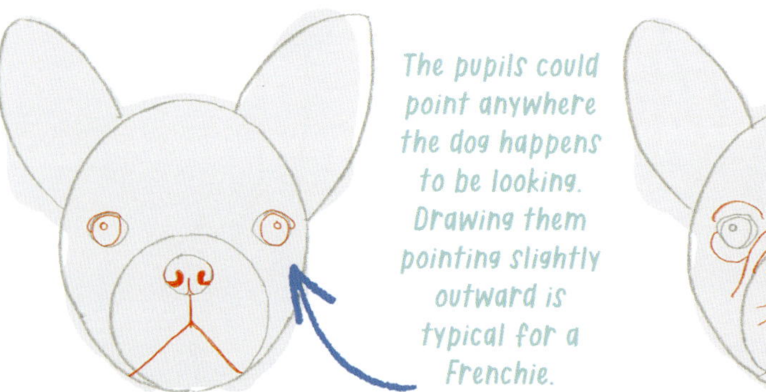
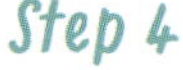

Step 3

Draw small circles in each eye for eyeballs, and even smaller ones in those for pupils. Add curved lines for upper eyelids. Also add two rounded U shapes in the nose and an upside-down Y shape below those for the mouth.

Step 4

Draw curved lines above and below each eye. Next, draw a couple of long, curved lines around the top of the muzzle, and a few more curved lines around the nose. Add a line down the forehead.

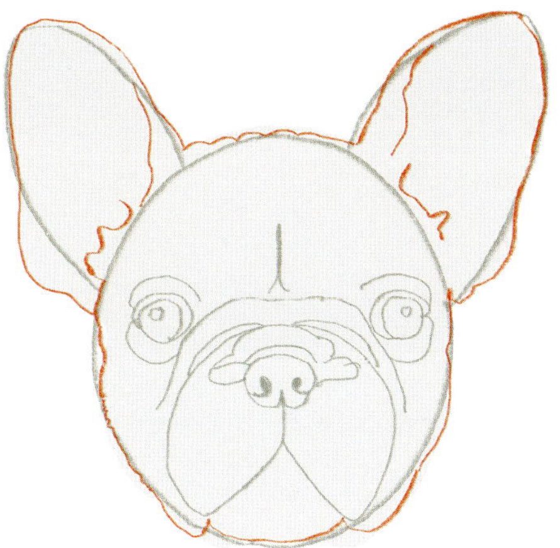 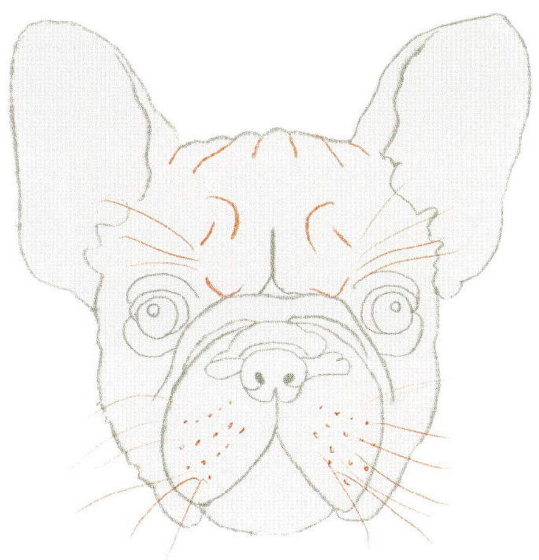

Step 5

Outline the head with a squiggly line between the ears and an uneven line around the bottom of the head. Draw a few more squiggly lines inside the bottom of each ear. About halfway up the base of the ear, draw a curved line toward the top of the ear to make it look like the ears are folding over.

Step 6

For whiskers, draw lines in the muzzle, on the jaw area and near the eyes. Next, let's add the forehead wrinkles: short lines across the top of the head and a few curved lines below them. Finally, draw three rows of dots on each side of the muzzle.

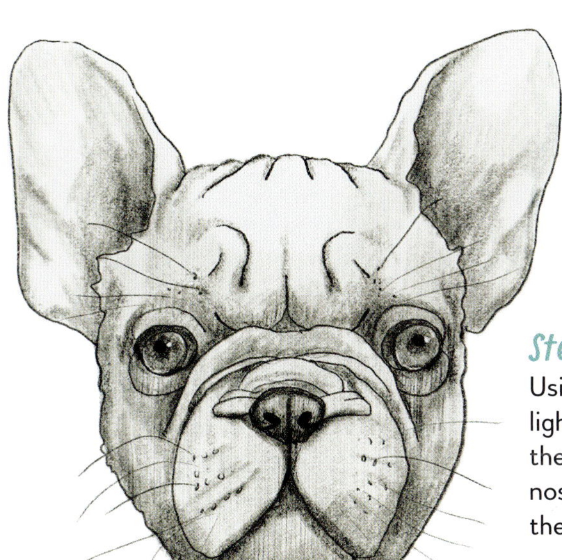

Step 7

Using the side of your pencil, lightly shade the sides of the head, the inside edges of the ears, the nostrils, the bottom of the muzzle, the eyelids and forehead wrinkles.

Reference: Dog

From short hair to long hair and floppy ears to pointy ones, dogs come in all shapes and sizes. Here are just a few of the more than 300 dog breeds out there.

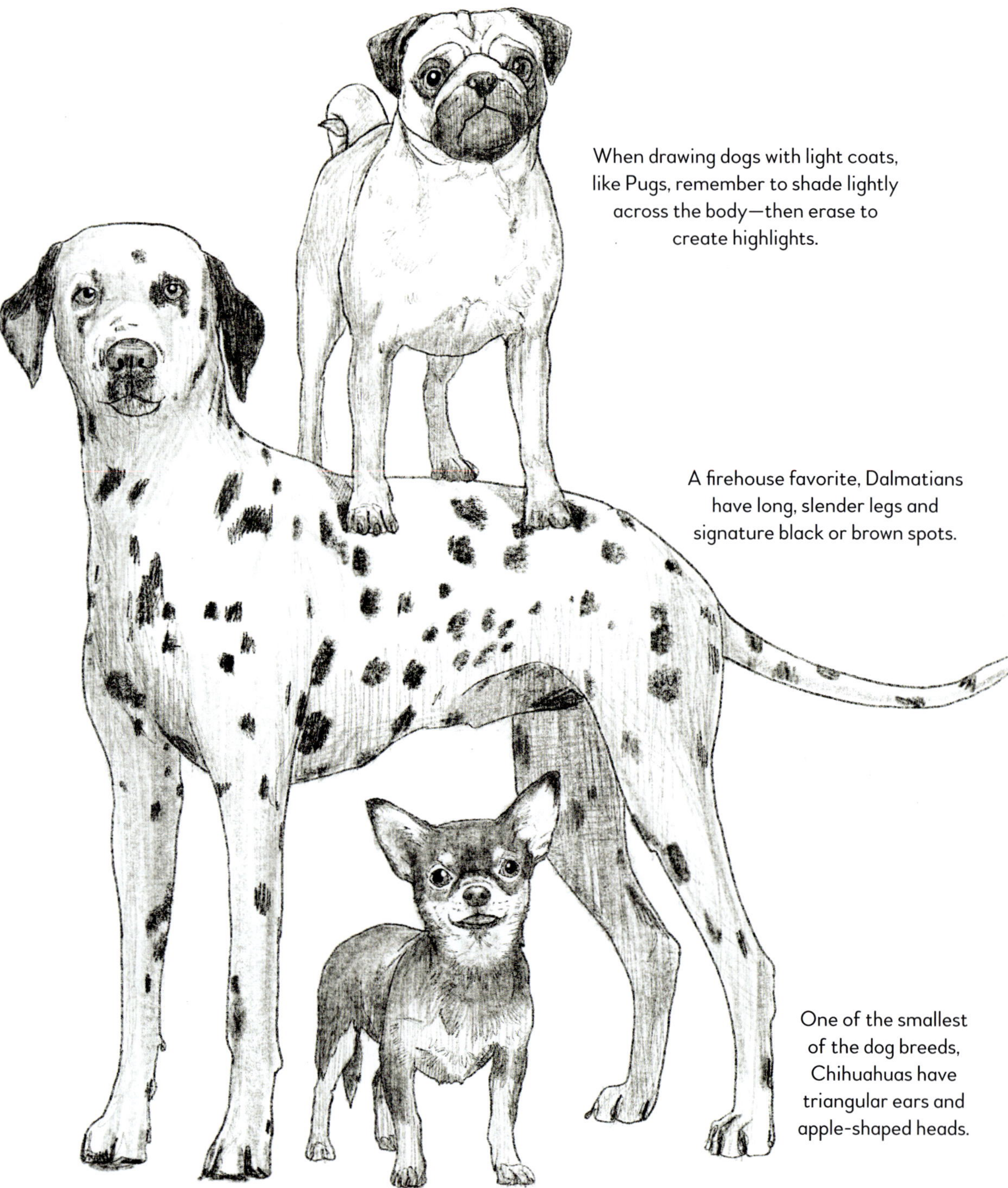

When drawing dogs with light coats, like Pugs, remember to shade lightly across the body—then erase to create highlights.

A firehouse favorite, Dalmatians have long, slender legs and signature black or brown spots.

One of the smallest of the dog breeds, Chihuahuas have triangular ears and apple-shaped heads.

Create the appearance of a shiny coat on
dark-haired dogs, such as Doberman Pinschers,
by leaving highlights very white.

When drawing dogs with their mouths open, like
with this Labrador Retriever, don't forget to draw
the shadow on their tongue.

For long-haired
dogs, such as
Pomeranians, use a
jagged line around
the outside to show
the length of the
hair.

CAT

Love them or hate them, it's undeniable: cats are a pleasure to draw. Unlike other animals, whose torsos are best drawn with one foundational shape, the slender torso of a cat is best drawn with two shapes.

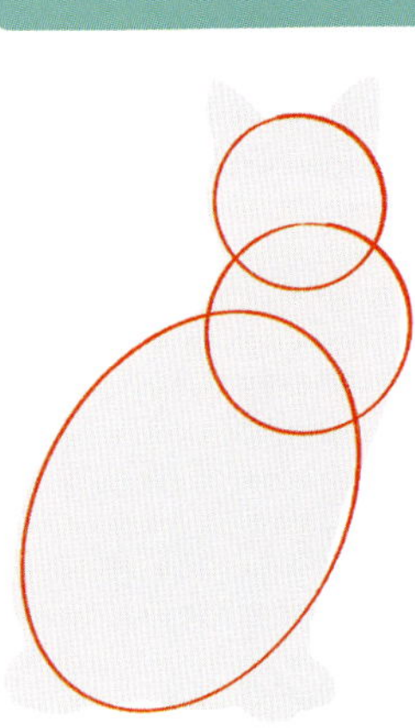

Step 1

Draw a large oval for the lower body. On top of the oval, add a small circle for the chest and then an even smaller circle for the head.

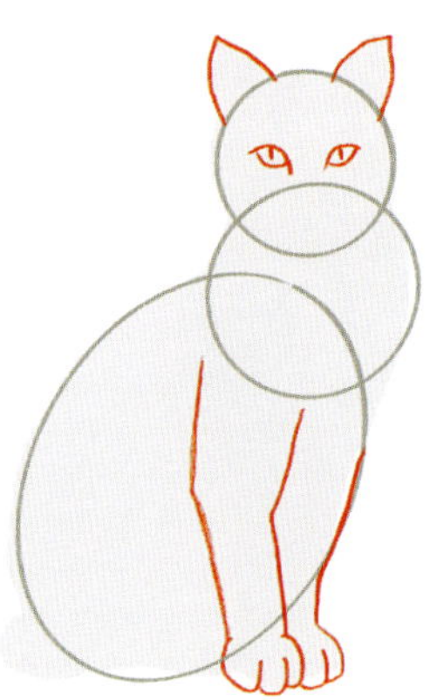

Step 2

Draw upside-down V shapes for ears, pointing them diagonally outward. About halfway down the head draw almond-shaped eyes. Add the front legs: slightly curved lines with three U shapes for the feet.

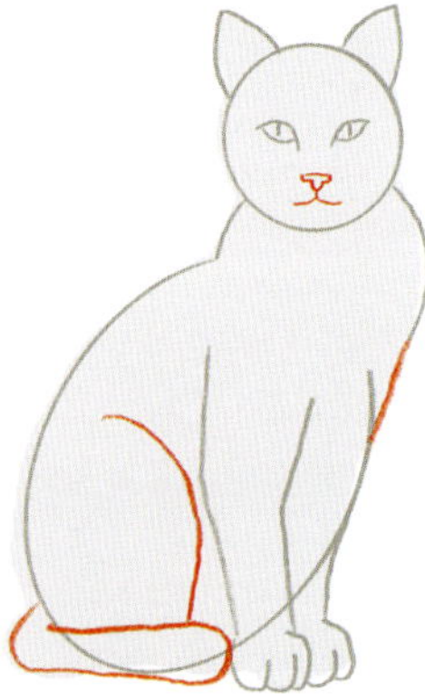

Step 3

Add a T shape for the nose and a curved line for the mouth. Connect the chest circle to the lower body oval, then erase your guidelines. Now draw a large curved line for the back leg and a sausage shape for the tail.

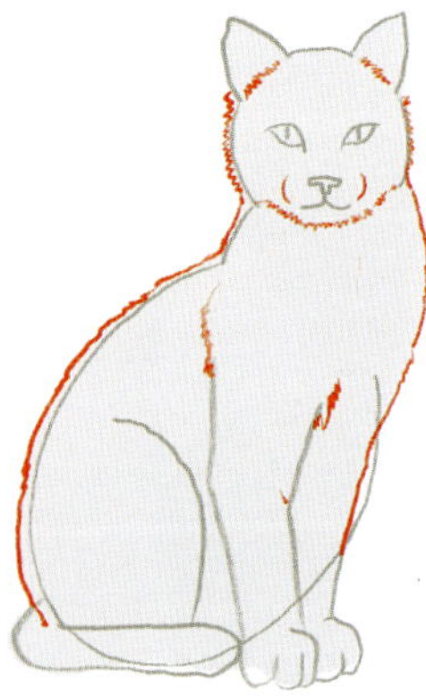

Step 4

Add very small zigzag lines around the body to create the appearance of fur. (See page 126 for an in-depth look at drawing fur.)

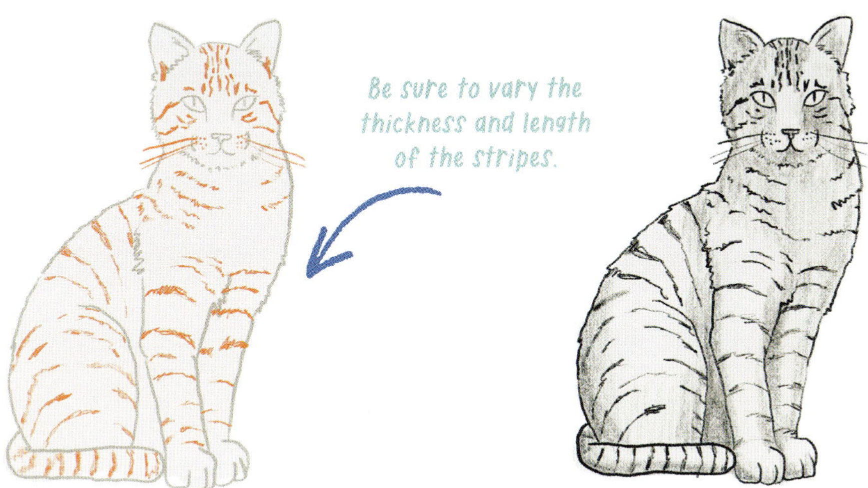

Step 5

Using the same small zigzag lines, draw stripes around the whole body. Add three or four whiskers on each side of the mouth. They should point slightly downward.

Step 6

Lightly shade the entire cat, making the areas between the legs and on the bottom of the tail and feet darkest.

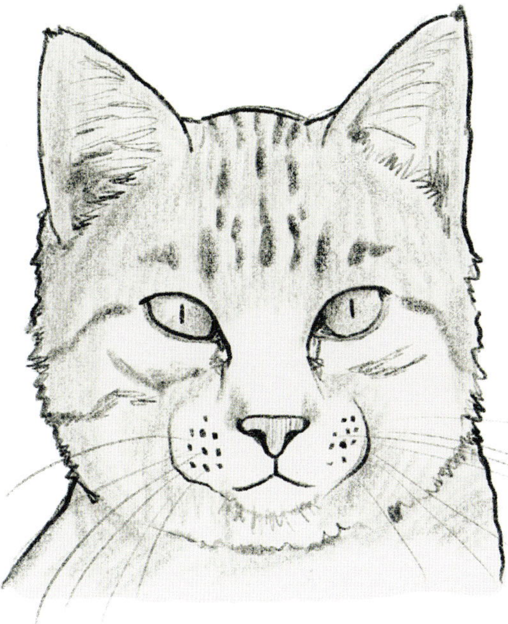

Here is a more detailed look at the cat's head. Remember to draw little dots where the whiskers start on the face. Also, notice that cats don't have circular pupils—their pupils look like vertical slits.

BONUS: FUR

Whether you're drawing cats, bunnies, lions or llamas, you're going to need a way to show their soft, fluffy coats. Though there is a distinction between fur and animal hair, it's all drawn in roughly the same way. Let's use a cat as an example.

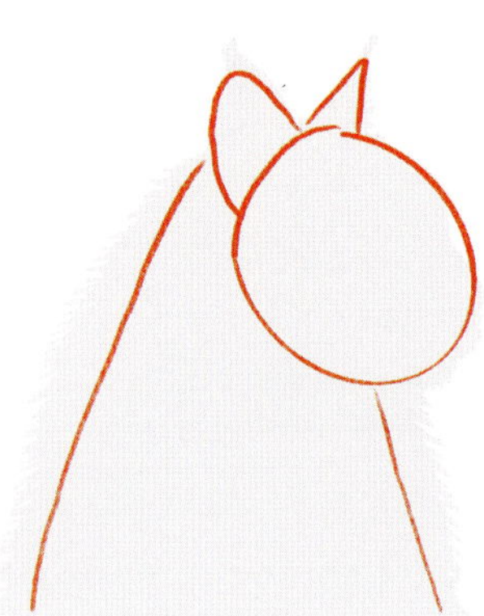

Step 1

Draw the basic shapes of the cat. Be sure to draw the guidelines very lightly, as we'll be covering them with fur in just a few steps.

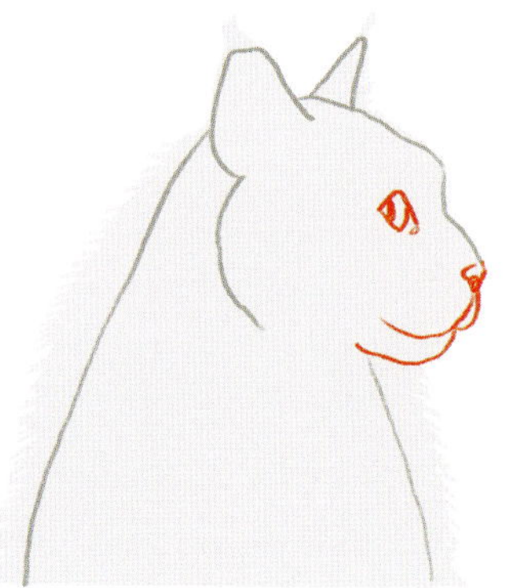

Step 2

Refine the shapes and draw the outline of the cat. Draw the features that don't have any fur, like the eyes and the nose, or only have very short fur, like the mouth.

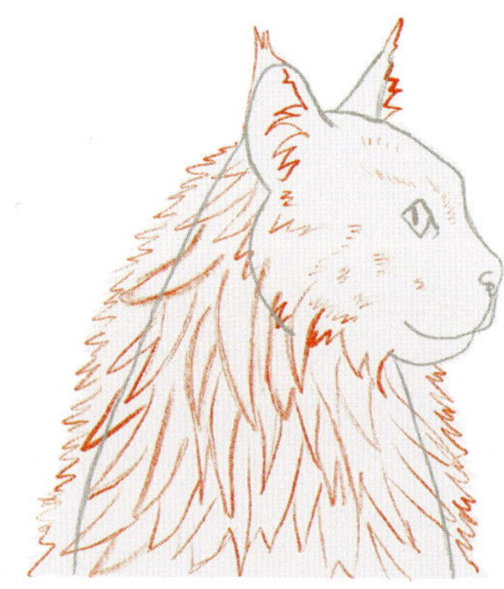

Step 3

Draw curved V shapes over the whole body. Pay attention to the direction of the V shapes. They should be pointing downward.

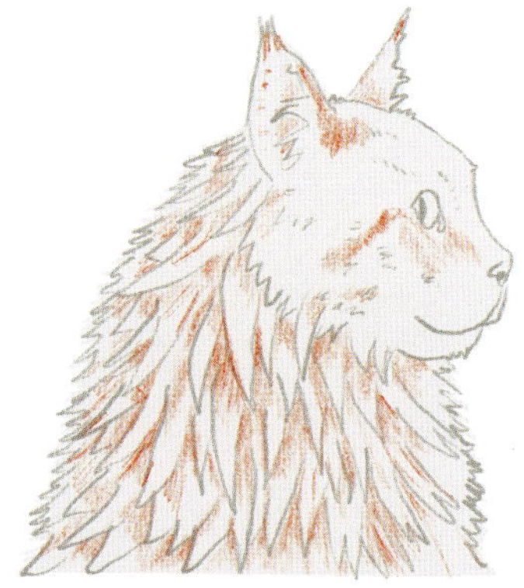

Step 4

Lightly shade the base of each V shape. Leave the tips quite light. This will create depth.

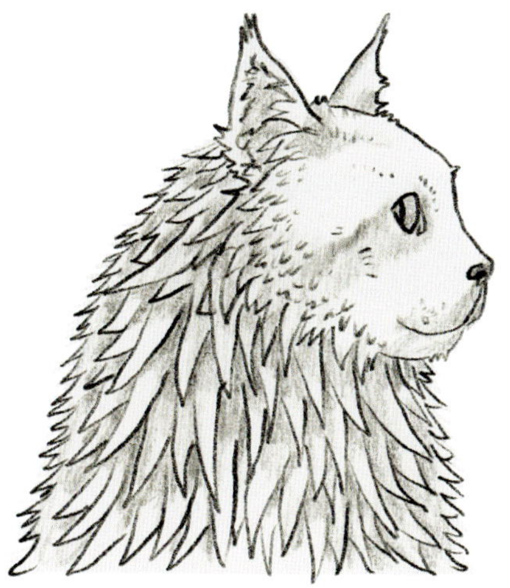

Step 5

Within each of the existing V shapes, make smaller V shapes. Also draw little lines in the areas that have short fur, like the cheeks and ears.

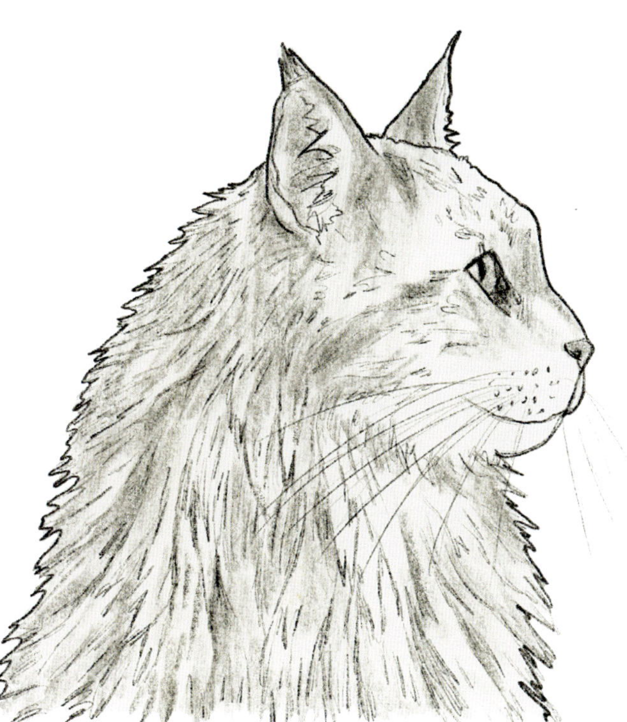

Step 6

Using a blending stump or tortillon, blend as many of the heavy V-shape lines as possible. This will give the illusion of softness. Add short lines and squiggles throughout to create more texture.

RABBIT

Rabbits may very well be the cutest animals out there, so it's a relief that they're fairly easy to draw. A tip for making your rabbit look extra furry: use small, jagged lines around the outside of its body.

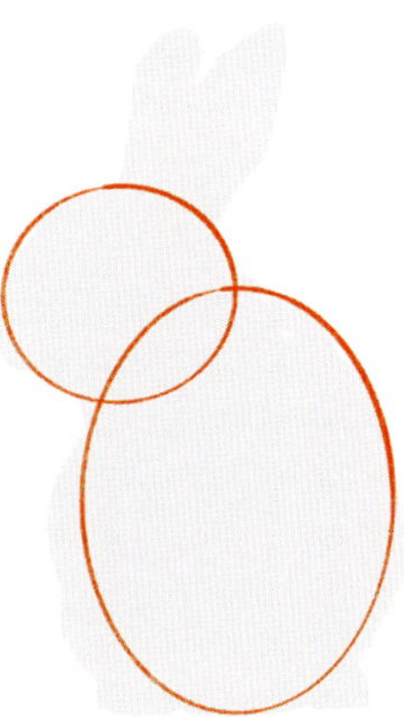

Step 1

Draw a large oval. This will be the rabbit's body. Add a circle over the top left part of the oval for the head.

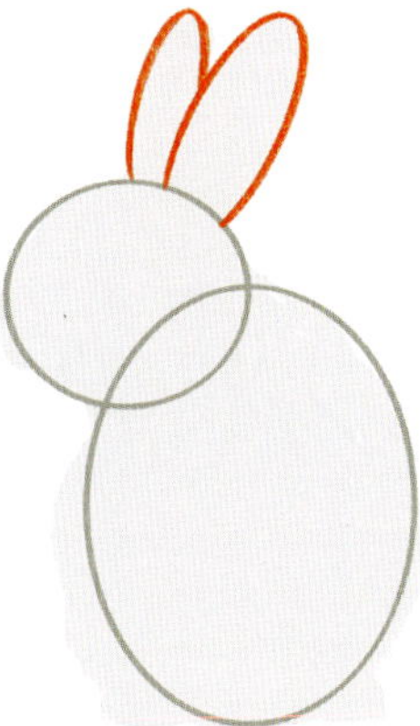

Step 2

Draw two upside-down U shapes on the top of the head. These will be the ears.

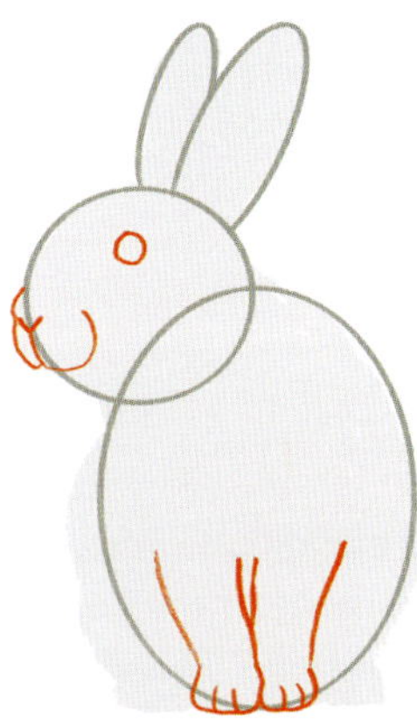

Step 3

Add a circle for the eye, a Y-shaped nose and three semicircles around it to complete the muzzle. The front legs are just two curved lines each. The front feet are U shapes, with little lines separating the toes.

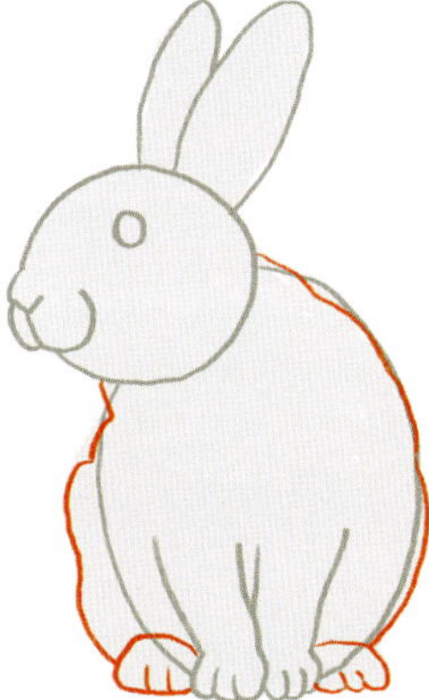

Step 4

Draw a wobbly line around the oval for the body. Add the back feet by drawing a circular shape for each foot, with little lines separating the toes.

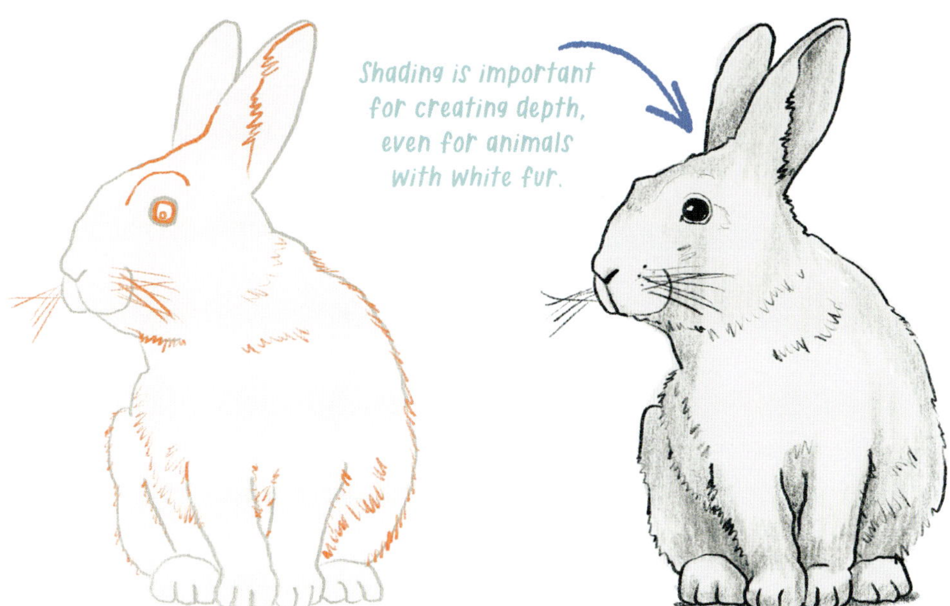

Step 5

Draw a jagged line inside the ears. This will look like fur. Now outline the eye and pupil, and draw whiskers around the nose. Add short, jagged lines around the body for fur.

Step 6

Shade all over the rabbit, making the areas around the legs, around the mouth and inside the ears darkest.

There are many different types of rabbits. Notice that some of them have large ears that droop down, while others have shorter ears that stick straight up.

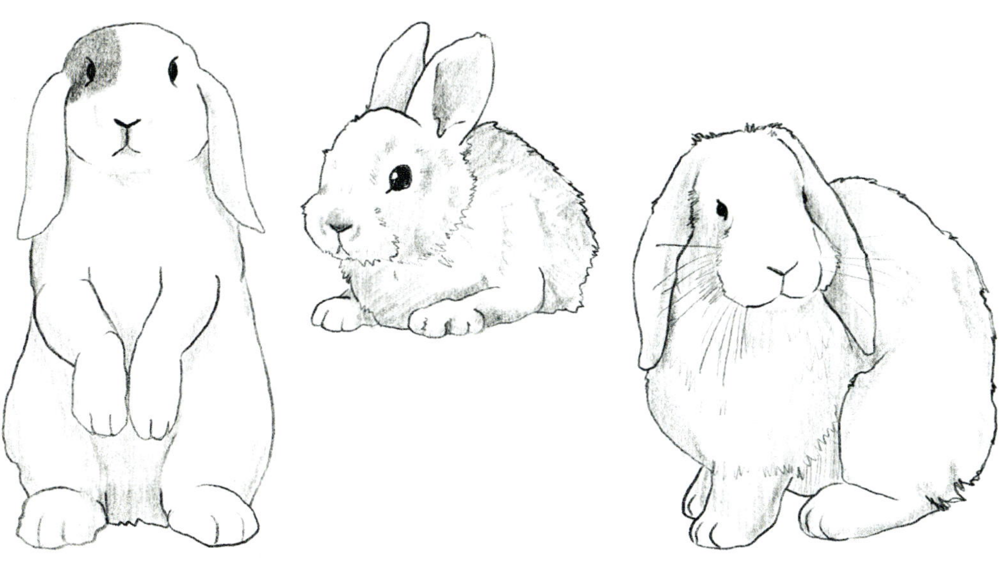

GIRAFFE

You're going to need a long piece of paper for this one! Giraffes share an underlying kite-shaped head with horses and goats, but they differ from their friends in that they have spots—not to mention their long legs and long, long neck.

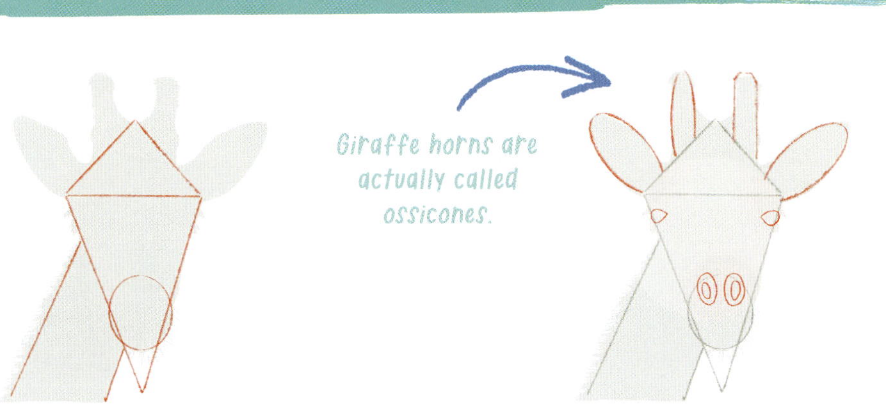

Step 1

Draw one small triangle and one large triangle together to make a kite shape. Now draw an oval toward the bottom of the large triangle. Add two lines for the neck.

Step 2

Draw two ovals that extend diagonally out from the base of the small triangle for ears, and two sausage shapes pointing upward near the tip of the triangle for horns. In the large triangle, make two sideways teardrop shapes for the eyes, and two sets of ovals for each nostril.

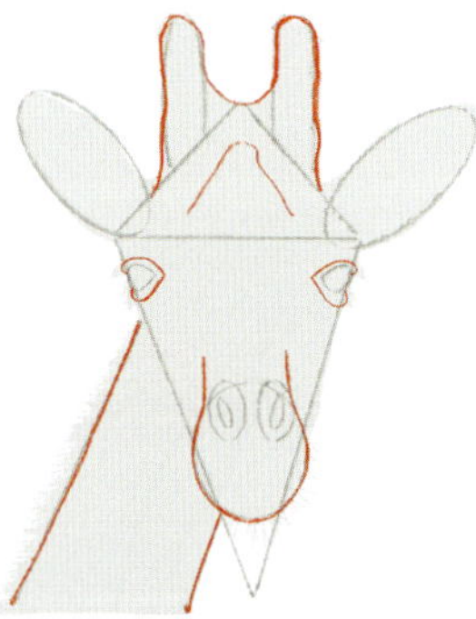

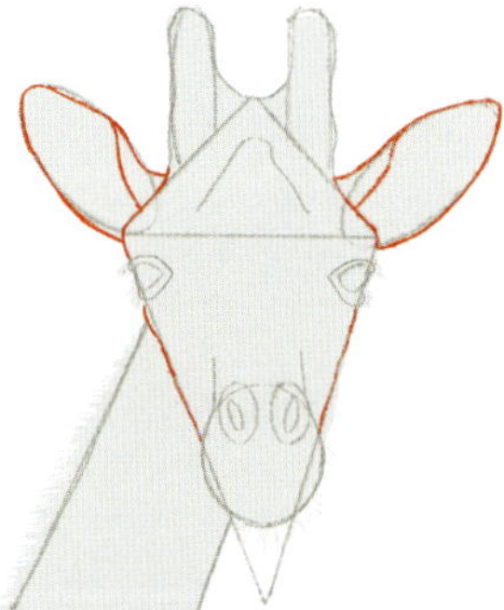

Step 3

Connect the horns with a U shape. Draw a small bump in the middle of the forehead—that will be the giraffe's third ossicone. Draw an outline around the eyes and a U shape around the mouth.

Step 4

Add slight curves to the lines on the sides of the head. Make the ears slightly pointy at the tips and wider at the bases. About halfway up the base of the ear, draw a curved line toward the top of the ear to make it look like the ears are folding over.

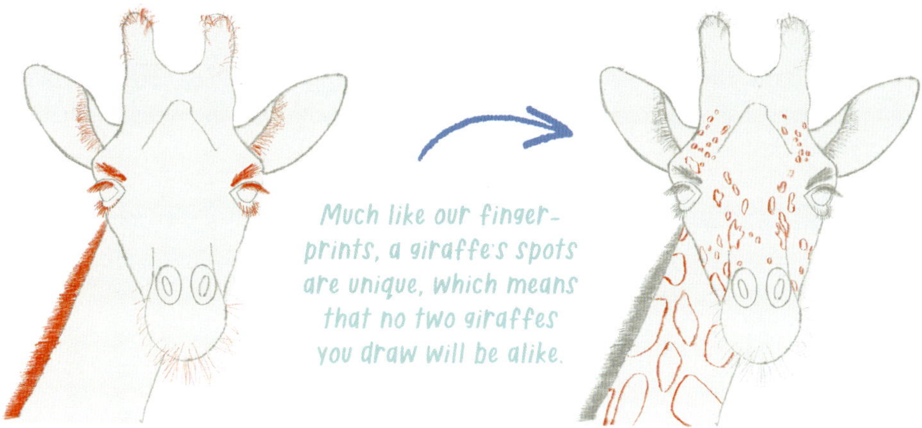

Step 5

Pressing down harder than usual on your pencil, draw thick hair down the back of the neck. Now, pressing down normally, draw thin hair along the bottom of the muzzle and fuzz around the ossicones and the insides of the ears. Draw in eyebrows and eyelashes.

Step 6

Let's outline the spots. They don't follow a pattern, but they are generally large on the neck, medium-sized around the nose and small on the forehead.

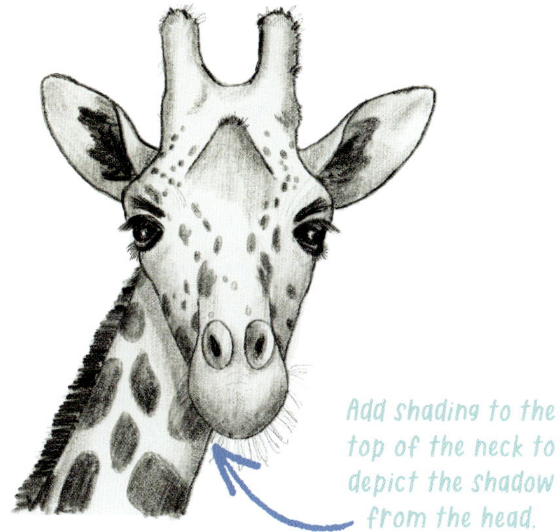

Step 7

Color in the spots that you just outlined, as well as the insides of the ears. Use the side of your pencil to lightly shade the sides of the head, the ears, the nostrils, the bottom of the muzzle and the ossicones.

TIGER

Fierce and majestic, tigers are widely known for their orange and white coats and black (or brown) stripes. The way to create the illusion of those colors with a single pencil is to use light and dark shading.

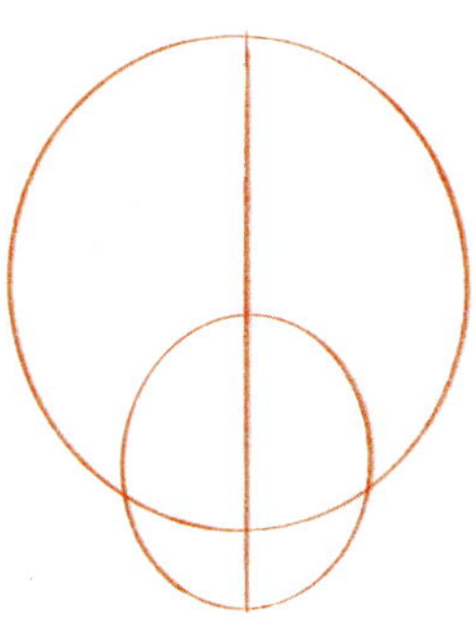

Step 1

Draw a large circle for the head. Split the circle in half. Next, starting just over halfway down the midline, draw a small oval. This will be the mouth and nose.

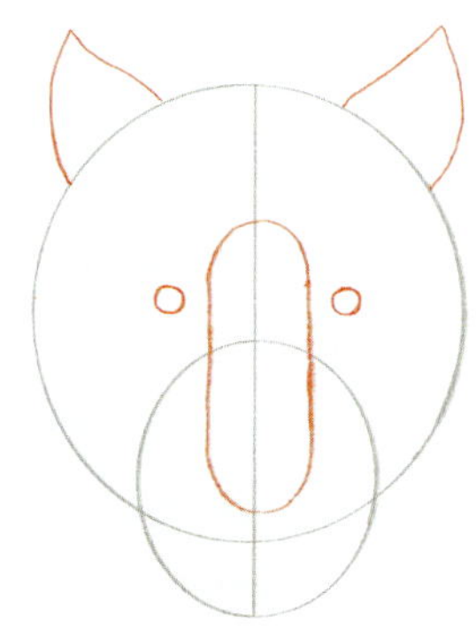

Step 2

Draw two upside-down V shapes for the ears. Rough in the eyes with two small circles halfway down the head. Draw a long pill-shape form along the midline for the nose.

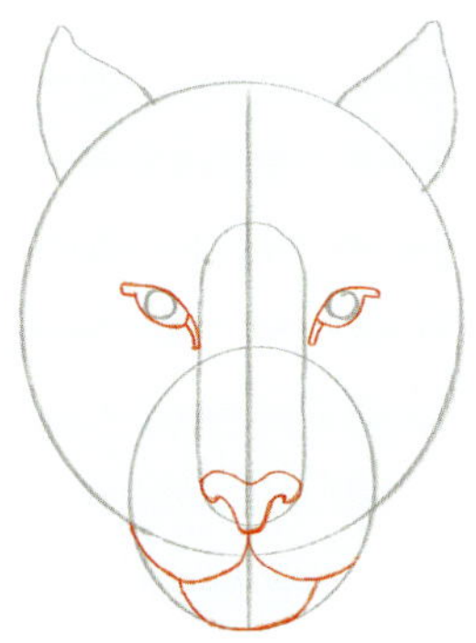

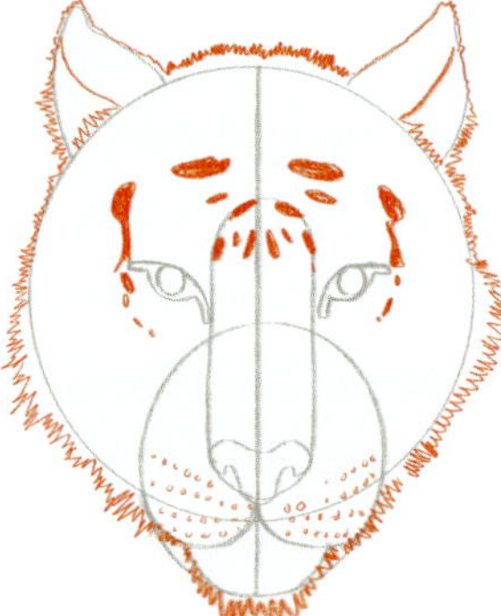

Step 3

Draw angled almond shapes for eyes, with little tail-like shapes around each one. Now, at the tip of the nose, draw a curvy T shape. At the bottom of the T, draw two U shapes for the top of the mouth, and then another U below those for the bottom of the mouth.

Step 4

Now outline the outside of the head with squiggly lines. Draw a curved line toward the top of the ear to make it look like the ears are folding over. Make a few oval-shaped stripes around the eyes. Draw four lines of small circles below the nose.

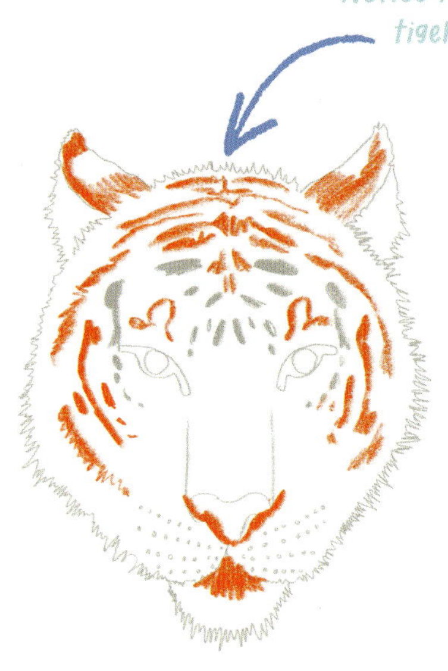

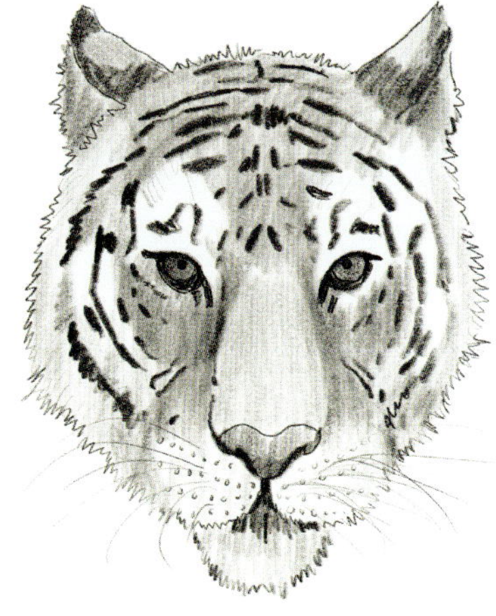

Step 5

Draw symmetrical stripes on both sides of the midline. Work your way down from the top of the head and around the eyes. Darken the areas inside the ears, under the nostrils and at the mouth.

Step 6

Darken the areas that represent orange fur, keeping the areas around the eyes and mouth light. Shade along the inside and bottom of the ears. Add long whiskers, and you're done!

Here's the rest of the tiger's body for reference. Think about the body roughly as a long oval shape extending back from the head, with front legs, hind legs and a tail. Ensure that your stripes follow the curvature of the body.

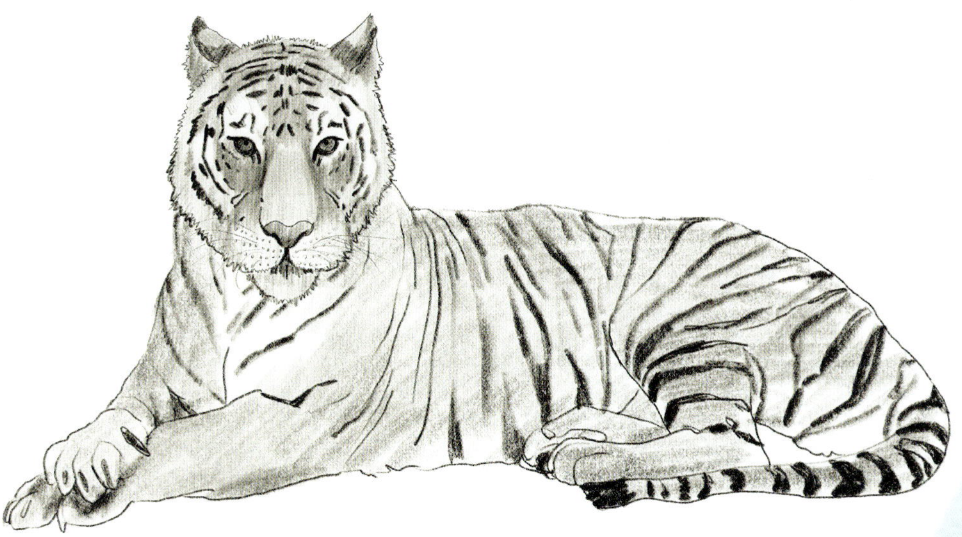

BUMBLEBEE

Stout and rounded, the bumblebee is the furriest and fluffiest of its insect cousins. Create their characteristic fur with short, light lines, and show their stripes with shading. Flip to the flowers on page 164 to learn how to give your bumblebee a soft landing.

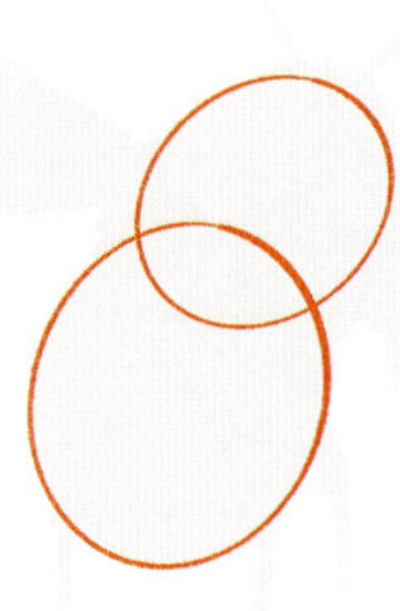

Step 1

Draw two ovals. Have them slightly overlapping.

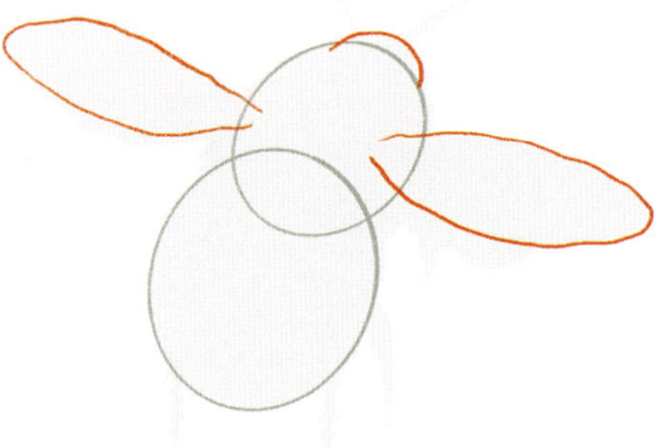

Step 2

Draw a small curved line at the top for the head. Now add two near ovals for the wings.

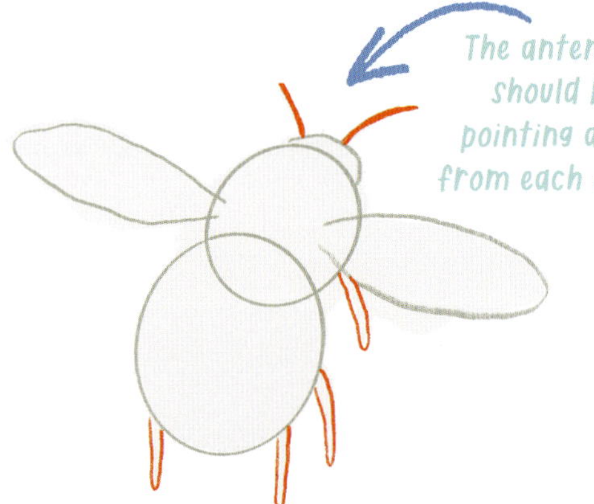

Step 3

The antennae are just two curved lines on top of the head. Draw four of the six legs. They look like very narrow U shapes.

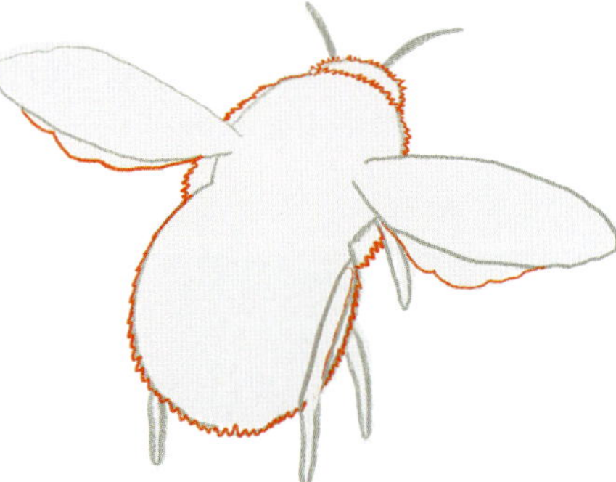

Step 4

Draw small zigzag lines around your guidelines on the body. This will give the illusion of fuzz.

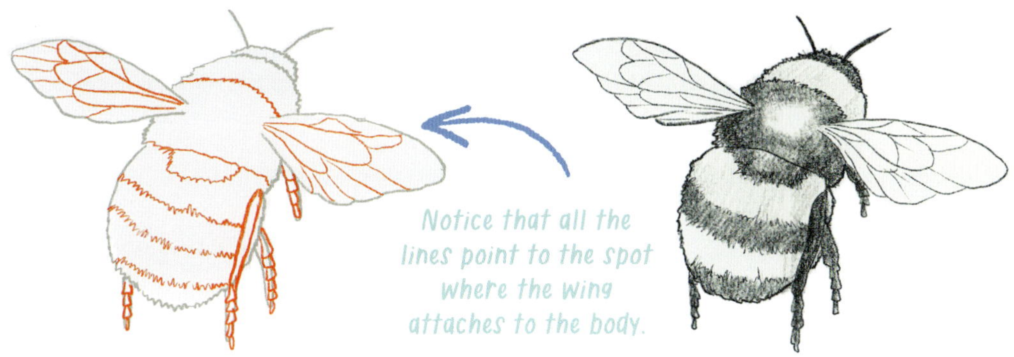

Step 5

In the wings, add one tier of tear shapes, and another of small lines. Draw stripes on the body using zigzag lines. Create little triangles on the legs to give them some detail.

Step 6

Add shading, alternating between dark and light areas. Create a highlight by erasing a rounded area in between the wings. You can lightly shade the wings, or leave them as is.

When the bumblebee is in the three-quarter position, we see one of its eyes. Bumblebee eyes are large and oval shaped. Include a highlight to show shine.

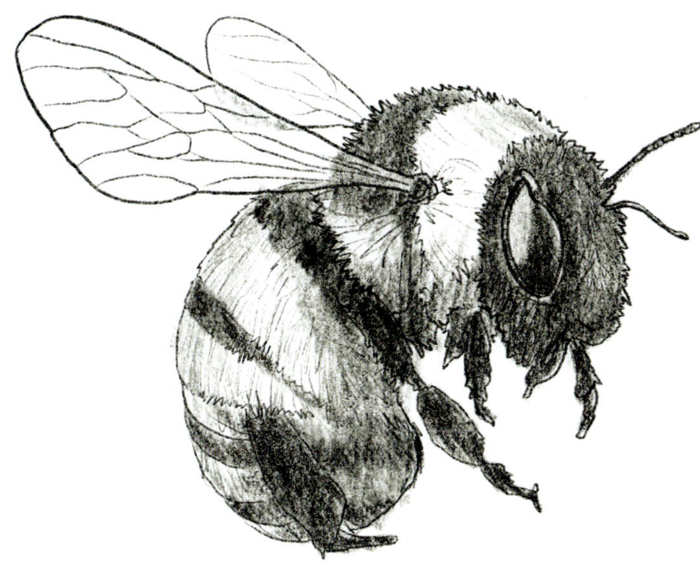

EAGLE

Known for its impressive flying ability, this great bird of prey presents a great opportunity to practice different textures. The beak and talons are drawn with smooth lines, while the feathers are drawn with bumpy ones.

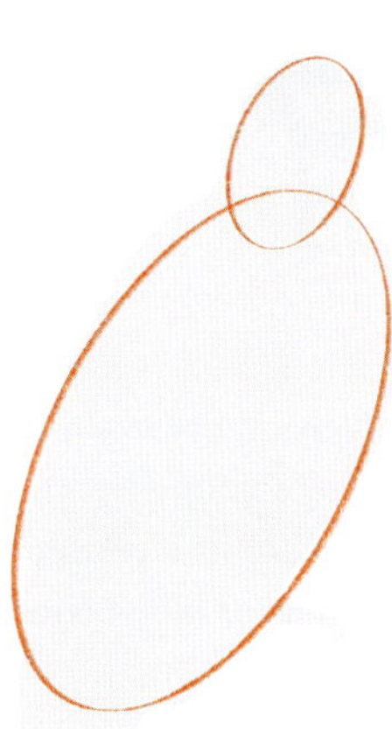

Step 1

Draw a large tilted oval for the body, and an overlapping vertical oval for the head. These are guidelines, so draw them in lightly—you'll erase them later before you do the details.

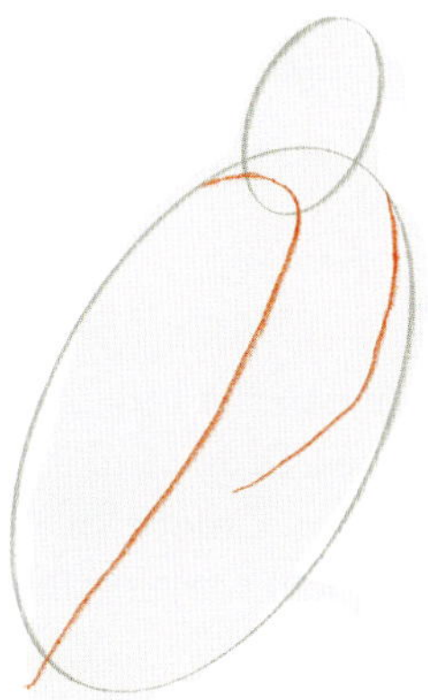

Step 2

Now for the wing. Draw a large curved line that turns sharply at the top and straightens out as it goes down the body. Draw a smaller curved line for the body. It should come down to about the halfway point of the oval.

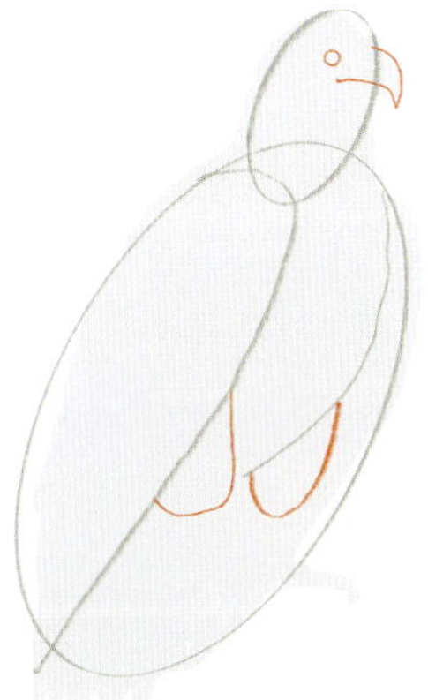

Step 3

Draw two U shapes for the tops of the legs. The eye is a small circle in the middle of the head. Add the beak, making the top line shorter than the bottom one.

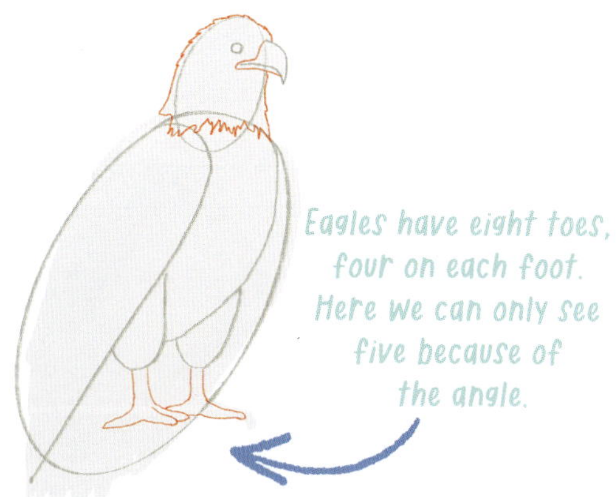

Step 4

Draw jagged lines around the head and neck. Now, to the feet: draw upside down T shapes below the legs.

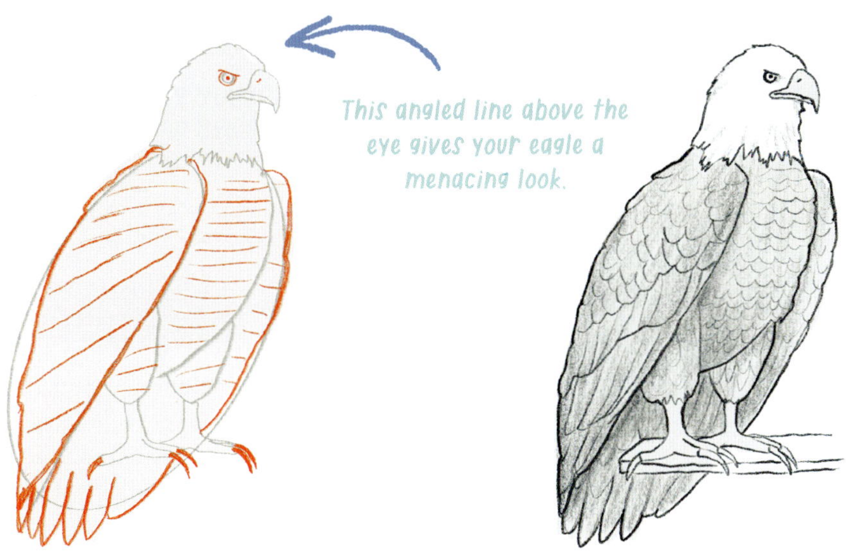

Step 5

Outline the wing with a few bumps and curves. Draw horizontal lines down the wings, chest and legs. Add a series of U shapes at the bottom for tail feathers. Draw a few circles around the eye, and add curved lines to the toes to make them into talons.

Step 6

Along the horizontal lines you just drew, draw rows of U shapes for feathers. Notice that the feathers become longer toward the tips of the wings. Very lightly shade the head with little lines. Shade the rest of the body.

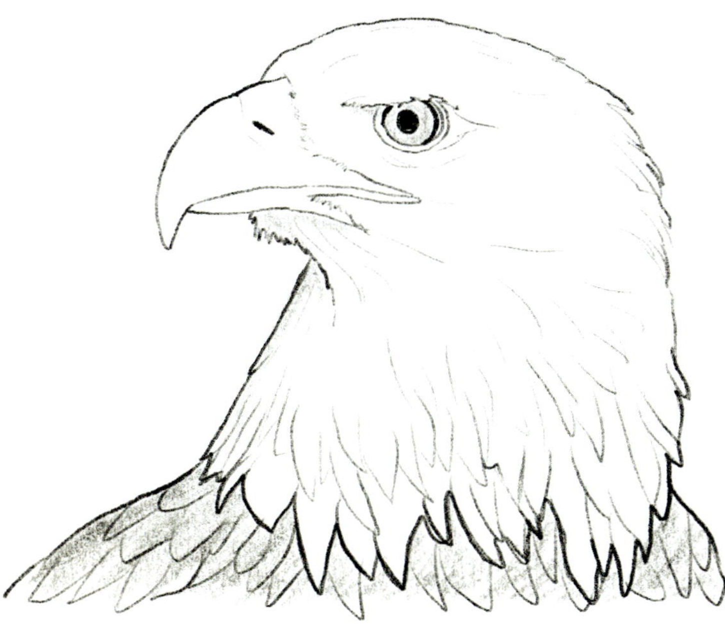

Because there are so few details on the eagle's face, do your best to get the details that *are* there correct. Notice the nostril is angled. There are circles around the eyes. The white feathers around the neck have more detail than those on the face and top of the head.

Reference: Animals

From pets to wild animals and insects to mammals, you can draw just about any animal you'd like once you get the hang of identifying the underlying shapes and lines. Here are a few more you can get inspired to draw.

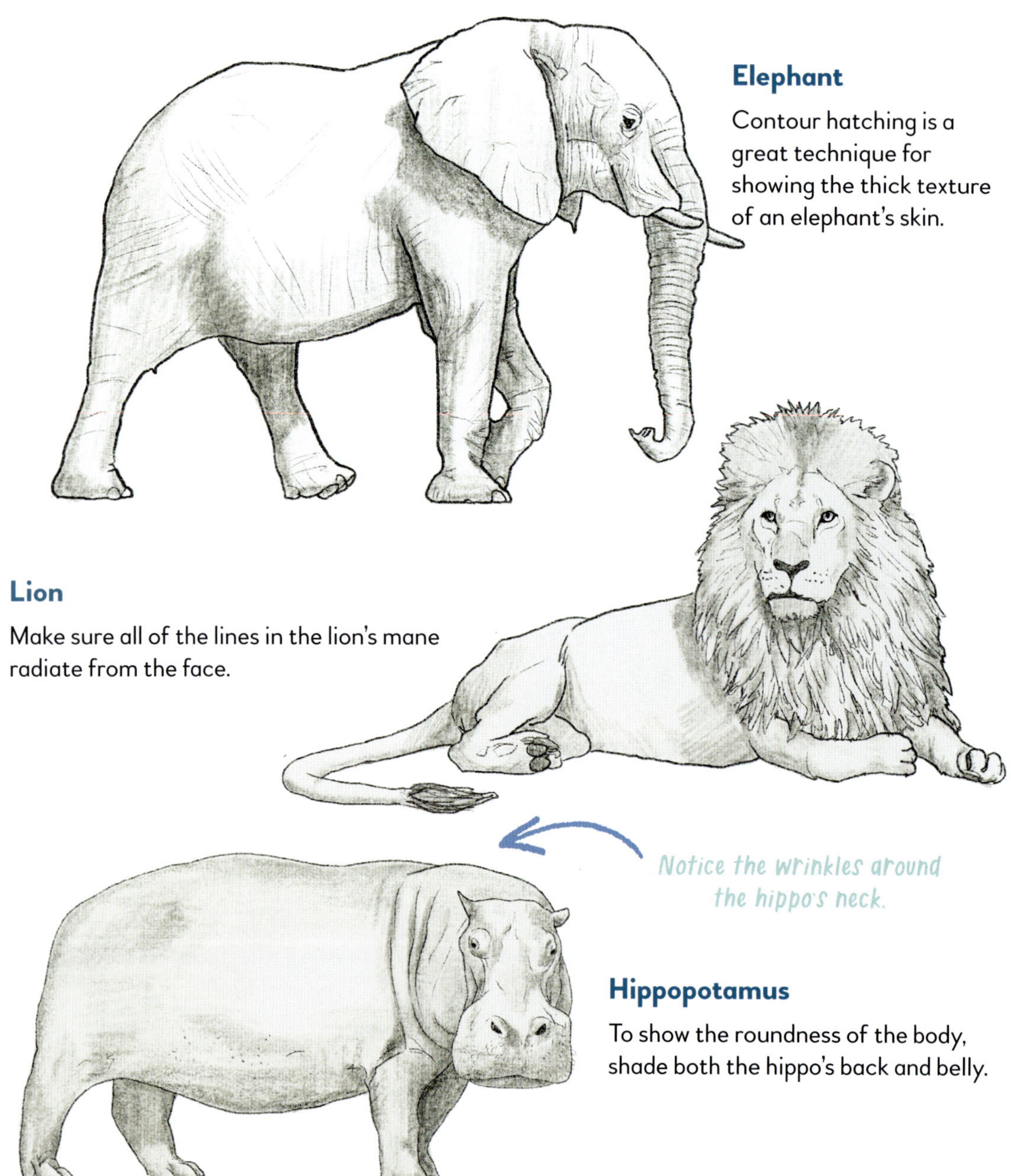

Elephant

Contour hatching is a great technique for showing the thick texture of an elephant's skin.

Lion

Make sure all of the lines in the lion's mane radiate from the face.

Hippopotamus

To show the roundness of the body, shade both the hippo's back and belly.

Hyena

Notice that the hind legs are much shorter than the forelegs.

Giraffe

The giraffe's neck is the same length as its legs.

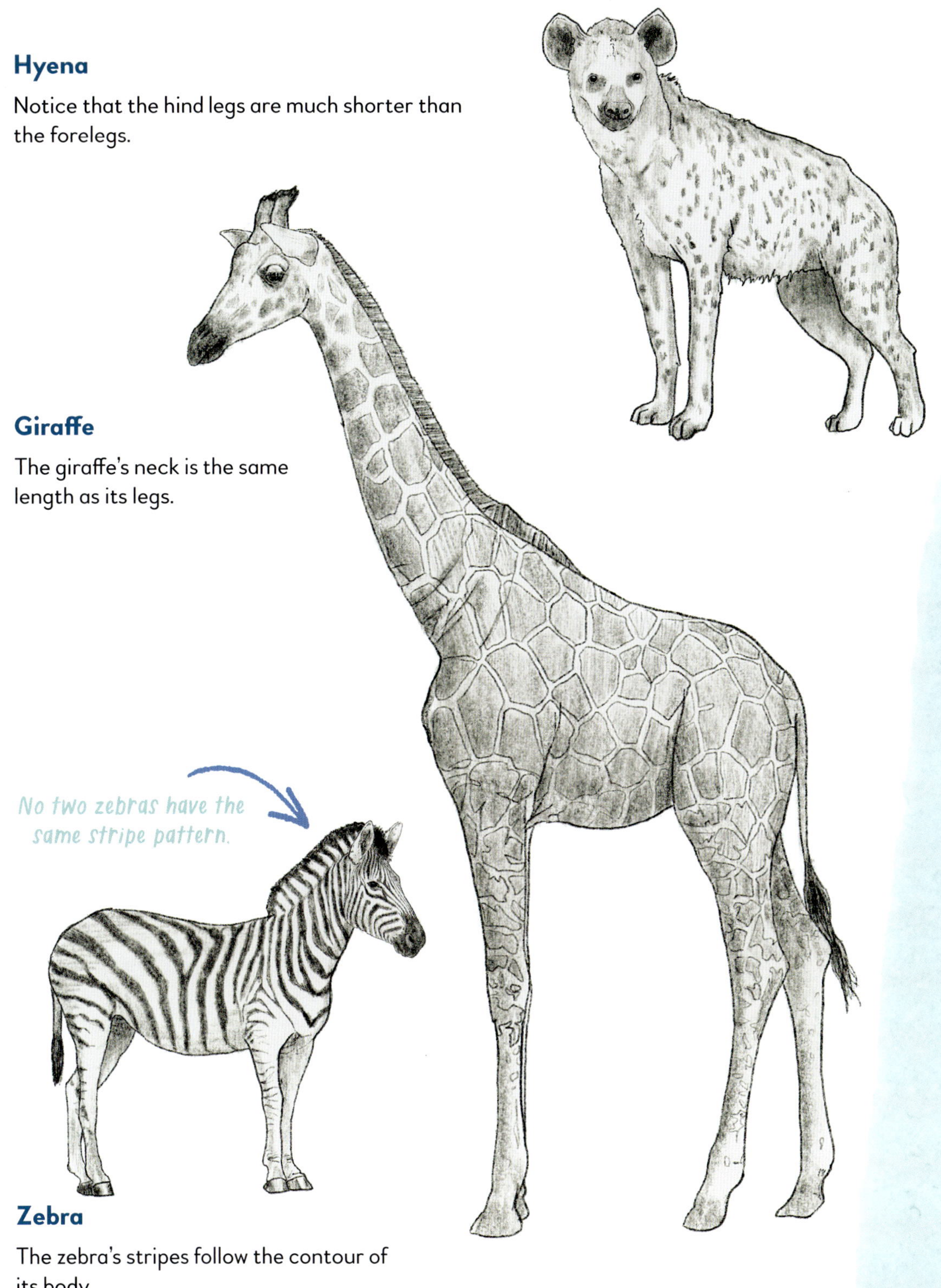

Zebra

The zebra's stripes follow the contour of its body.

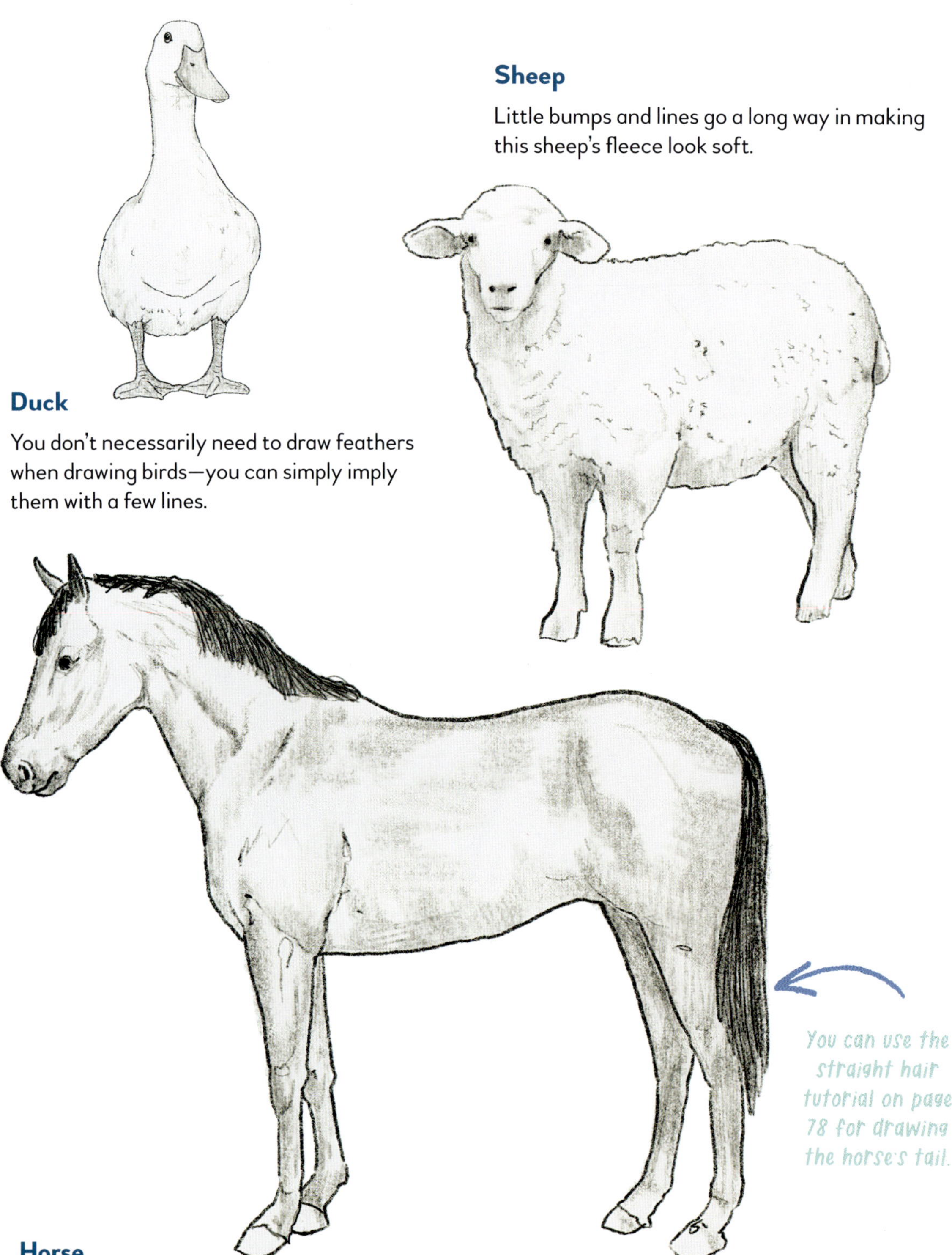

Sheep

Little bumps and lines go a long way in making this sheep's fleece look soft.

Duck

You don't necessarily need to draw feathers when drawing birds—you can simply imply them with a few lines.

Horse

Sharp transitions between light and dark help to make the horse's coat look shiny.

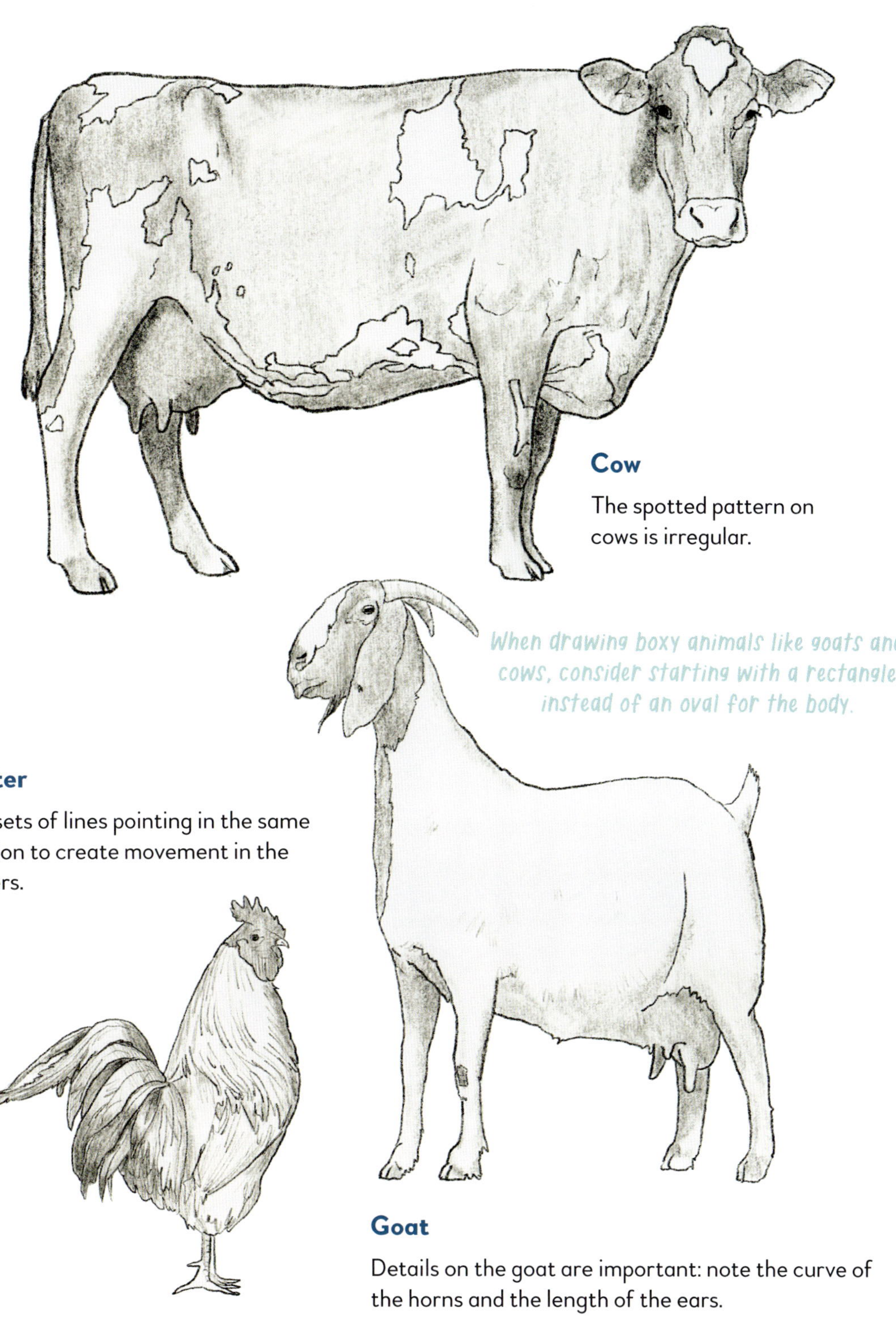

Cow

The spotted pattern on cows is irregular.

Rooster

Draw sets of lines pointing in the same direction to create movement in the feathers.

Goat

Details on the goat are important: note the curve of the horns and the length of the ears.

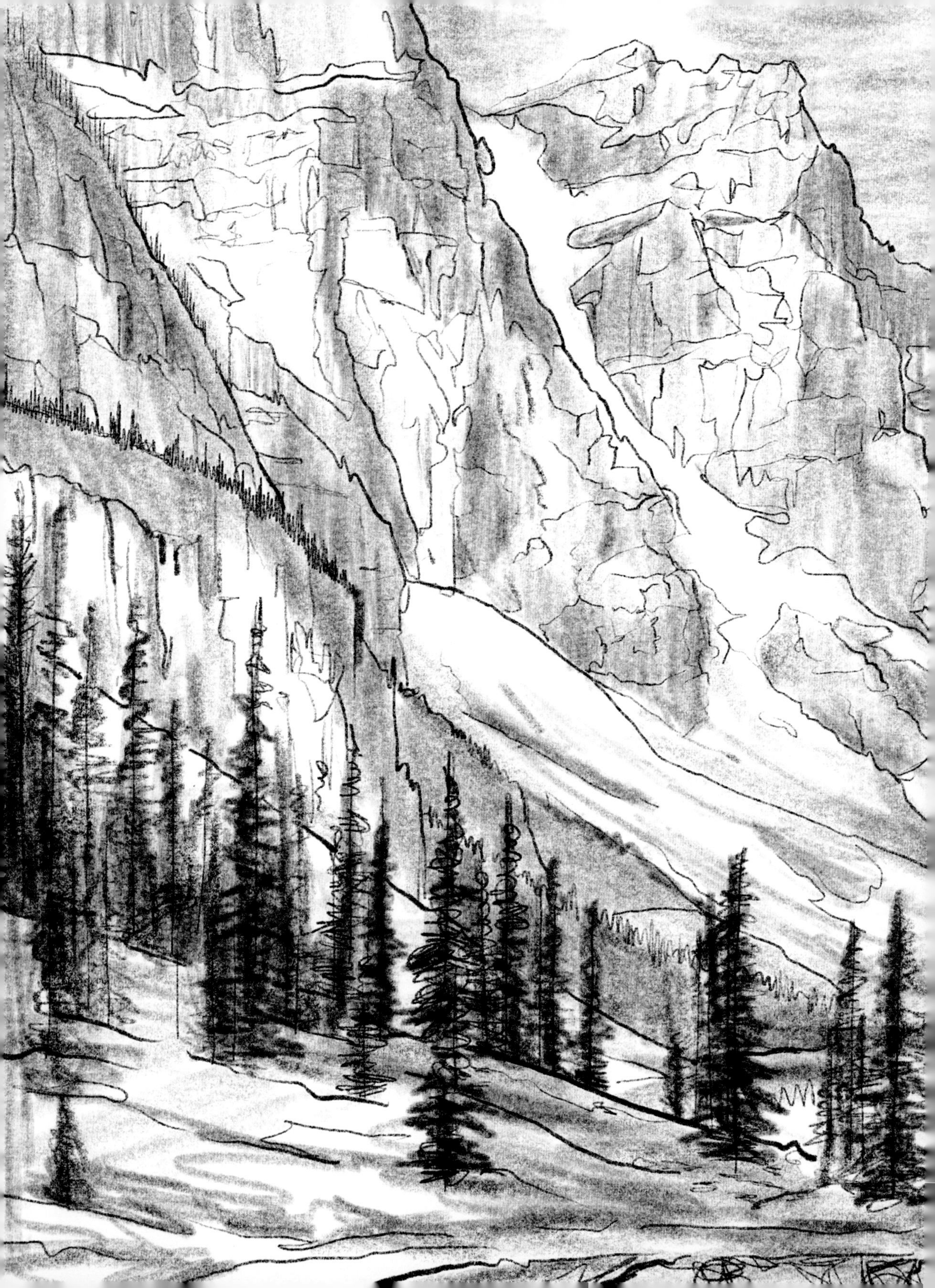

LANDSCAPES

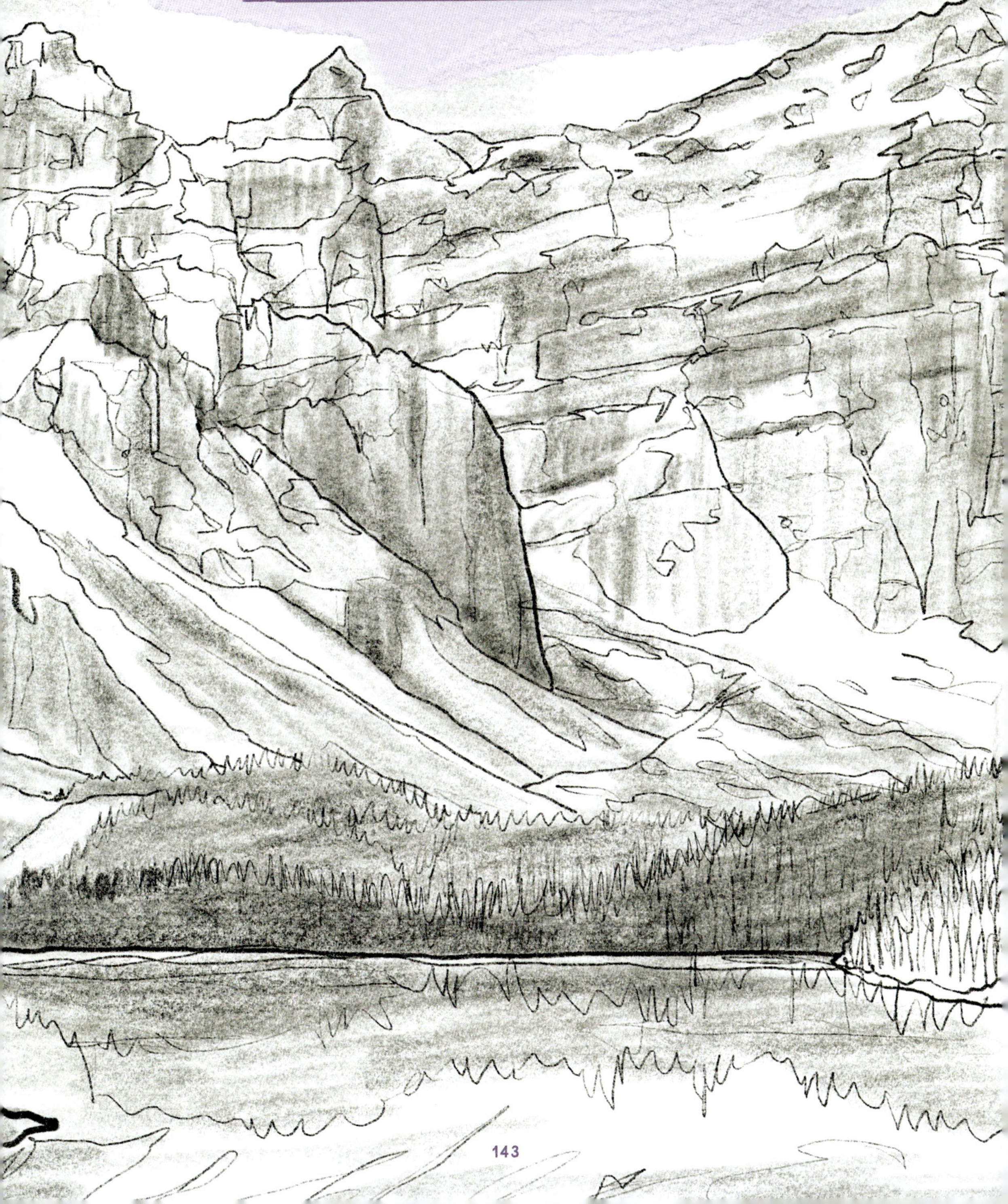

OAK TREE

As artists, we have a special relationship with trees—after all, it's thanks to them that we have the paper we draw on and most of the pencils we use. Generally speaking, the shape of a tree is defined by the shape of its trunk and branches. Let's look at how to draw an oak tree.

The first set of offshoots that extend from the trunk aren't called branches, but rather limbs. Branches are offshoots that extend from those limbs. Limbs are generally thicker than branches.

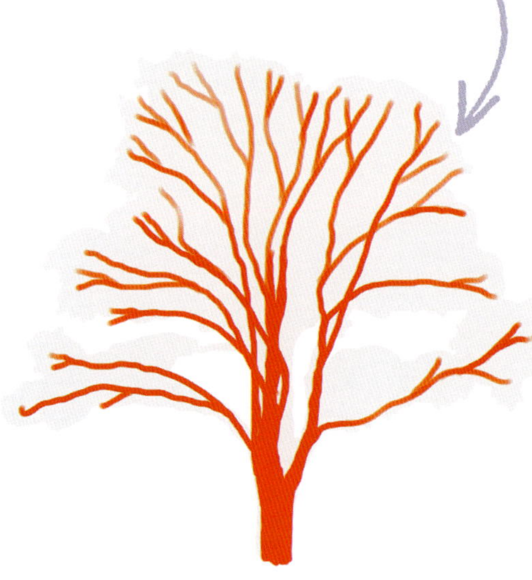

Don't make perfect ovals, and don't be afraid to leave a few gaps, too.

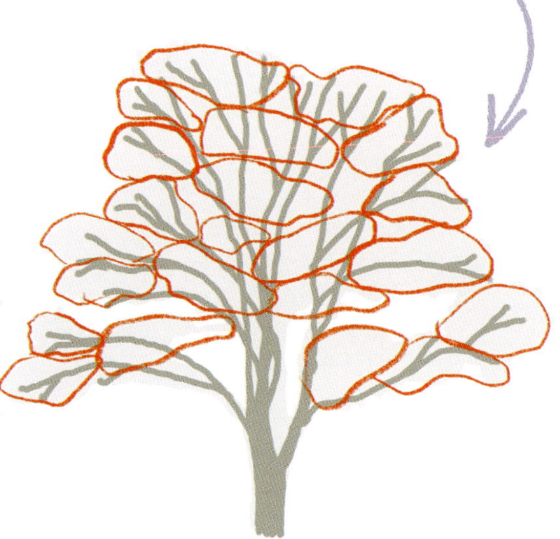

Step 1

Start by drawing a thick line for the trunk. From there, draw various thinner lines upward and to the sides. Then, go back and draw lines coming off those lines to fill your tree with branches.

Step 2

Now, create oval-like shapes along the limbs and branches, beginning just above the trunk and extending to the top of the tree. These indicate clusters of leaves.

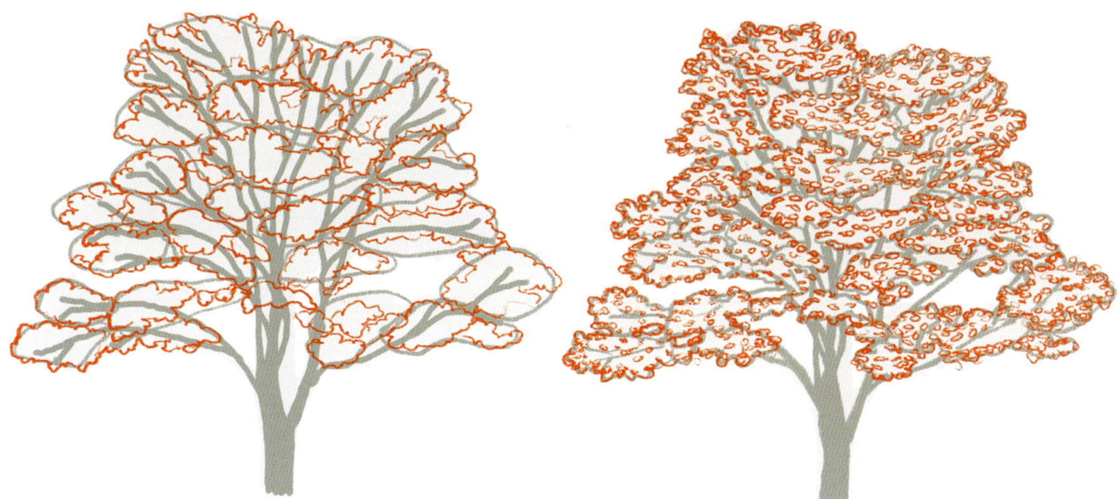

Step 3

Let's define the leaves a bit more. Outline each oval shape with uneven squiggly lines.

Step 4

Within each cluster of leaves, draw several small ovals. These will indicate individual leaves.

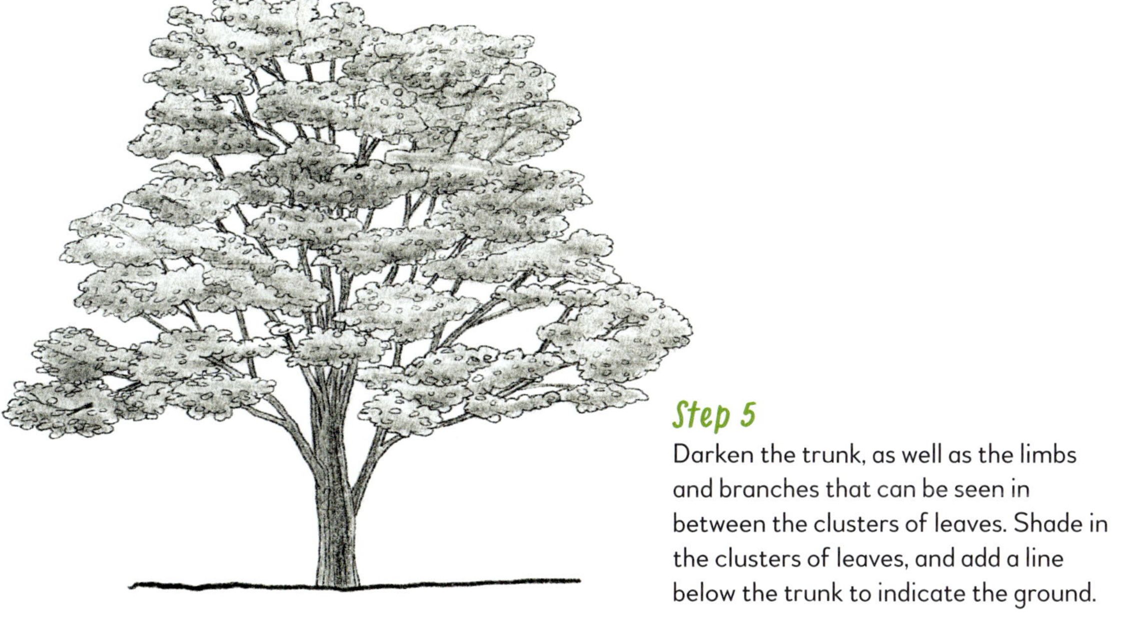

Step 5

Darken the trunk, as well as the limbs and branches that can be seen in between the clusters of leaves. Shade in the clusters of leaves, and add a line below the trunk to indicate the ground.

PALM TREE

A must-have in every tropical landscape, the palm is one of the most beloved trees. It resembles a flower, not only in how it is structured but in how it is drawn. There are many species of palm trees, but let's draw one of the classics.

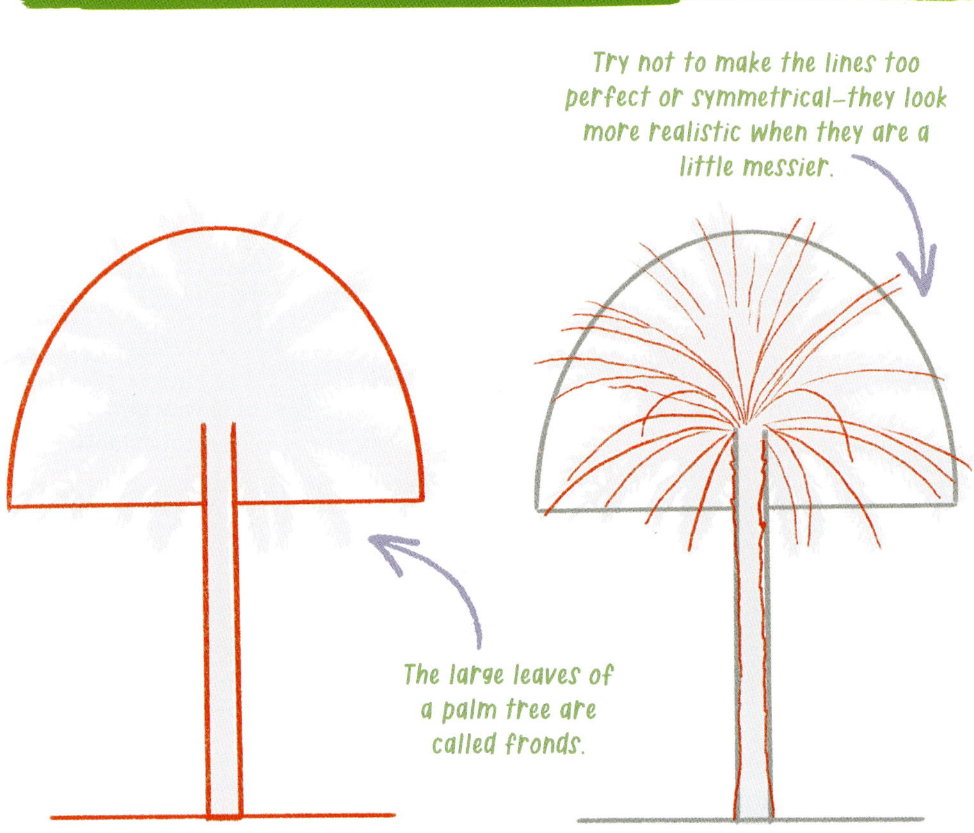

Step 1

Draw a horizontal line toward the bottom of the page for the ground. Draw two vertical lines coming off those lines for the trunk. Now draw a semicircle as a guideline for the leaves.

Step 2

Draw curved lines from the top of the trunk to the edge of the semicircle. Each line will be the middle of a frond.

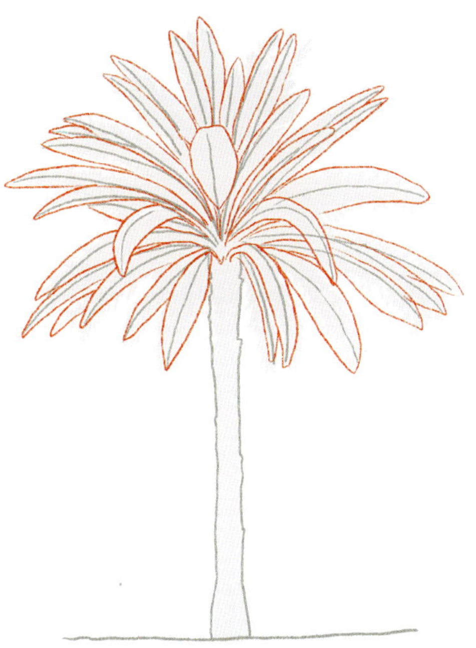

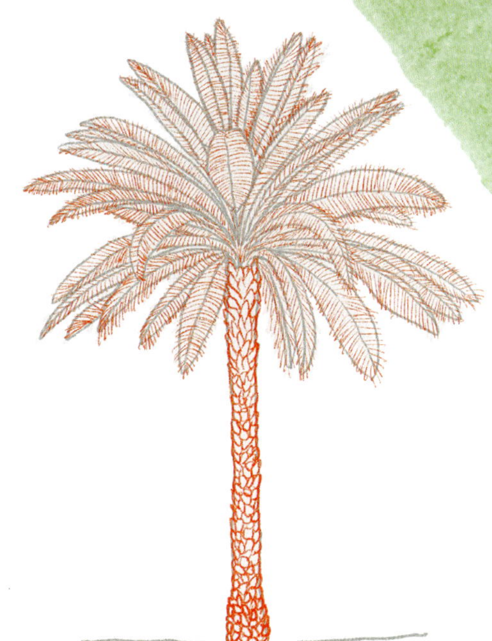

Step 3

Draw a tear shape around each of the frond lines you drew in the last step, making some of them overlap. There are no rules here other than to try to have the fronds all pointing to the middle of the tree.

Step 4

Cover the trunk in little ovals and circles to show texture. For each frond, draw lines from the midline to the outside of the tear shape.

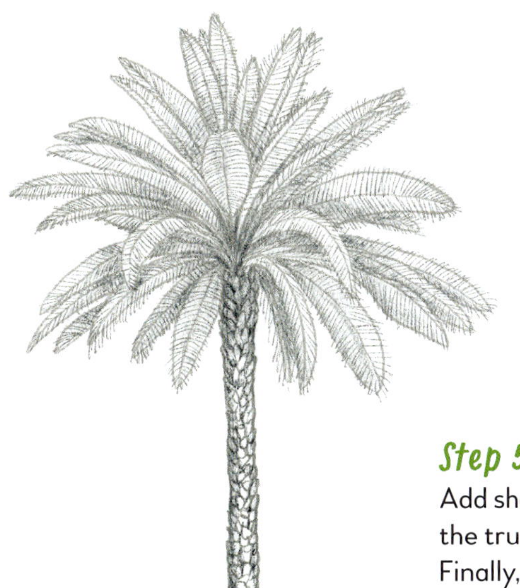

Step 5

Add shading to the sides of the trunk. Leave the center of the trunk light. Add shading to the middle of the palm tree. Finally, very lightly shade each frond on its bottom side.

Reference: Trees

There are more than 70,000 different species of trees on Earth. Here are just a few more from which to draw inspiration.

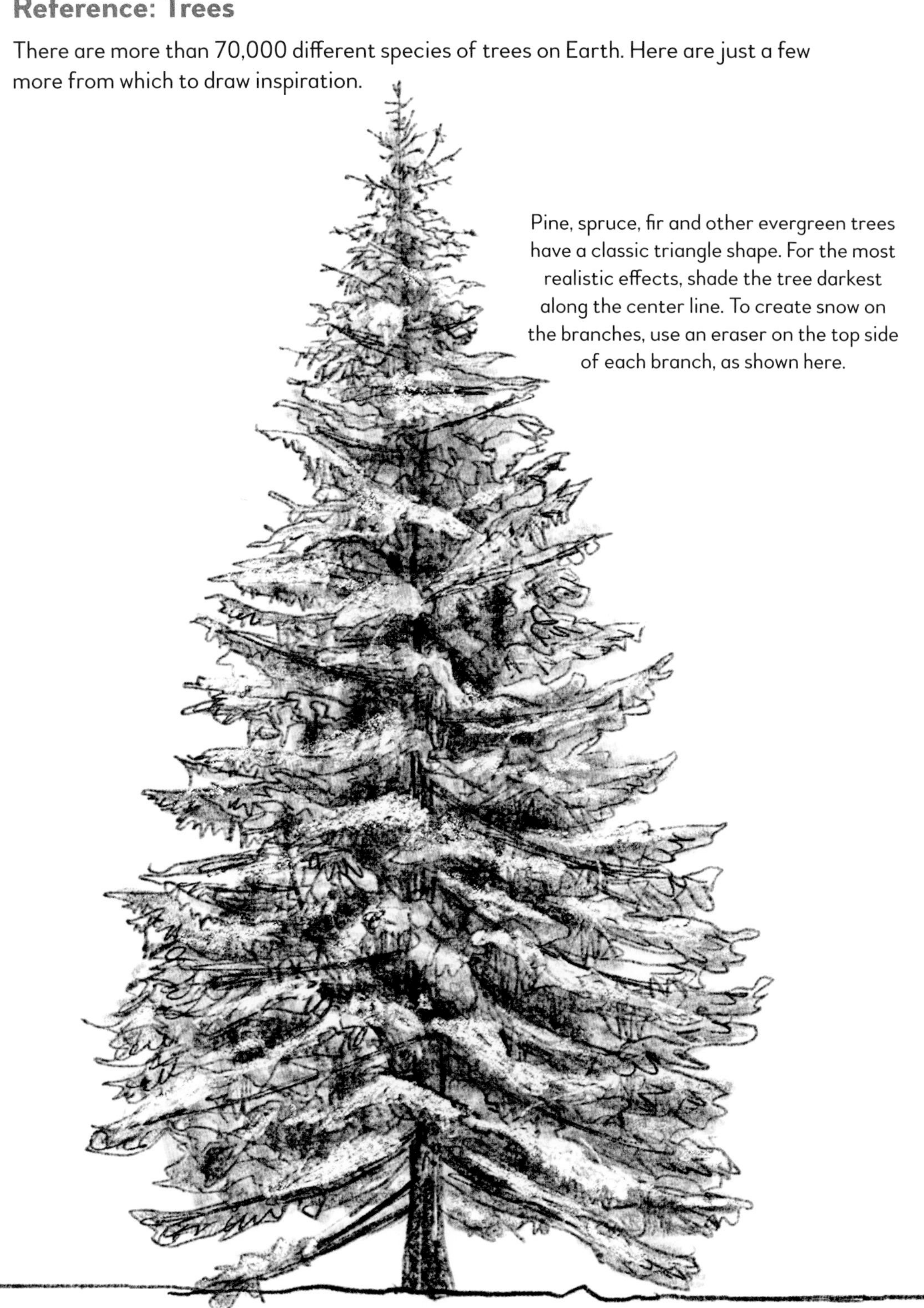

Pine, spruce, fir and other evergreen trees have a classic triangle shape. For the most realistic effects, shade the tree darkest along the center line. To create snow on the branches, use an eraser on the top side of each branch, as shown here.

Weeping willows are defined by their drooping branches and leaves, which can be represented through vertical lines. Those lines give the willow not only form and texture, but also movement. Also note that, unlike other trees, weeping willows are generally asymmetrical.

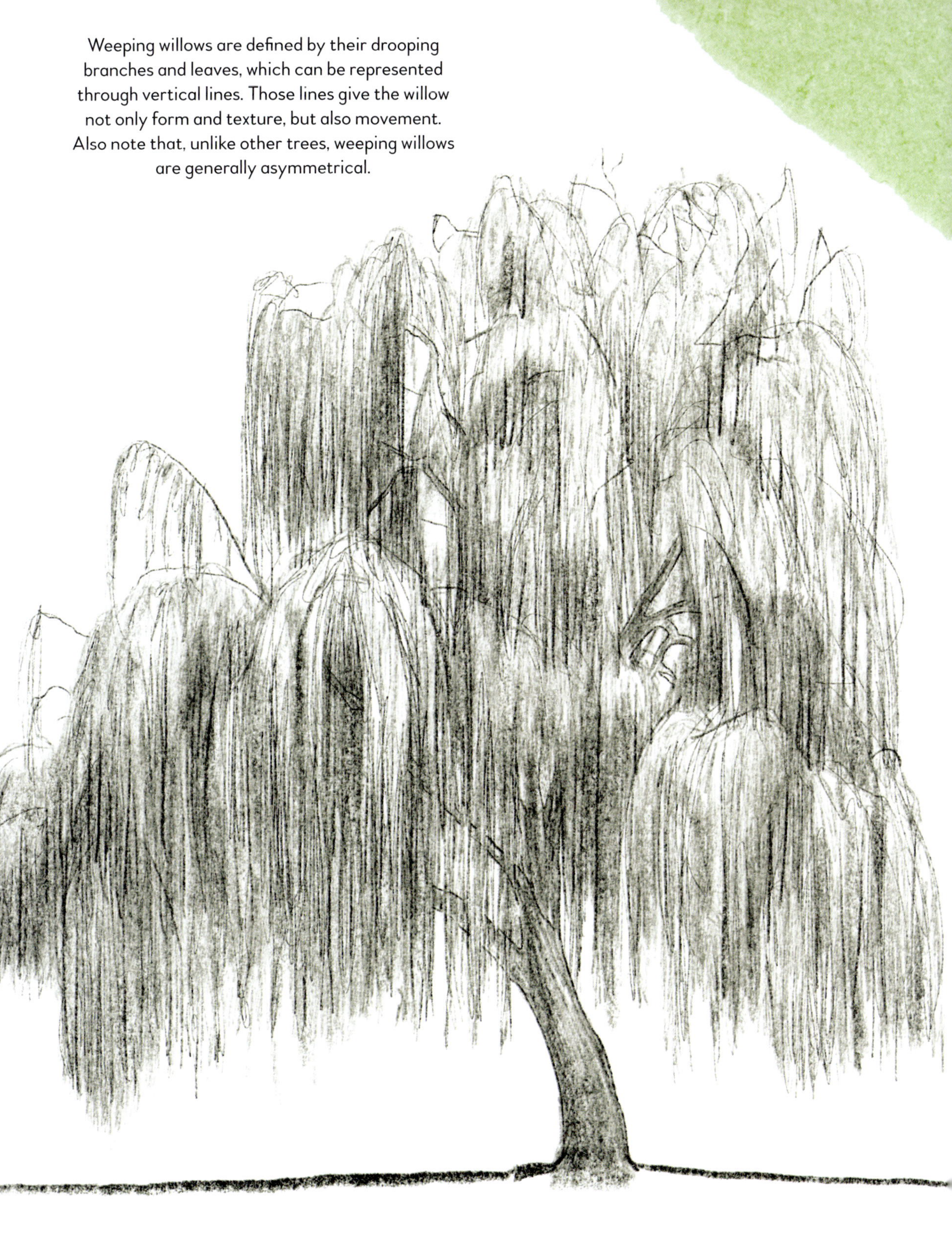

FOREST

Drawing a realistic forest involves placing a few very detailed trees in the foreground and many, *many* less detailed other ones in the background. In this particular forest, we start with a shaded page and erase away certain areas. This is an example of subtractive drawing.

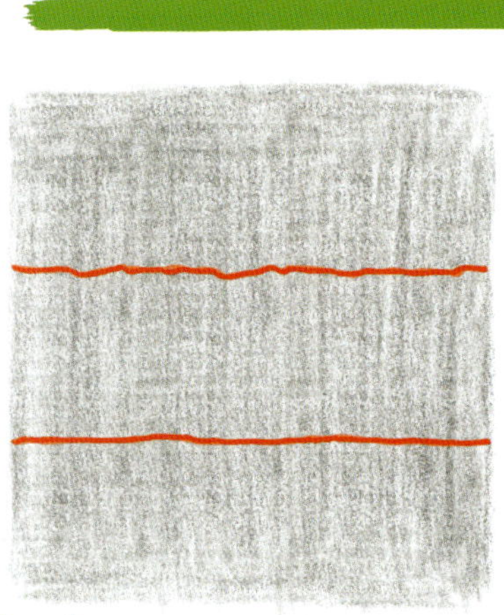

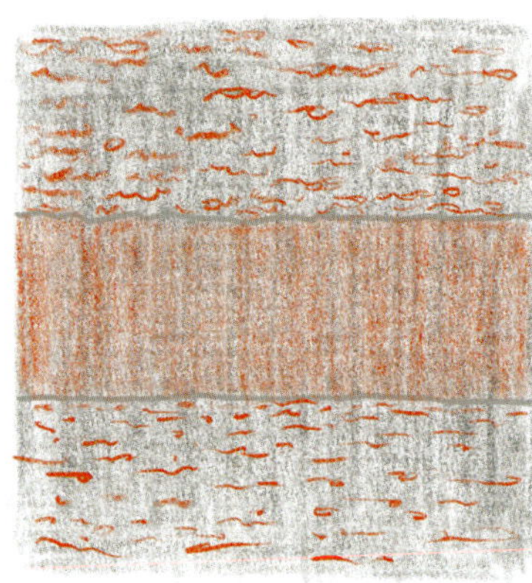

Step 1

With the side of your pencil, lightly shade your entire page. Next, draw two horizontal lines across the shaded area. Make the top line slightly uneven to represent clusters of leaves.

Step 2

Shade in the area between the two horizontal lines. Draw squiggly lines across the bottom and top thirds of your drawing. Add oval-like shapes in the top third to indicate leaves.

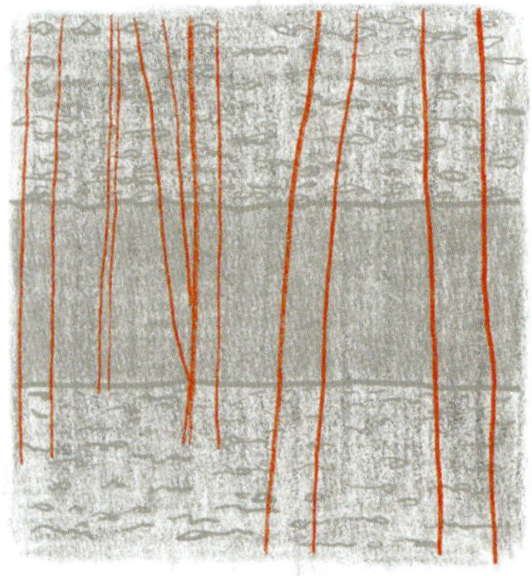

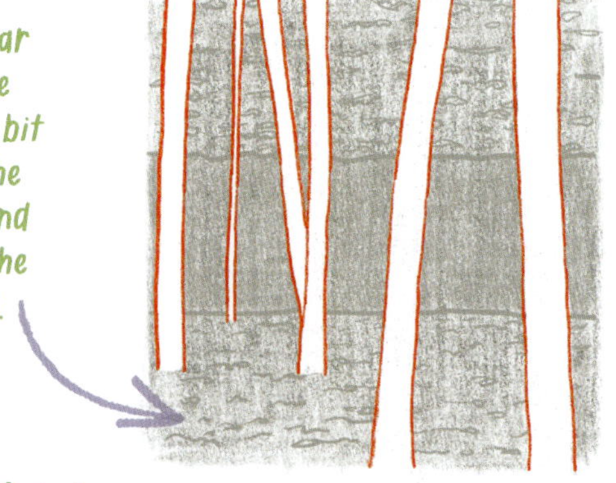

Step 3

Draw a few sets of parallel lines extending up from the bottom of your page. These will be tree trunks in the foreground. Draw a few narrower ones extending up from the bottom third—those will be trees in the midground.

Step 4

Get out your erasers! (No, you haven't made a mistake.) Erase the shading in between the parallel lines to make this into a forest of birch trees with white bark.

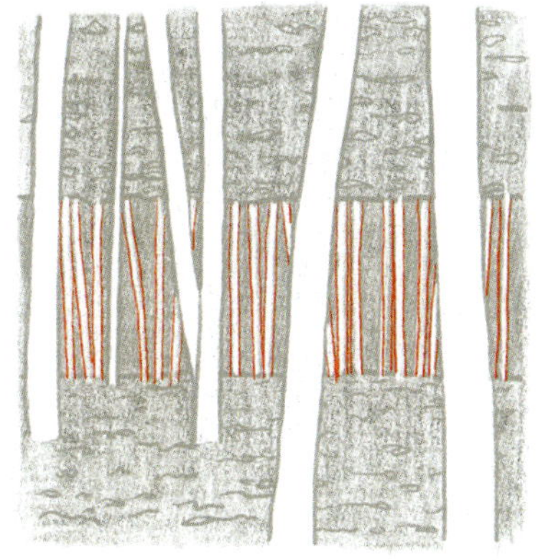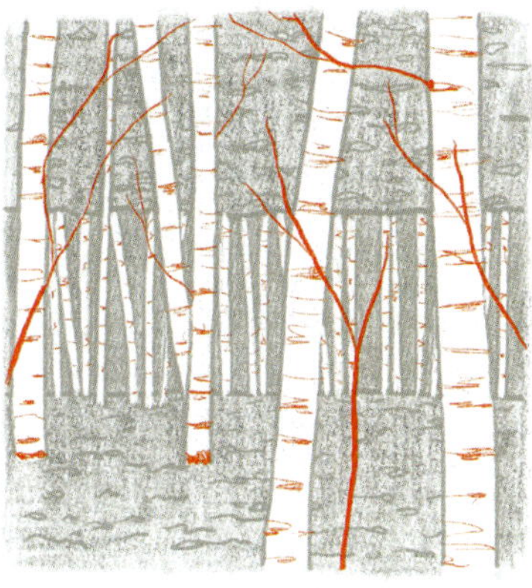

Step 5

Draw another series of even narrower parallel lines in the middle third of your drawing, and, again, erase the shading in between each set of lines. These trees are in the background.

Step 6

Add horizontal lines up and down the trunks of the trees. Throughout the forest, make a series of Y shapes to indicate branches and twigs.

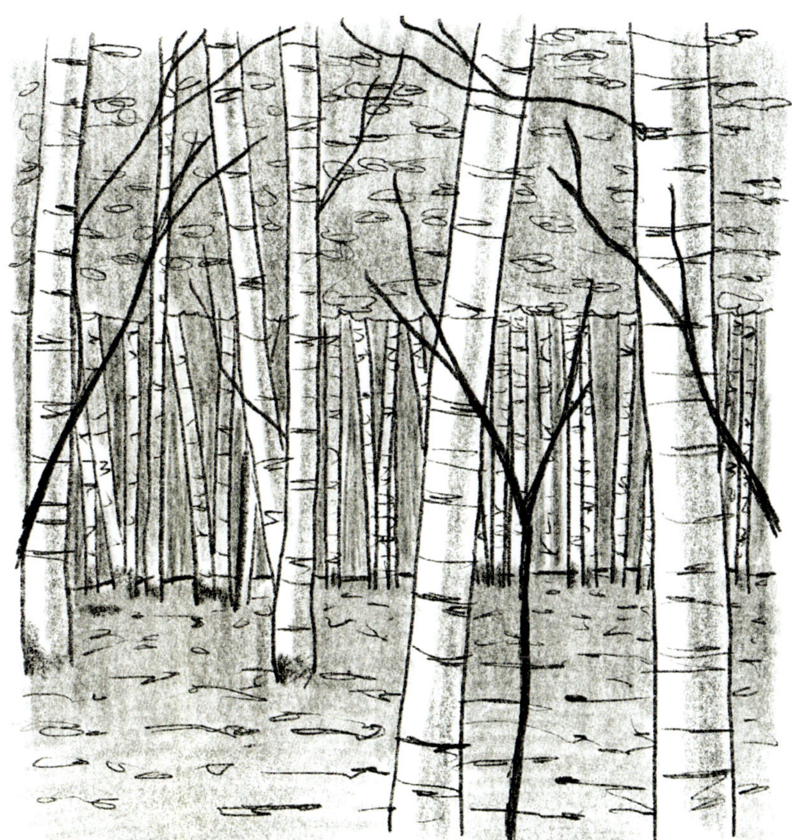

Step 7

Add more shading in between the trees in the background. If you'd like to add more leaves to the trees, this is the time. You can also add more leaves to the ground.

MOUNTAINS

When most people picture mountains, they picture giant, rocky triangles. But mountains can also take on diamond, hourglass and inverted pyramid shapes. Below, let's look at a mountain range with broad peaks and not-so-sharp slopes.

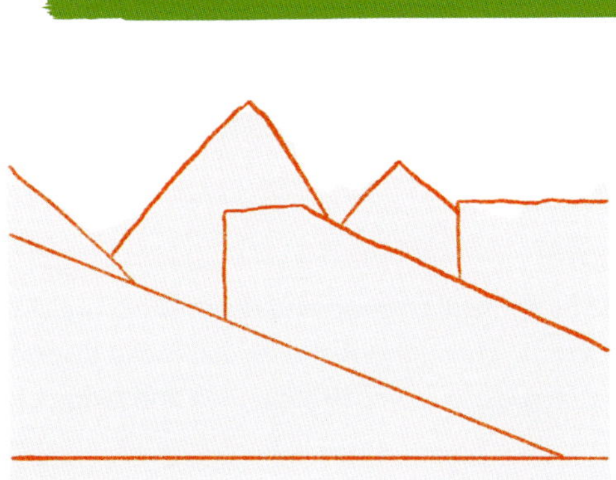

Step 1

Draw a line across the bottom of your page. Everything below that is ground level. Halfway up the left side of your page, draw a diagonal line down to make a large triangle. This will be a mountain in the foreground. Now, fill the page with overlapping triangles, rectangles and other four-sided shapes.

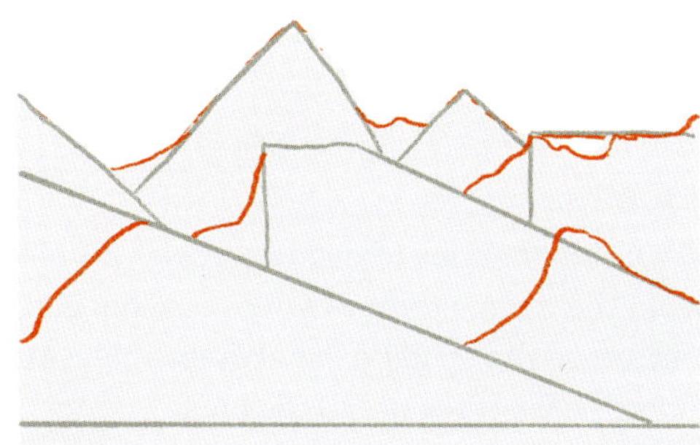

Step 2

Add more peaks and ridges to your mountain range by drawing slightly curved lines in between your shapes.

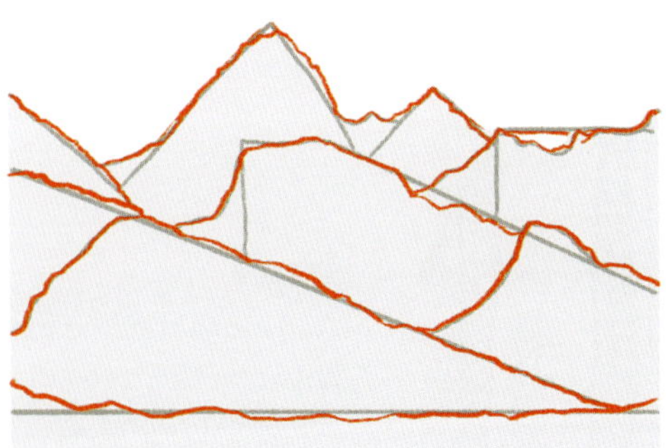

Step 3

Mountain terrain is rugged, not smooth, so using uneven lines, loosely retrace the lines that are in place.

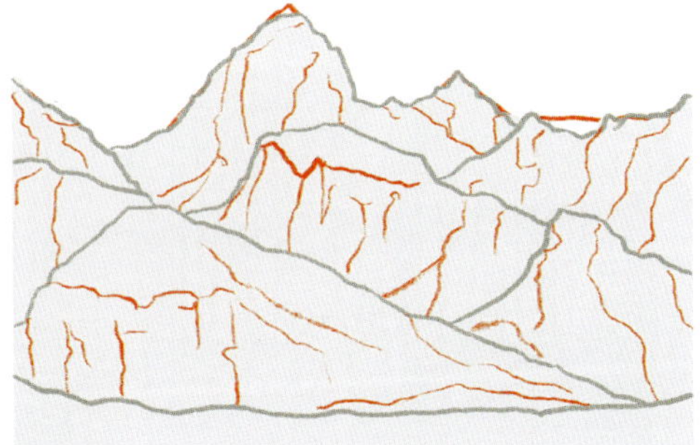

Step 4

Draw more uneven lines—a few horizontal ones below the peaks to represent flatter landings and vertical ones extending down from those to create different slopes.

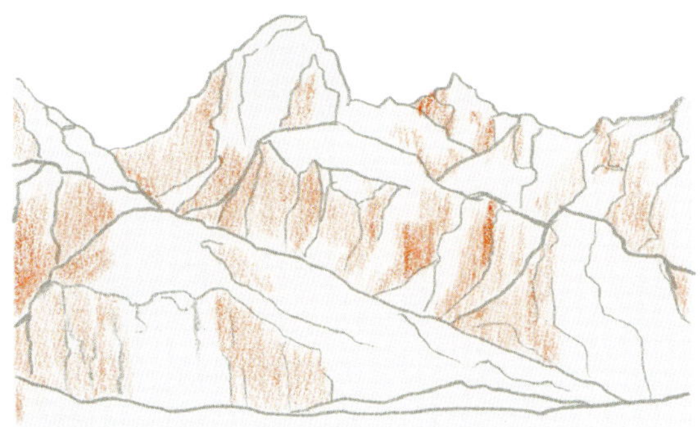

Step 5

Using the side of your pencil, shade in most of the slopes, leaving a few unshaded to imply they're in direct sunlight.

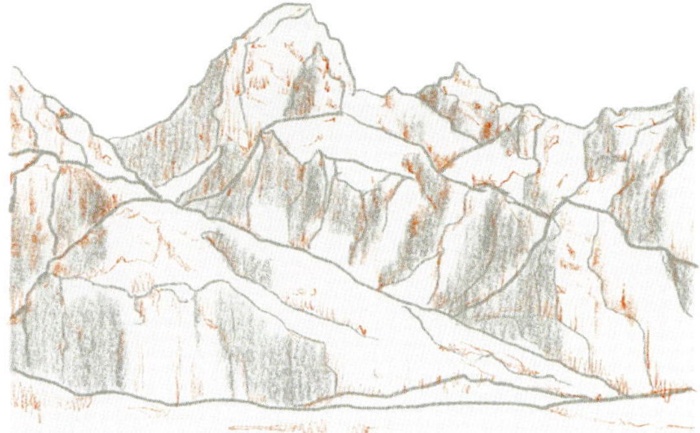

Step 6

Let's add some more texture to the mountains. Make a series of short lines along the slopes and some scribbles in the flatter areas.

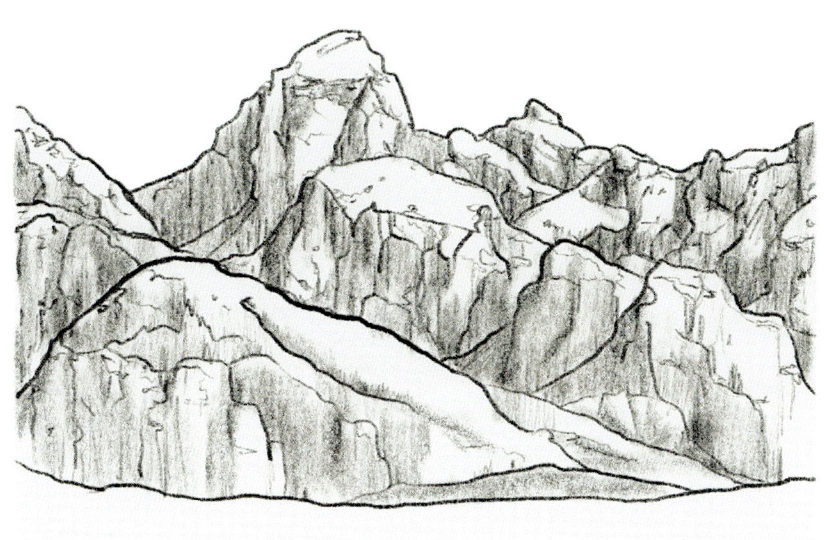

Step 7

Add more shading to some of the slopes of the mountains—leave others partially shaded or not shaded at all. Also leave the peaks and flatter surfaces free of shading, as they'll be in full light.

CLOUDS

No landscape would be complete without a few well-placed clouds in the sky. In addition to adding to the mood of a landscape, clouds can be a great way to add visual weight and create movement in your drawings (refer to page 168 for tips on composition).

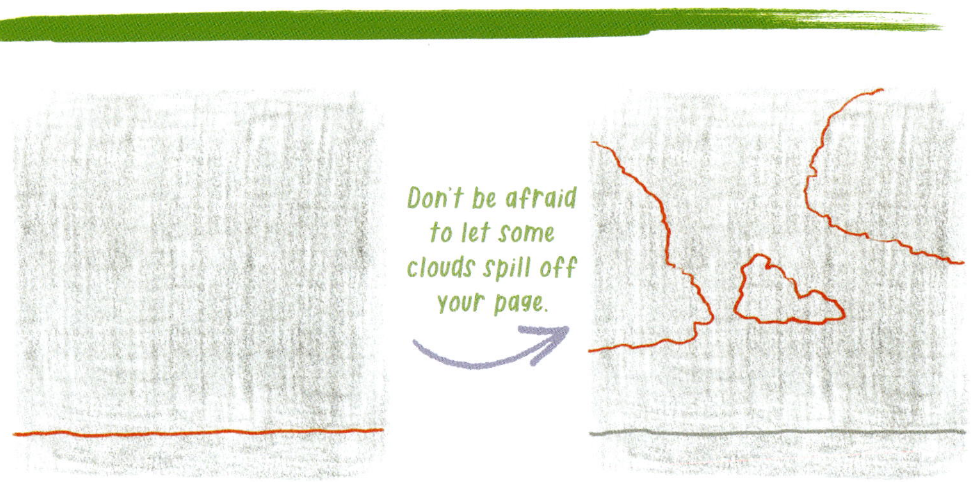

Step 1

With the side of your pencil, lightly shade your entire page. Now draw a horizontal line across the bottom of your drawing. This will be the horizon line.

Step 2

Outline a few main clouds across your page using bumpy lines. Play with different sized shapes—no two clouds are alike, so flex your creativity here.

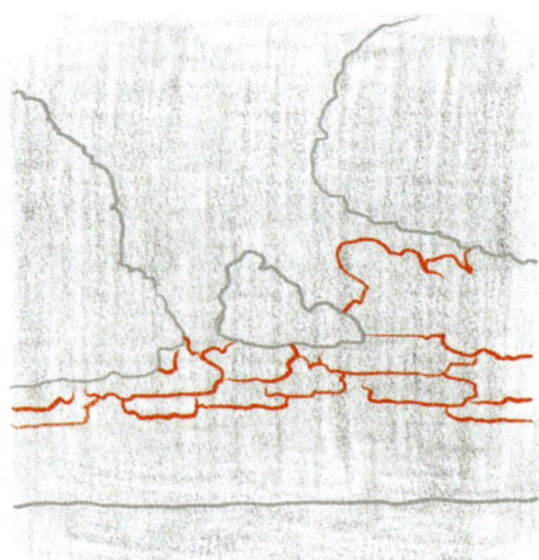

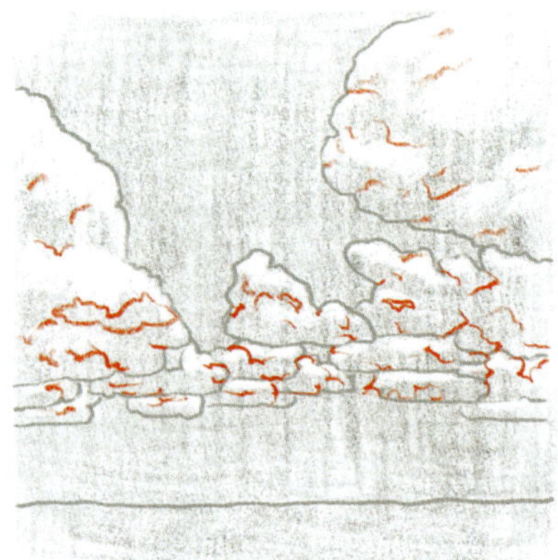

Step 3

Add more cloud outlines in the midground and background, making them smaller as they fall into the distance.

Step 4

Add some short squiggly lines within the outlines for clumps. Next, erase the areas above the squiggly lines to create highlights.

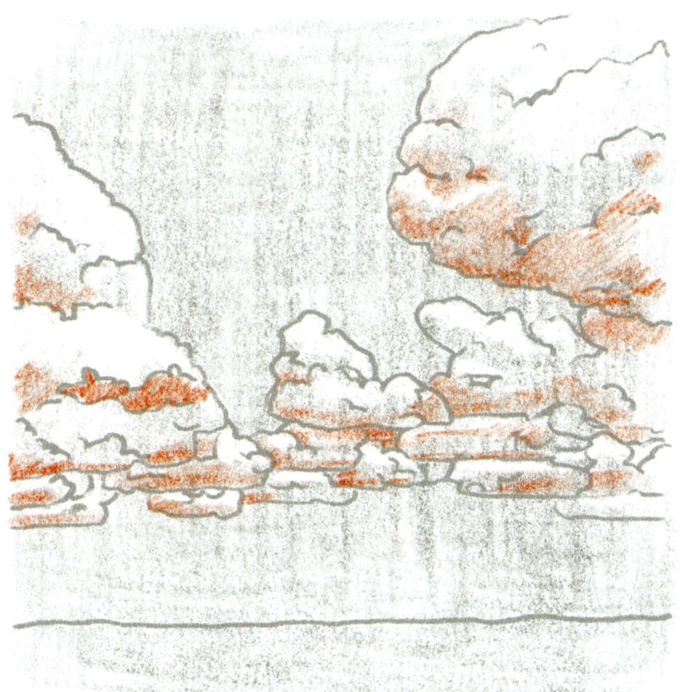

Shade along the bottom of the clouds and some of the clumps.

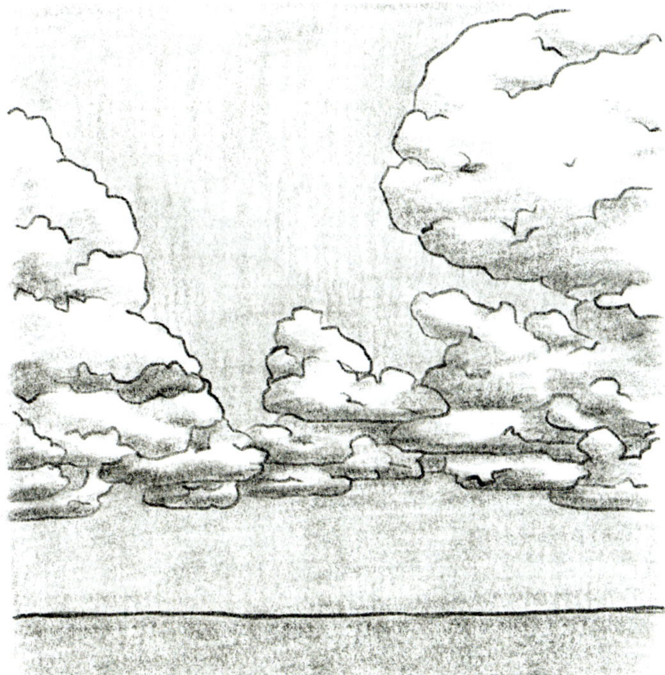

Make those clouds white! Grab your eraser again, and erase the shading at the tops of the clouds.

WAVES

Popularized by the Japanese printer and printmaker Katsushika Hokusai, the image of the giant wave has become a classic of art history. Shading is the trick to drawing waves: alternate between light and dark areas to create the illusion of depth.

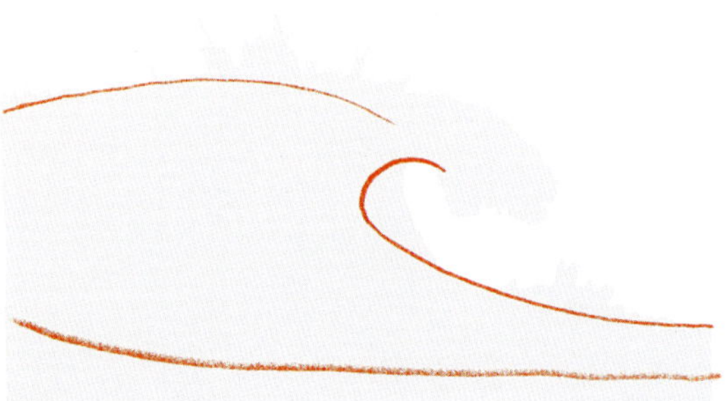

Step 1

For the inside of the wave, draw a C shape with a long tail. For the crest of the wave, draw a curved line. The bottom is a straight line with a slight curve on the left side.

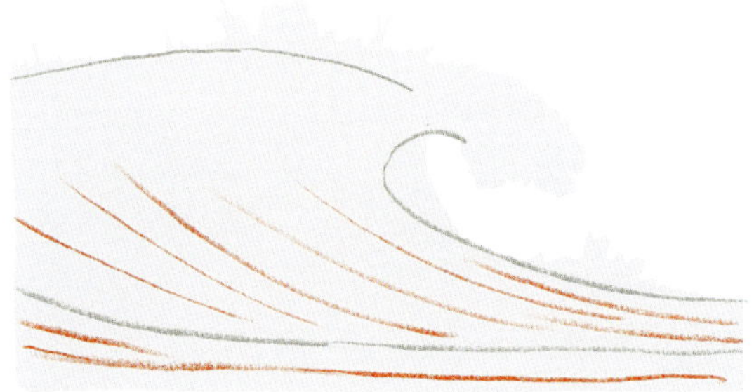

Step 2

Add a set of wispy, diagonal curved lines inside the shape you've made, leaving some clear space at the top.

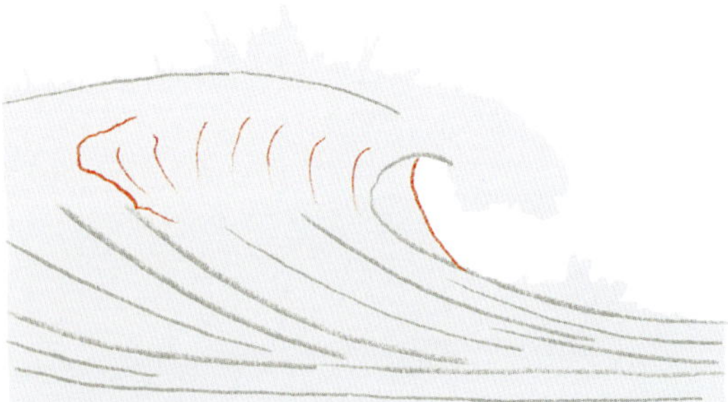

Step 3

Add a smaller set of wisps above those, extending nearly to the crest of the wave.

Add another crashing wave in the backdrop if you'd like.

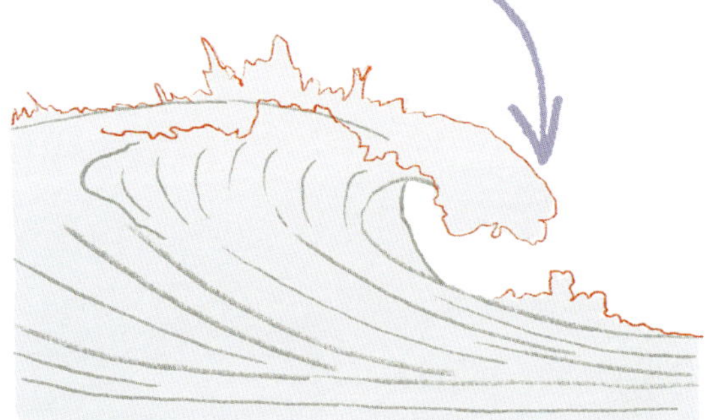

Step 4

Let loose! Draw some squiggly lines along the crest of the wave, adding a few peaks throughout. Straighten things out a bit toward the front of the crest, and continue the squiggly lines back the other way.

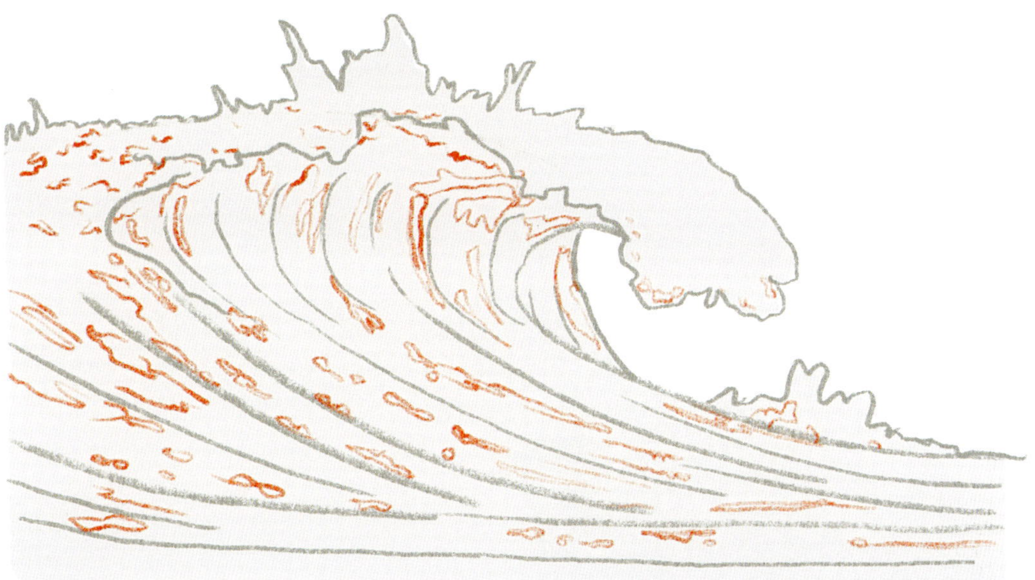

Step 5

This part isn't an exact science, so have some fun with it. Following the direction of the lines you've made inside the wave, make oval-like shapes throughout and smaller squiggles toward the top.

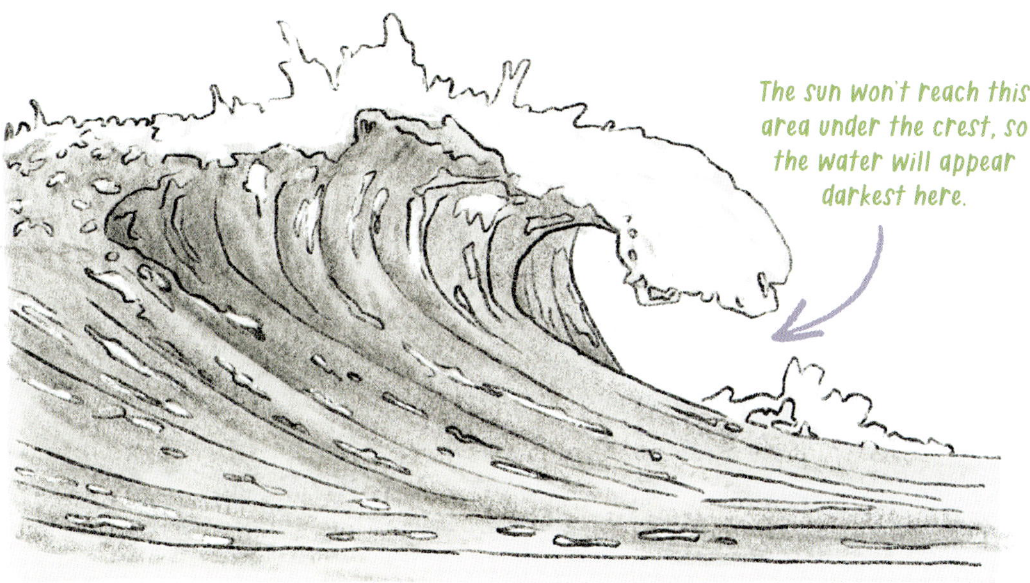

Step 6

Time to shade. Darken everything except the top of the crest and the inside of the oval-like shapes.

STILL LIFES

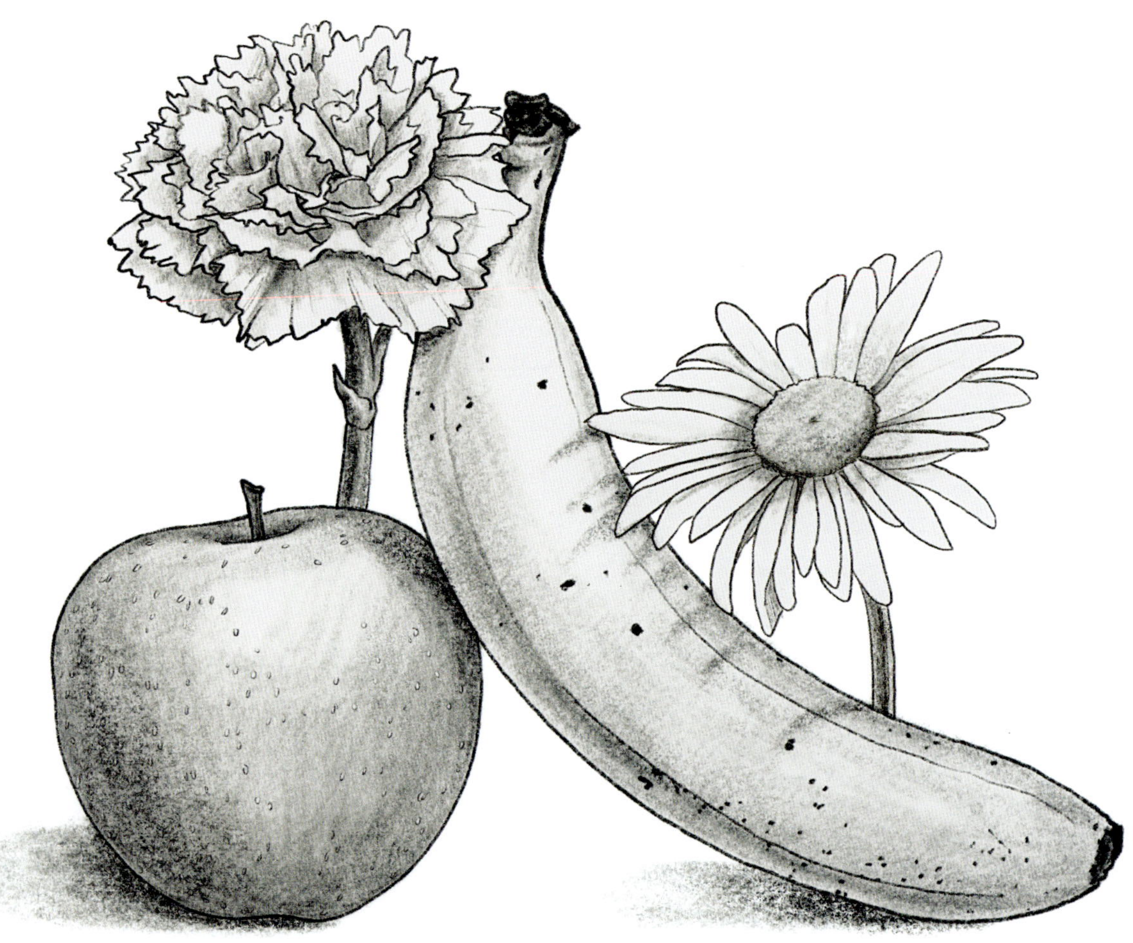

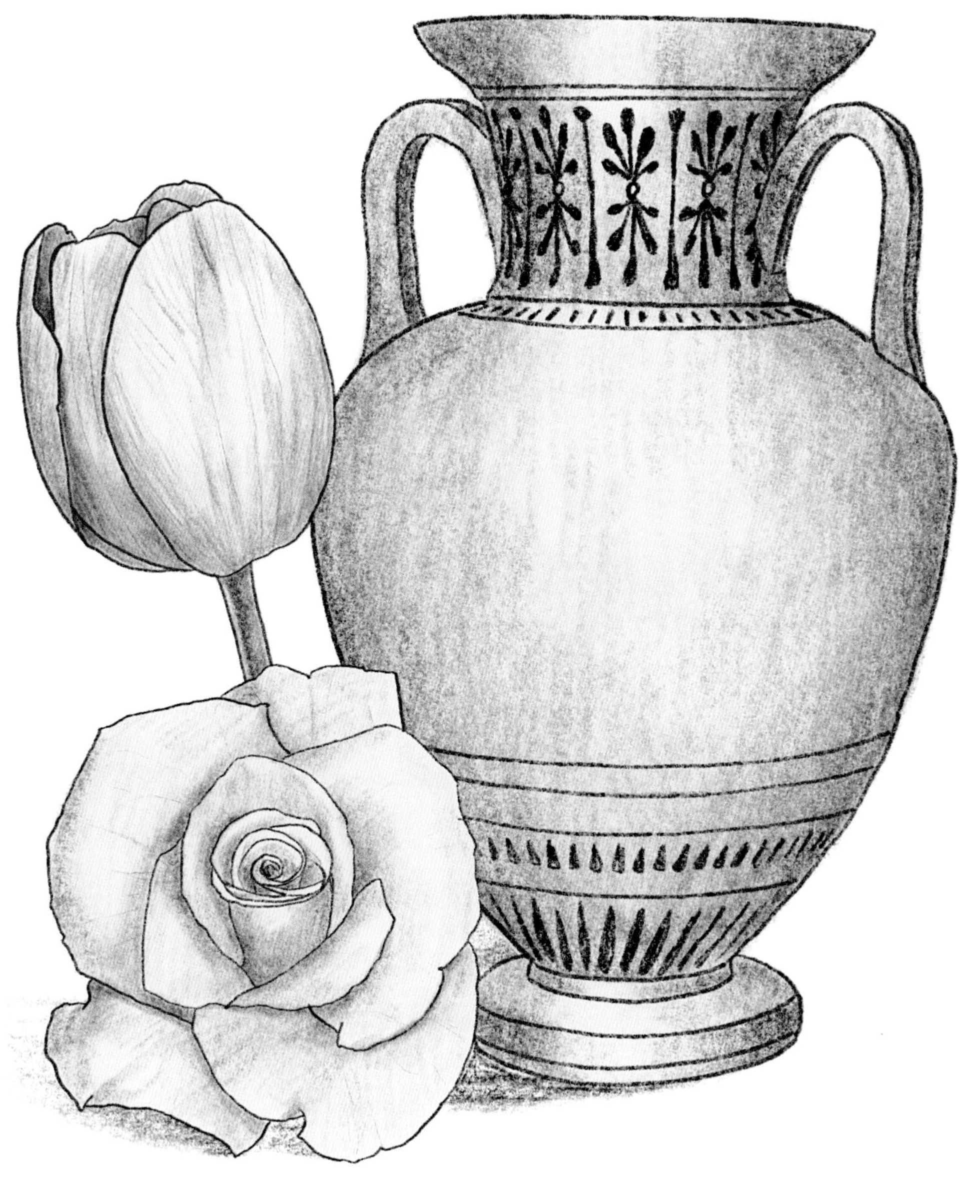

FRUIT

Fruit is an essential feature of still life drawing—and as a result, art education. Most fruits have simple underlying shapes. Once you get the hang of identifying those shapes, the rest of the details will fall into place.

Banana

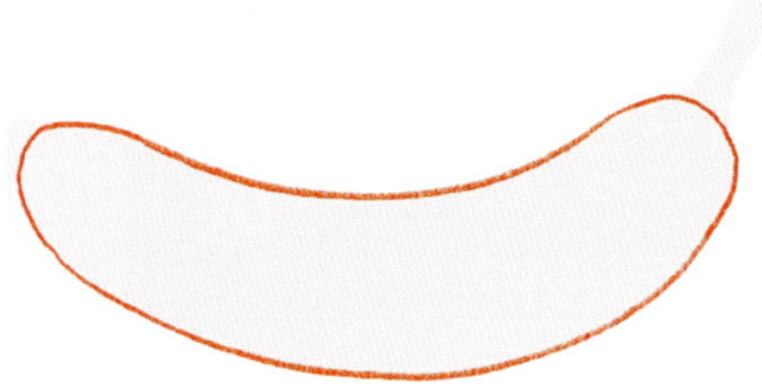

Step 1

Draw a long bean shape.

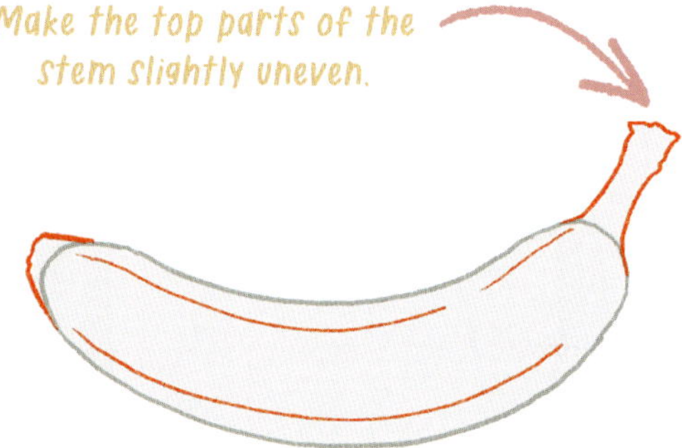

Step 2

Add a rectangular stem to the top, and add a small U shape to the bottom. Draw a few lines down the sides of the banana.

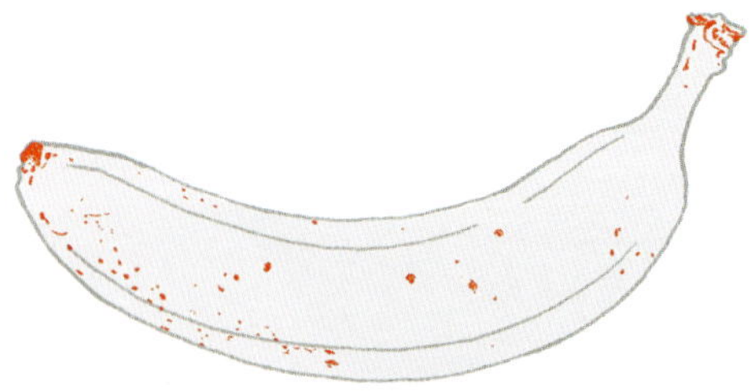

Step 3

Darken the tip of the stem and the bottom of the banana. Add spots of varying sizes across the banana.

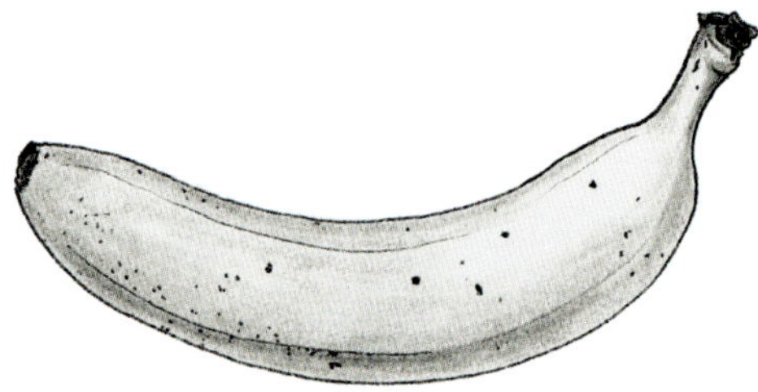

Step 4

Further darken the tip of the stem and the bottom of the banana. Shade the middle of the banana lightly, the short side a bit more and the long side the darkest.

Apple

Step 1

Draw a large circle.

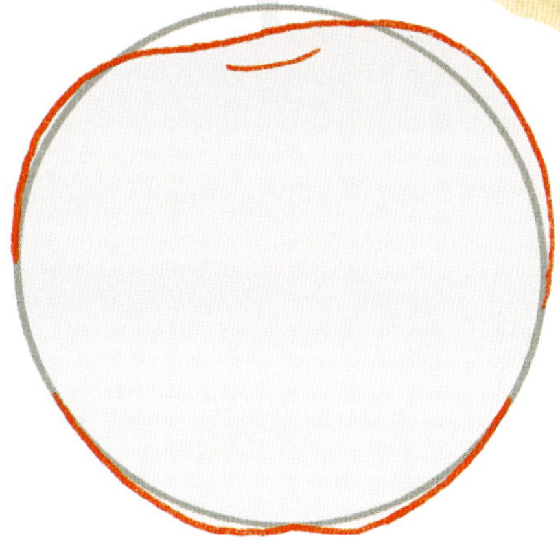

Step 2

Flatten the top slightly, and draw a small indentation at the bottom. Add a small line near the top where the stem will go.

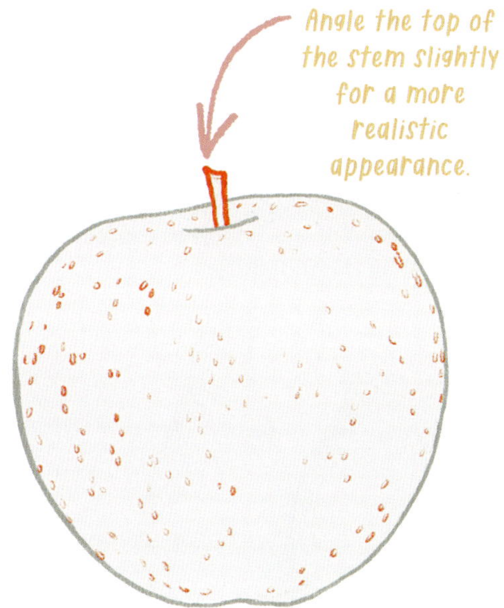

Step 3

Erase your guidelines. Draw a small stem at the top. Add small circles across the apple for details.

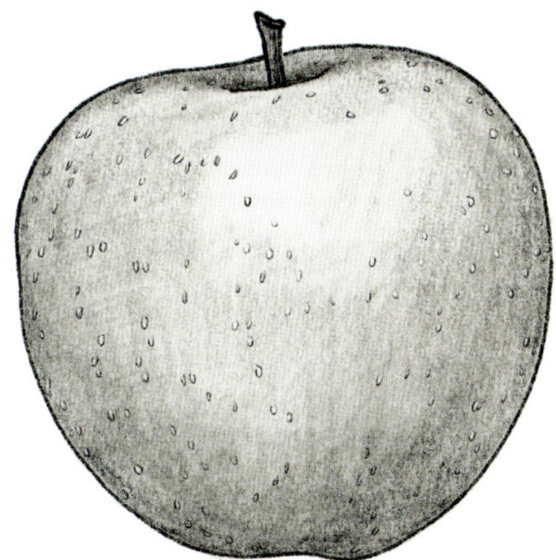

Step 4

Shade along the top, bottom and sides of the apple. Leave a highlight just above the middle of the apple.

VASES

Another classic feature of a still life drawing is the vase. Vases come in many shapes and sizes, and can be plain or detailed, smooth or textured, matte or shiny. Once you get a handle on drawing them, flip to page 164 to learn how to fill them up with flowers.

Let's draw two differently shaped vases side by side.

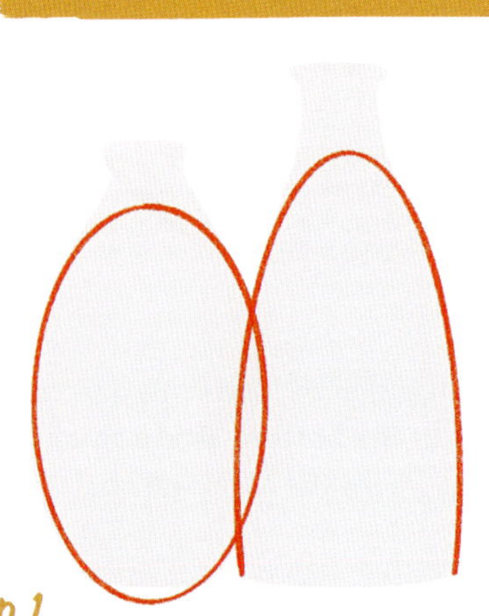

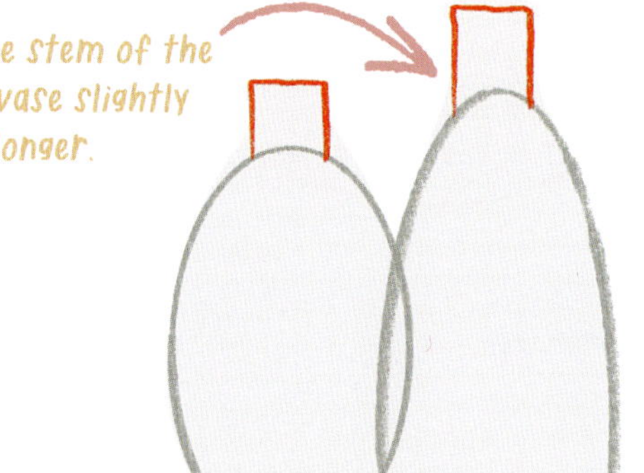

Step 1

Draw an oval. Next to it, draw the top half of a bigger oval. Let the vases overlap slightly.

Step 2

Draw three sides of a rectangle at the top of both ovals. These will be the stems. Add lines at the bottom of both ovals to represent the base. Curve them slightly.

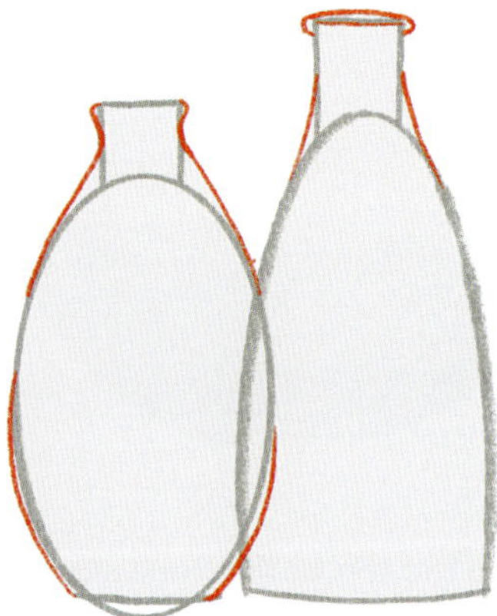

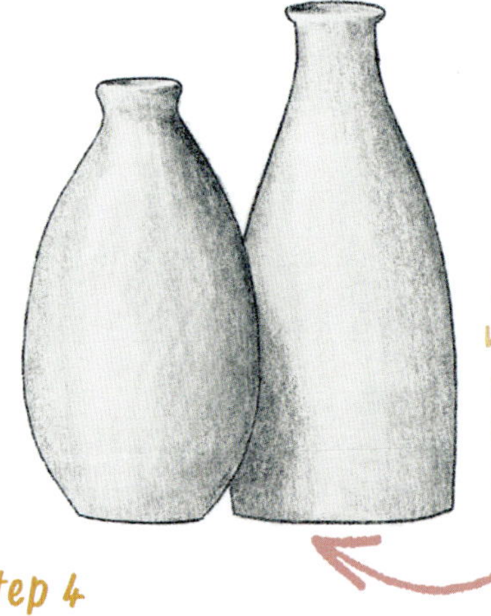

Step 3

Use rounded lines to connect the stems to the ovals. Also, add a small curved line at the top of the stems. These rims will give the vases a more realistic feel.

Step 4

The light source is up and to the left here, so shade on the right sides of both vases. Add a cast shadow on the lower left side of the right vase.

Play with different underlying shapes to create a range of vases. You don't even need to add flowers for them to be beautiful.

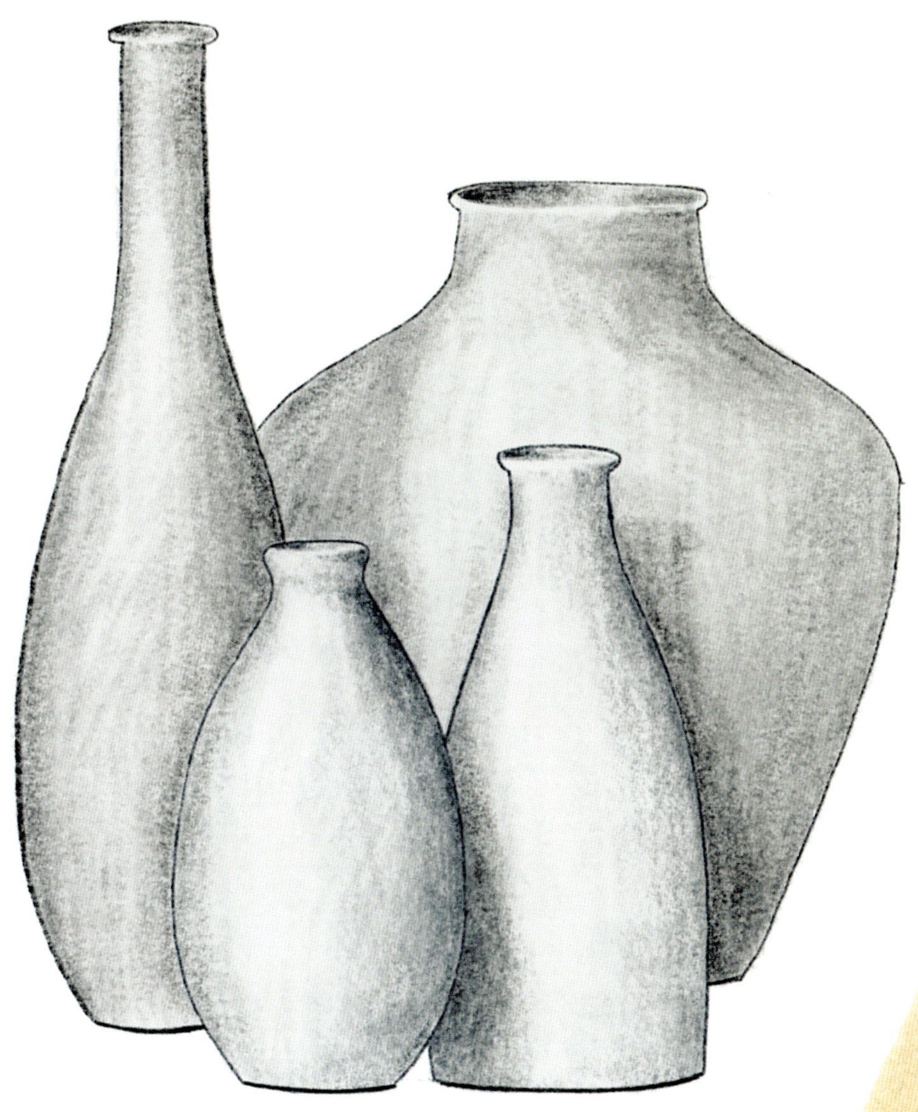

FLOWERS

Of all the flowers, roses are among the hardest to master. They're also among the most beautiful. Take pride in knowing that once you're able to draw this classic flower, you'll be well on your way to drawing a bouquet. (Turn the page for more floral inspiration.)

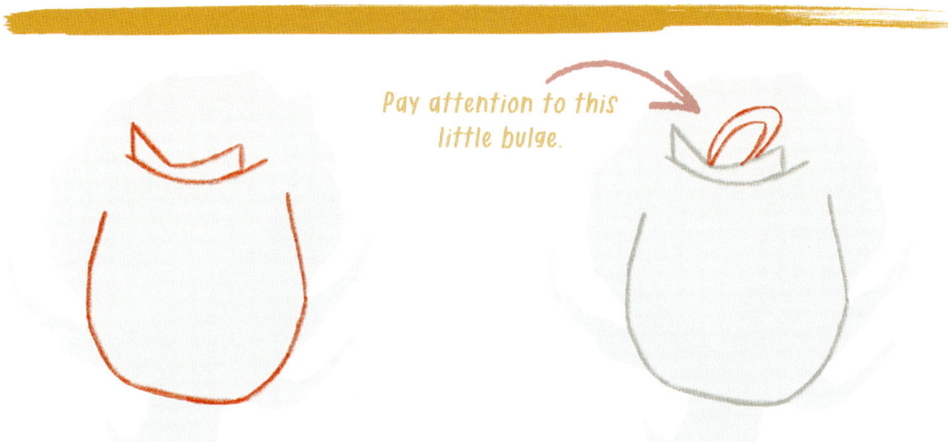

Step 1

Draw a large U shape. This will be the main body of the rose. Above that, draw a wide and shallow M shape, and then a curved line below it.

Step 2

Draw a small upside-down U shape on top of the M shape. Now, draw another one inside it. This will be the center of the rose.

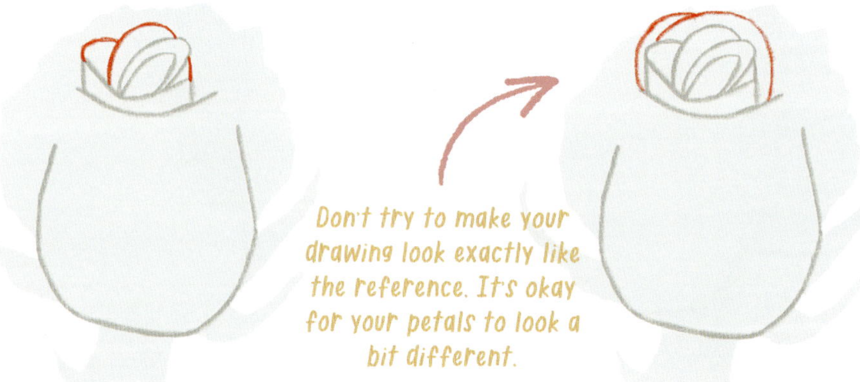

Step 3

Add a few more curved lines around the center of the rose. These will be petals.

Step 4

Add two more larger petals around the ones you just drew. Notice that the petals are getting bigger—that's because we're moving from the center of the rose to the outside.

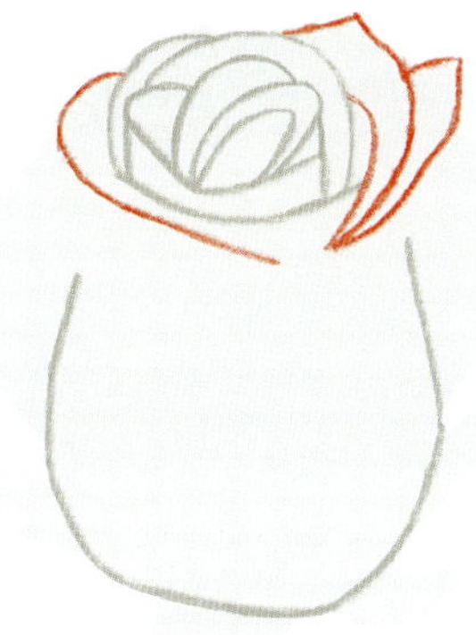

Step 5

Draw three more petals. Make the petals on the right pointed.

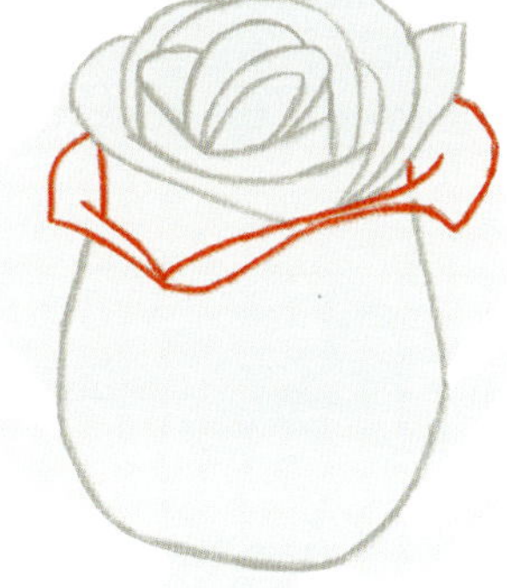

Step 6

Add a few curved lines that connect the main U shape to the petals you've just drawn. This is the hardest step, so take your time.

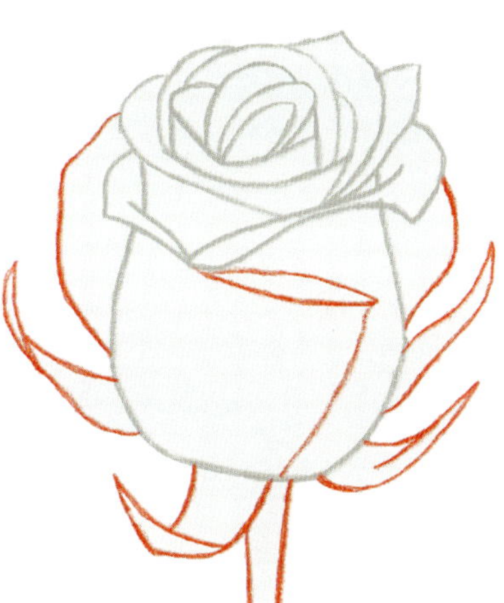

Step 7

Add the two largest petals behind the rose. Don't forget the petal right at the front. Outline the stem and the leaves.

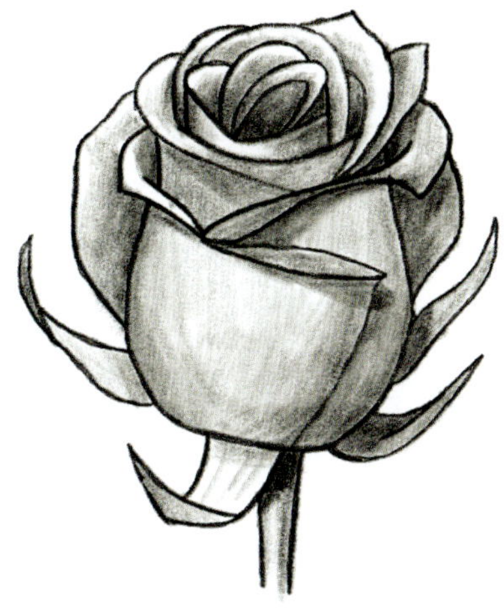

Step 8

Now let's shade. Build the shading up slowly on this one. The center of the rose is darkest, and the outer petals lightest. For a more realistic look, add cast shadows underneath the overlapping petals.

Reference: Flowers

What if you want to fill those vases you learned to draw with a bouquet? Here are a few more flowers you can learn to draw by applying some of the basic principles you've learned in this book.

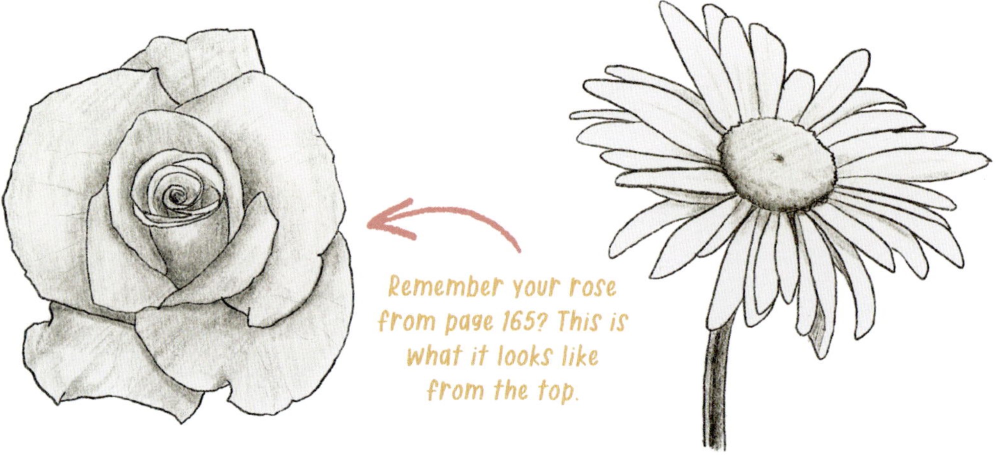

Rose

Notice how rose petals are smallest in the center and get larger as you move toward the outside.

Daisy

Try not to make your petals look perfectly identical. A little asymmetry will make your daisy look more realistic.

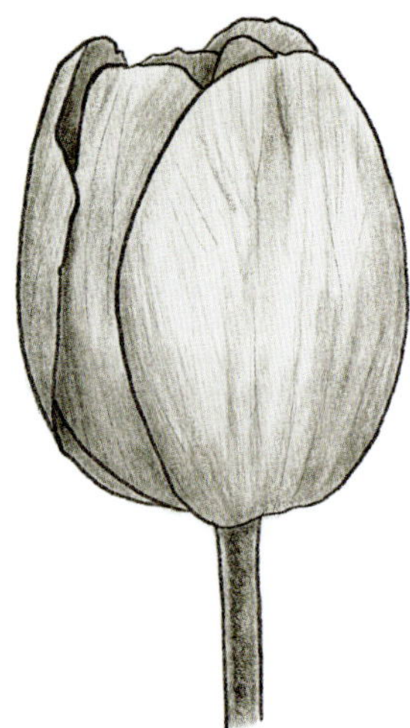

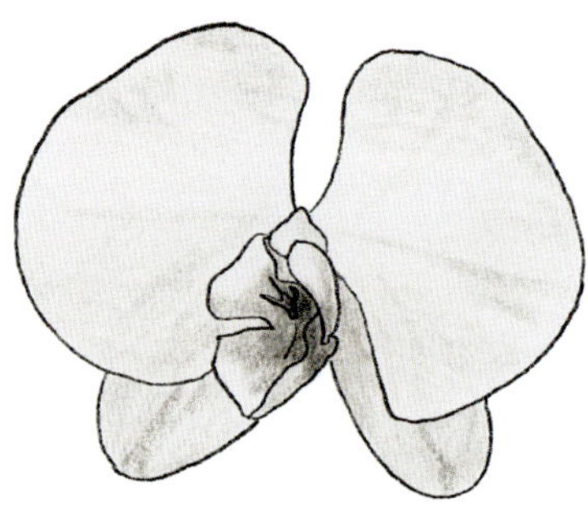

Tulip

Tulips may very well be the easiest flower to draw: start with an oval, and add a few C shapes.

Orchid

Another relatively easy flower to draw, orchids are known for their symmetrical, bean-shaped petals.

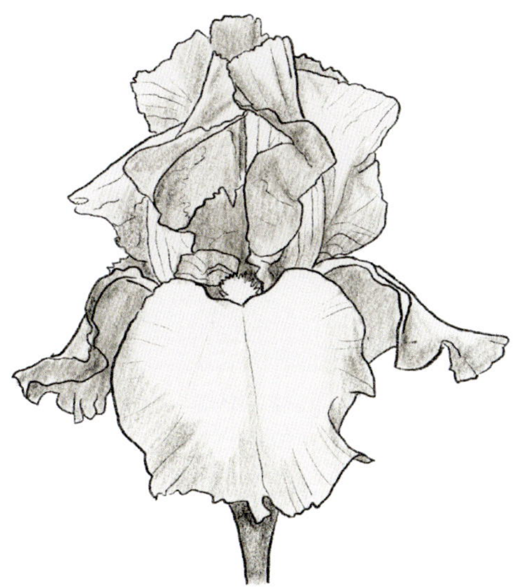

Iris

Irises have a complex structure, placing them among the hardest flowers to draw.

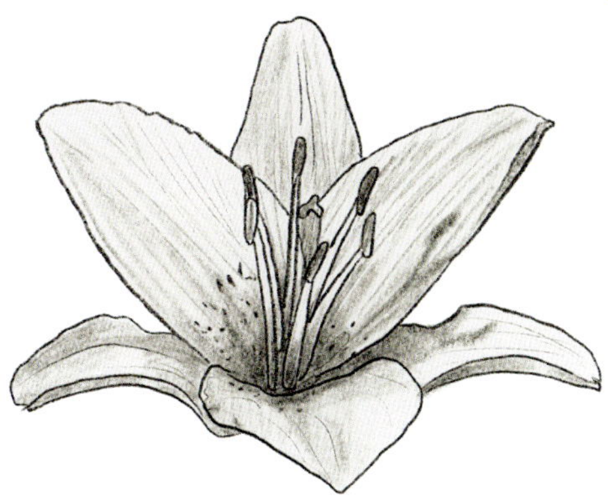

Lily

Lilies are known for their six long stamens (the long stem-like parts in the center).

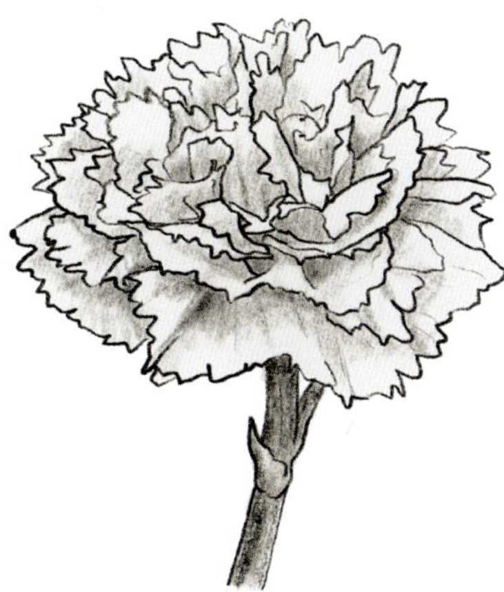

Carnation

Carnations have multiple layers of ruffled petals.

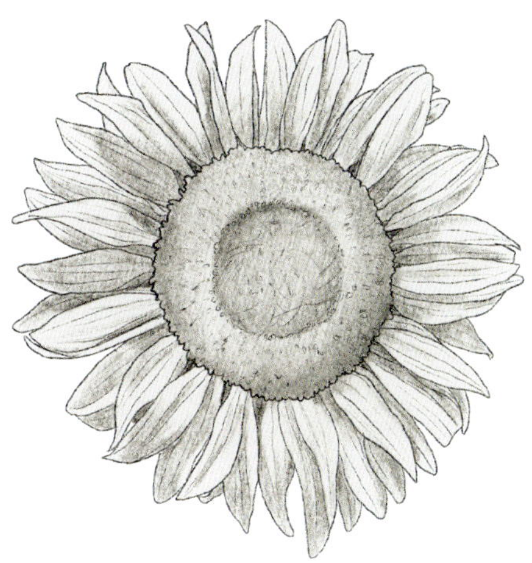

Sunflower

A fan favorite among artists, sunflowers are all about their large center and small petals.

BONUS: COMPOSITION

Now that you know how to draw a few still life elements, like fruit, vases and flowers, you might want to put them all into a single drawing. The word *composition* refers to the way things are arranged in your drawing. Here are the main factors to think about when building your own composition.

Focus

In art, the areas of *focus*, or focal points, are the parts of your drawing that attract a viewer's eye. If you're doing it right, it's where you *want* the viewer to spend most of their time looking. Areas of focus typically have more details than other areas—for example, the eyes and mouth of a portrait, the patterns on a vase or the centers of flowers in a still life.

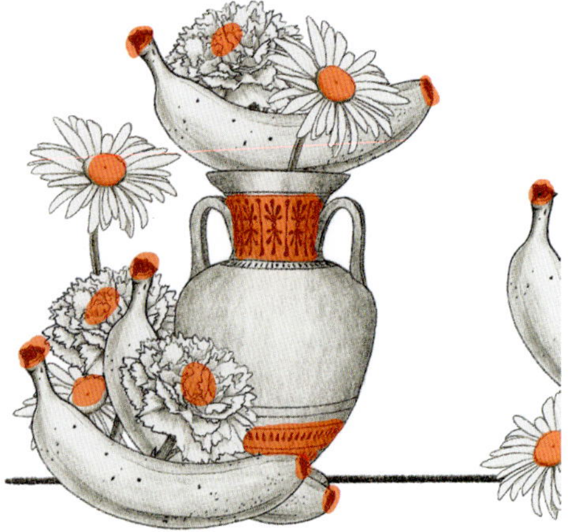

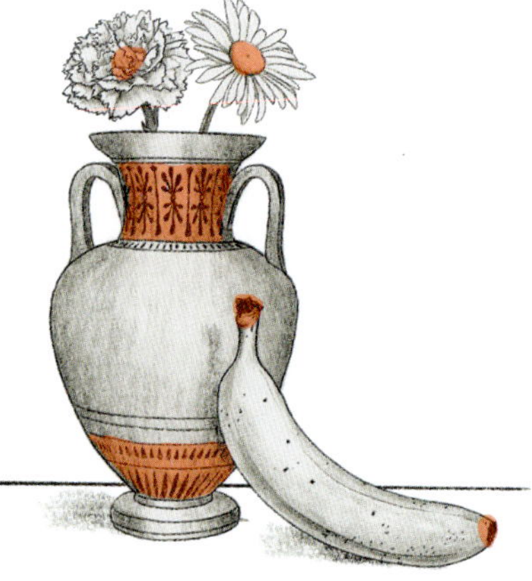

X   **Too many focal points create confusion in this composition. The viewer doesn't know where to settle their gaze.**

✔   **In this composition, there are just a few focal points. The viewer is not overwhelmed and knows where to look.**

Movement

Movement refers to where and how your viewer's eyes move through your drawing—usually toward areas of focus. You can create movement with shapes, actual lines and *implied* lines (like the direction flower stems are pointing).

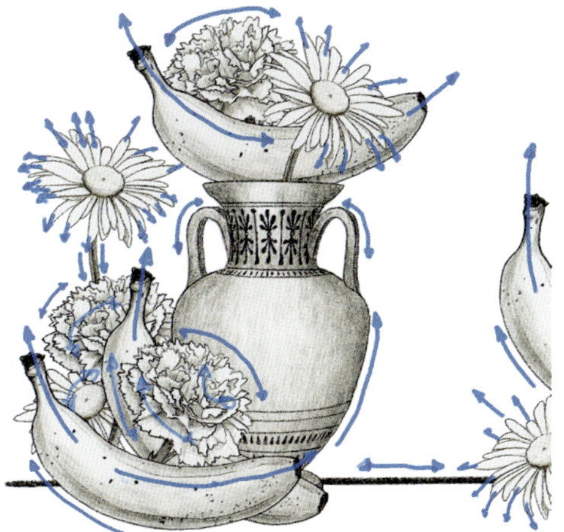

X   Too much movement creates chaos, leaving the viewer confused as to where to direct their gaze.

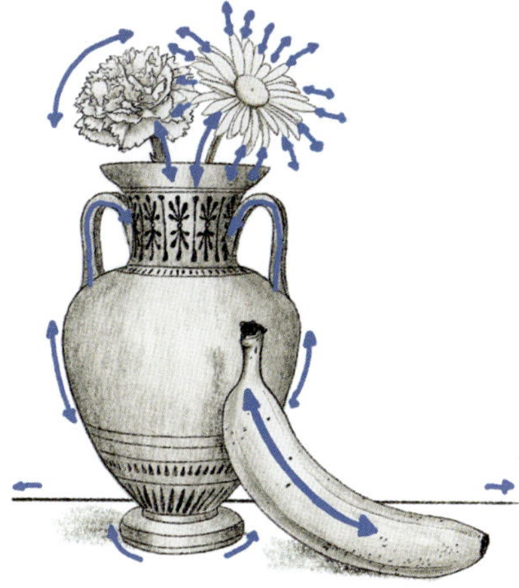

✓   Good movement invites the viewer's eye to move steadily through the artwork and settle on an area or areas of focus.

Balance

Balance is how visual weight is distributed in your artwork—in other words, the ratio of stuff to no stuff. The two types of spaces are sometimes referred to as positive space (stuff) and negative space (no stuff).

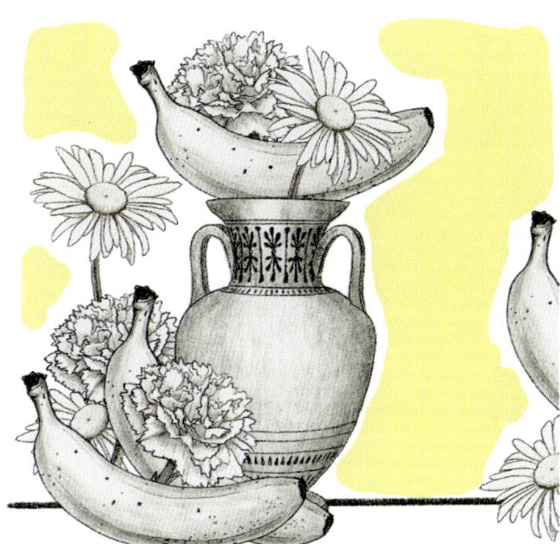

X   Although there is some negative space in this composition, there's not enough to let the viewer's eye rest, creating a sense of overwhelm.

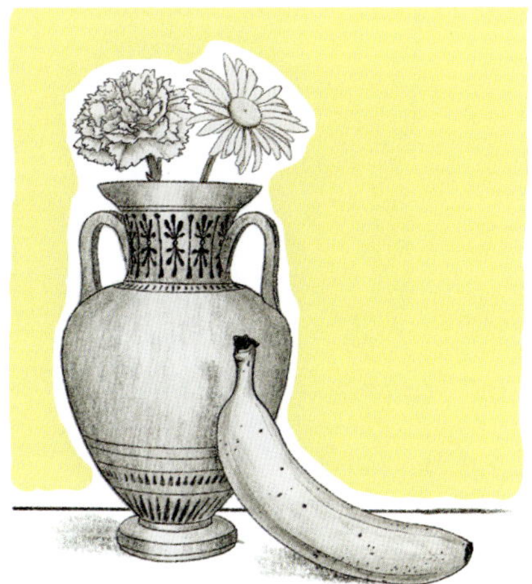

✓   This composition has a healthy amount of negative space in relation to positive space, so the viewer's eye may both focus and rest.

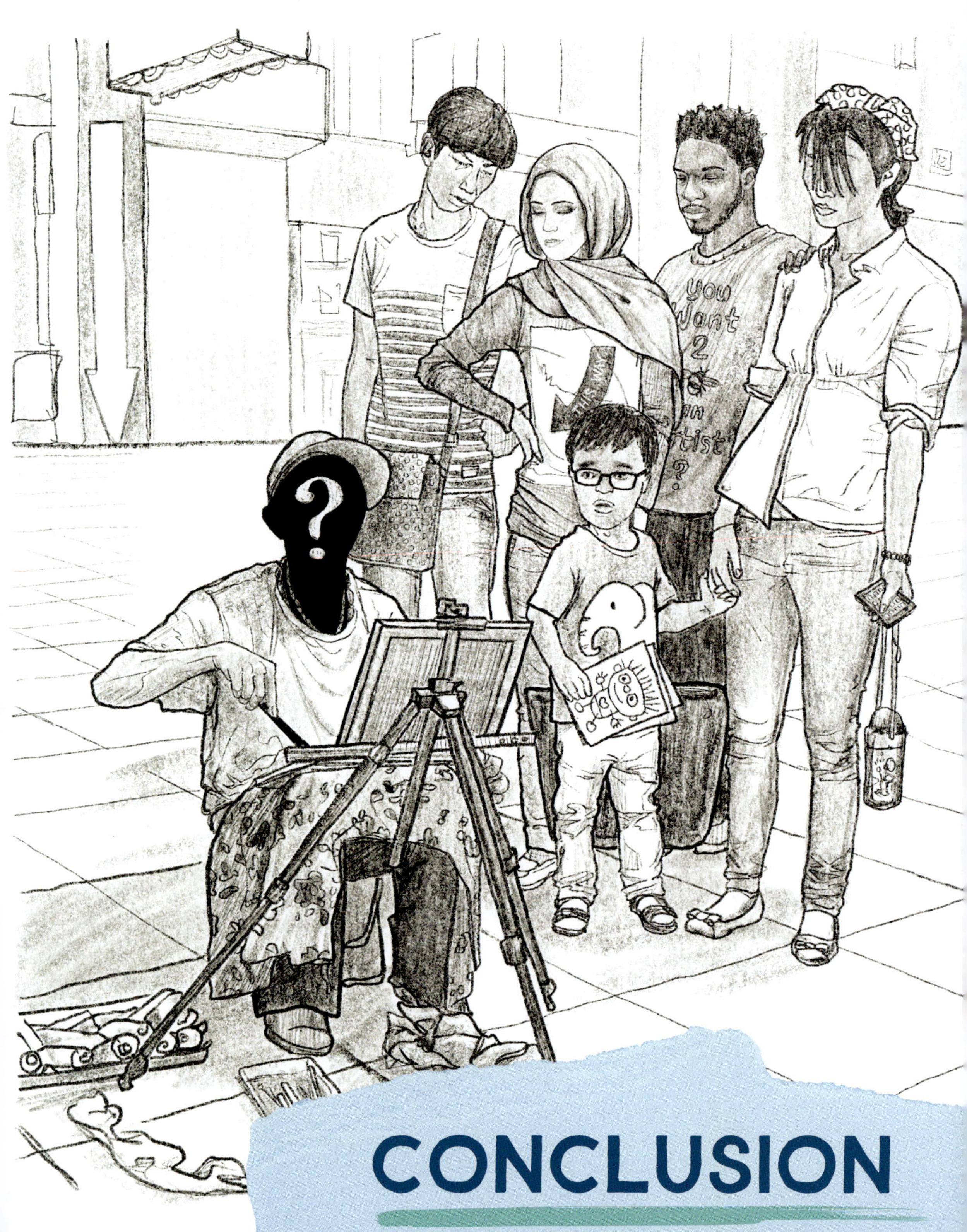

CONCLUSION

BEFORE YOU GO

There are some things you can't learn in a book. Here are a few more lessons that drawing will teach you as you continue along your artistic journey.

1   **Pause before picking up your pencil.**

Carefully look at what you want to draw before beginning to draw. When you slow down to truly examine an object, you see things you've never seen before—and your drawings will reflect it.

2   **Draw on a napkin if you must.**

Ideally, it's not a napkin, but the point is you don't need the latest pencil, sketchpad or tablet to draw. The materials you use matter a lot less than how you use them.

3   **Compare your drawings today to your drawings from yesterday.**

And definitely don't compare them to other people's drawings. Everybody starts in their own time and progresses at their own pace. Focus on *your* journey.

4   **Drawing realism isn't magic.**

Many people think realist artists just pick up a pencil for the first time and create masterpieces. That's not how it works. Successful artists put in the time and effort needed to develop their skills. You can, too.

5   **Half a drawing is better than no drawing.**

Don't feel the need to finish every drawing. *Do* feel the need to learn from every drawing—and carry it with you into the next one.

6   **Everybody can draw.**

Maybe you grew up thinking that you couldn't, or maybe somebody told you that you couldn't. Now you know that you can. Remember that as you encounter other hard things in life.

7   **Drawing makes you a better person.**

Especially drawing hard things. The humility, patience and confidence that you'll gain through drawing will carry into everything that you do.

8   **Art unites us.**

There are around 7,000 languages spoken in the world. Art is the only one spoken by us all. It's up to you to decide what you want to say.

ACKNOWLEDGMENTS

I would like to express my gratitude to everyone who has picked up a pencil and tried my drawing lessons on social media.

Thank you to my editors, Madeline Greenhalgh and Franny Donington, and to the team at Page Street Publishing for giving me the opportunity to teach my art with this book.

Thank you to my friends and family for their endless support and encouragement.

Thank you to my parents for believing in me before I even knew how to believe in myself.

Thank you to my wife, Sabiha, for being my muse and for helping me become the artist I am today.

And to my son, Xavier, thank you for our drawing sessions, which inspire me more than you'll ever know.

ABOUT THE AUTHOR

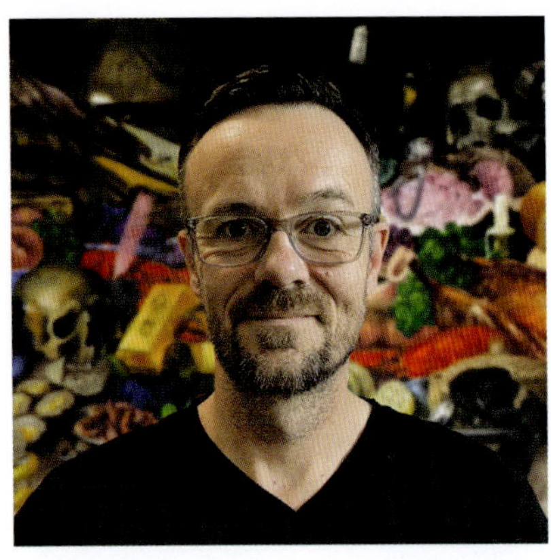

Mark Liam Smith is a professional artist and art educator. He is passionate about teaching art to millions of beginner artists through his social media platforms.

When he's not teaching art, he's creating it. Smith is an accomplished, gallery-represented oil painter. His work has been exhibited internationally in galleries in Montreal, Toronto, London, New York, Miami, Los Angeles, and at art fairs such as SCOPE Basel, Affordable Art Fair NYC, PULSE Miami, Art Seattle, Art Toronto and more.

He has been granted the Emerging Artist Award by the Federation of Canadian Artists and three Ontario Arts Council grants. His art has been featured in *The Jealous Curator*, the *Toronto Star*, the CBC, *Hi-Fructose* magazine, *Booooooom* and *Create!* magazine, among many others.

He lives in Toronto, Canada with his wife and son.

You can find more of Mark's art and tutorials at **markliamsmith.com** and on social media @markliamsmith.